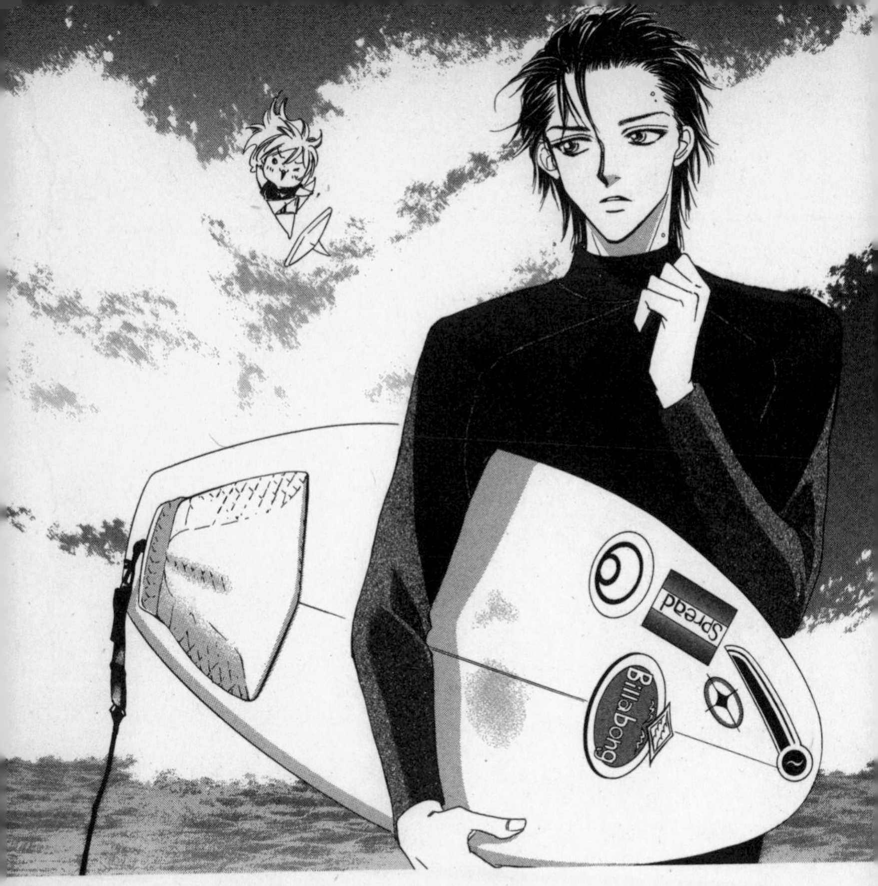
Spread
Billabong

HAPPY HUSTLE HIGH

3

story and art by **Rie Takada**

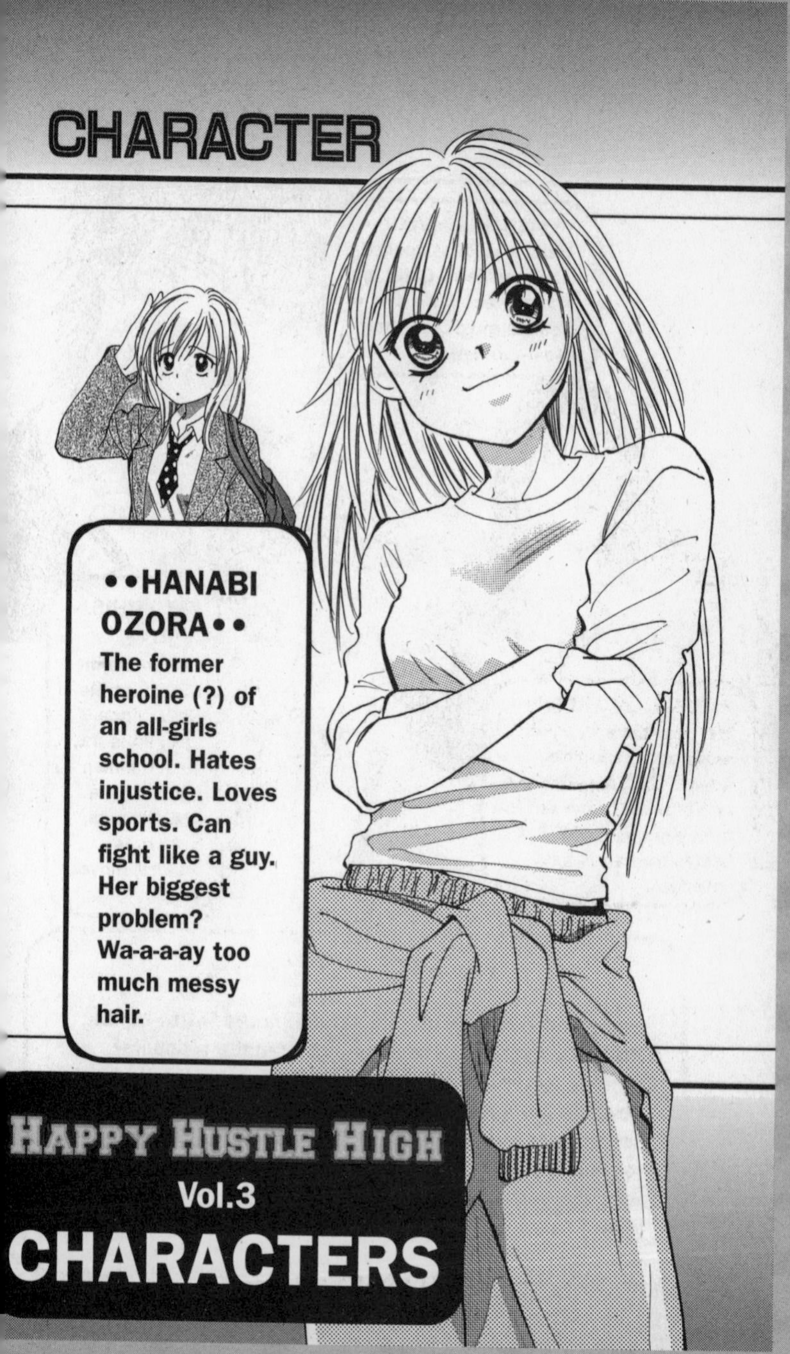

CHARACTER

••HANABI OZORA••

The former heroine (?) of an all-girls school. Hates injustice. Loves sports. Can fight like a guy. Her biggest problem? Wa-a-a-ay too much messy hair.

HAPPY HUSTLE HIGH
Vol.3
CHARACTERS

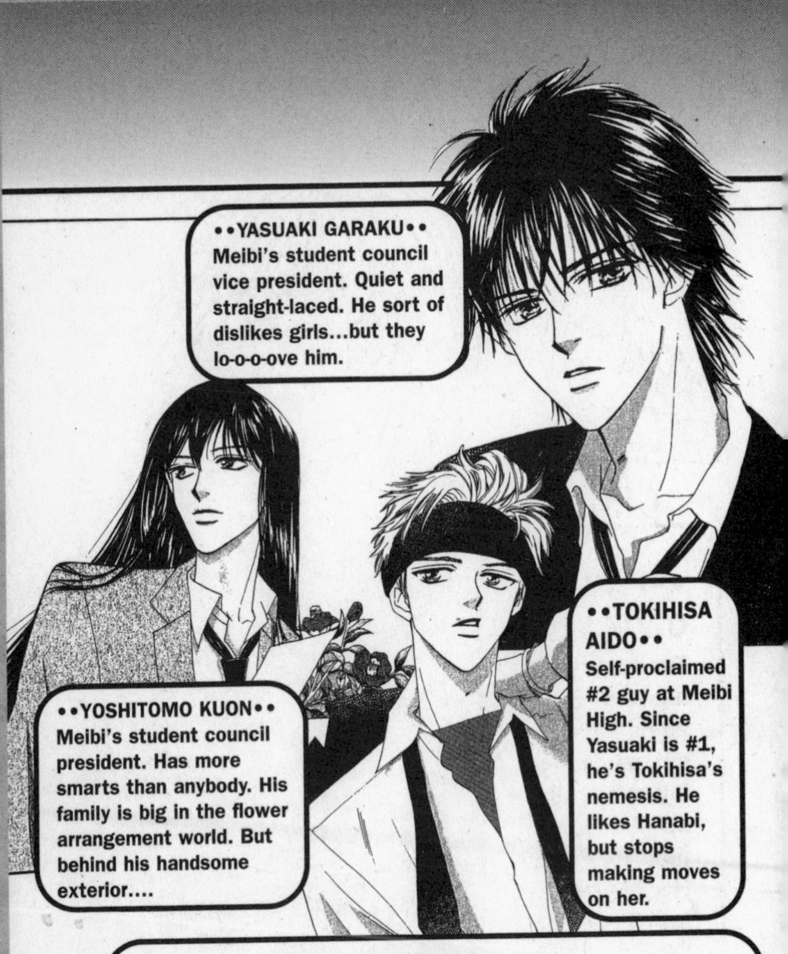
••YASUAKI GARAKU•• Meibi's student council vice president. Quiet and straight-laced. He sort of dislikes girls...but they lo-o-o-ove him.
••TOKIHISA AIDO•• Self-proclaimed #2 guy at Meibi High. Since Yasuaki is #1, he's Tokihisa's nemesis. He likes Hanabi, but stops making moves on her.
••YOSHITOMO KUON•• Meibi's student council president. Has more smarts than anybody. His family is big in the flower arrangement world. But behind his handsome exterior....

•••STORY•••

Earlier, an ordinary all-girls school merged with Meibi High, a very elite all-boys school. Hanabi, a popular tomboy, is the girls' rep on a student council full of hot guys. To her surprise, she starts dating Yasuaki, who seems cold but is actually very nice! They get past a terrible first meeting, near-expulsion from school, Tokihisa's love for Hanabi...and their first make out session. It's true love, but weird stuff always happens between them....

HAPPY HUSTLE HIGH

™

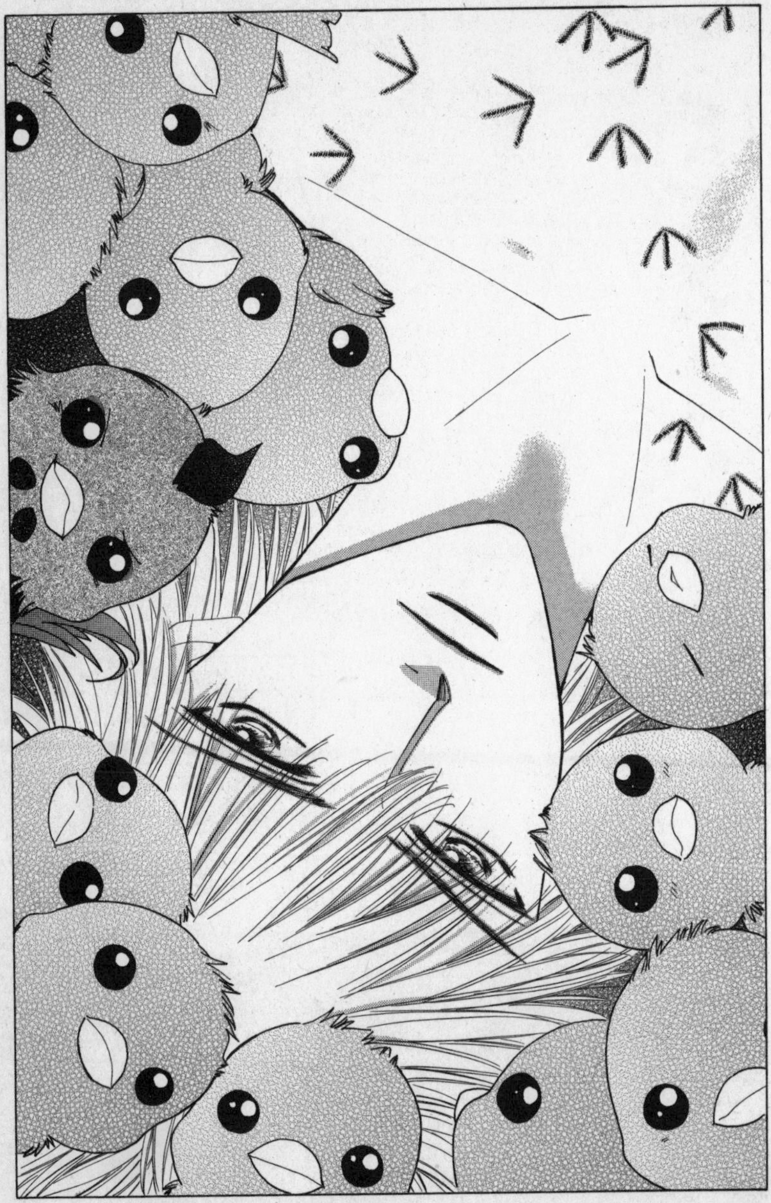

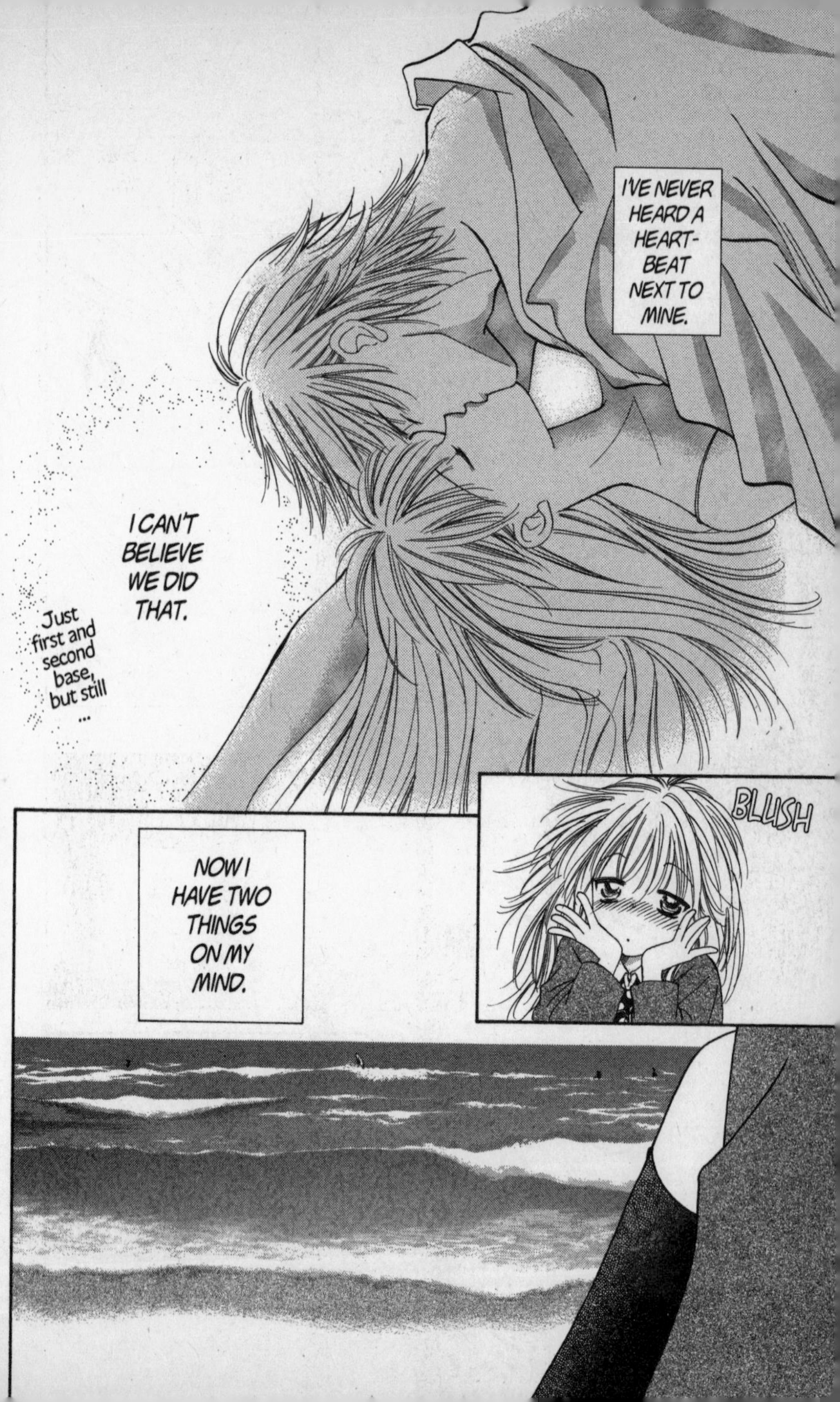
I'VE NEVER HEARD A HEART-BEAT NEXT TO MINE.
I CAN'T BELIEVE WE DID THAT.
Just first and second base, but still ...
BLUSH
NOW I HAVE TWO THINGS ON MY MIND.

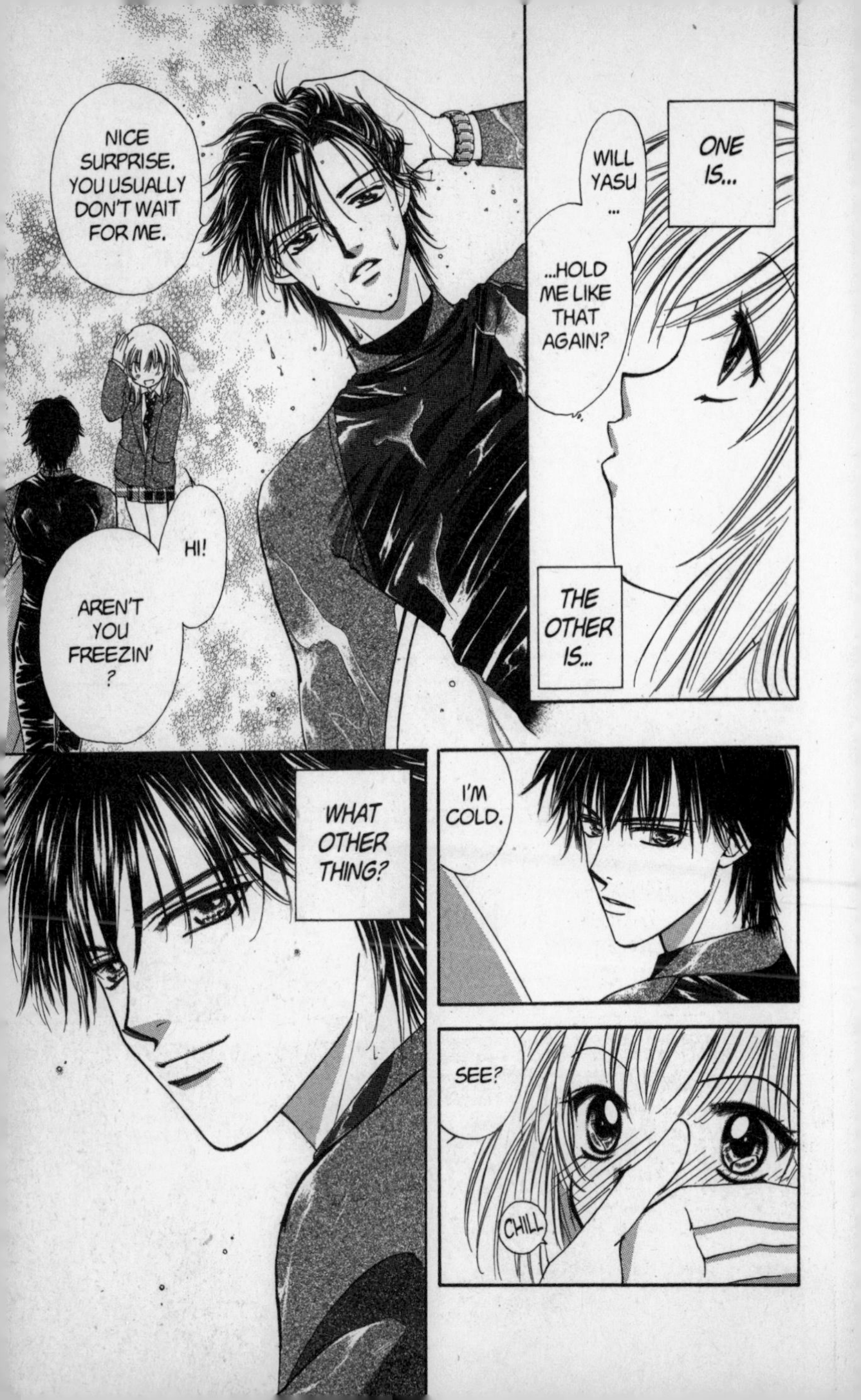
ONE IS...
WILL YASU ...
...HOLD ME LIKE THAT AGAIN?
THE OTHER IS...
NICE SURPRISE. YOU USUALLY DON'T WAIT FOR ME.
HI!
AREN'T YOU FREEZIN'?
I'M COLD.
SEE?
CHILL
WHAT OTHER THING?

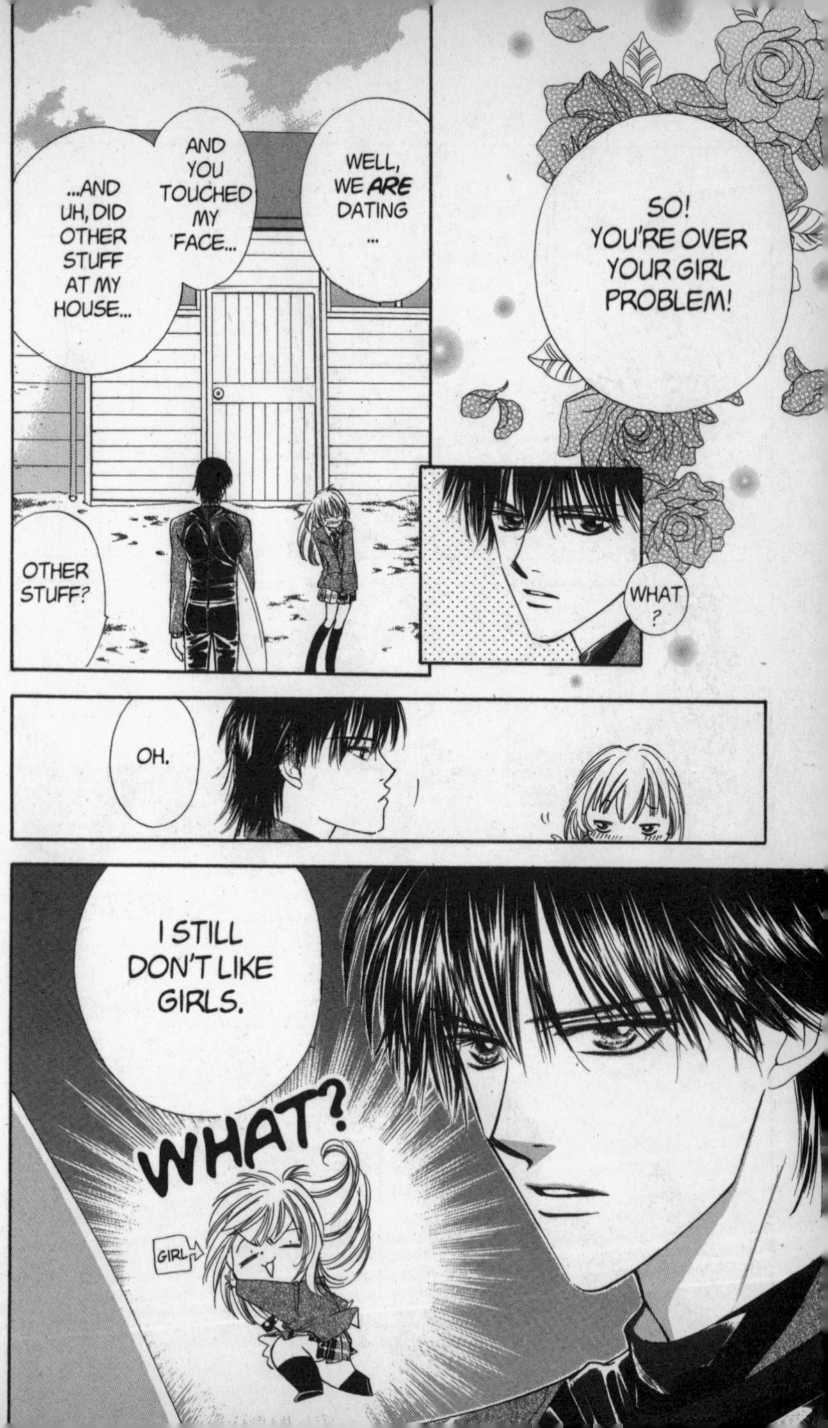

SO! YOU'RE OVER YOUR GIRL PROBLEM!
WHAT?
WELL, WE ARE DATING ...
AND YOU TOUCHED MY FACE...
...AND UH, DID OTHER STUFF AT MY HOUSE...
OTHER STUFF?
OH.
I STILL DON'T LIKE GIRLS.
WHAT?
GIRL

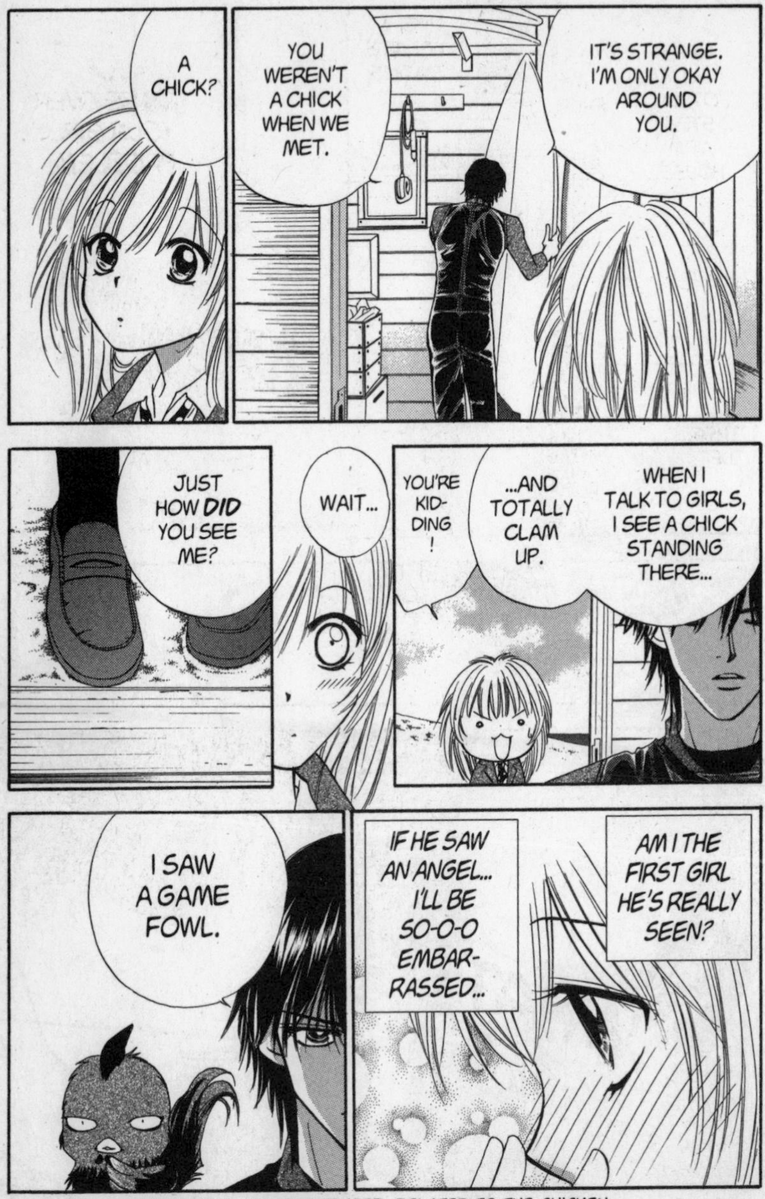
IT'S STRANGE. I'M ONLY OKAY AROUND YOU.
YOU WEREN'T A CHICK WHEN WE MET.
A CHICK?
WHEN I TALK TO GIRLS, I SEE A CHICK STANDING THERE...
...AND TOTALLY CLAM UP.
YOU'RE KID-DING!
WAIT...
JUST HOW **DID** YOU SEE ME?
AM I THE FIRST GIRL HE'S REALLY SEEN?
IF HE SAW AN ANGEL... I'LL BE SO-O-O EMBAR-RASSED...
I SAW A GAME FOWL.

GAME FOWL: STURDY BUILD, VIOLENT TEMPER, RELATED TO THE CHICKEN.

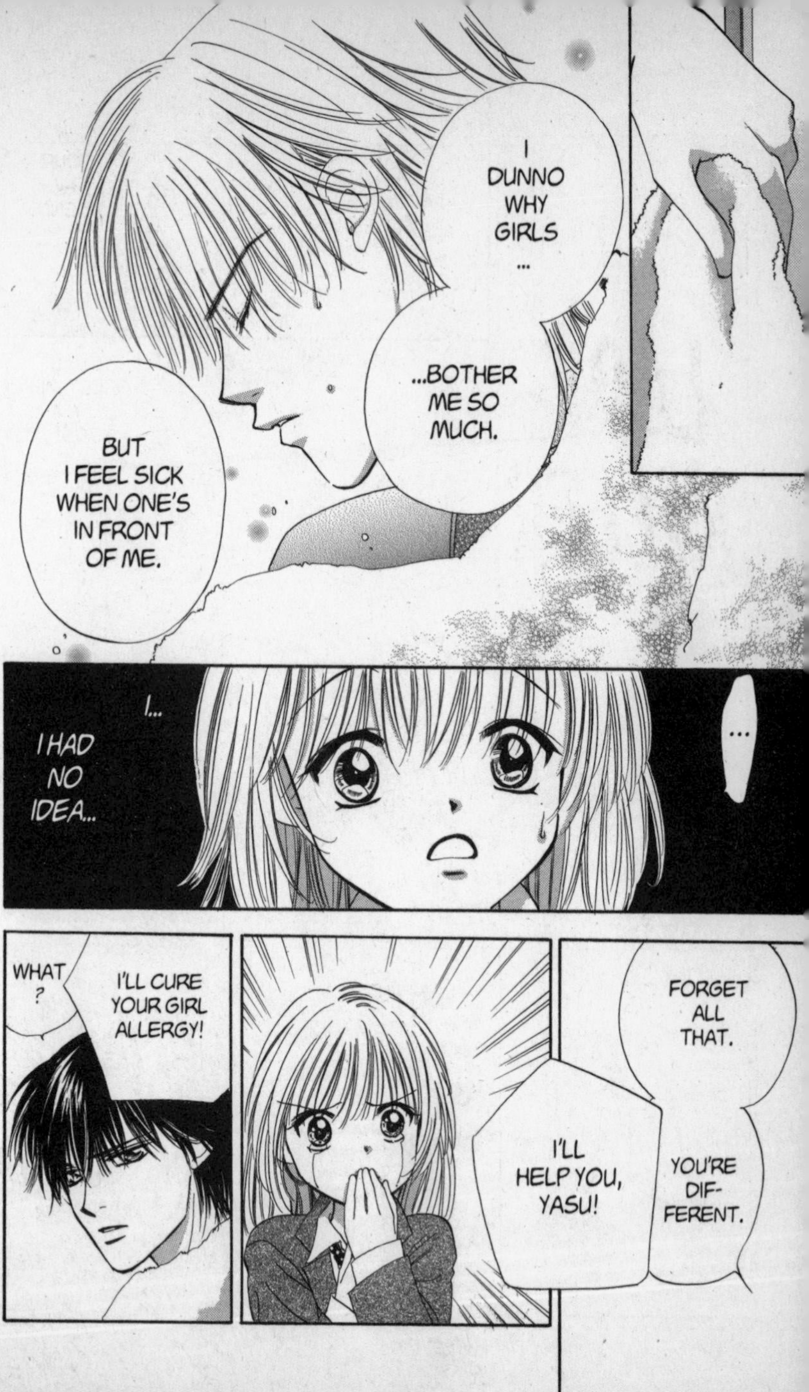
I DUNNO WHY GIRLS ...
...BOTHER ME SO MUCH.
BUT I FEEL SICK WHEN ONE'S IN FRONT OF ME.
...
I... I HAD NO IDEA...
FORGET ALL THAT.
YOU'RE DIF-FERENT.
I'LL HELP YOU, YASU!
I'LL CURE YOUR GIRL ALLERGY!
WHAT?

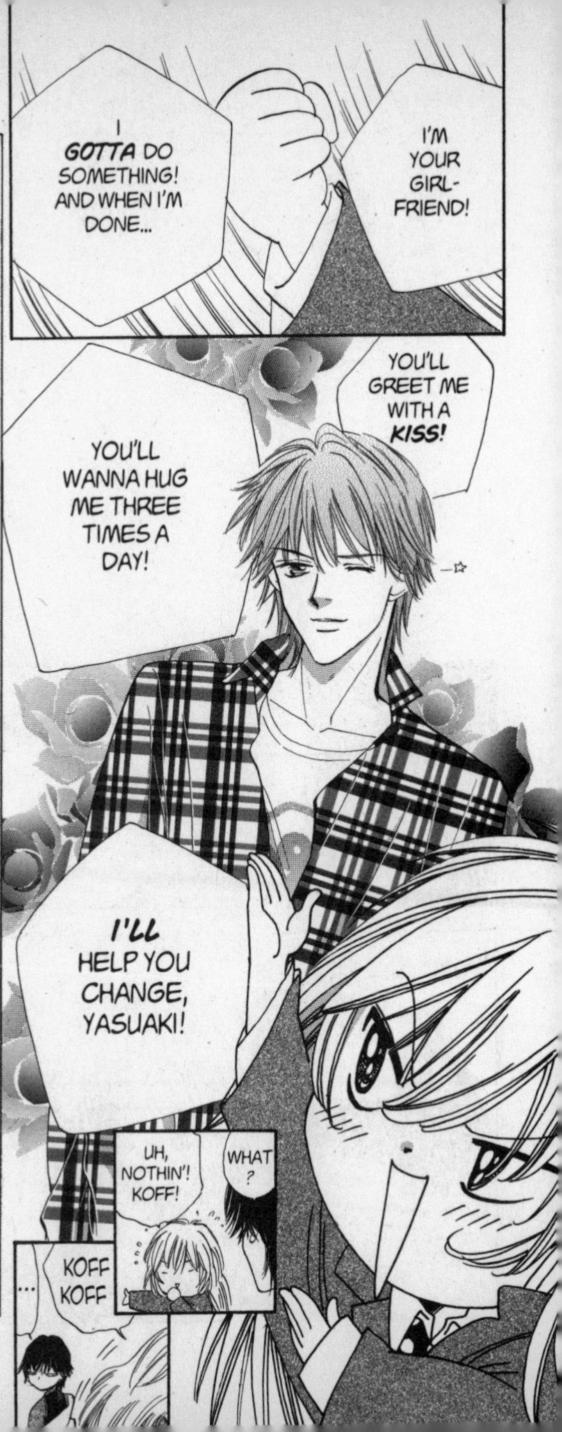
I'M YOUR GIRL-FRIEND!
I GOTTA DO SOMETHING! AND WHEN I'M DONE...
YOU'LL GREET ME WITH A KISS!
YOU'LL WANNA HUG ME THREE TIMES A DAY!
I'LL HELP YOU CHANGE, YASUAKI!
WHAT?
UH, NOTHIN'! KOFF!
KOFF KOFF
...

LADY-KILLER

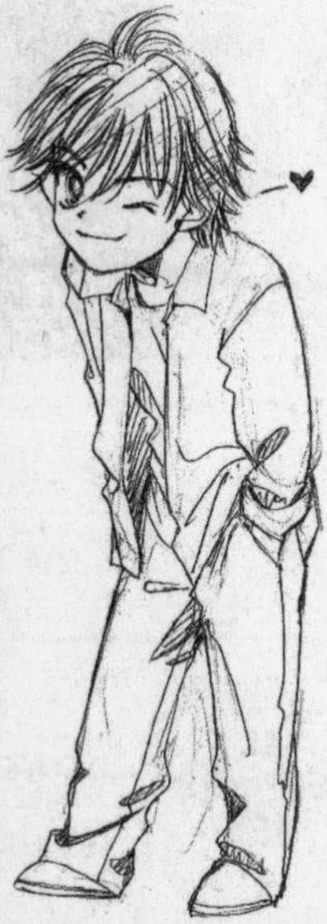

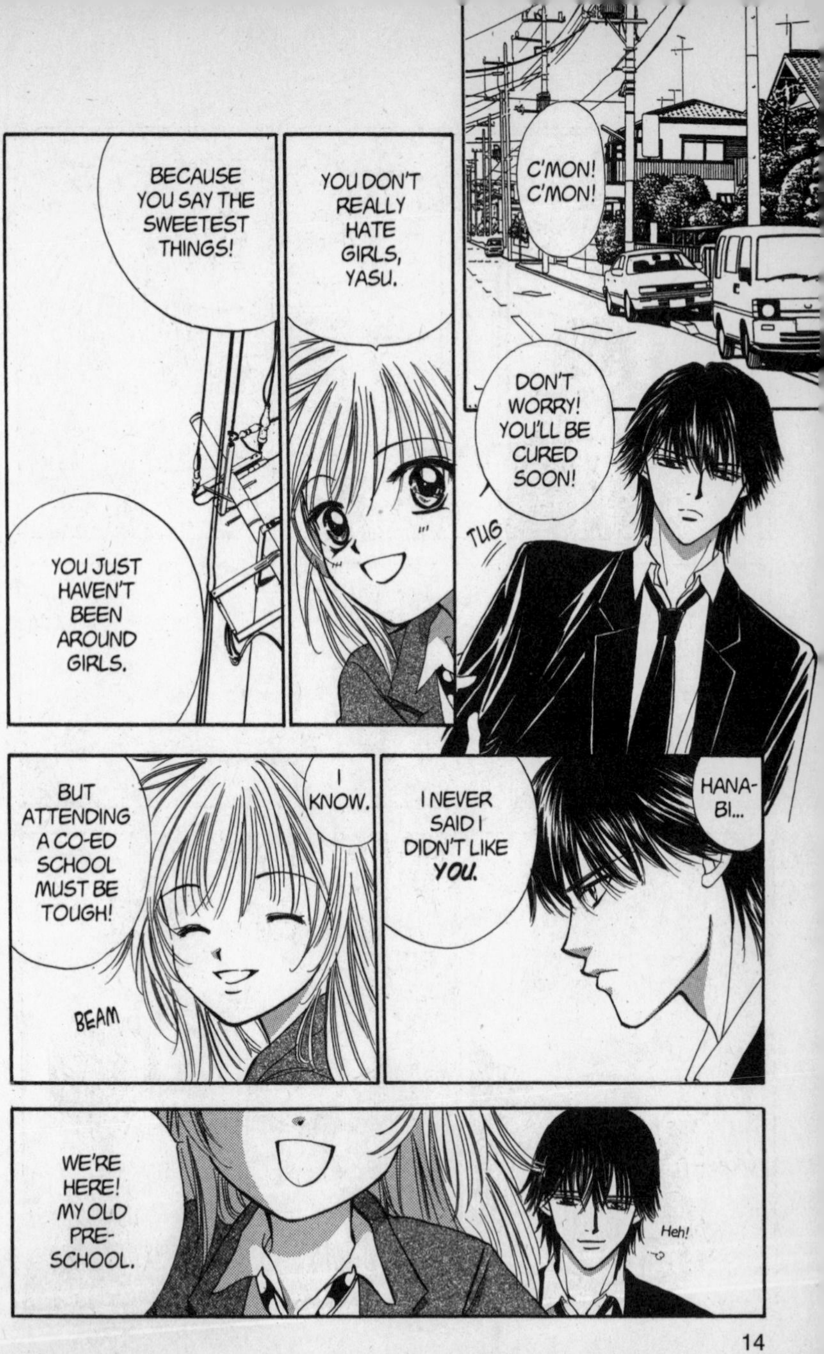
C'MON! C'MON!
DON'T WORRY! YOU'LL BE CURED SOON!
TUG
YOU DON'T REALLY HATE GIRLS, YASU.
BECAUSE YOU SAY THE SWEETEST THINGS!
YOU JUST HAVEN'T BEEN AROUND GIRLS.
HANA-BI...
I NEVER SAID I DIDN'T LIKE **YOU.**
I KNOW.
BUT ATTENDING A CO-ED SCHOOL MUST BE TOUGH!
BEAM
Heh!
WE'RE HERE! MY OLD PRE-SCHOOL.

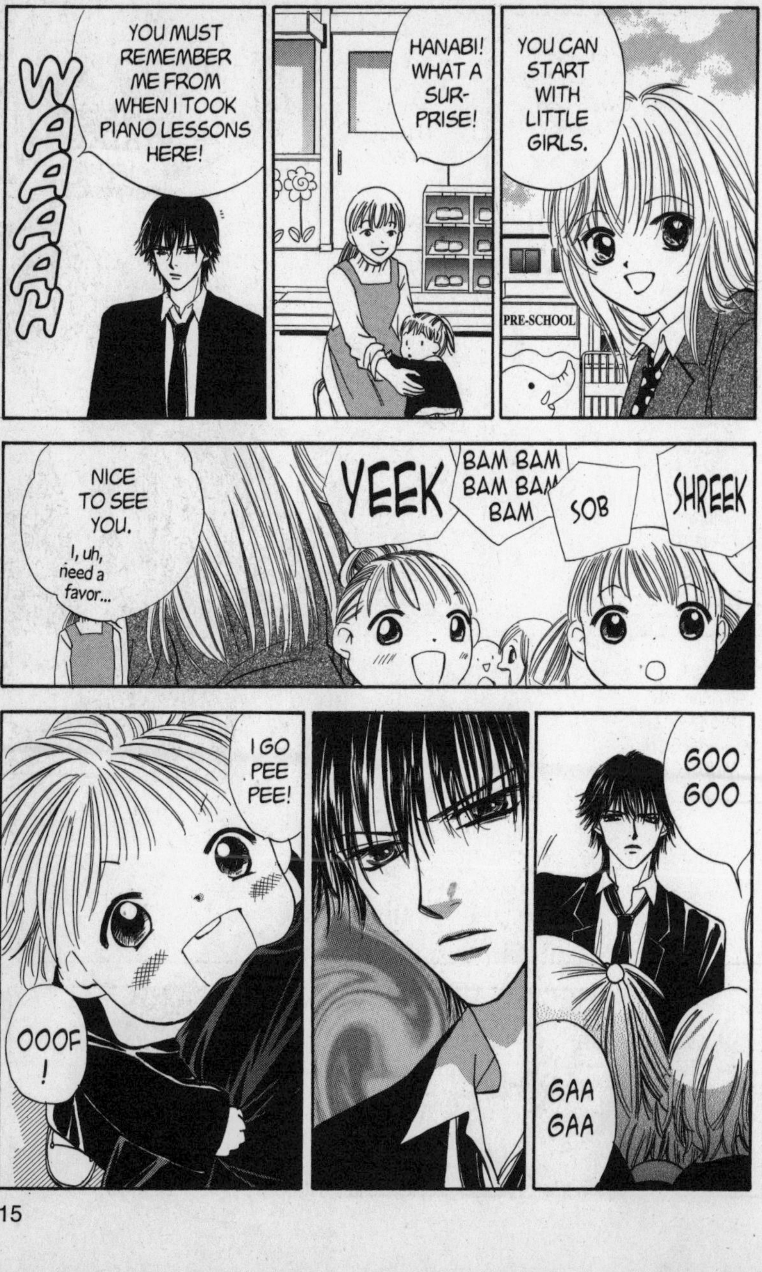
YOU CAN START WITH LITTLE GIRLS.
PRE-SCHOOL
HANABI! WHAT A SUR-PRISE!
YOU MUST REMEMBER ME FROM WHEN I TOOK PIANO LESSONS HERE!
WAAAAAH
SHREEK
SOB
BAM BAM BAM BAM BAM
YEEK
NICE TO SEE YOU.
I, uh, need a favor...
GOO GOO
GAA GAA
I GO PEE PEE!
OOOF!

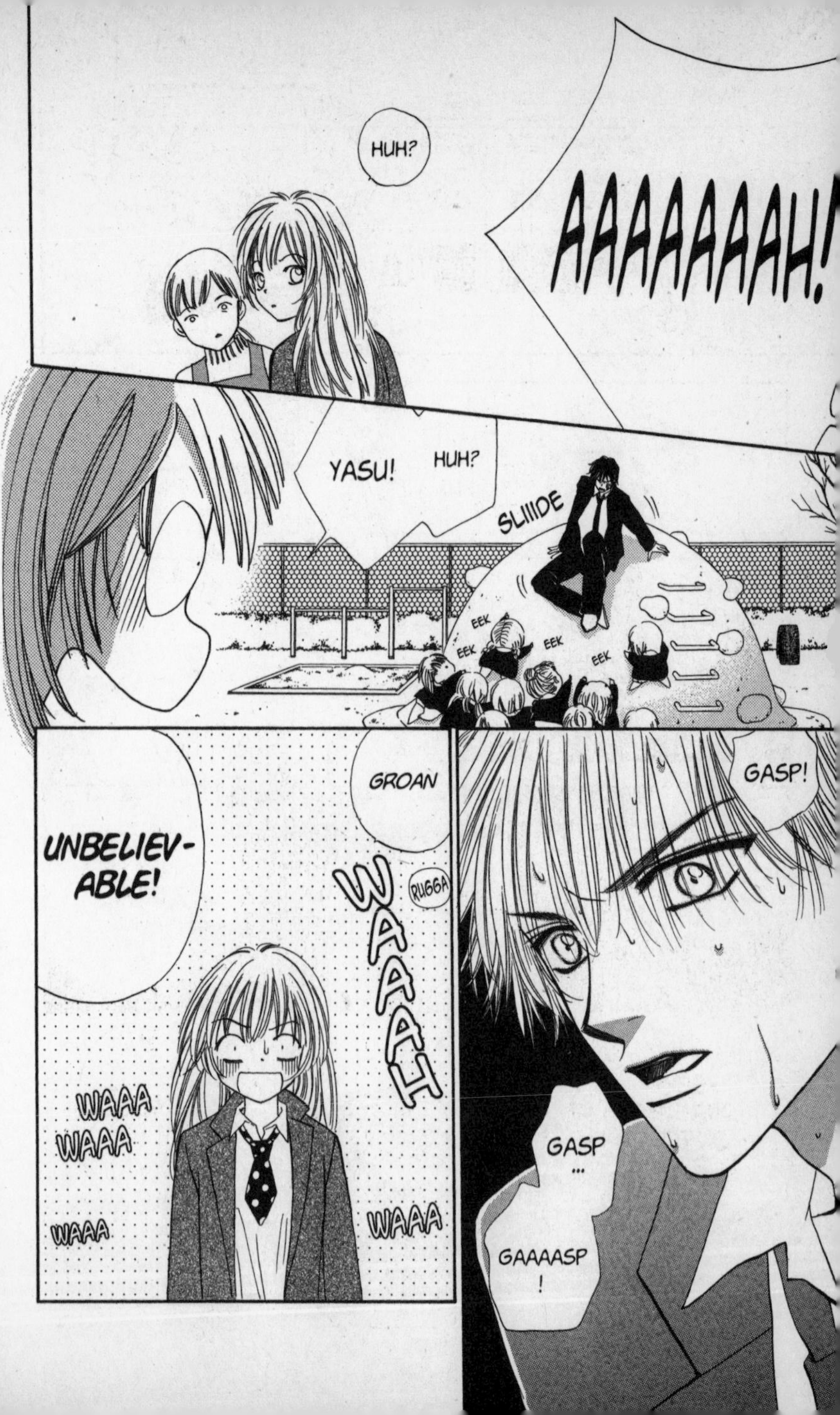
AAAAAAAH!
HUH?
YASU! HUH?
SLIIDE
EEK
EEK
EEK
EEK
GASP!
GASP ...
GAAAASP !
GROAN
RUGGA
WAAAAH
UNBELIEV-ABLE!
WAAA
WAAA
WAAA
WAAA

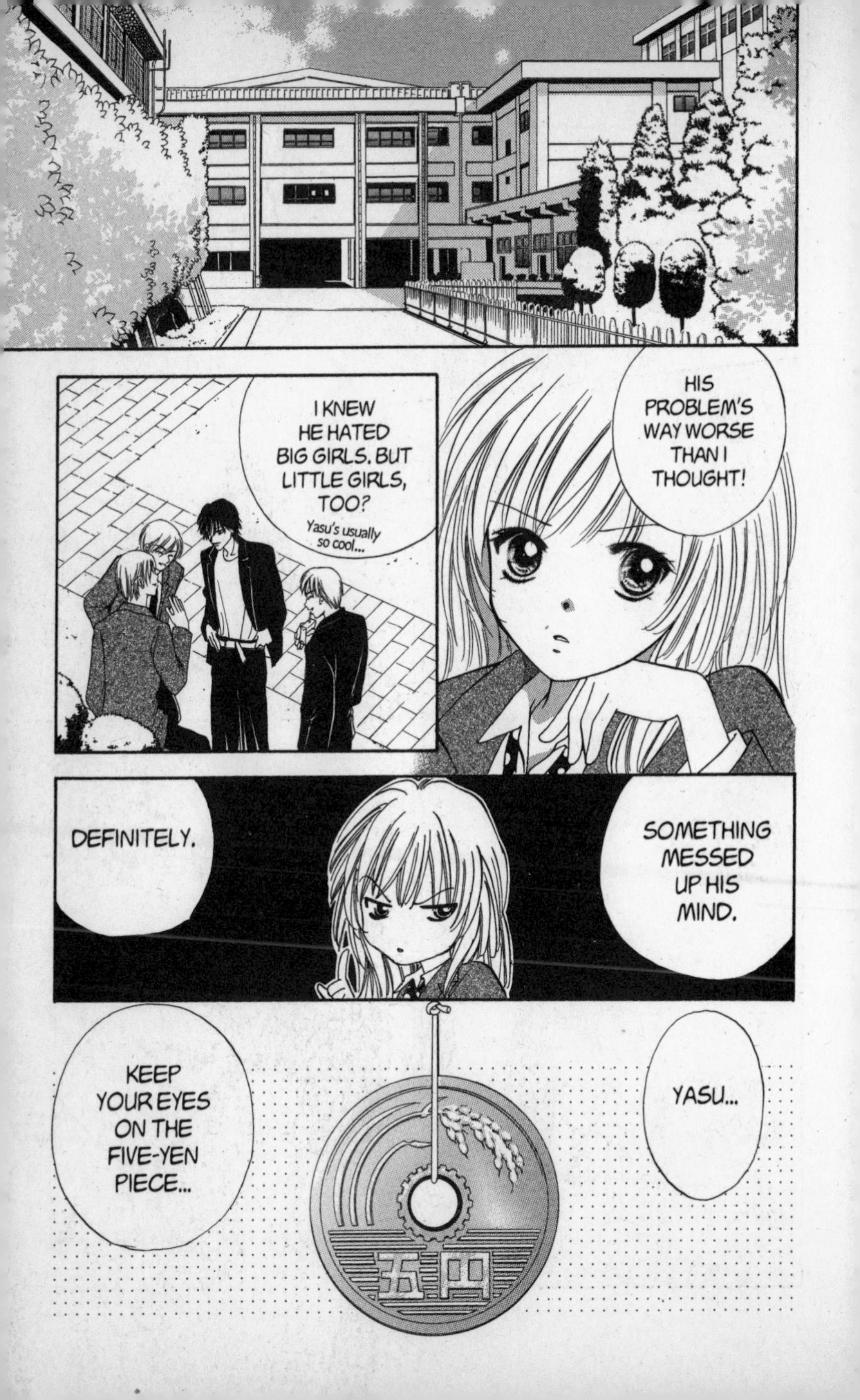
HIS PROBLEM'S WAY WORSE THAN I THOUGHT!
I KNEW HE HATED BIG GIRLS. BUT LITTLE GIRLS, TOO?
Yasu's usually so cool...
SOMETHING MESSED UP HIS MIND.
DEFINITELY.
YASU...
KEEP YOUR EYES ON THE FIVE-YEN PIECE...
五円

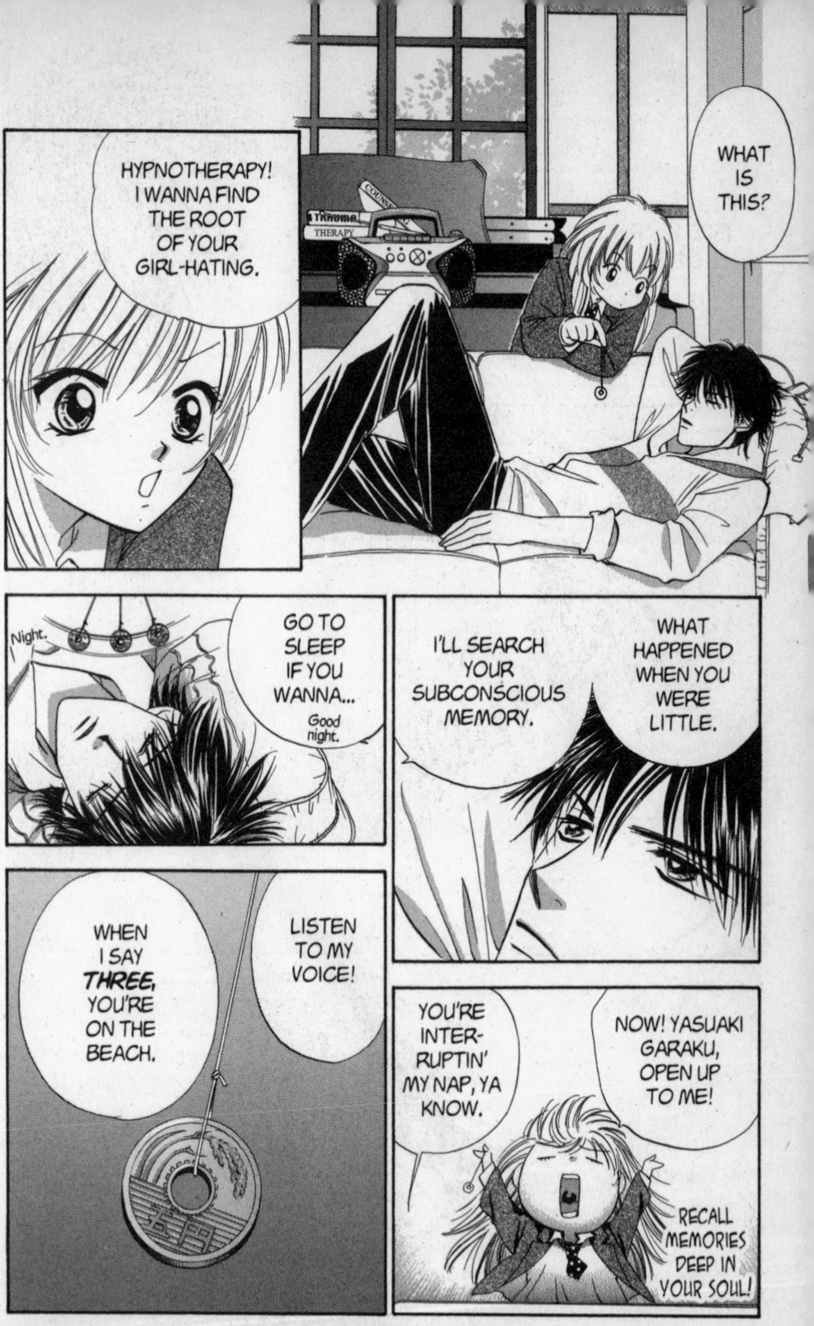
WHAT IS THIS?
HYPNOTHERAPY! I WANNA FIND THE ROOT OF YOUR GIRL-HATING.
WHAT HAPPENED WHEN YOU WERE LITTLE.
I'LL SEARCH YOUR SUBCONSCIOUS MEMORY.
GO TO SLEEP IF YOU WANNA...
Good night.
Night.
NOW! YASUAKI GARAKU, OPEN UP TO ME!
YOU'RE INTER-RUPTIN' MY NAP, YA KNOW.
RECALL MEMORIES DEEP IN YOUR SOUL!
LISTEN TO MY VOICE!
WHEN I SAY **THREE**, YOU'RE ON THE BEACH.

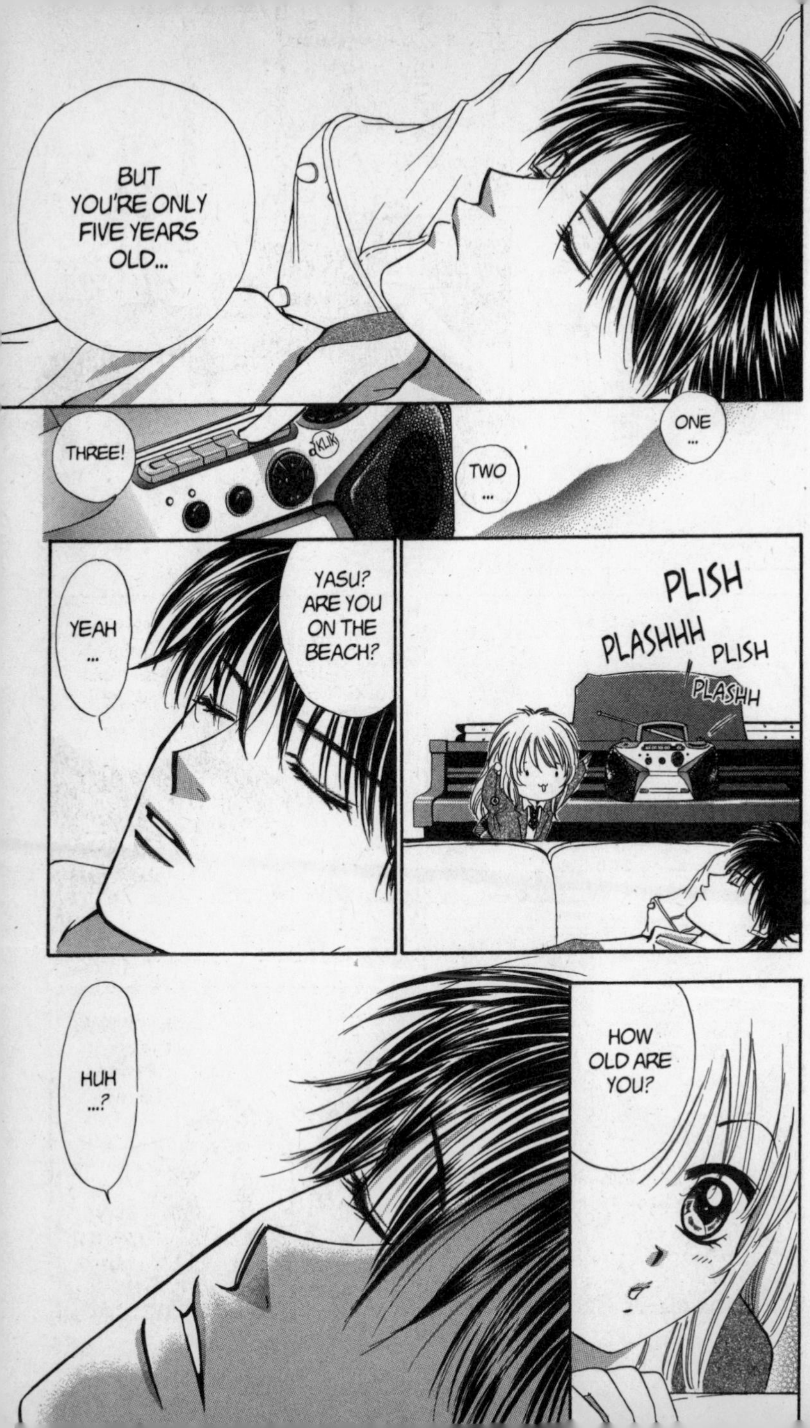
BUT YOU'RE ONLY FIVE YEARS OLD...
ONE ...
TWO ...
KLIK
THREE!
PLISH
PLASHHH
PLISH
PLASHH
YASU? ARE YOU ON THE BEACH?
YEAH ...
HOW OLD ARE YOU?
HUH ...?

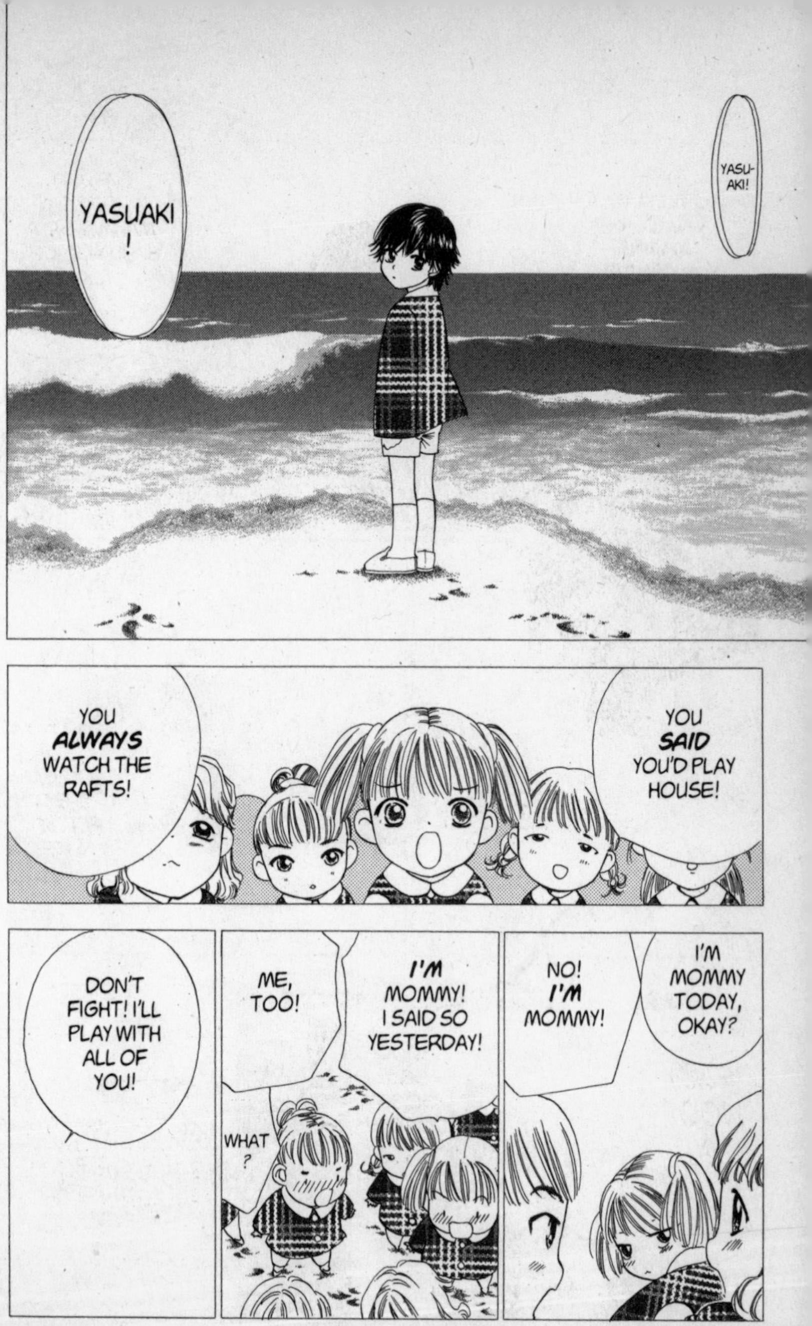
YASU-AKI!
YASUAKI!
YOU SAID YOU'D PLAY HOUSE!
YOU ALWAYS WATCH THE RAFTS!
I'M MOMMY TODAY, OKAY?
NO! I'M MOMMY!
I'M MOMMY! I SAID SO YESTERDAY!
ME, TOO!
WHAT?
DON'T FIGHT! I'LL PLAY WITH ALL OF YOU!

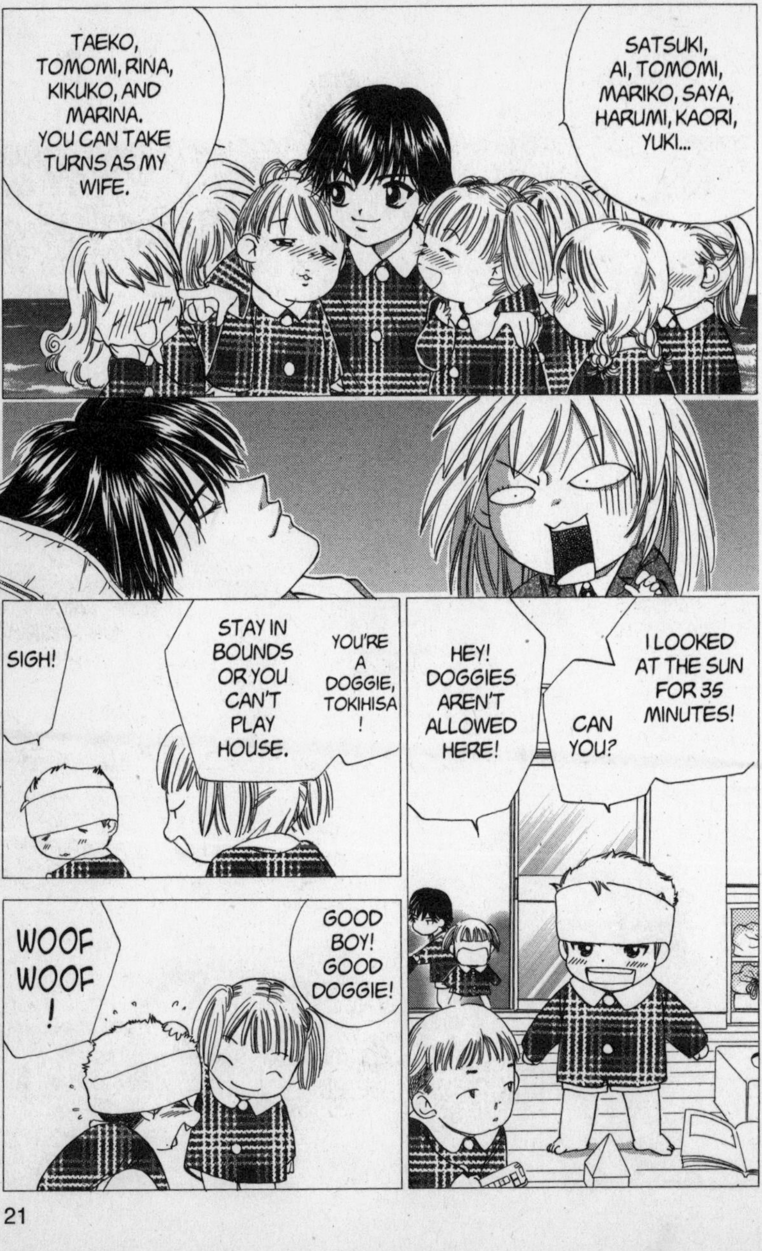
SATSUKI, AI, TOMOMI, MARIKO, SAYA, HARUMI, KAORI, YUKI...
TAEKO, TOMOMI, RINA, KIKUKO, AND MARINA. YOU CAN TAKE TURNS AS MY WIFE.
I LOOKED AT THE SUN FOR 35 MINUTES!
CAN YOU?
HEY! DOGGIES AREN'T ALLOWED HERE!
YOU'RE A DOGGIE, TOKIHISA!
STAY IN BOUNDS OR YOU CAN'T PLAY HOUSE.
SIGH!
GOOD BOY! GOOD DOGGIE!
WOOF WOOF!

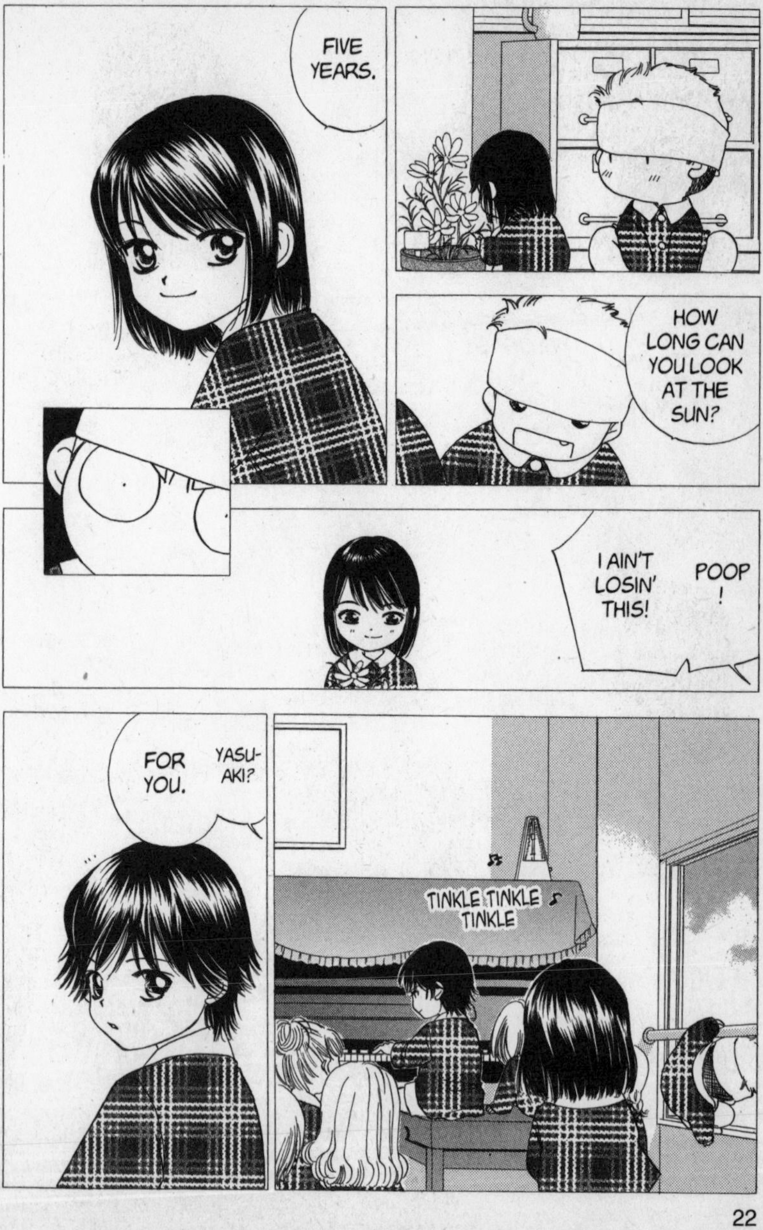
HOW LONG CAN YOU LOOK AT THE SUN?
FIVE YEARS.
POOP!
I AIN'T LOSIN' THIS!
TINKLE TINKLE TINKLE
YASU-AKI?
FOR YOU.
...

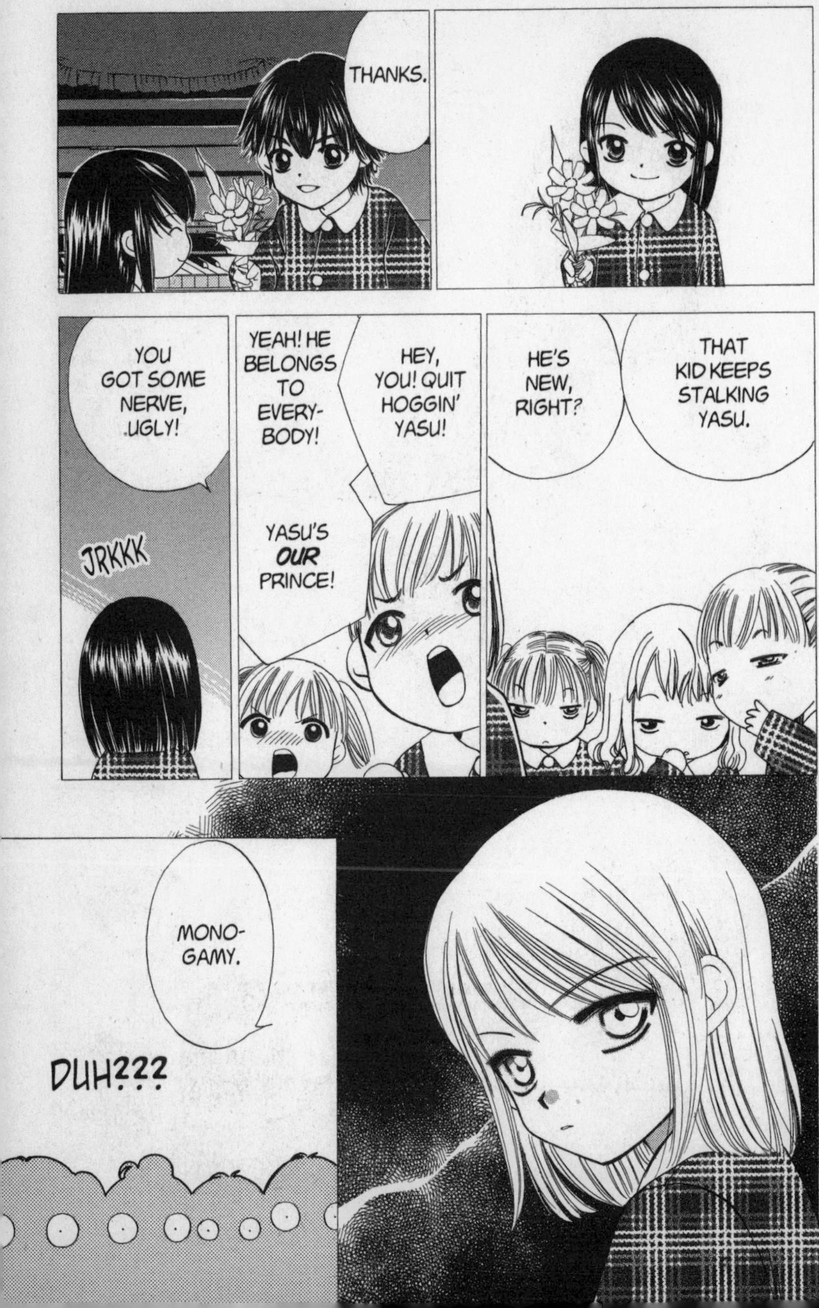
THANKS.
THAT KID KEEPS STALKING YASU.
HE'S NEW, RIGHT?
HEY, YOU! QUIT HOGGIN' YASU!
YEAH! HE BELONGS TO EVERY-BODY!
YASU'S **OUR** PRINCE!
YOU GOT SOME NERVE, UGLY!
JRKKK
MONO-GAMY.
DUH???

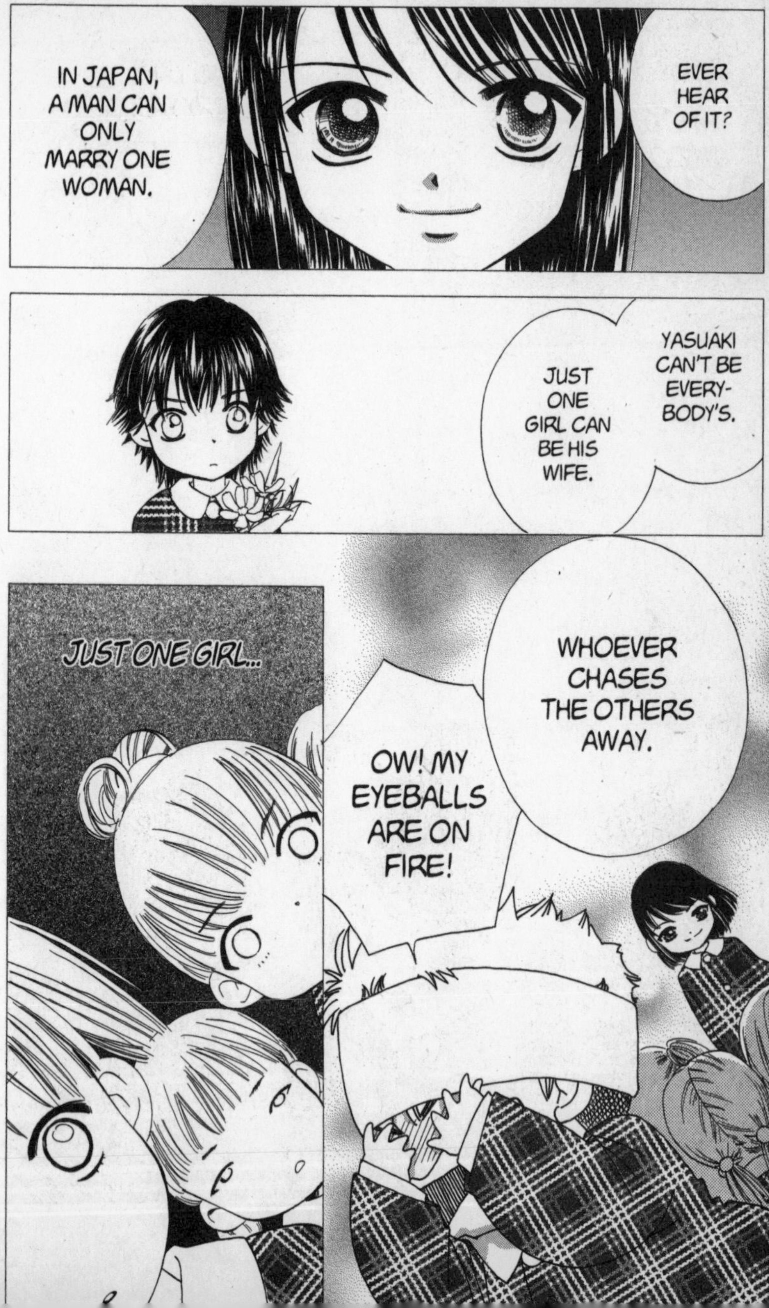
EVER HEAR OF IT?
IN JAPAN, A MAN CAN ONLY MARRY ONE WOMAN.
YASUAKI CAN'T BE EVERY-BODY'S.
JUST ONE GIRL CAN BE HIS WIFE.
WHOEVER CHASES THE OTHERS AWAY.
OW! MY EYEBALLS ARE ON FIRE!
JUST ONE GIRL...

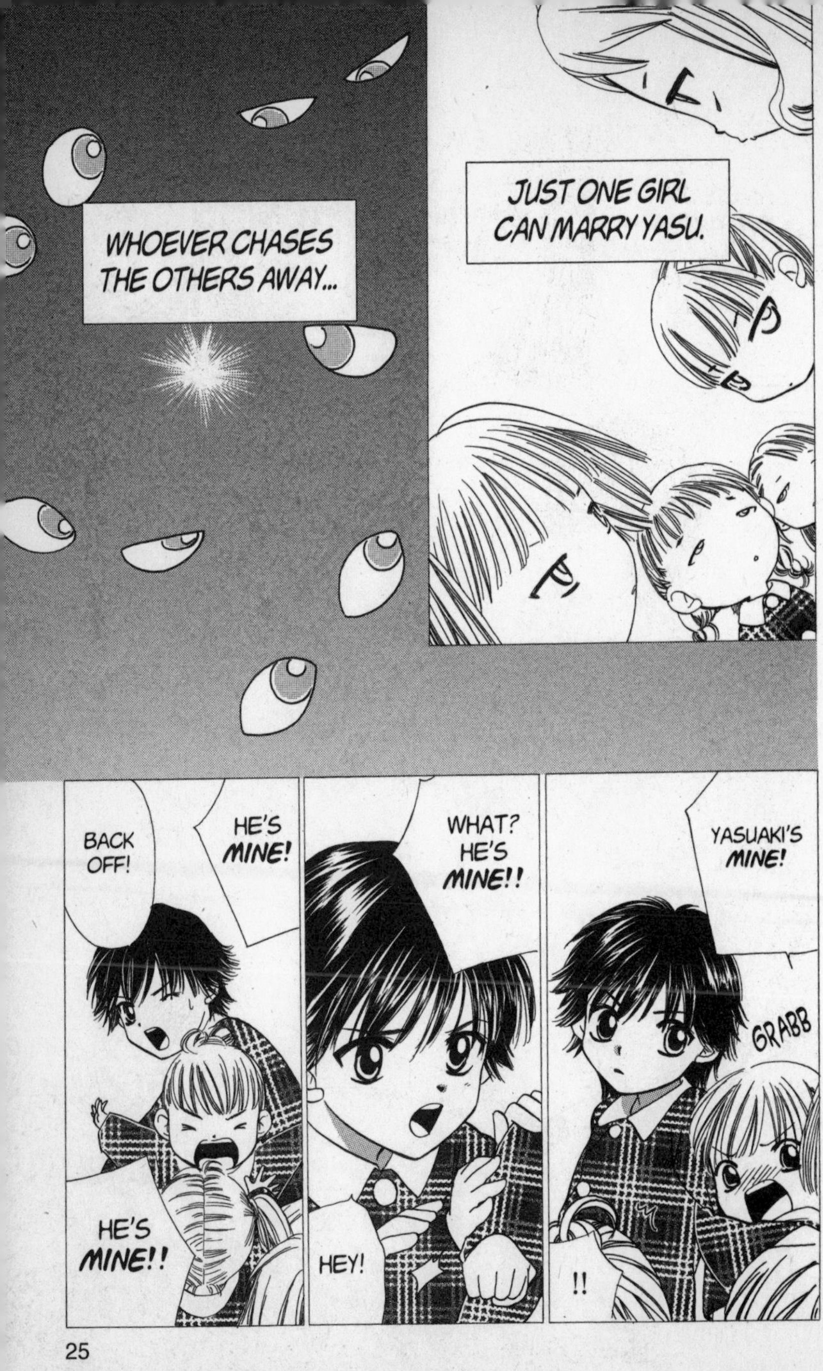
JUST ONE GIRL CAN MARRY YASU.
WHOEVER CHASES THE OTHERS AWAY...
YASUAKI'S MINE!
GRABB
!!
WHAT? HE'S MINE!!
HEY!
HE'S MINE!
BACK OFF!
HE'S MINE!!

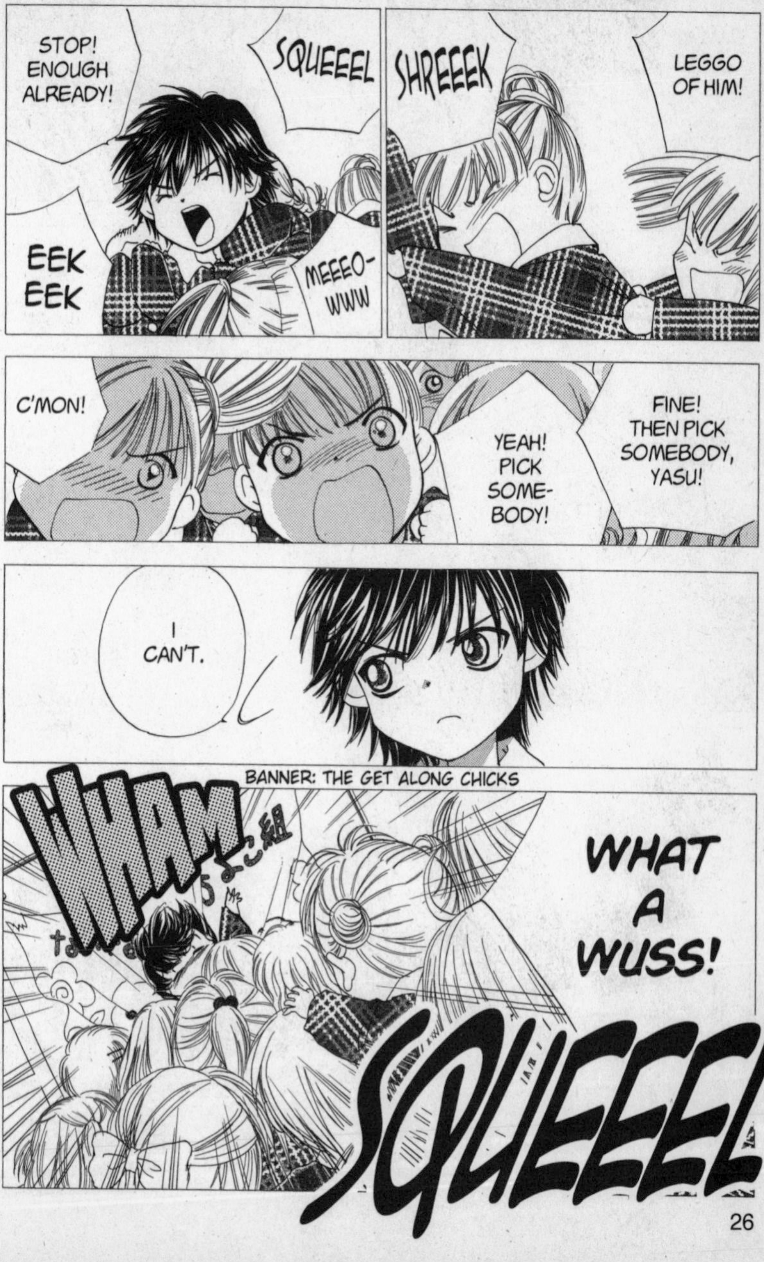
LEGGO OF HIM!
SHREEEK
SQUEEEL
STOP! ENOUGH ALREADY!
MEEEO-WWW
EEK EEK
FINE! THEN PICK SOMEBODY, YASU!
YEAH! PICK SOME-BODY!
C'MON!
I CAN'T.
BANNER: THE GET ALONG CHICKS
WHAT A WUSS!
WHAM
SQUEEEL

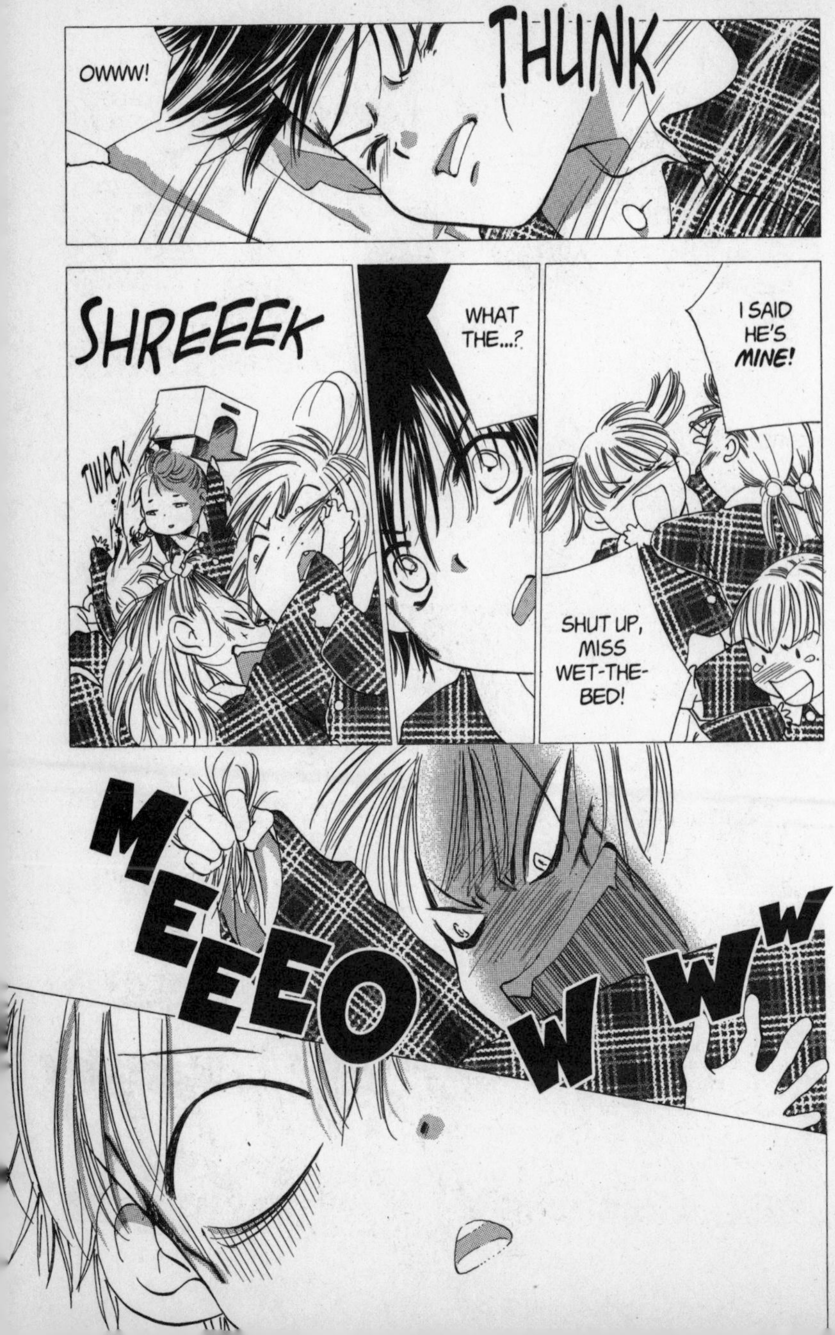
THUNK
OWWW!
I SAID HE'S MINE!
SHUT UP, MISS WET-THE-BED!
WHAT THE...?
SHREEEK
TWACK
MEEEOWWWW

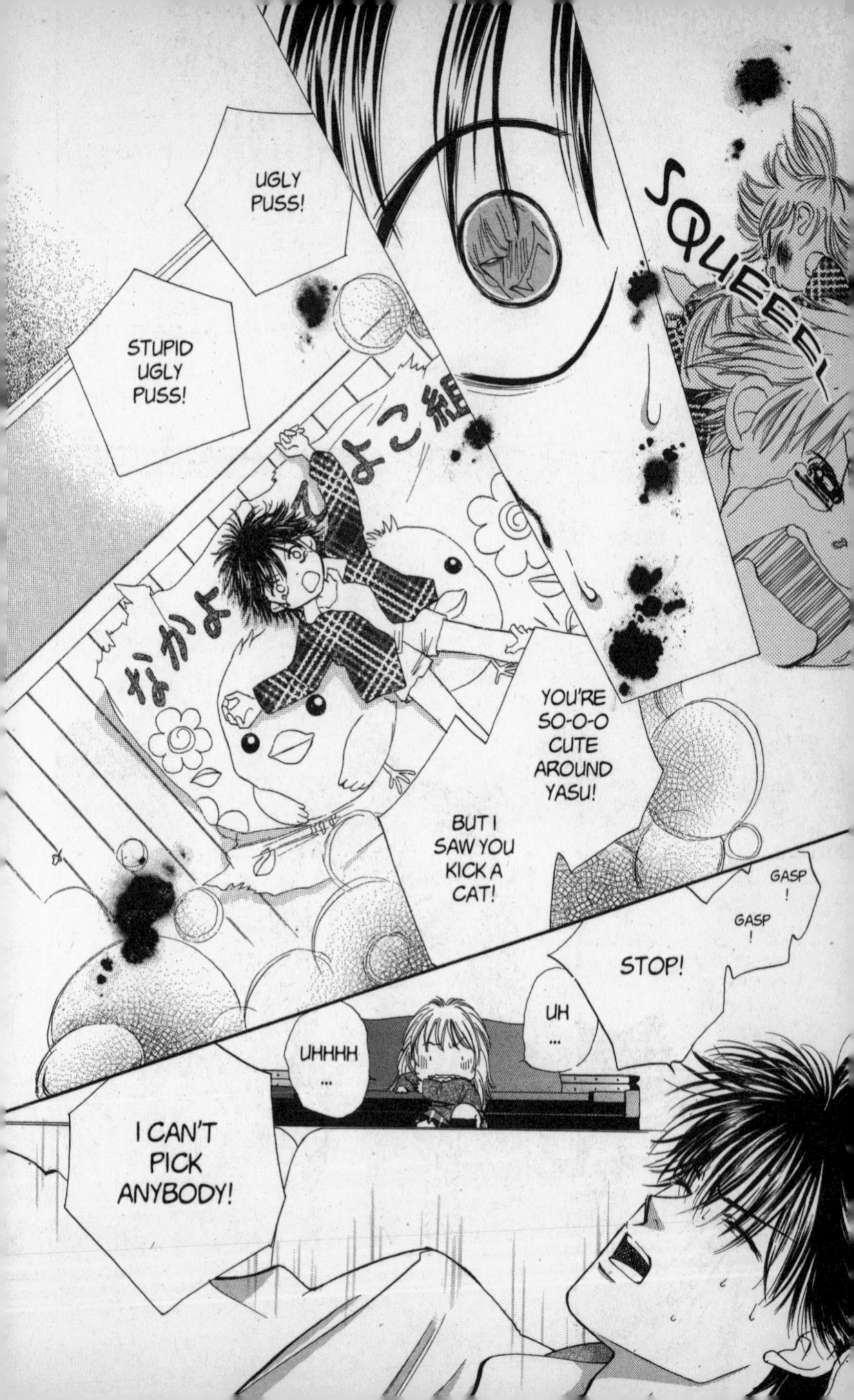
SQUEEEE!
UGLY PUSS!
STUPID UGLY PUSS!
よこ組
なかよ
YOU'RE SO-O-O CUTE AROUND YASU!
BUT I SAW YOU KICK A CAT!
GASP!
GASP!
STOP!
UH...
UHHHH...
I CAN'T PICK ANYBODY!

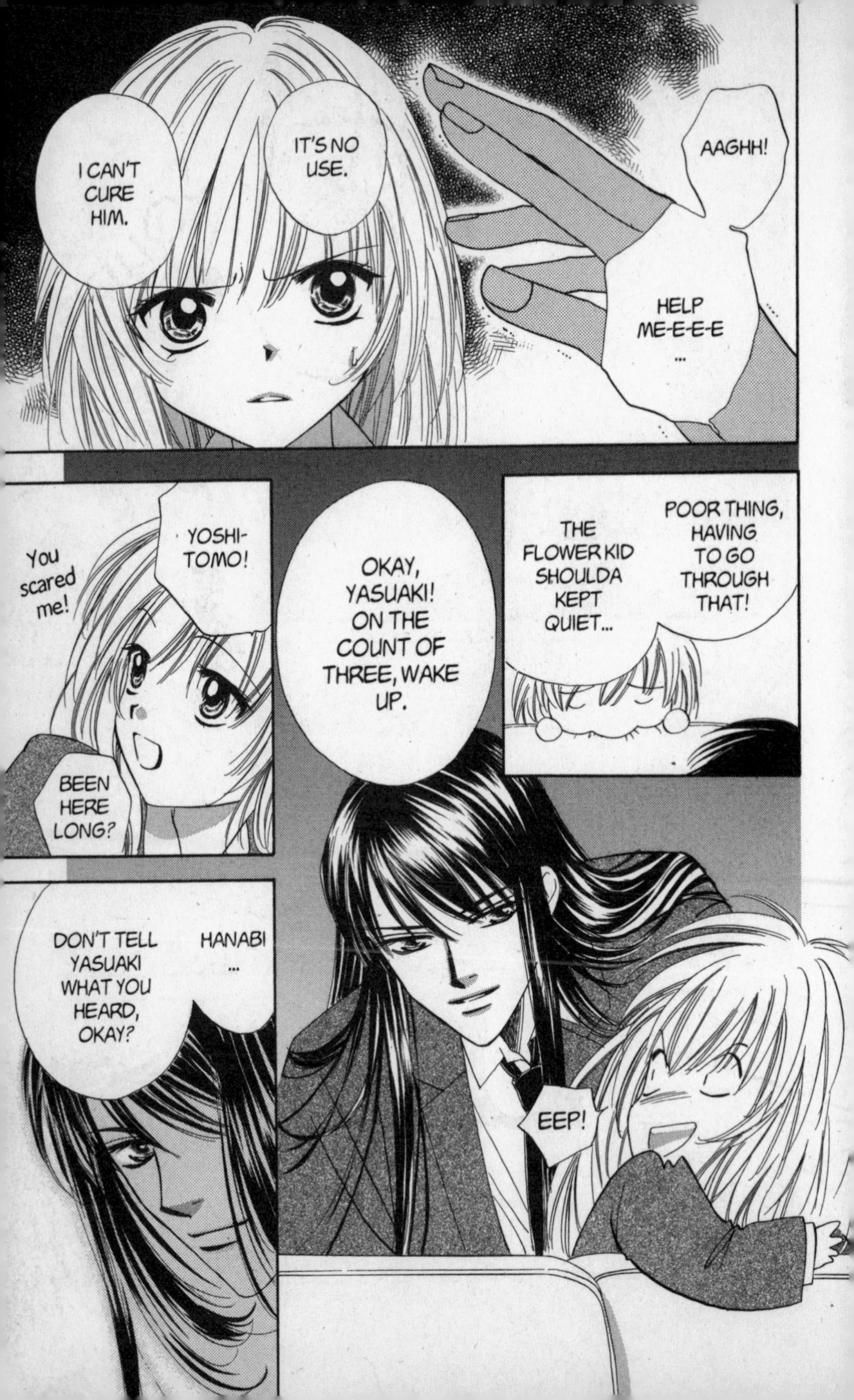
AAGHH!
HELP ME-E-E-E ...
IT'S NO USE.
I CAN'T CURE HIM.
POOR THING, HAVING TO GO THROUGH THAT!
THE FLOWER KID SHOULDA KEPT QUIET...
OKAY, YASUAKI! ON THE COUNT OF THREE, WAKE UP.
EEP!
YOSHI-TOMO!
You scared me!
BEEN HERE LONG?
HANABI ...
DON'T TELL YASUAKI WHAT YOU HEARD, OKAY?

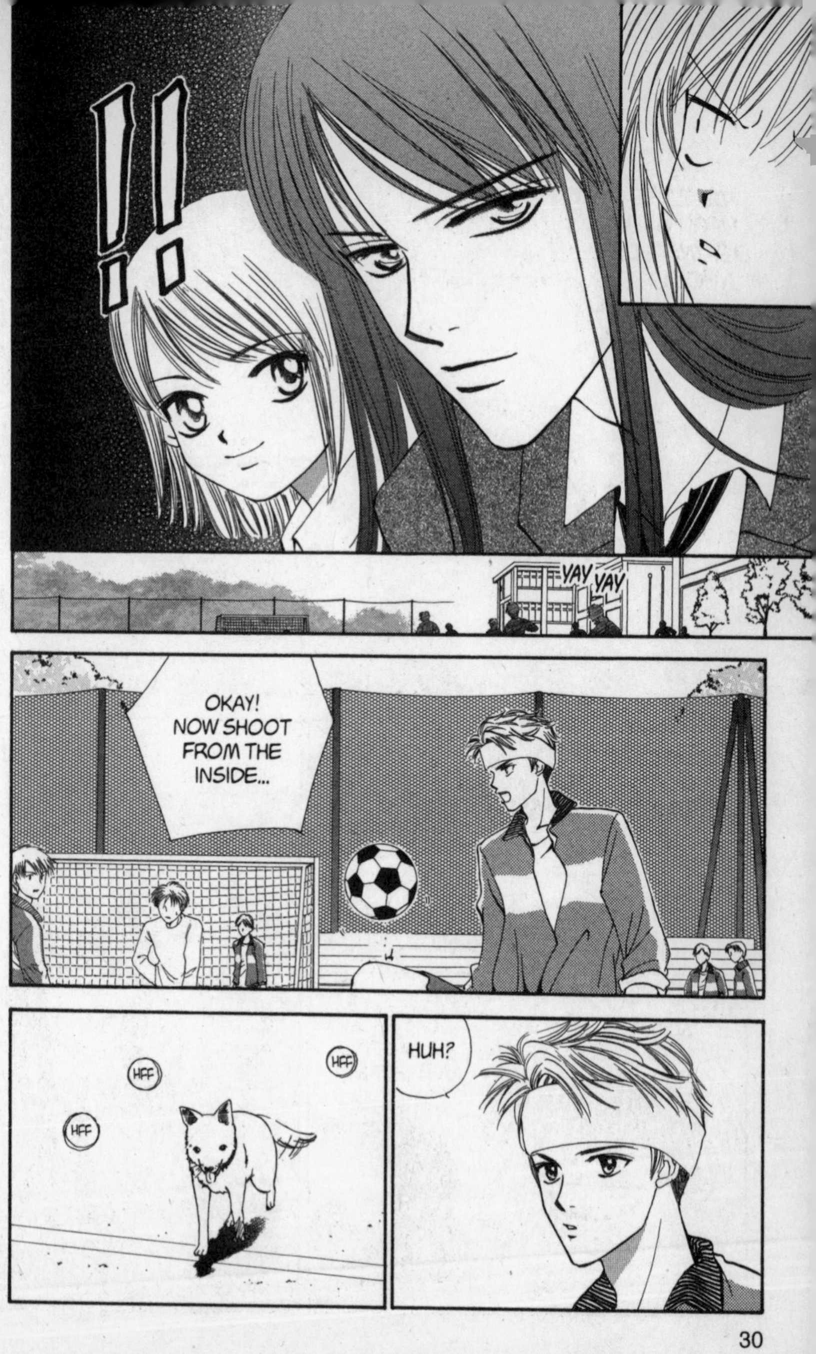
!!
YAY YAY
OKAY! NOW SHOOT FROM THE INSIDE...
HUH?
HFF
HFF
HFF

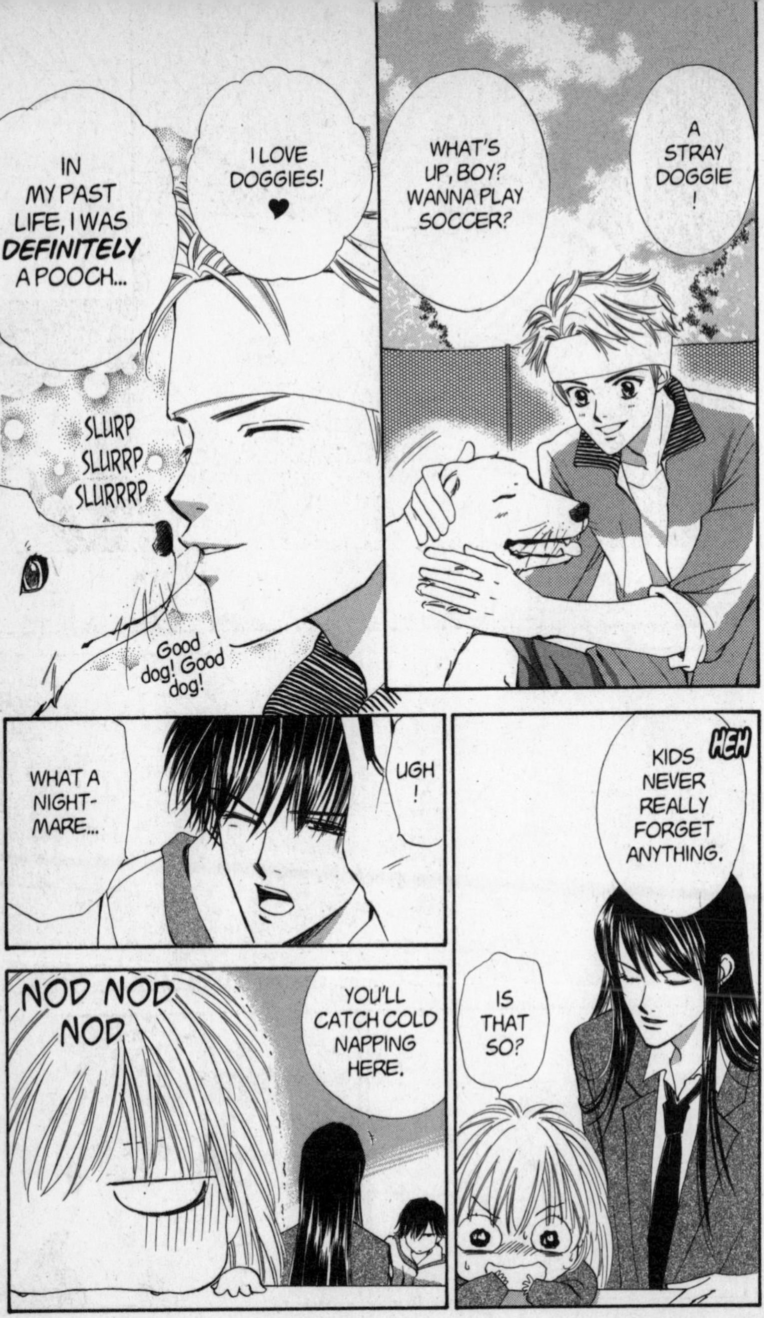
A STRAY DOGGIE!
WHAT'S UP, BOY? WANNA PLAY SOCCER?
I LOVE DOGGIES! ♥
IN MY PAST LIFE, I WAS DEFINITELY A POOCH...
SLURP SLURRP SLURRRP
Good dog! Good dog!
HEH
KIDS NEVER REALLY FORGET ANYTHING.
IS THAT SO?
UGH!
WHAT A NIGHTMARE...
YOU'LL CATCH COLD NAPPING HERE.
NOD NOD NOD

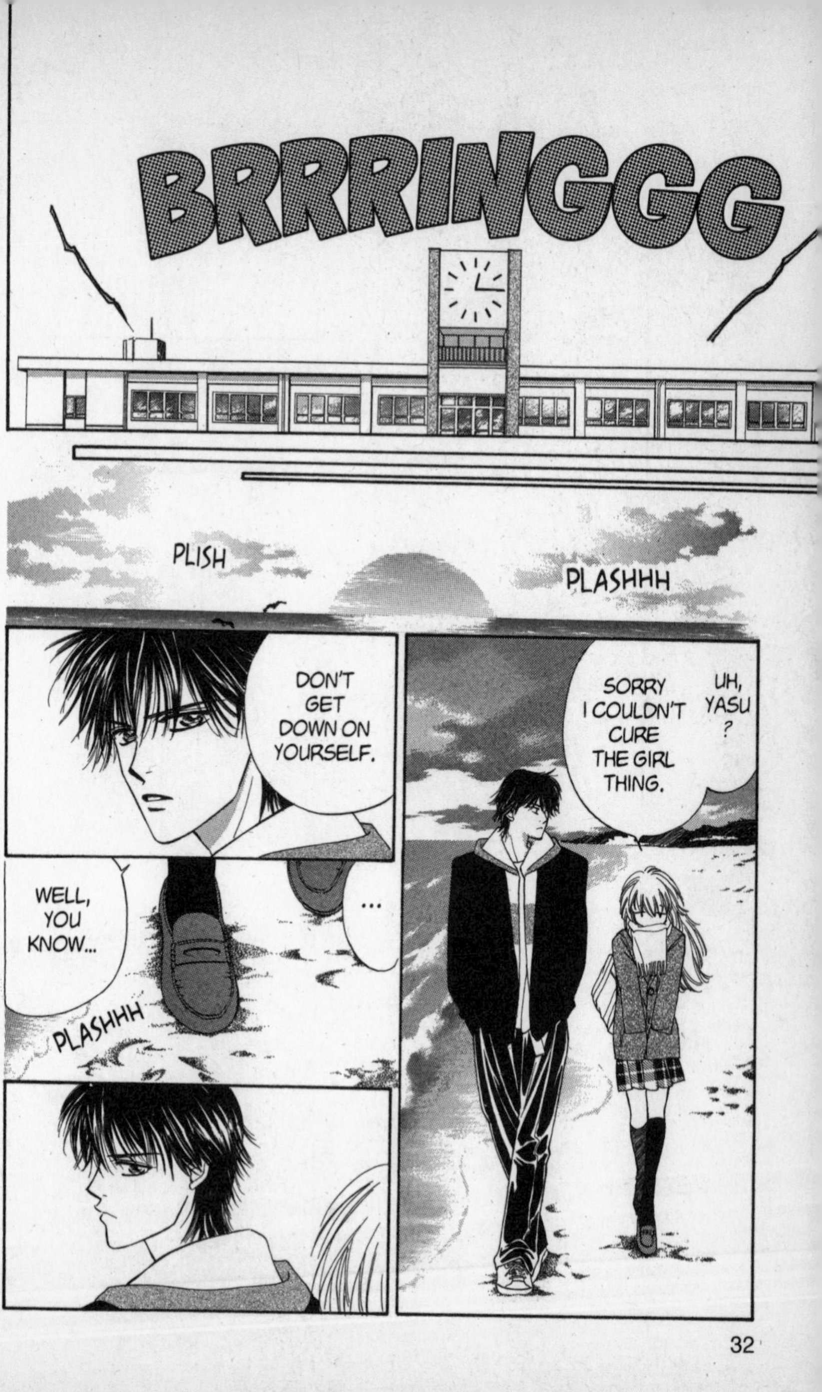
BRRRINGGG
PLASHHH
PLISH
UH, YASU?
SORRY I COULDN'T CURE THE GIRL THING.
DON'T GET DOWN ON YOURSELF.
...
WELL, YOU KNOW...
PLASHHH

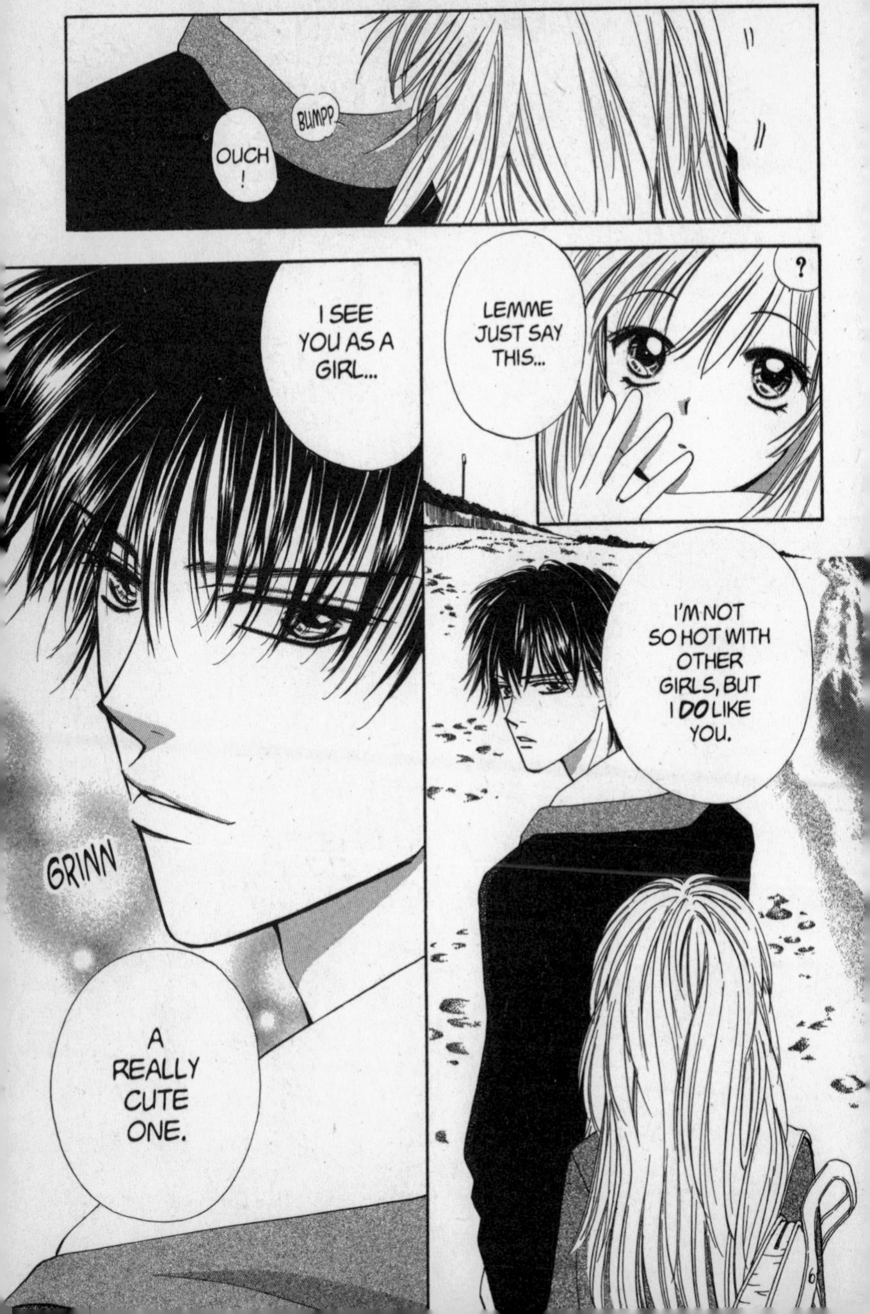
BUMPP
OUCH !
?
LEMME JUST SAY THIS...
I'M NOT SO HOT WITH OTHER GIRLS, BUT I **DO** LIKE YOU.
I SEE YOU AS A GIRL...
GRINN
A REALLY CUTE ONE.

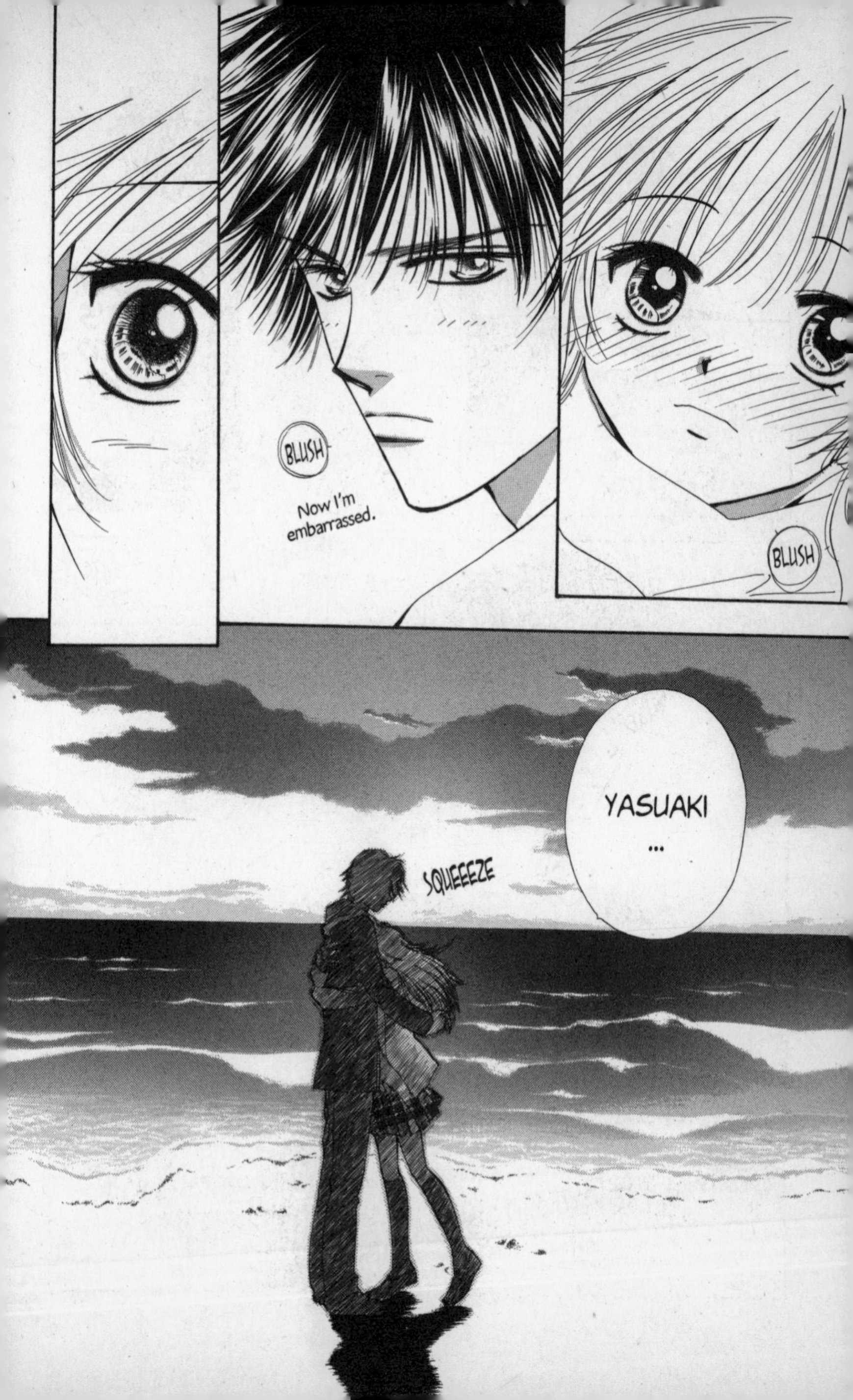
BLUSH
BLUSH
Now I'm embarrassed.
YASUAKI ...
SQUEEEZE

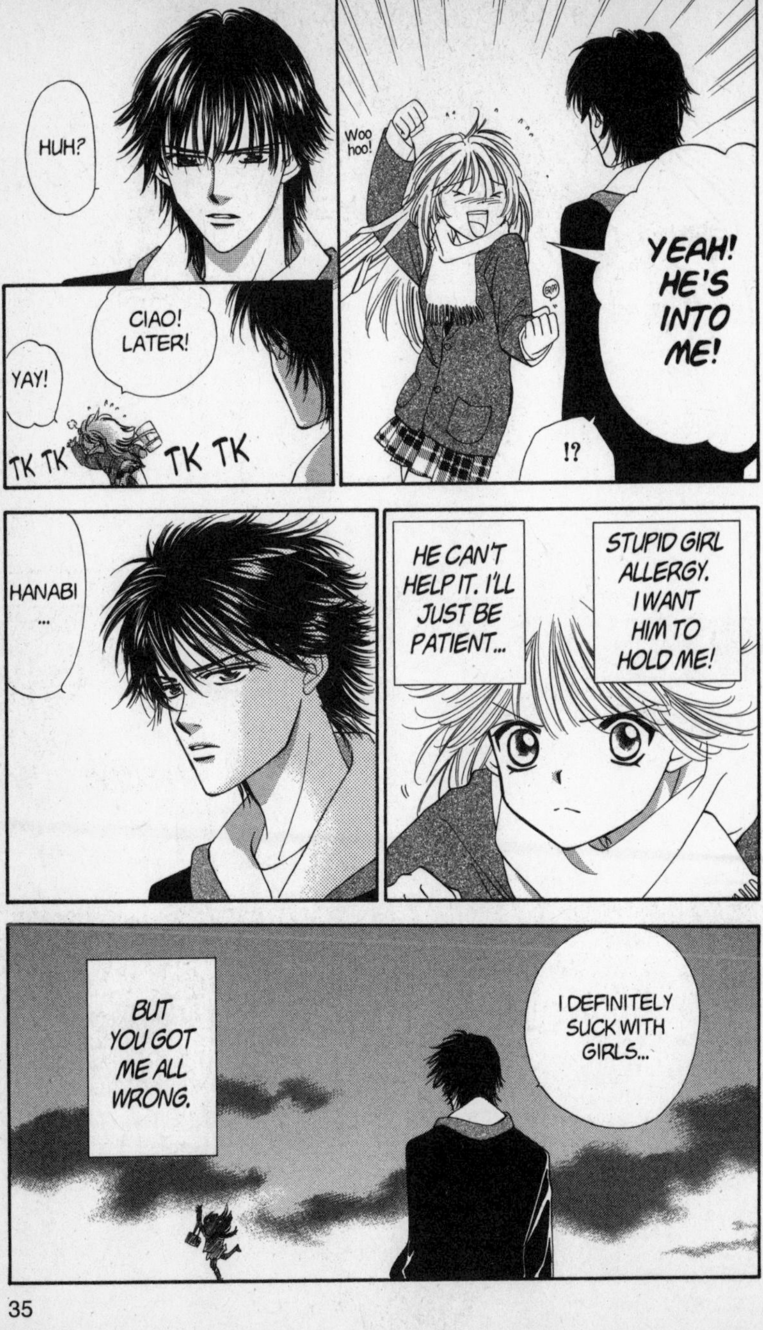
YEAH! HE'S INTO ME!
Woo hoo!
!?
HUH?
CIAO! LATER!
YAY!
TK TK
TK TK
STUPID GIRL ALLERGY. I WANT HIM TO HOLD ME!
HE CAN'T HELP IT. I'LL JUST BE PATIENT...
HANABI ...
I DEFINITELY SUCK WITH GIRLS...
BUT YOU GOT ME ALL WRONG.

HAPPY HUSTLE HIGH

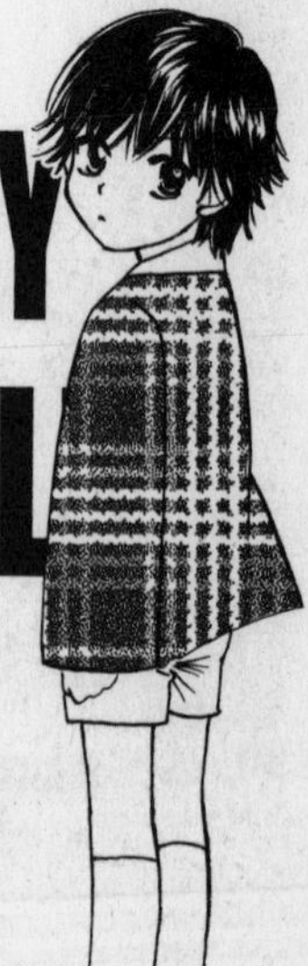

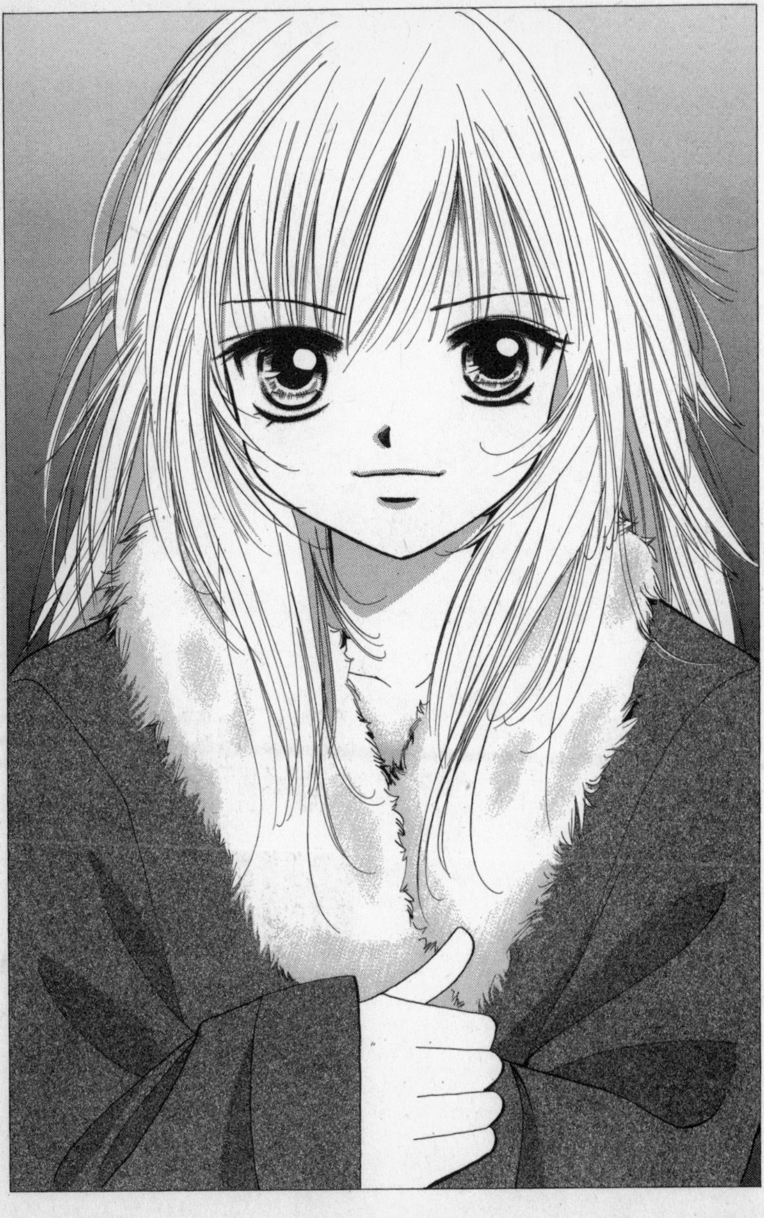

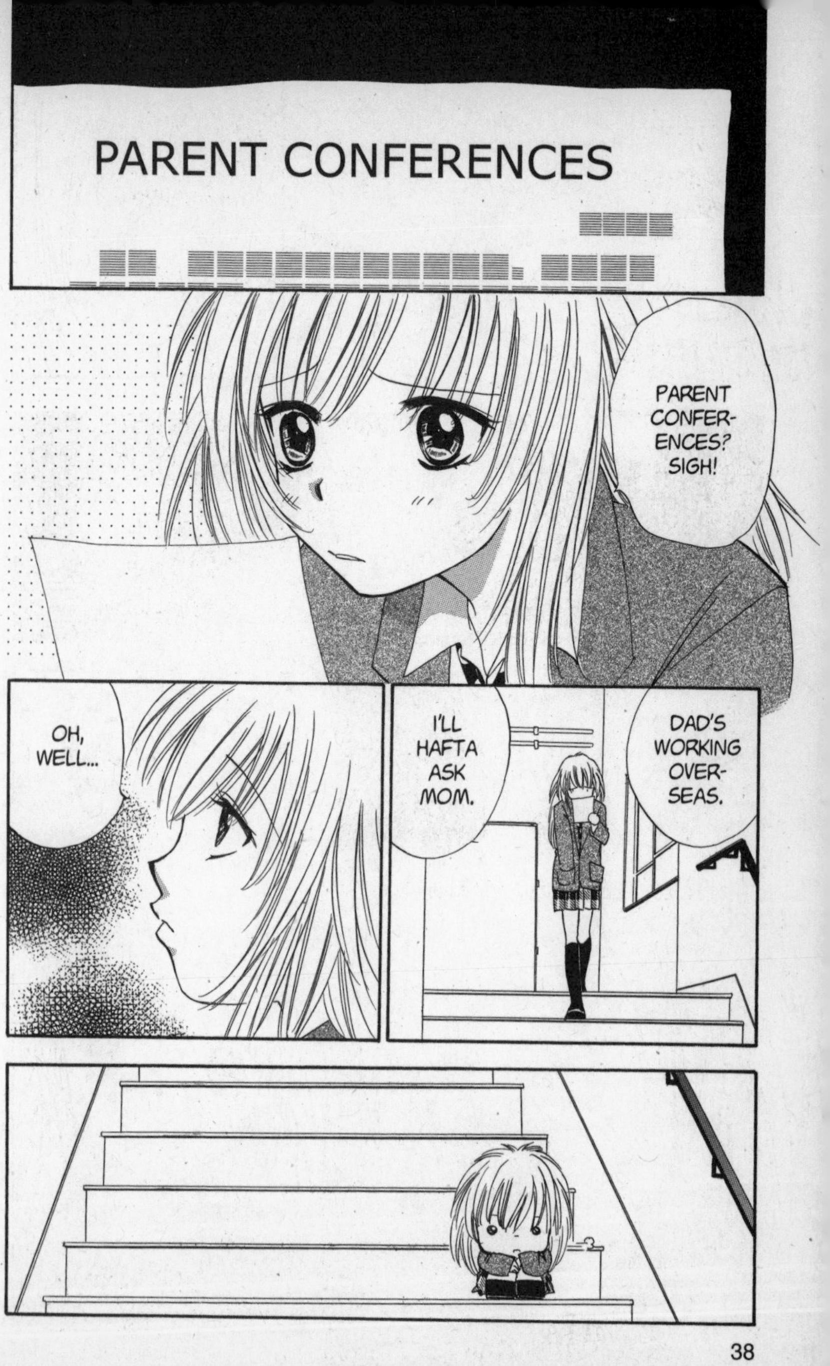
PARENT CONFERENCES
PARENT CONFERENCES? SIGH!
DAD'S WORKING OVERSEAS.
I'LL HAFTA ASK MOM.
OH, WELL...

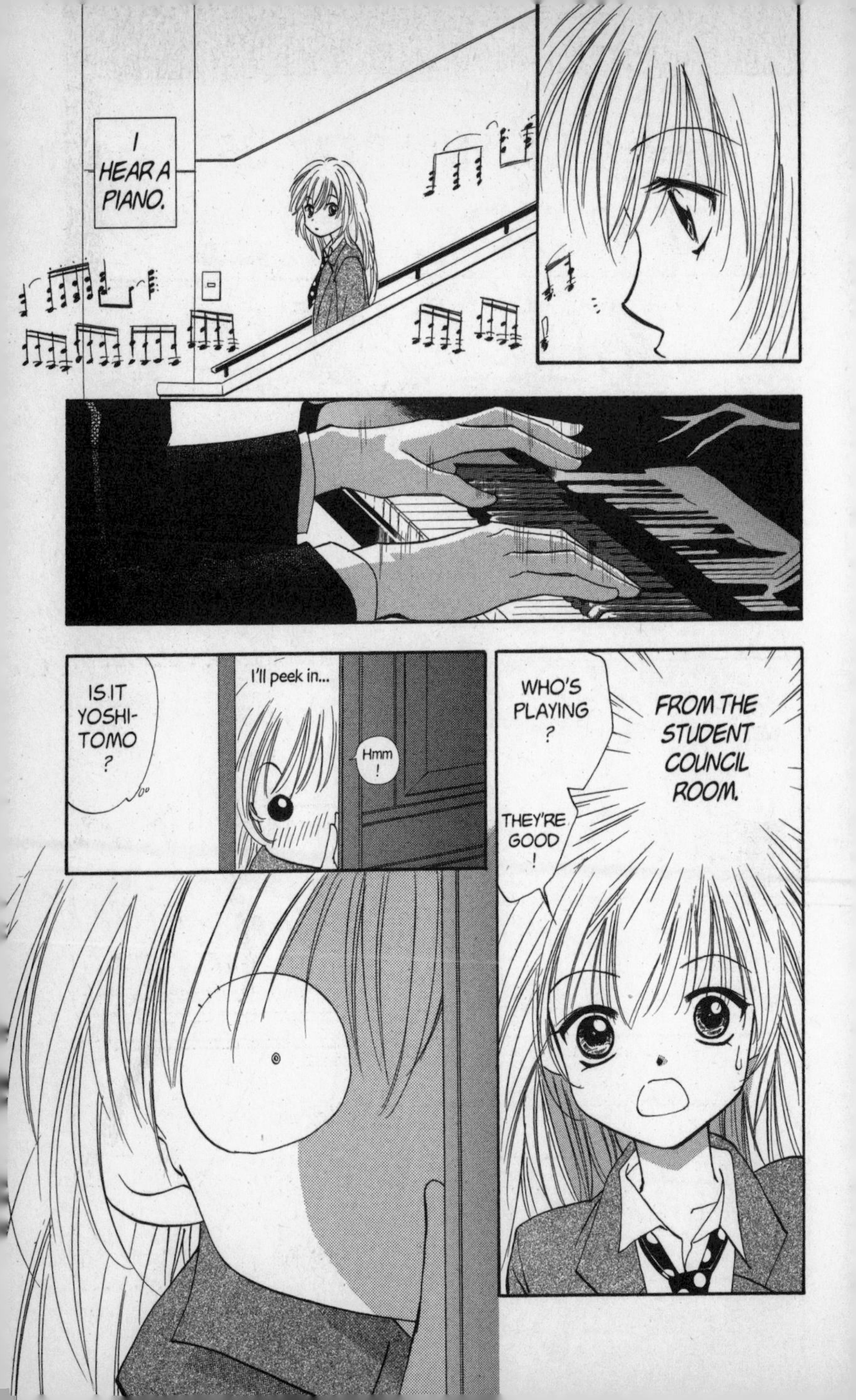
I HEAR A PIANO.
FROM THE STUDENT COUNCIL ROOM.
WHO'S PLAYING?
THEY'RE GOOD!
I'll peek in...
Hmm!
IS IT YOSHI-TOMO?

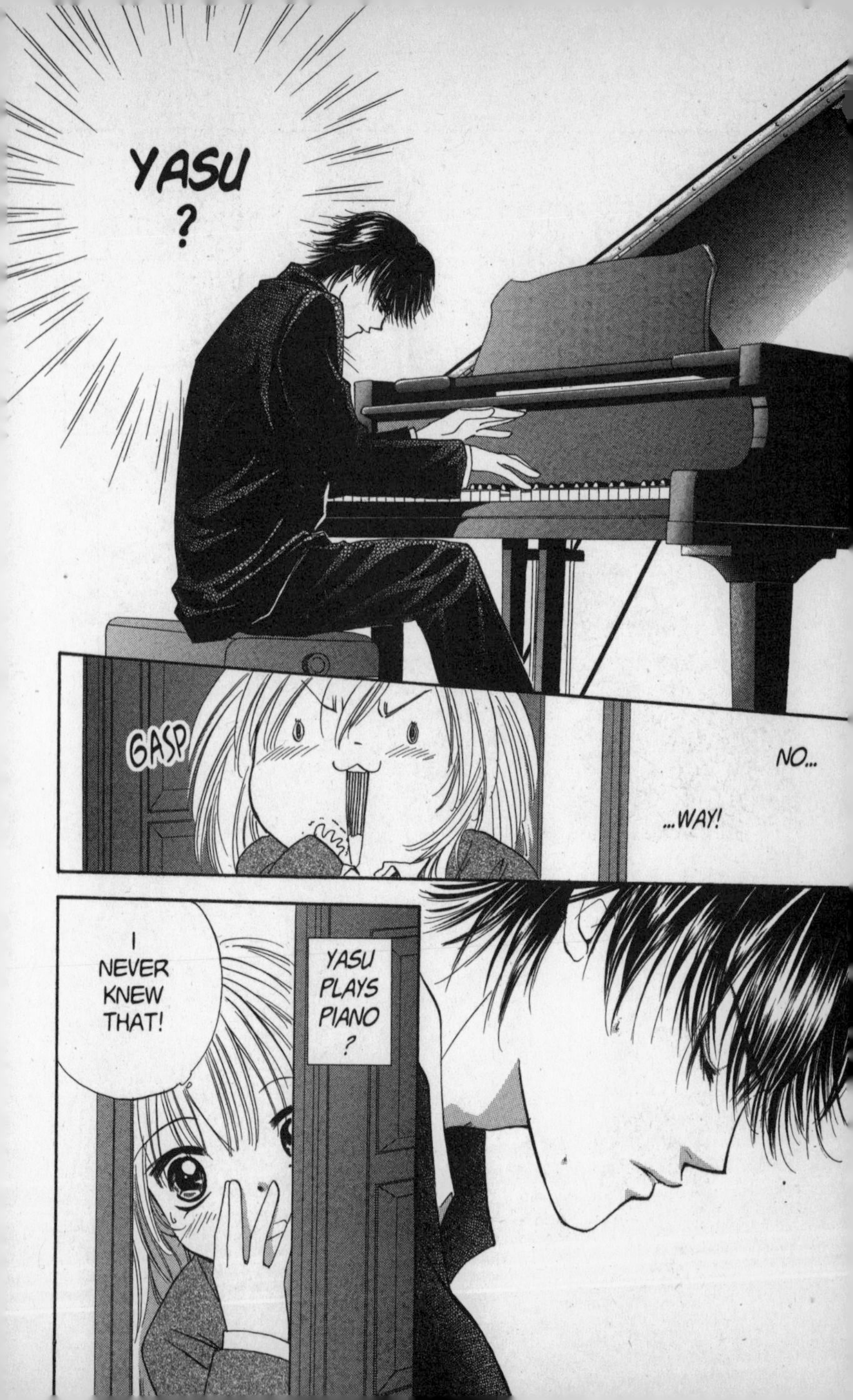
YASU ?
NO...
...WAY!
GASP
YASU PLAYS PIANO ?
I NEVER KNEW THAT!

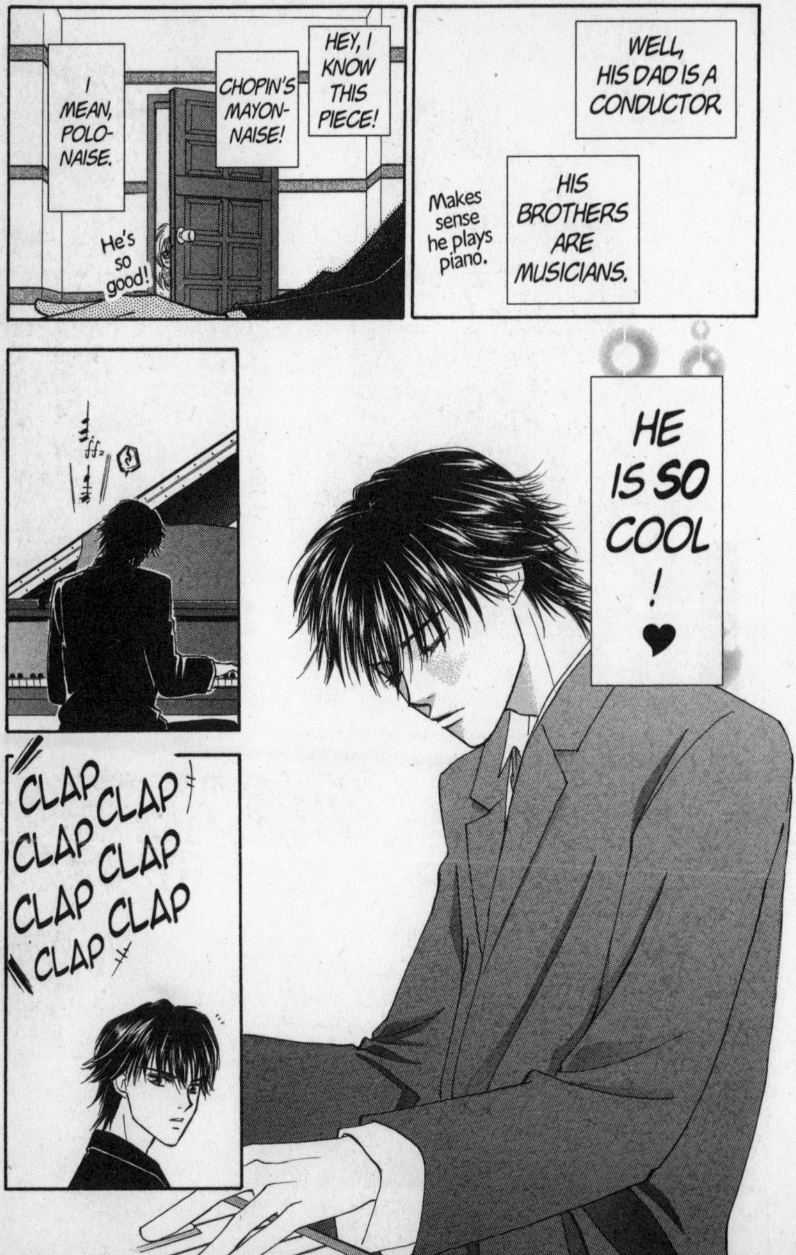
WELL, HIS DAD IS A CONDUCTOR.
HIS BROTHERS ARE MUSICIANS.
Makes sense he plays piano.
HEY, I KNOW THIS PIECE!
CHOPIN'S MAYON-NAISE!
I MEAN, POLO-NAISE.
He's so good!
HE IS SO COOL! ♥
CLAP CLAP CLAP CLAP CLAP CLAP CLAP CLAP

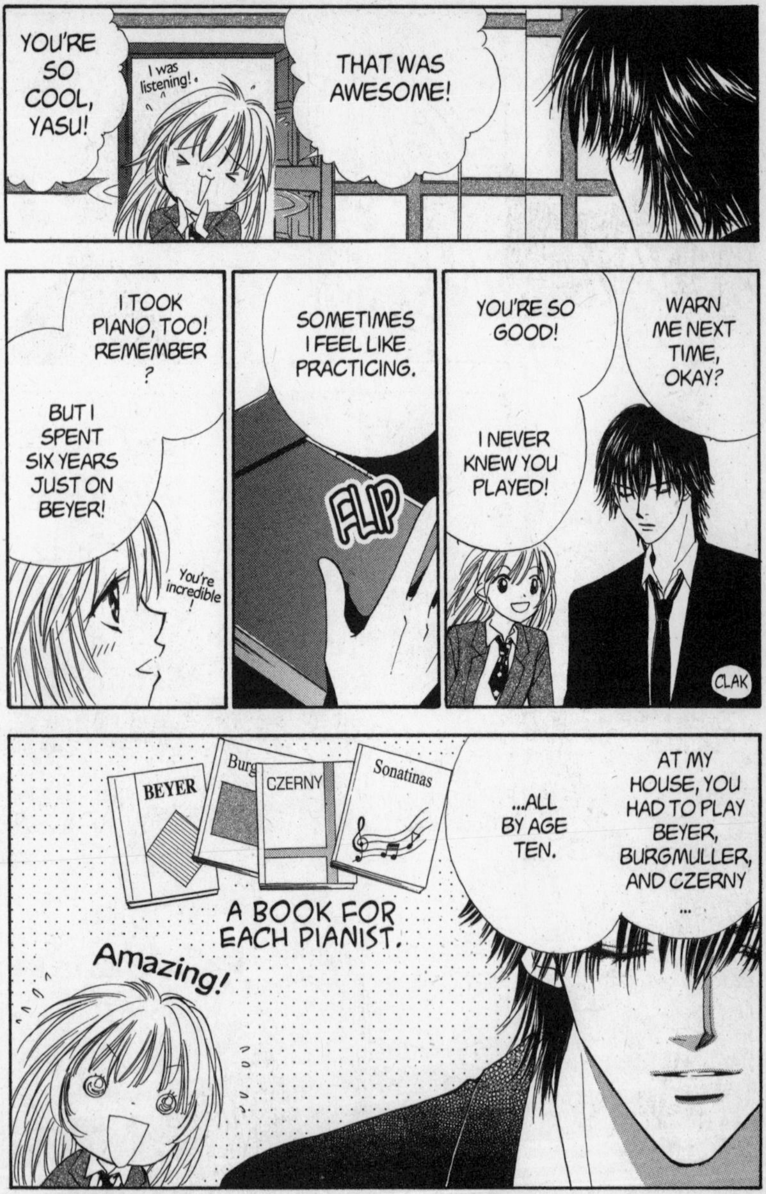
THAT WAS AWESOME!
YOU'RE SO COOL, YASU!
I was listening!
WARN ME NEXT TIME, OKAY?
YOU'RE SO GOOD!
I NEVER KNEW YOU PLAYED!
CLAK
SOMETIMES I FEEL LIKE PRACTICING.
FLIP
I TOOK PIANO, TOO! REMEMBER?
BUT I SPENT SIX YEARS JUST ON BEYER!
You're incredible!
AT MY HOUSE, YOU HAD TO PLAY BEYER, BURGMULLER, AND CZERNY ...
...ALL BY AGE TEN.
Sonatinas
CZERNY
Burg
BEYER
A BOOK FOR EACH PIANIST.
Amazing!

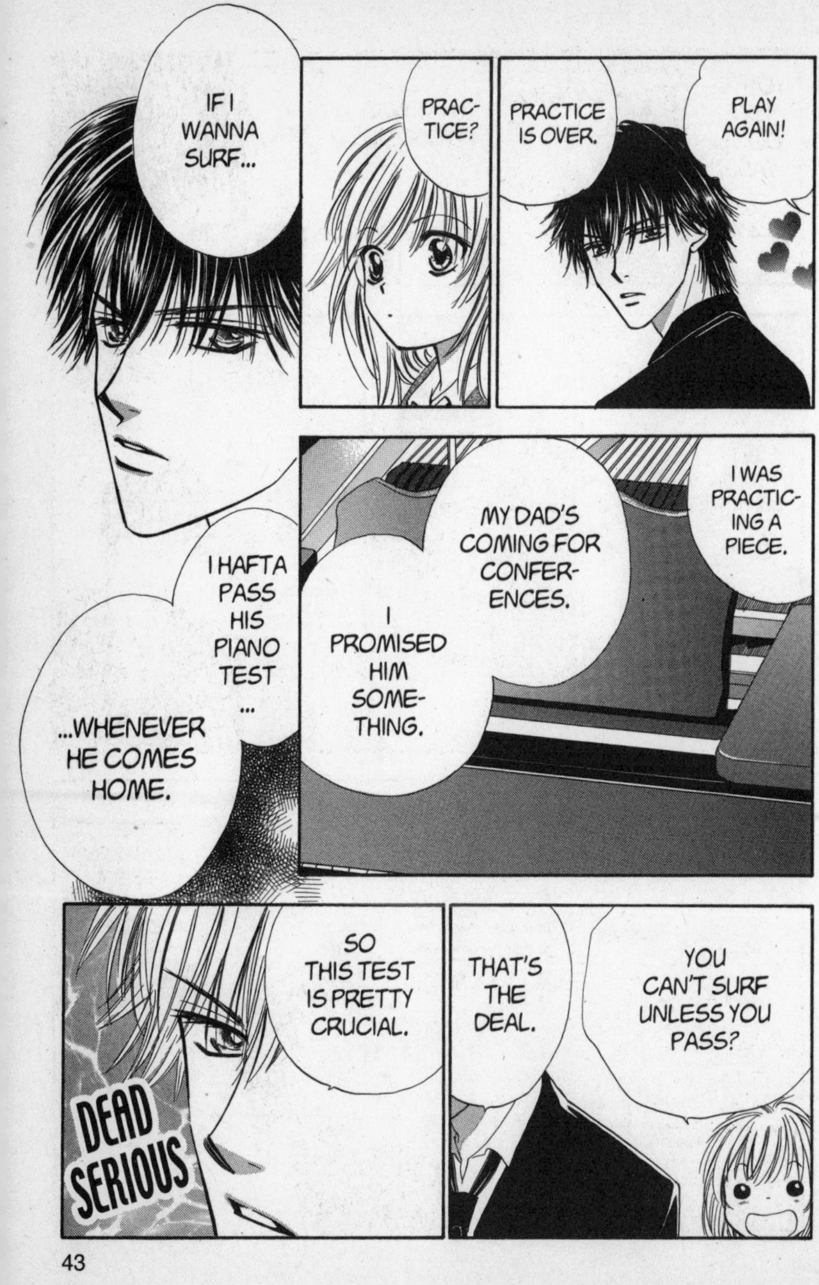
PLAY AGAIN!
PRACTICE IS OVER.
PRAC-TICE?
I WAS PRACTIC-ING A PIECE.
MY DAD'S COMING FOR CONFER-ENCES.
I PROMISED HIM SOME-THING.
IF I WANNA SURF...
I HAFTA PASS HIS PIANO TEST ...
...WHENEVER HE COMES HOME.
YOU CAN'T SURF UNLESS YOU PASS?
THAT'S THE DEAL.
SO THIS TEST IS PRETTY CRUCIAL.
DEAD SERIOUS

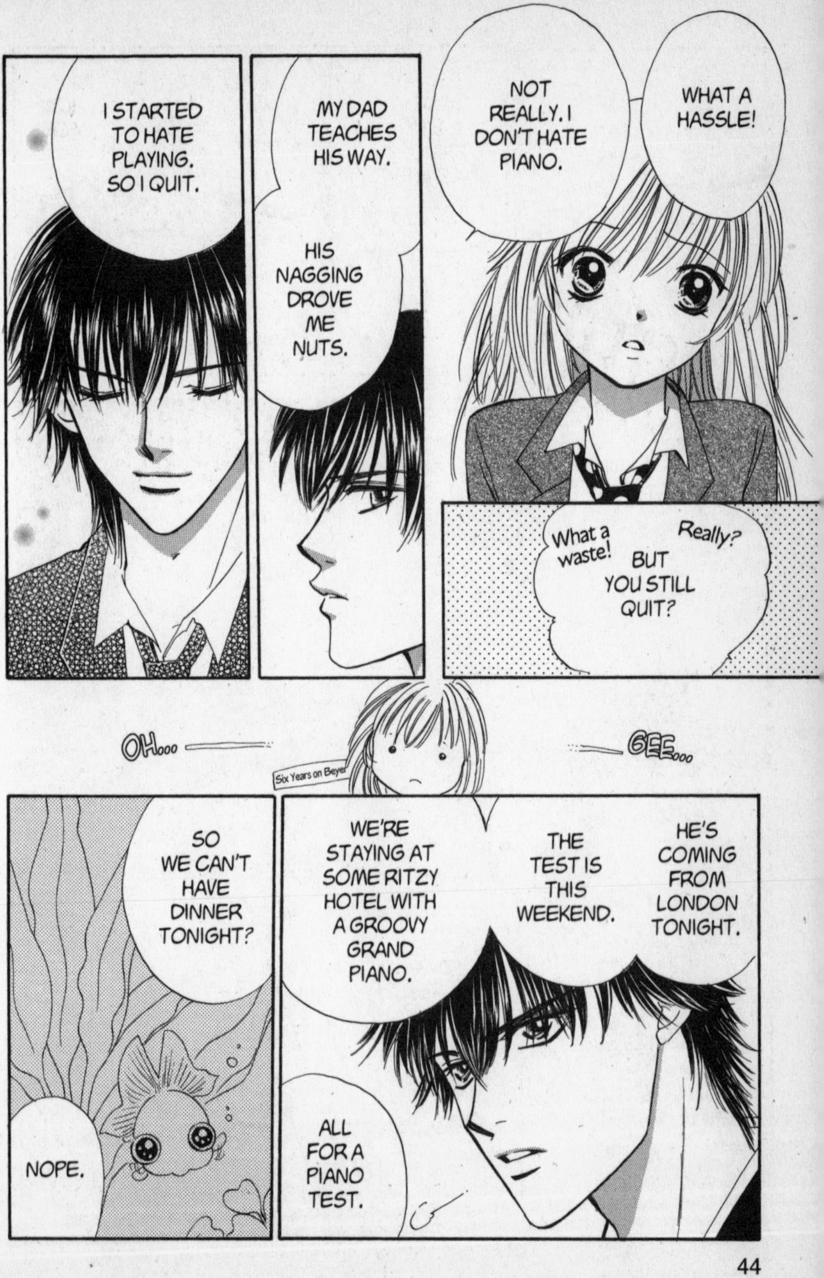
WHAT A HASSLE!
NOT REALLY. I DON'T HATE PIANO.
Really?
BUT YOU STILL QUIT?
What a waste!
MY DAD TEACHES HIS WAY.
HIS NAGGING DROVE ME NUTS.
I STARTED TO HATE PLAYING. SO I QUIT.
GEE...
Six Years on Beyer
OH...
HE'S COMING FROM LONDON TONIGHT.
THE TEST IS THIS WEEKEND.
WE'RE STAYING AT SOME RITZY HOTEL WITH A GROOVY GRAND PIANO.
ALL FOR A PIANO TEST.
SO WE CAN'T HAVE DINNER TONIGHT?
NOPE.

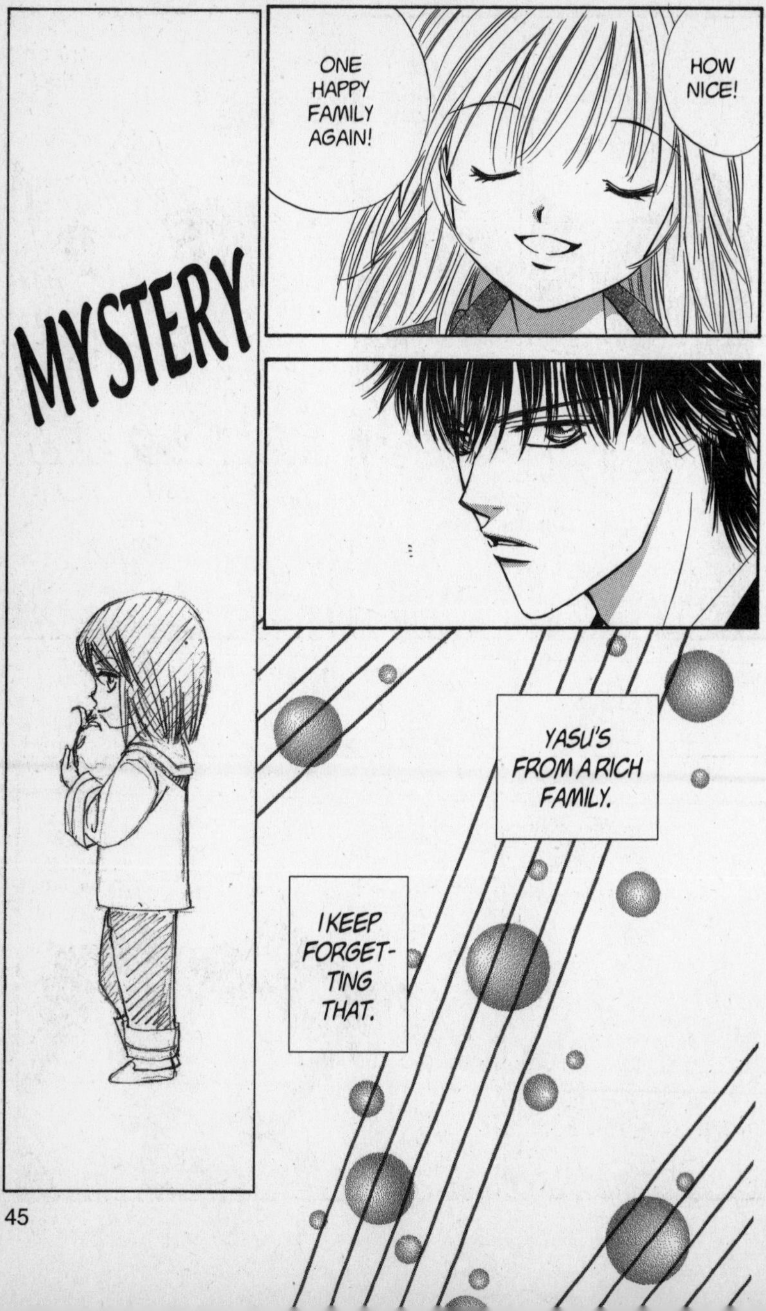
HOW NICE!
ONE HAPPY FAMILY AGAIN!
YASU'S FROM A RICH FAMILY.
I KEEP FORGET-TING THAT.
MYSTERY

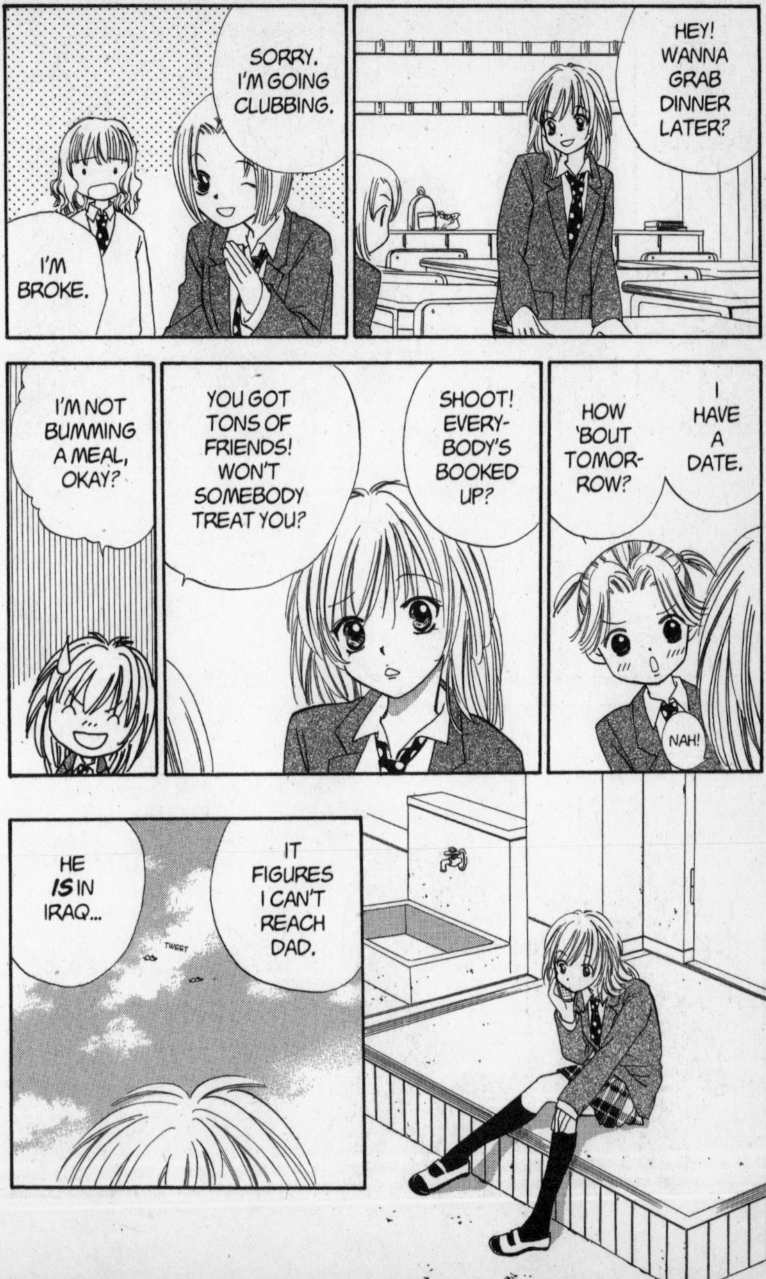
HEY! WANNA GRAB DINNER LATER?
SORRY. I'M GOING CLUBBING.
I'M BROKE.
I HAVE A DATE.
HOW 'BOUT TOMOR-ROW?
NAH!
SHOOT! EVERY-BODY'S BOOKED UP?
YOU GOT TONS OF FRIENDS! WON'T SOMEBODY TREAT YOU?
I'M NOT BUMMING A MEAL, OKAY?
IT FIGURES I CAN'T REACH DAD.
HE *IS* IN IRAQ...
TWEET

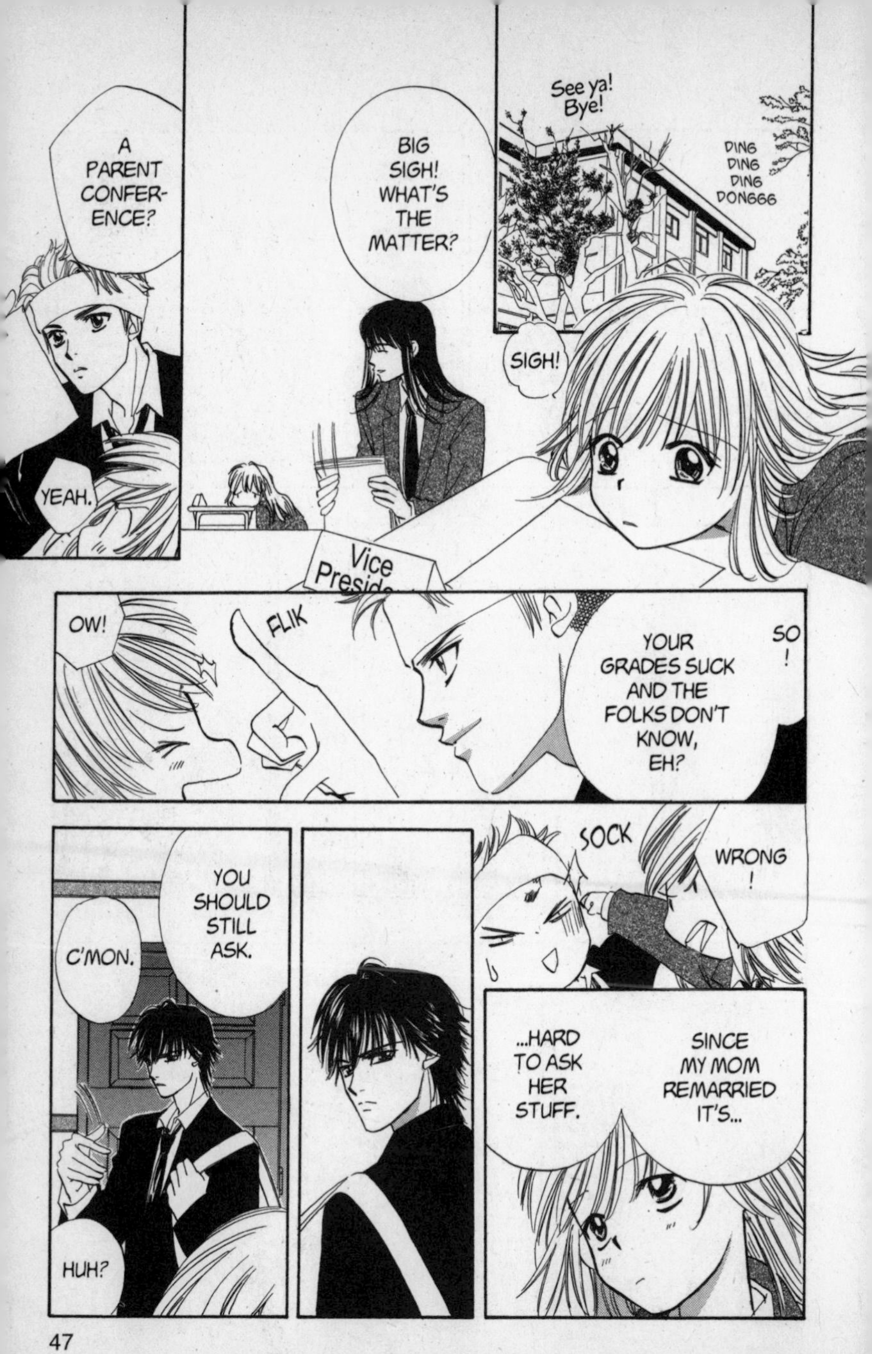
See ya! Bye!
DING DING DING DONGGG
SIGH!
BIG SIGH! WHAT'S THE MATTER?
Vice Preside
A PARENT CONFER-ENCE?
YEAH.
SO!
YOUR GRADES SUCK AND THE FOLKS DON'T KNOW, EH?
FLIK
OW!
WRONG!
SOCK
SINCE MY MOM REMARRIED IT'S...
...HARD TO ASK HER STUFF.
YOU SHOULD STILL ASK.
C'MON.
HUH?

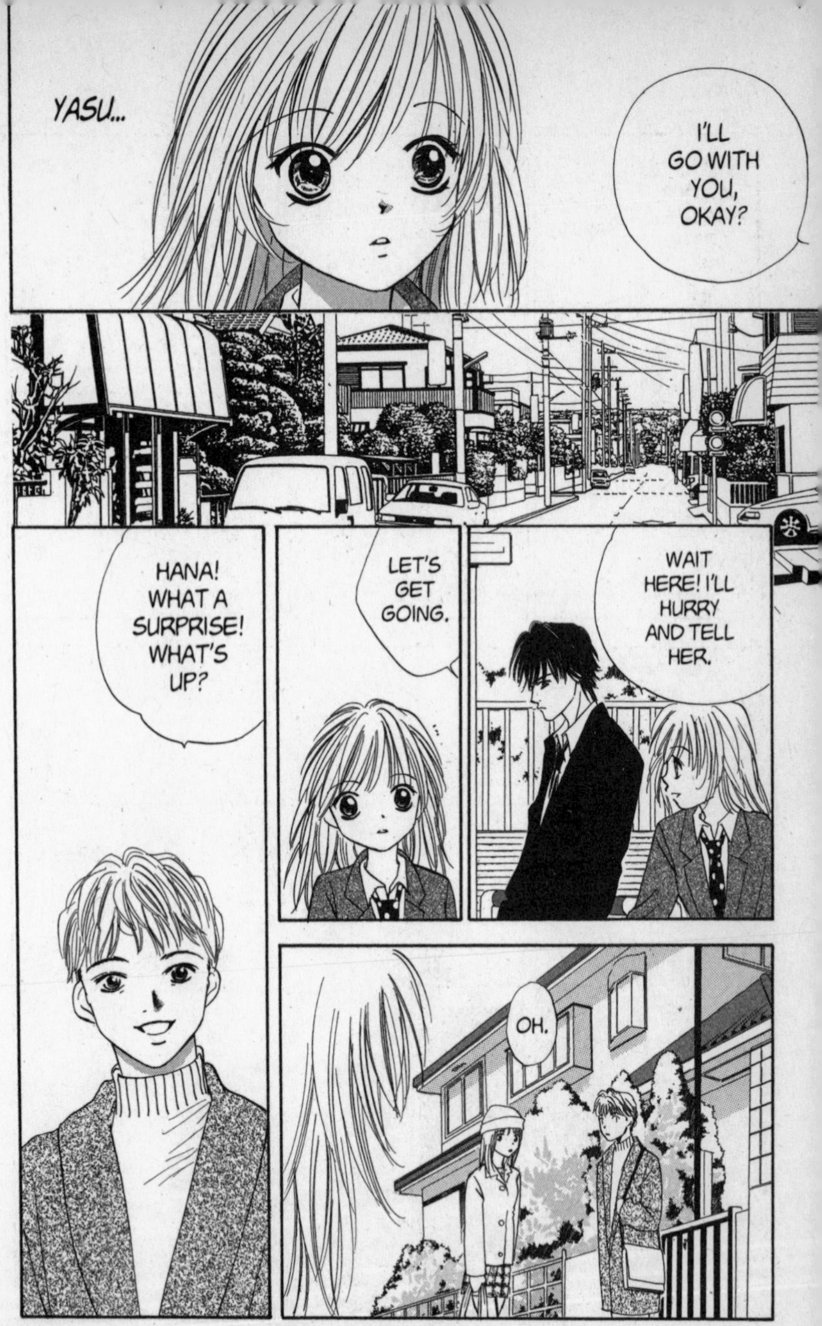
I'LL GO WITH YOU, OKAY?
YASU...
WAIT HERE! I'LL HURRY AND TELL HER.
LET'S GET GOING.
OH.
HANA! WHAT A SURPRISE! WHAT'S UP?

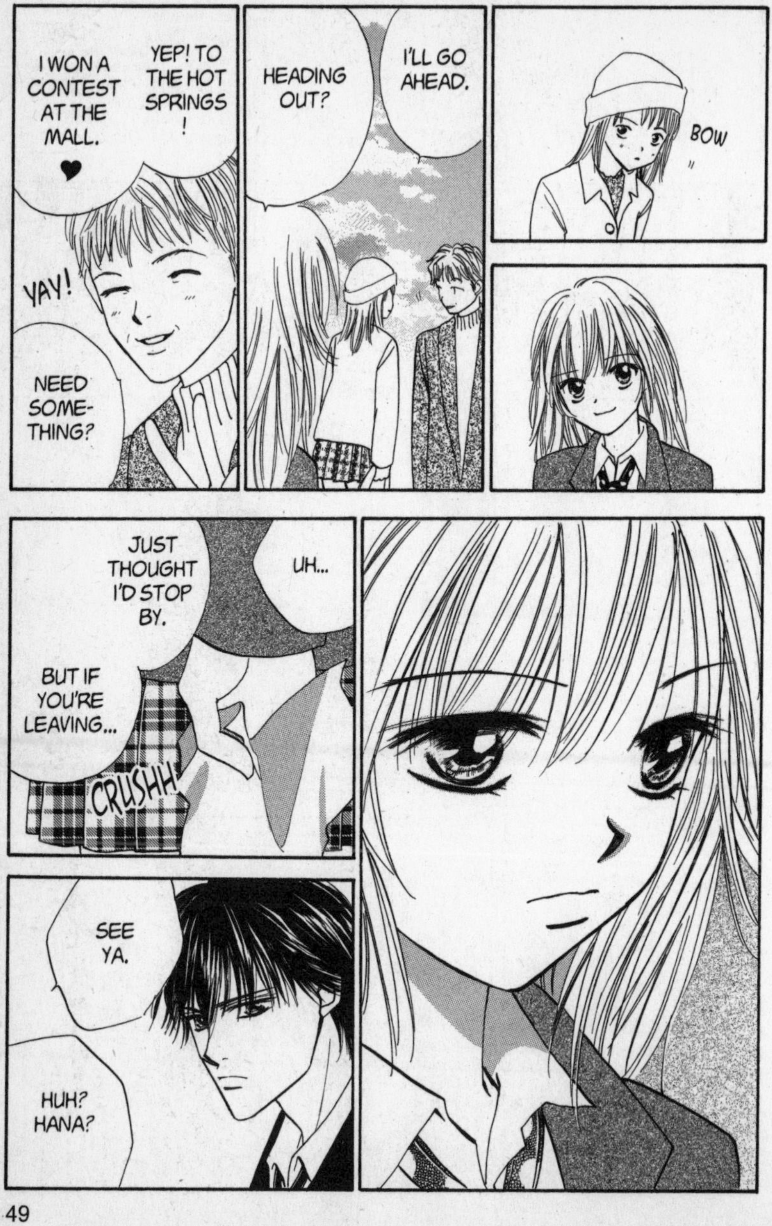
BOW
I'LL GO AHEAD.
HEADING OUT?
YEP! TO THE HOT SPRINGS!
I WON A CONTEST AT THE MALL. ♥
YAY!
NEED SOMETHING?
UH...
JUST THOUGHT I'D STOP BY.
BUT IF YOU'RE LEAVING...
CRUSHH
SEE YA.
HUH? HANA?

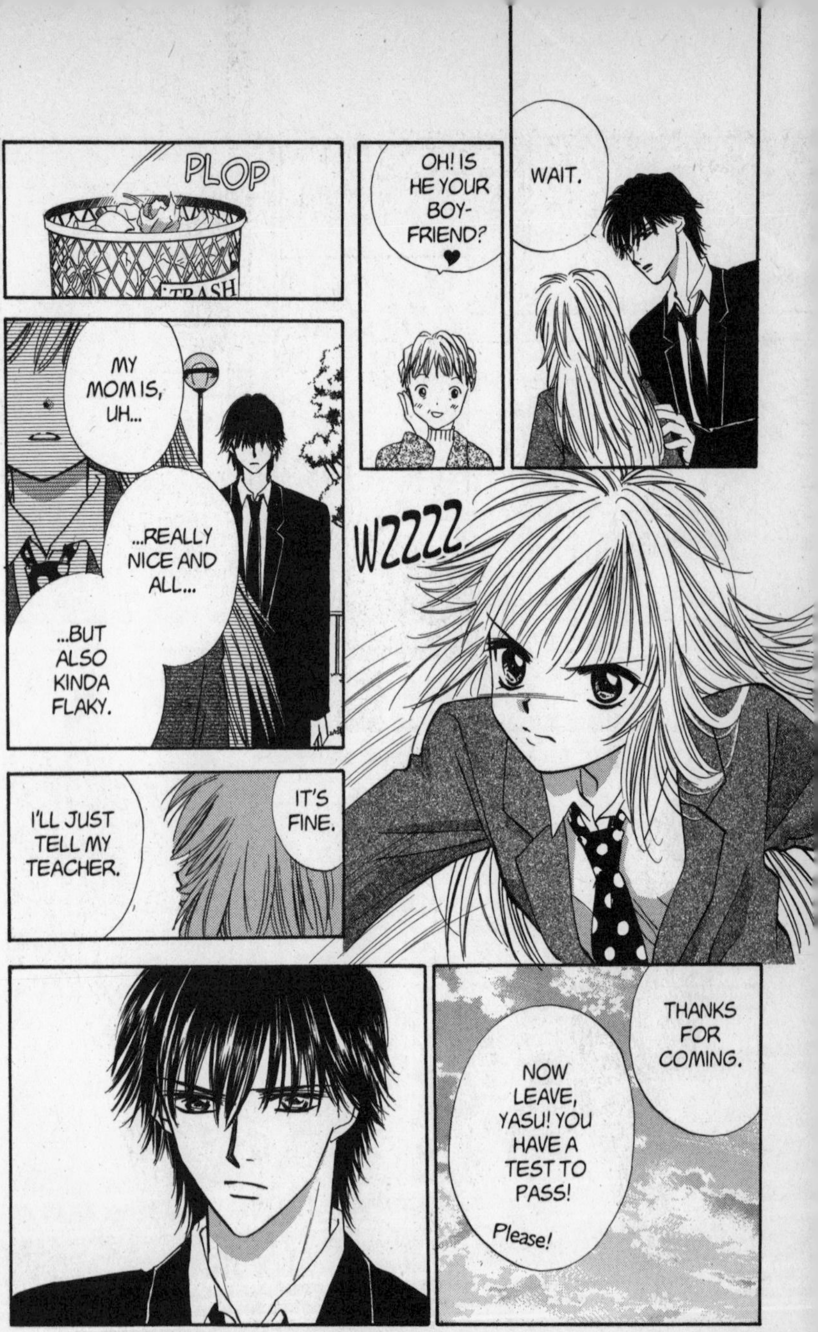
WAIT.
OH! IS HE YOUR BOY-FRIEND? ♥
WZZZZ
PLOP
TRASH
MY MOM IS, UH...
...REALLY NICE AND ALL...
...BUT ALSO KINDA FLAKY.
IT'S FINE.
I'LL JUST TELL MY TEACHER.
THANKS FOR COMING.
NOW LEAVE, YASU! YOU HAVE A TEST TO PASS!
Please!

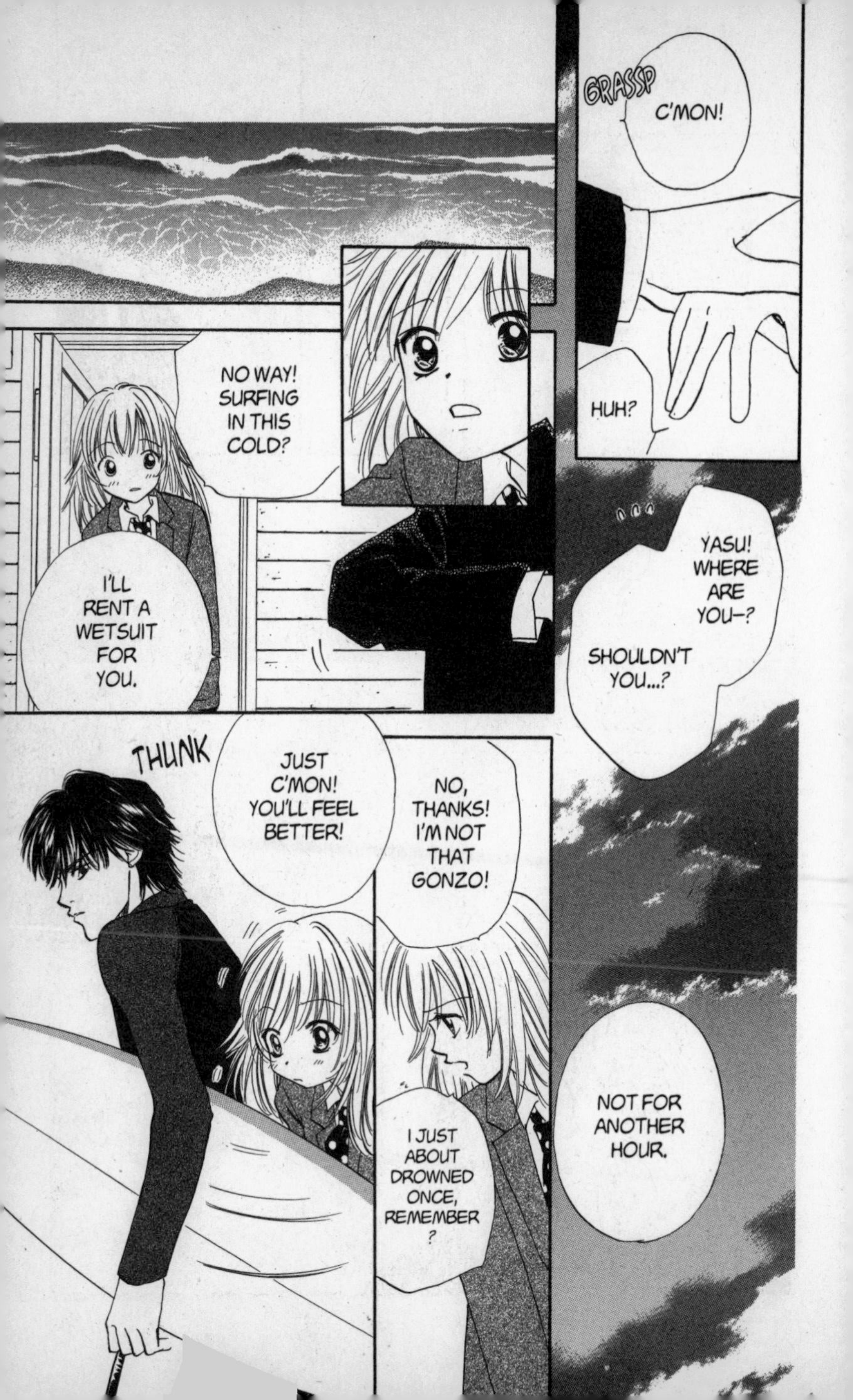
I'LL RENT A WETSUIT FOR YOU.
NO WAY! SURFING IN THIS COLD?
THUNK
JUST C'MON! YOU'LL FEEL BETTER!
NO, THANKS! I'M NOT THAT GONZO!
I JUST ABOUT DROWNED ONCE, REMEMBER?
GRASSP
C'MON!
HUH?
...
YASU! WHERE ARE YOU–?
SHOULDN'T YOU...?
NOT FOR ANOTHER HOUR.

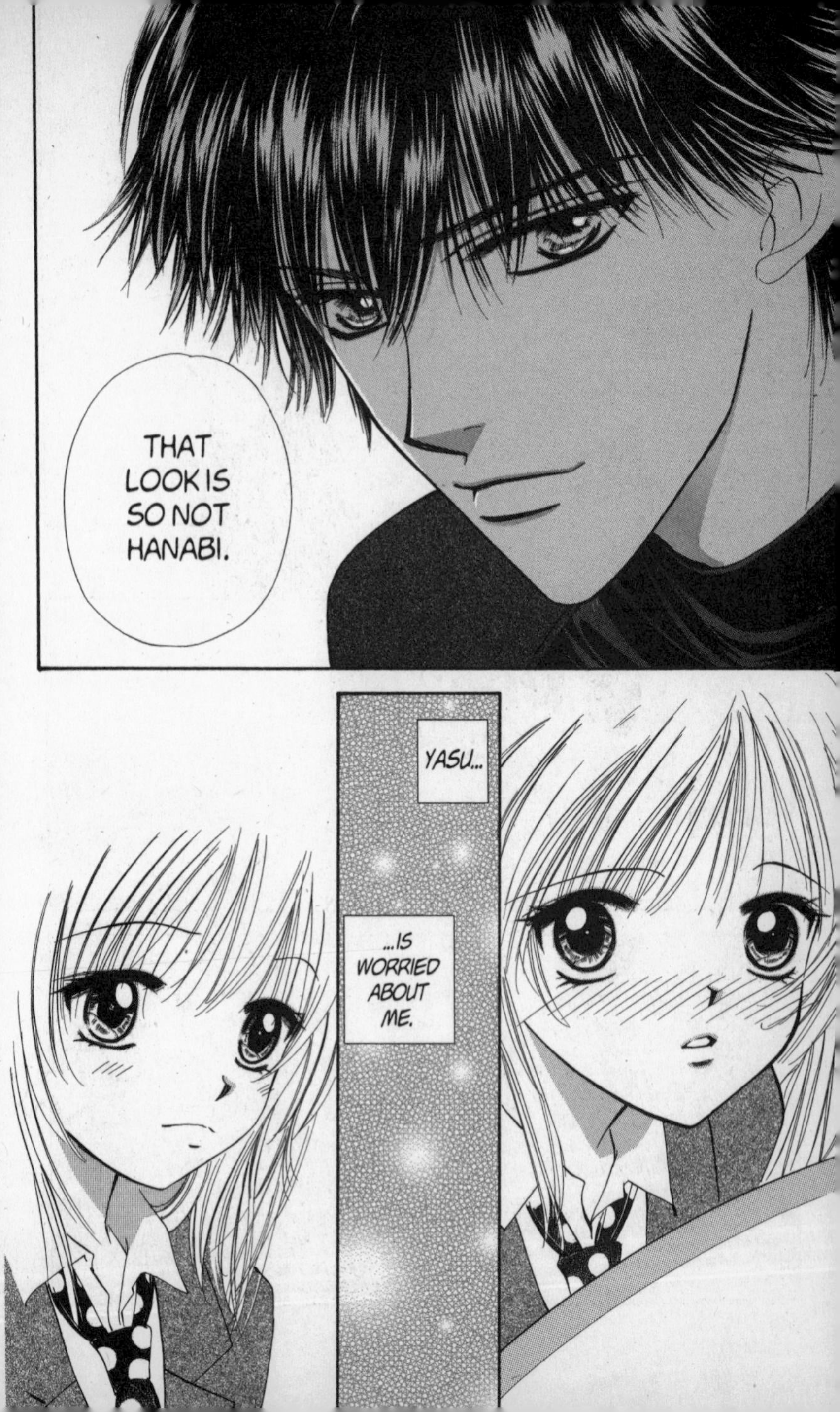
THAT LOOK IS SO NOT HANABI.
YASU...
...IS WORRIED ABOUT ME.

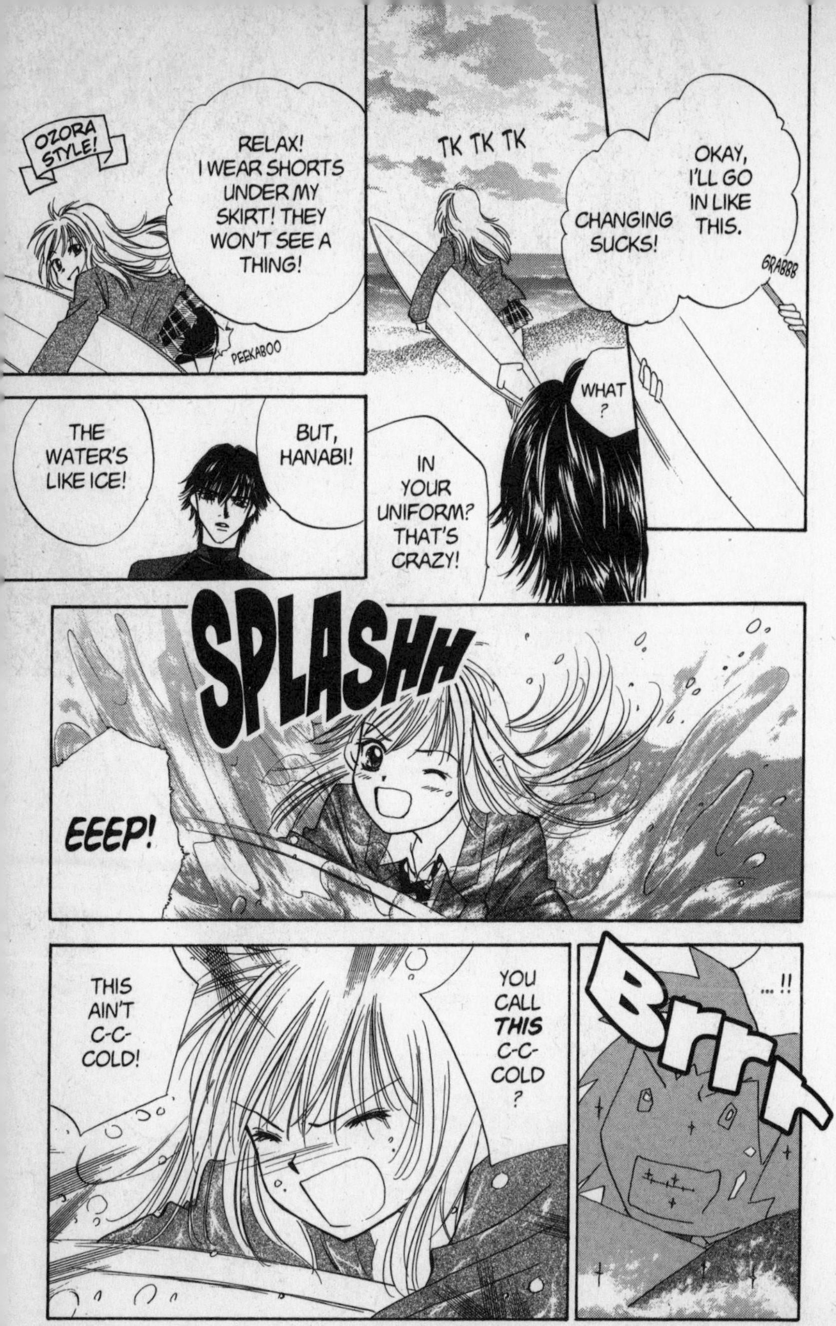
TK TK TK
OKAY, I'LL GO IN LIKE THIS.
CHANGING SUCKS!
GRABBB
WHAT?
OZORA STYLE!
RELAX! I WEAR SHORTS UNDER MY SKIRT! THEY WON'T SEE A THING!
PEEKABOO
BUT, HANABI!
IN YOUR UNIFORM? THAT'S CRAZY!
THE WATER'S LIKE ICE!
SPLASHH
EEEP!
Brrr
...!!
YOU CALL THIS C-C-COLD?
THIS AIN'T C-C-COLD!

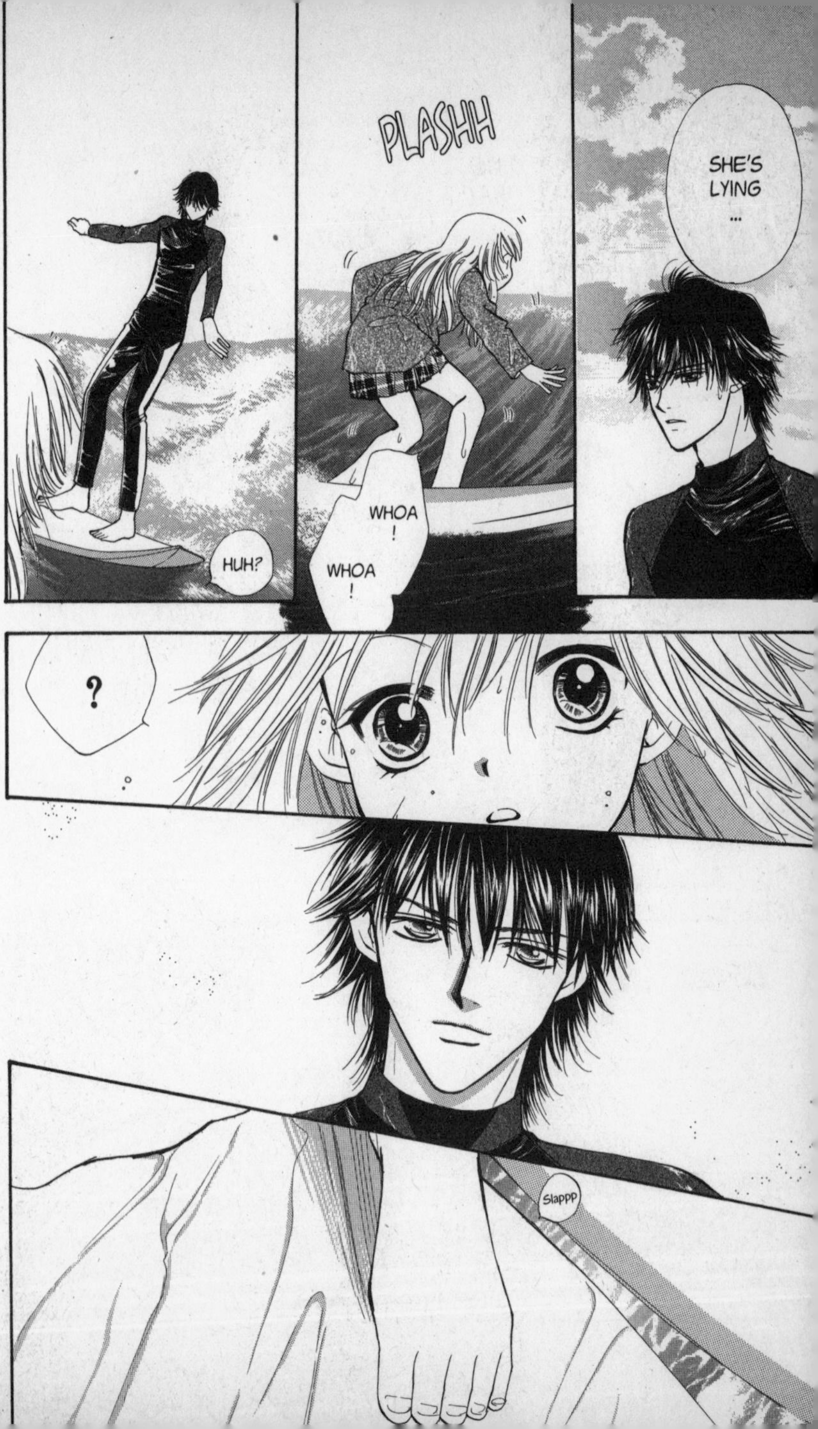
SHE'S LYING ...
PLASHH
WHOA! WHOA!
HUH?
?
Slappp

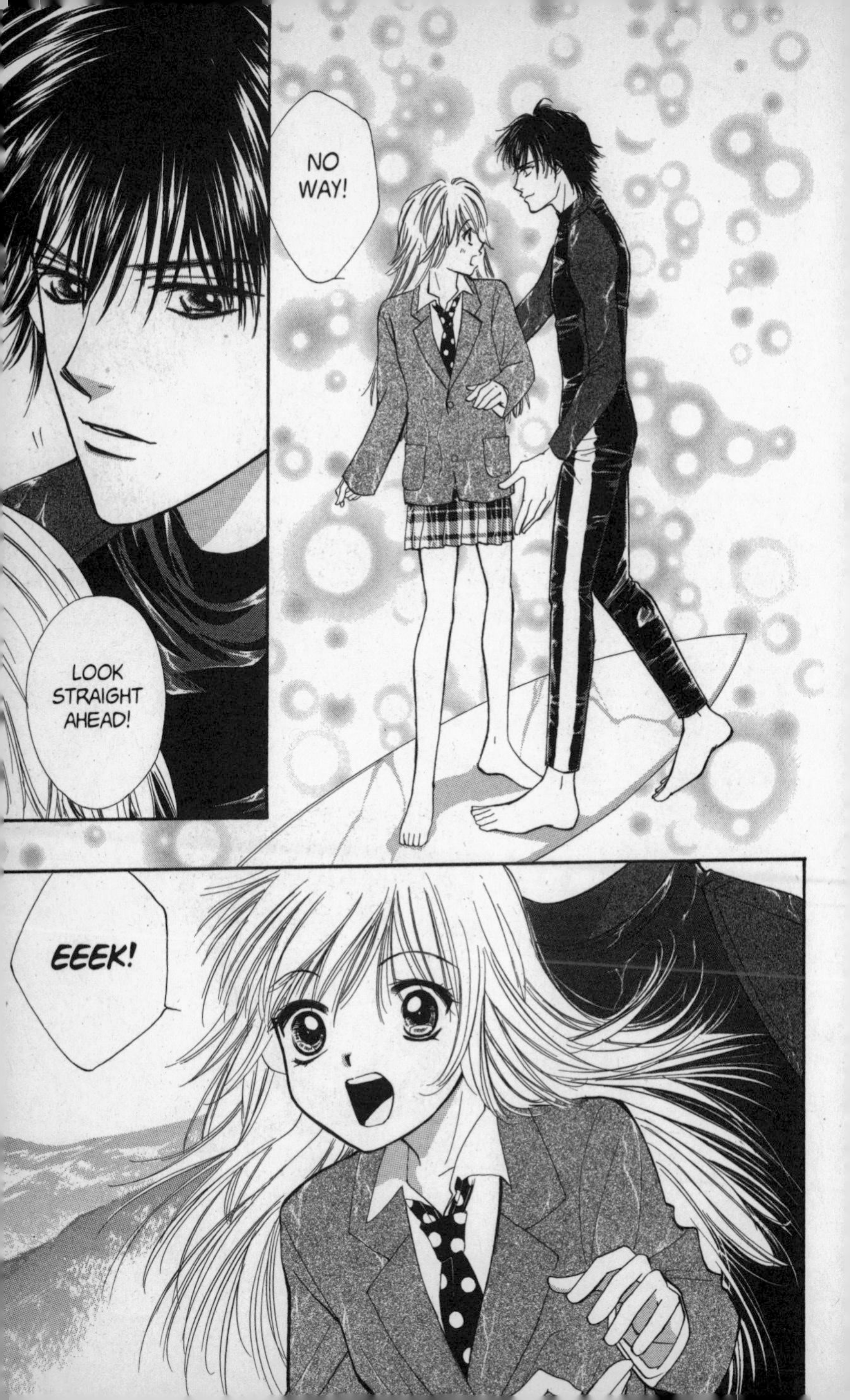
NO WAY!
LOOK STRAIGHT AHEAD!
EEEK!

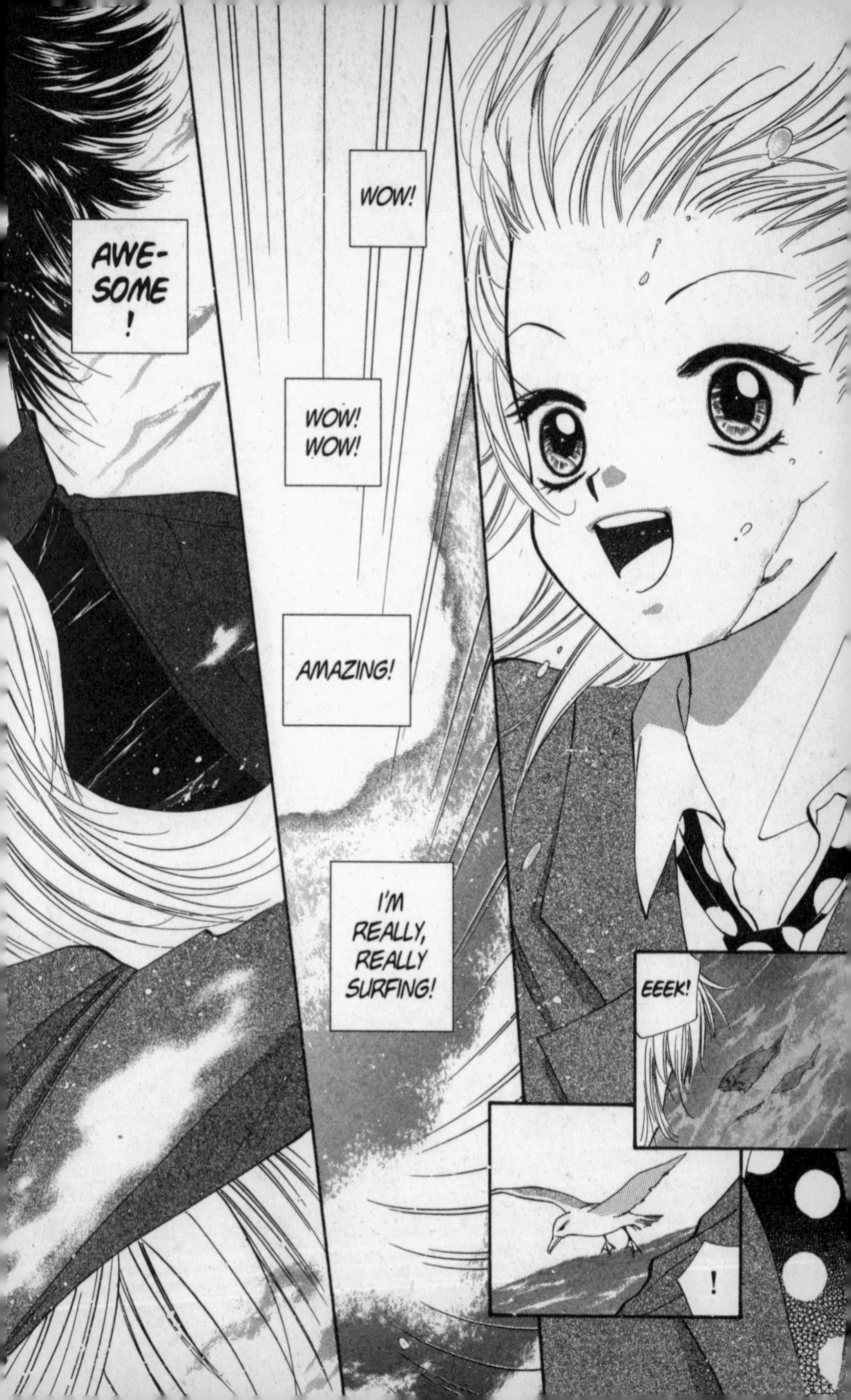
WOW!
AWE-SOME!
WOW! WOW!
AMAZING!
I'M REALLY, REALLY SURFING!
EEEK!
!

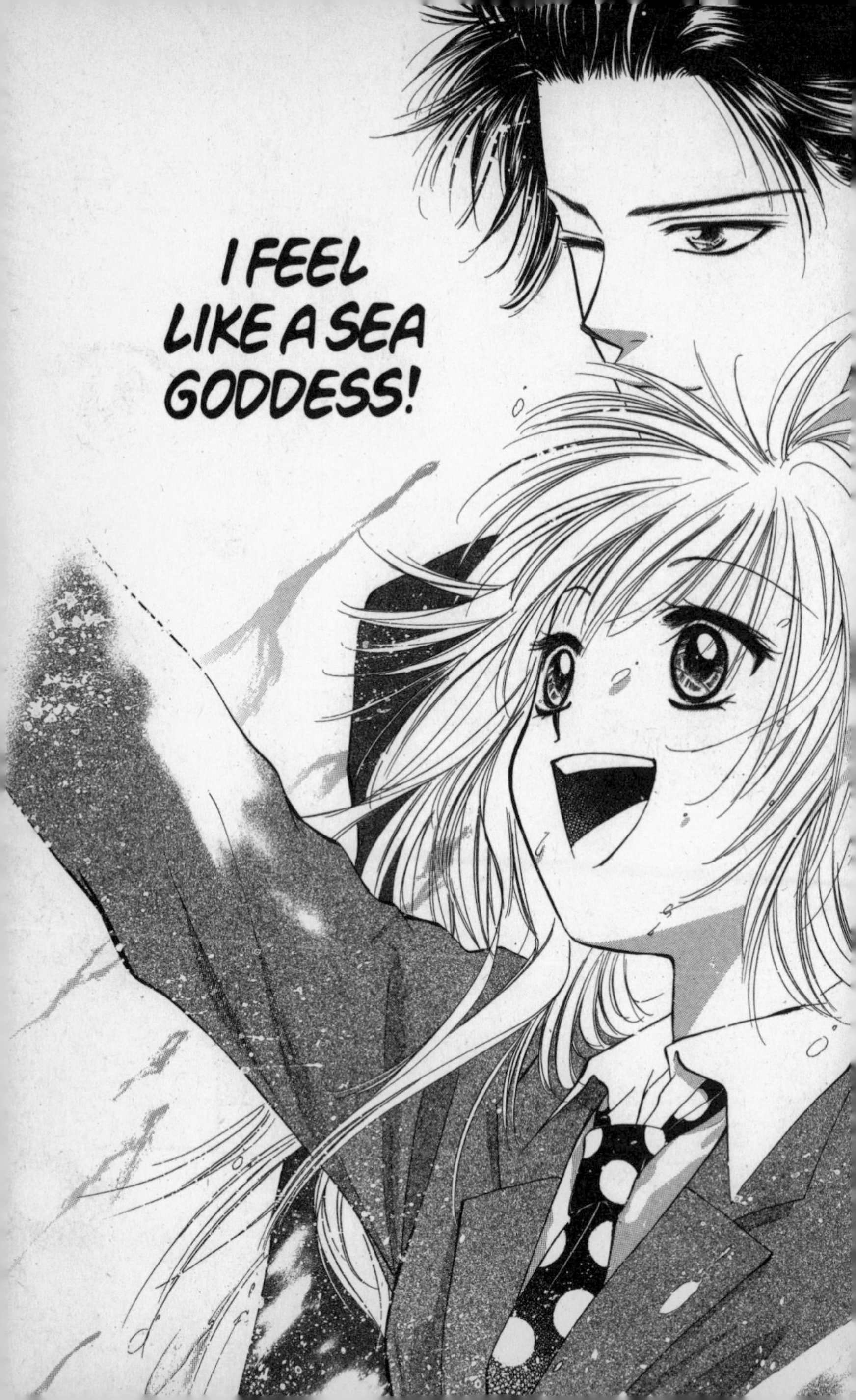
I FEEL LIKE A SEA GODDESS!

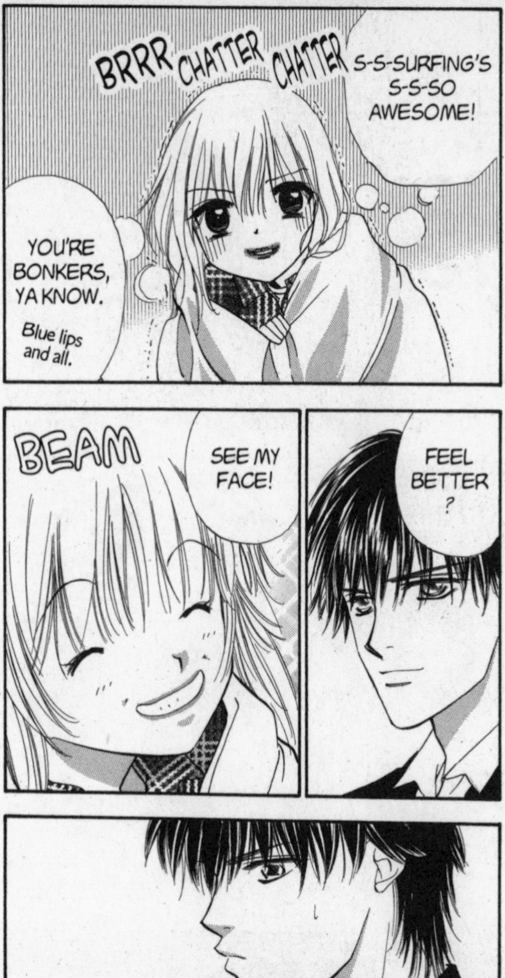
S-S-SURFING'S S-S-SO AWESOME!
BRRR
CHATTER
CHATTER
YOU'RE BONKERS, YA KNOW.
Blue lips and all.
FEEL BETTER ?
SEE MY FACE!
BEAM
!
DAMN! GOTTA GO!

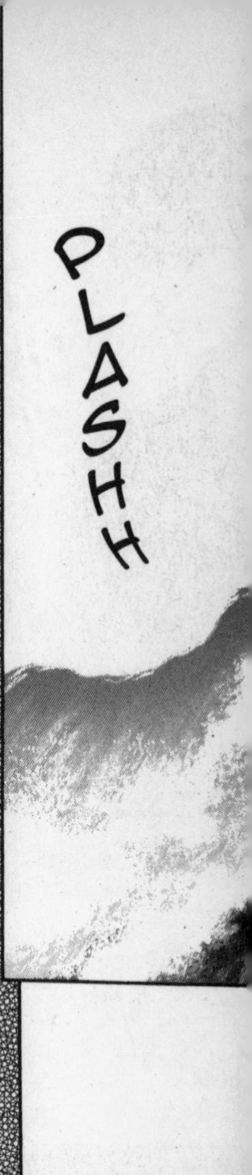
PLASHH

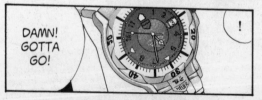

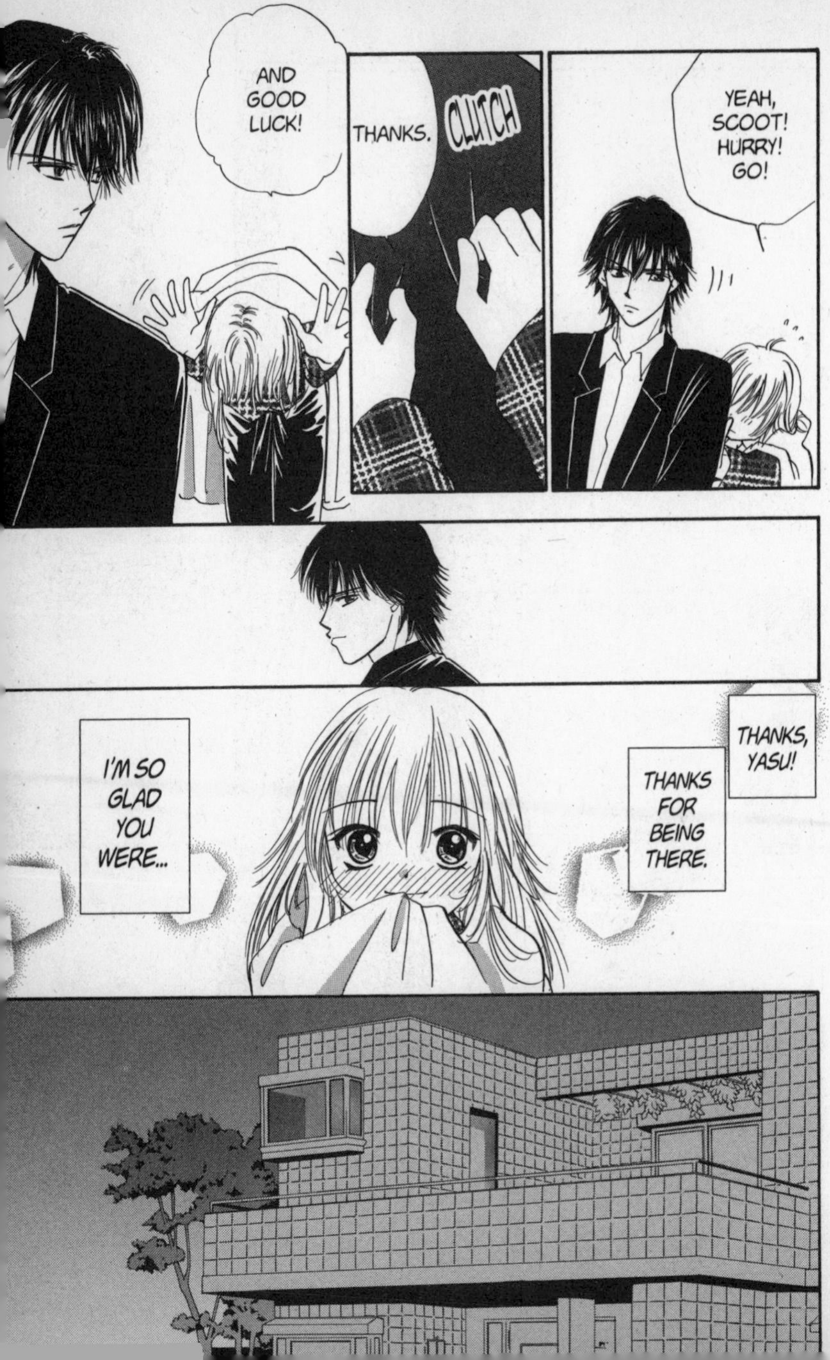
YEAH, SCOOT! HURRY! GO!
THANKS.
CLUTCH
AND GOOD LUCK!
THANKS, YASU!
THANKS FOR BEING THERE.
I'M SO GLAD YOU WERE...

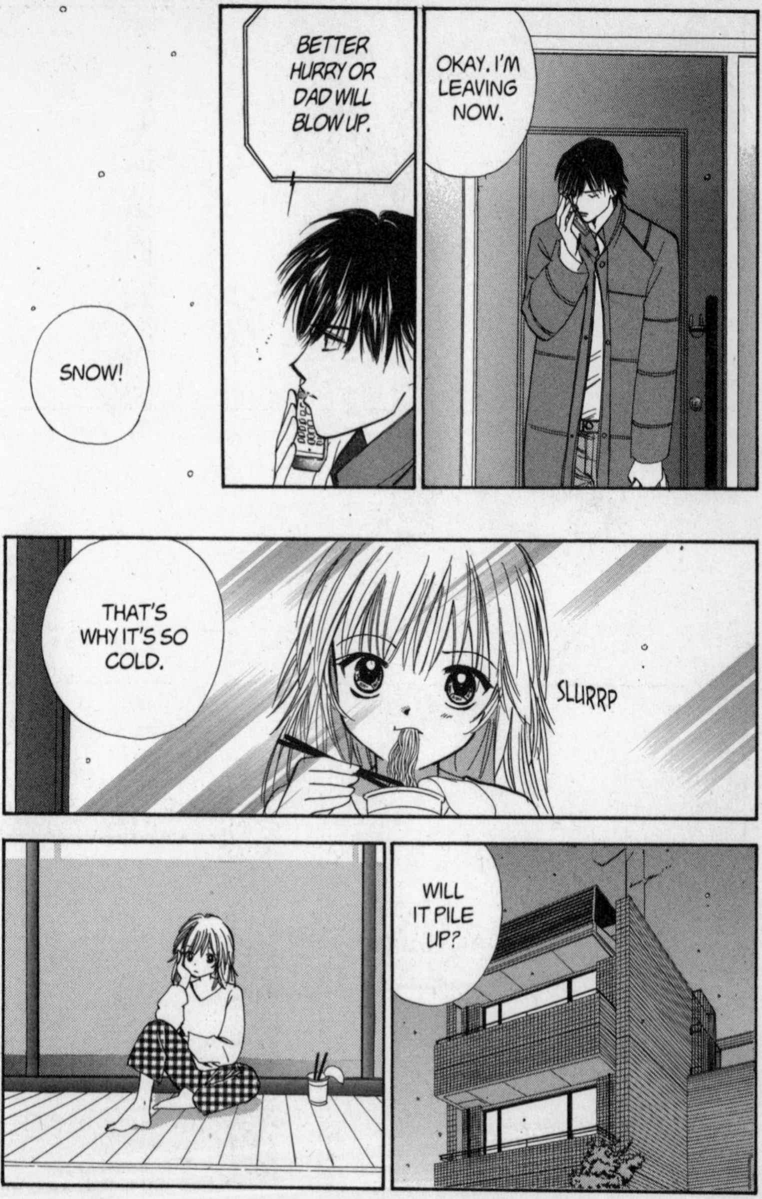
OKAY. I'M LEAVING NOW.
BETTER HURRY OR DAD WILL BLOW UP.
SNOW!
THAT'S WHY IT'S SO COLD.
SLURRP
WILL IT PILE UP?

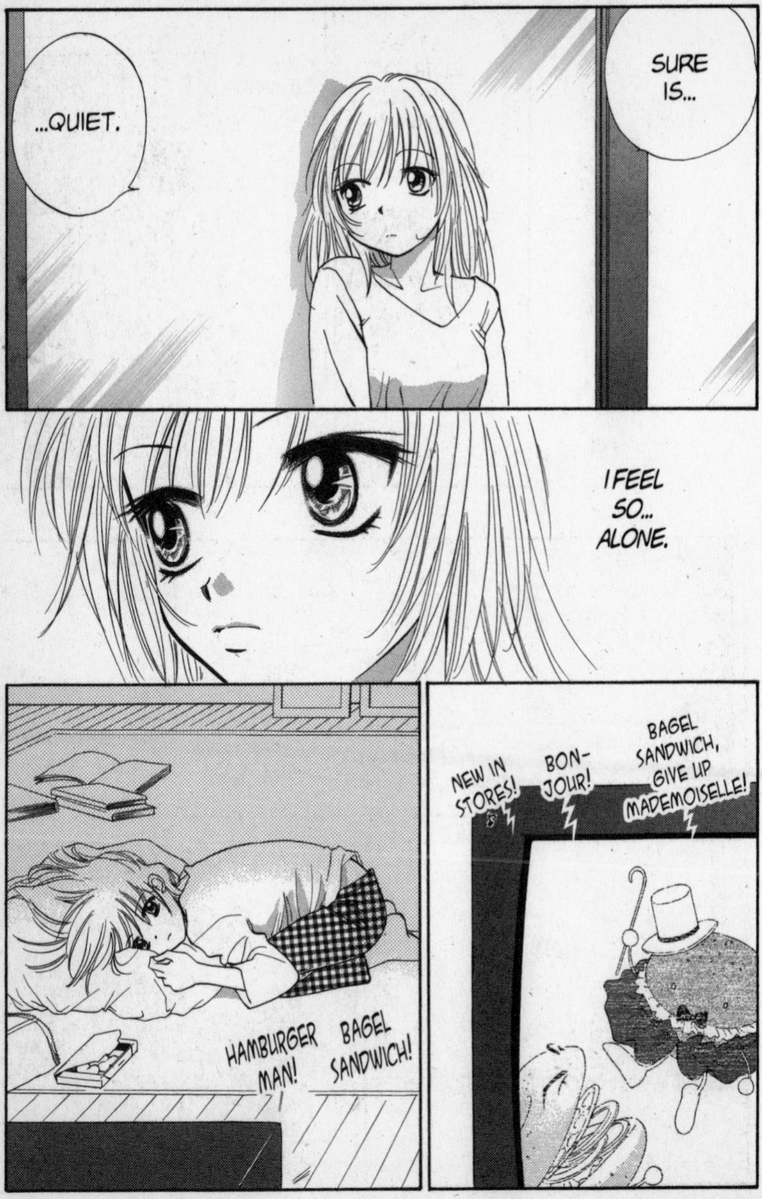
SURE IS...
...QUIET.
I FEEL SO... ALONE.
BAGEL SANDWICH, GIVE UP MADEMOISELLE!
BON-JOUR!
NEW IN STORES!
BAGEL SANDWICH!
HAMBURGER MAN!

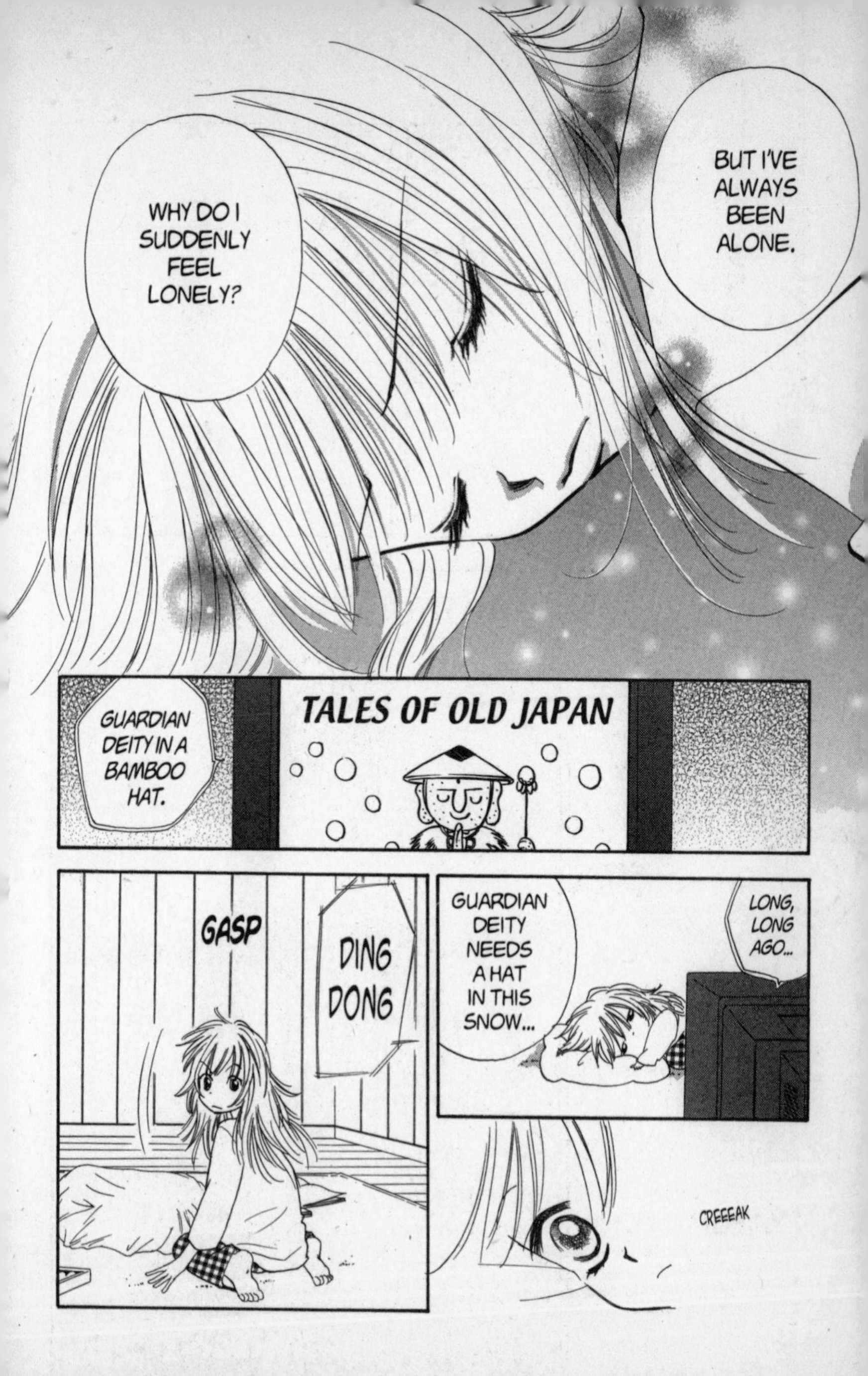

BUT I'VE ALWAYS BEEN ALONE.
WHY DO I SUDDENLY FEEL LONELY?
TALES OF OLD JAPAN
GUARDIAN DEITY IN A BAMBOO HAT.
LONG, LONG AGO...
GUARDIAN DEITY NEEDS A HAT IN THIS SNOW...
CREEEAK
DING DONG
GASP

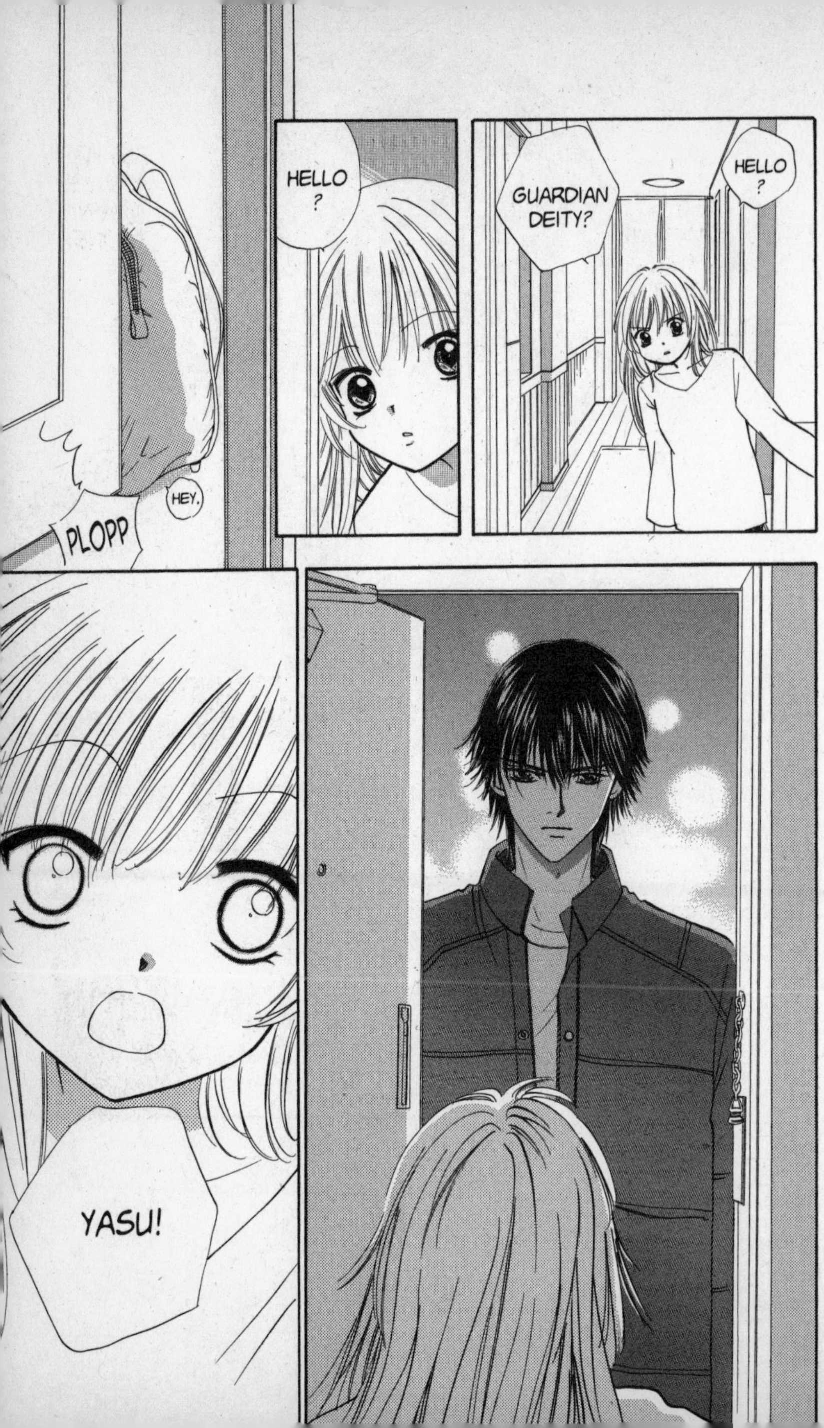
HELLO?
GUARDIAN DEITY?
HELLO?
HEY.
PLOPP
YASU!

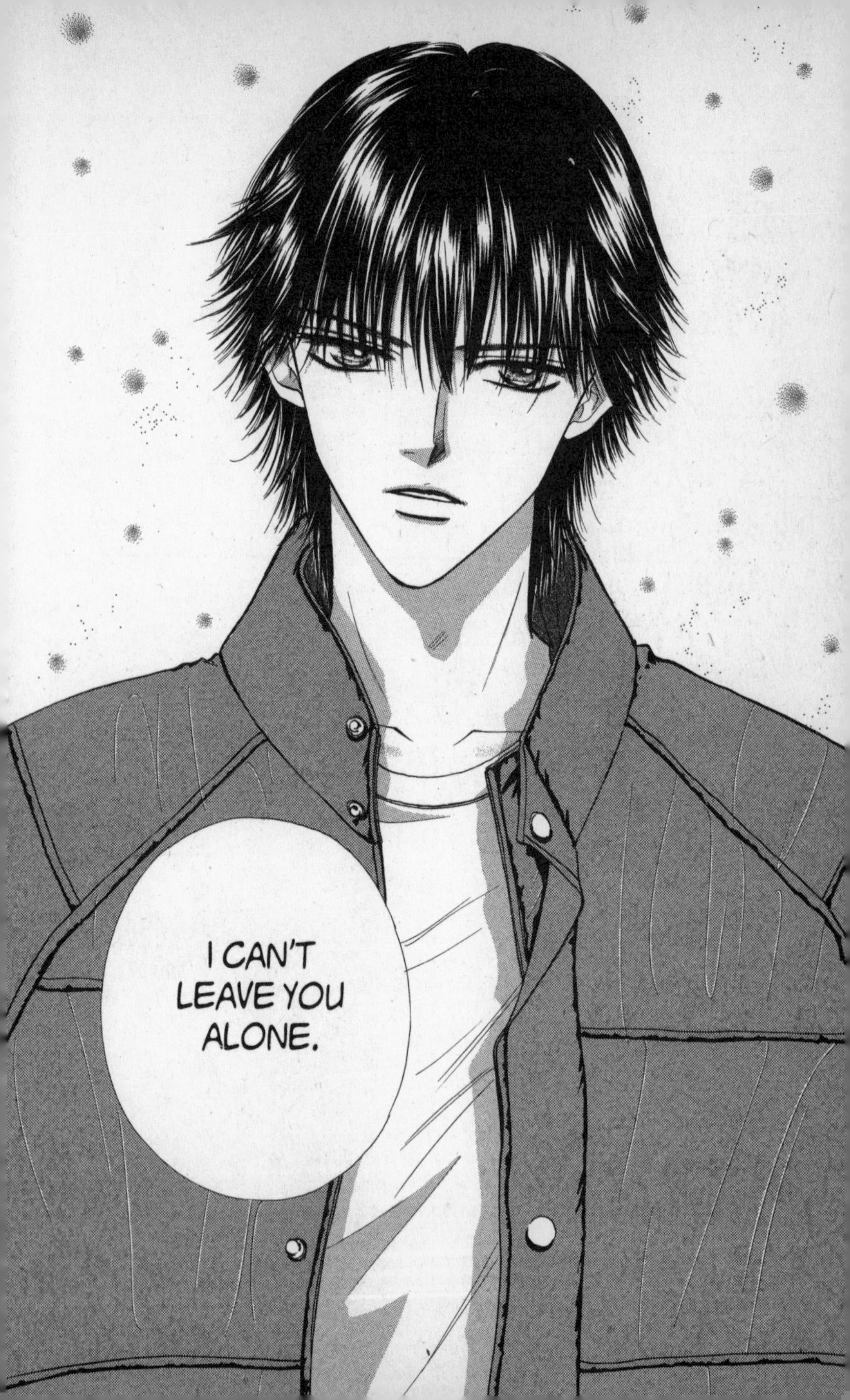
I CAN'T LEAVE YOU ALONE.

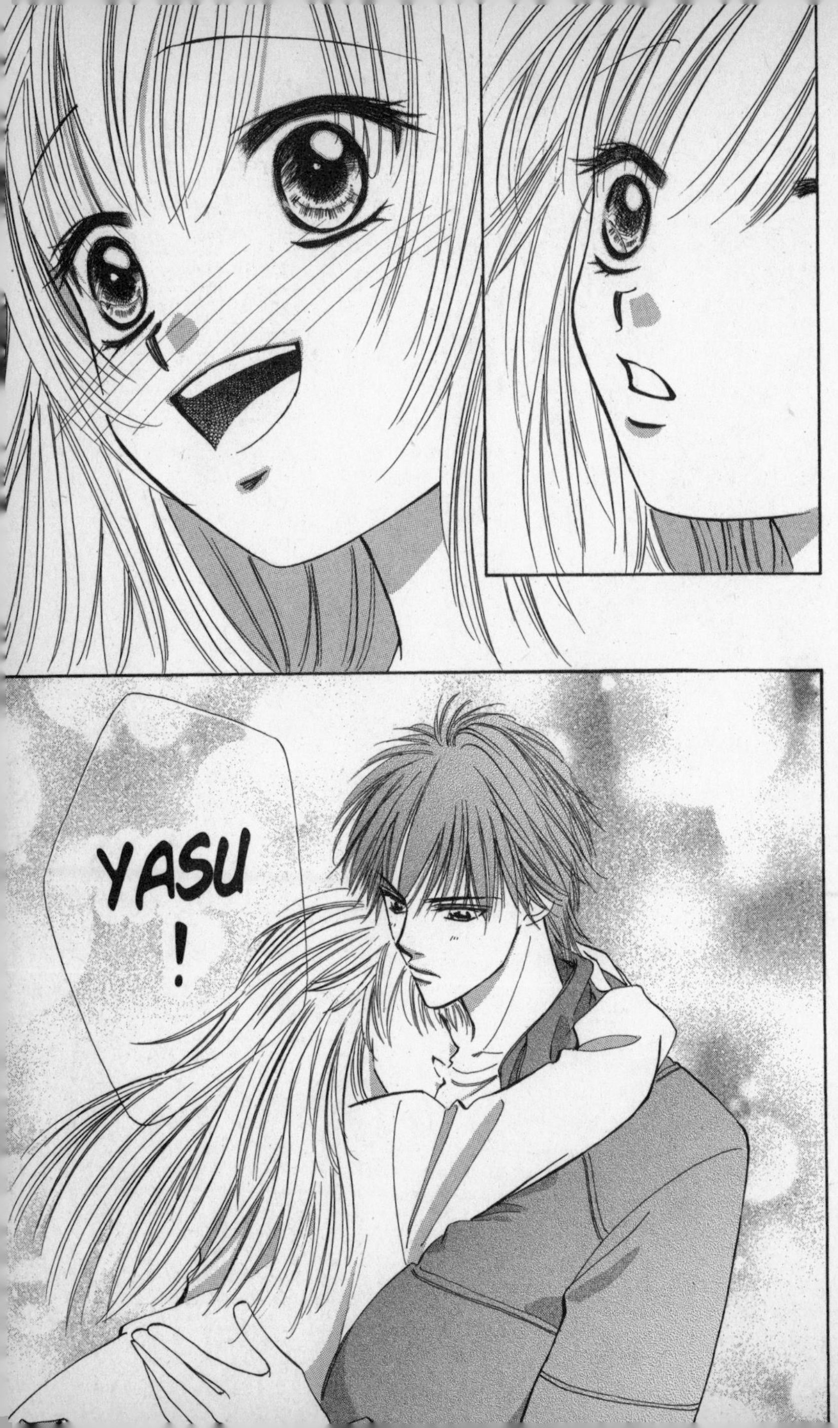
YASU
!

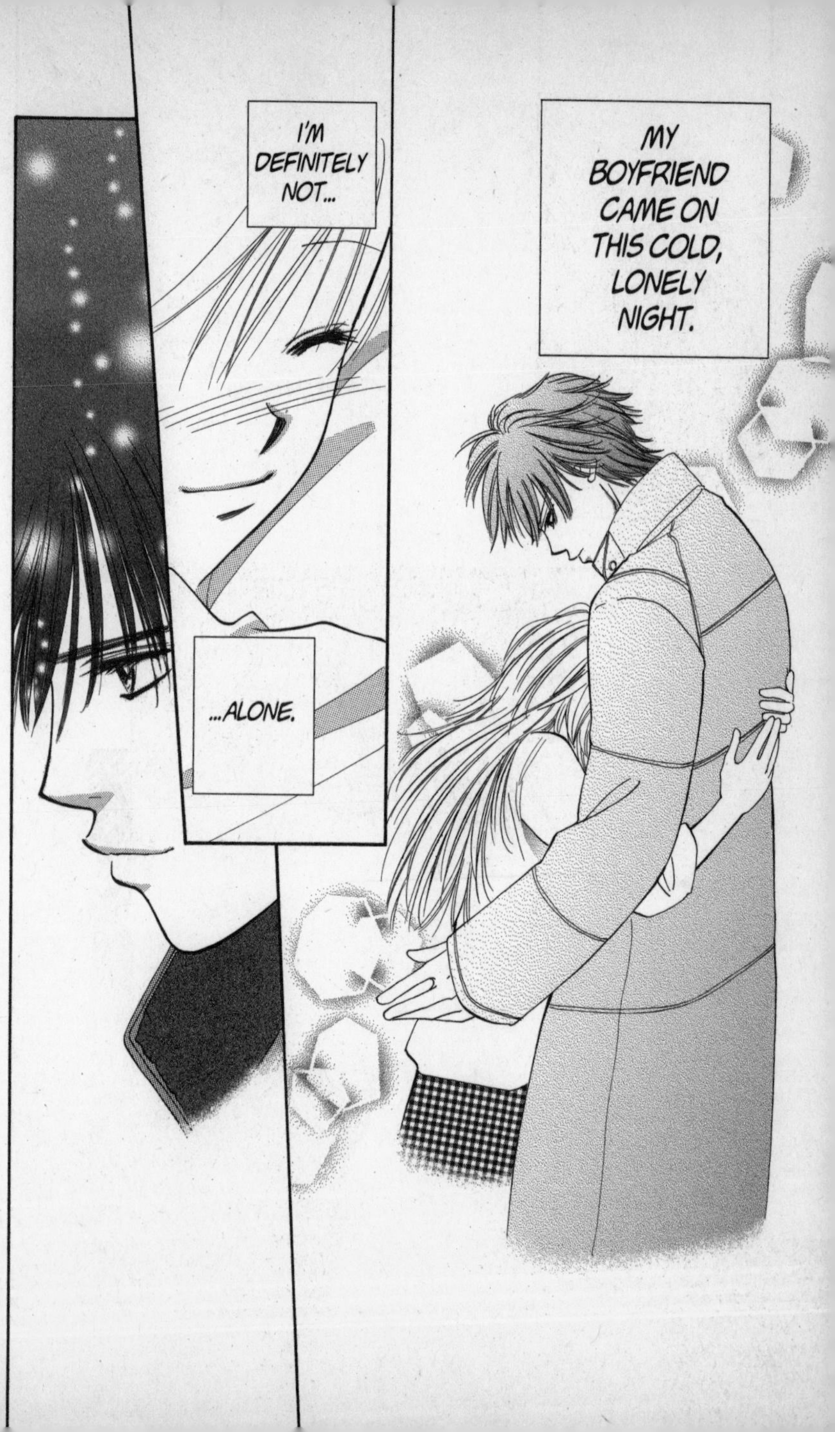
MY BOYFRIEND CAME ON THIS COLD, LONELY NIGHT.
I'M DEFINITELY NOT...
...ALONE.

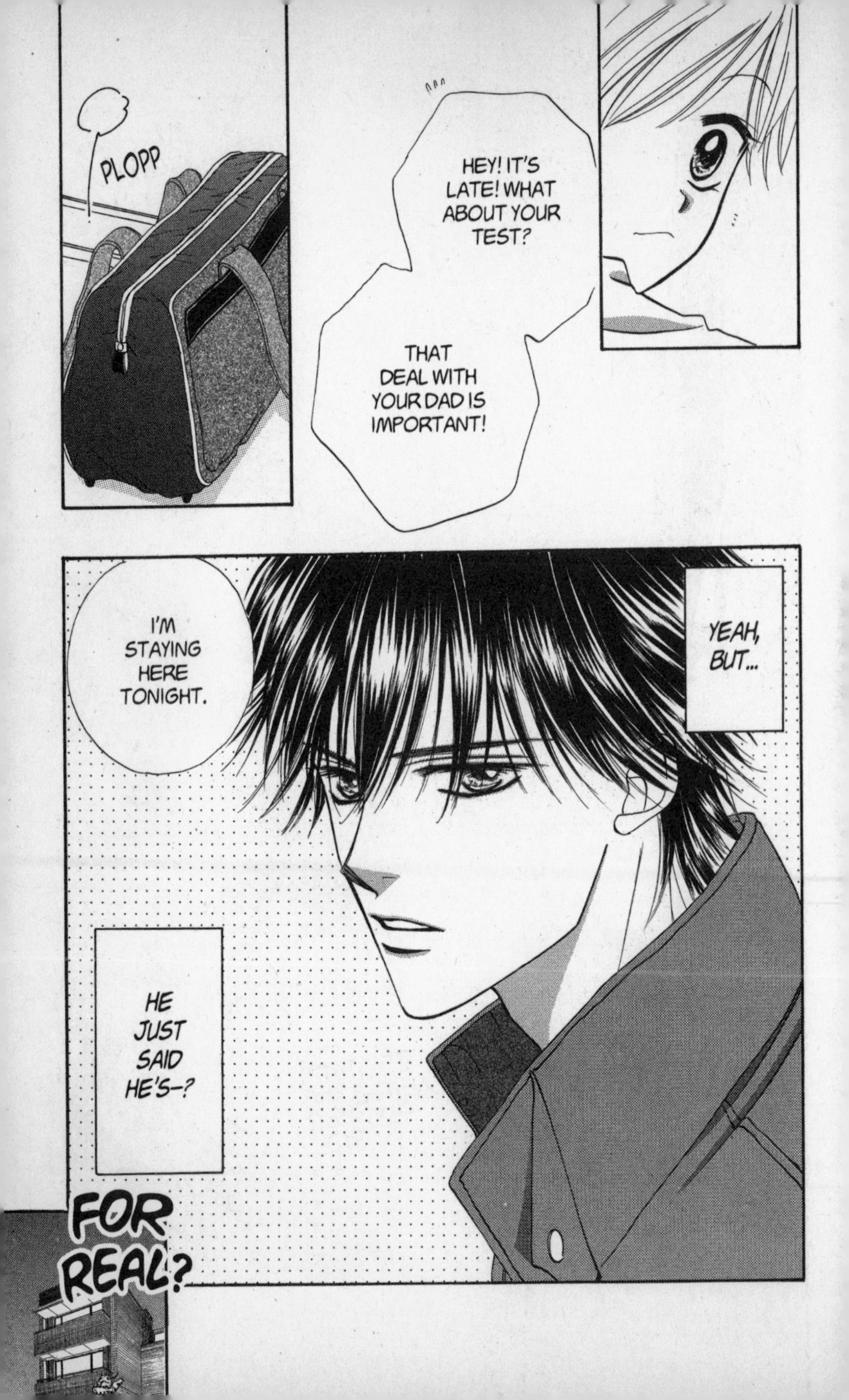
HEY! IT'S LATE! WHAT ABOUT YOUR TEST?
THAT DEAL WITH YOUR DAD IS IMPORTANT!
PLOPP
YEAH, BUT...
I'M STAYING HERE TONIGHT.
HE JUST SAID HE'S--?
FOR REAL?

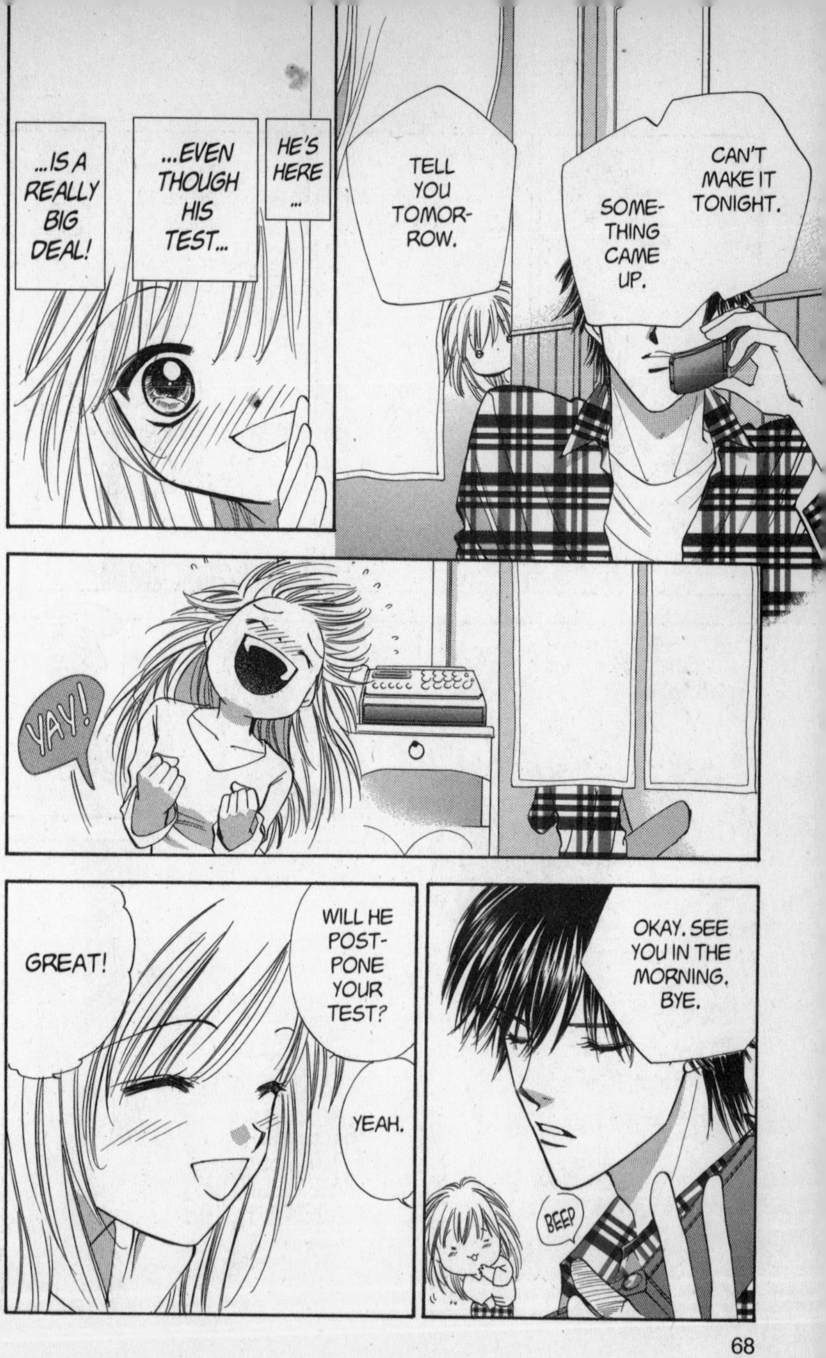
CAN'T MAKE IT TONIGHT.
SOMETHING CAME UP.
TELL YOU TOMORROW.
HE'S HERE...
...EVEN THOUGH HIS TEST...
...IS A REALLY BIG DEAL!
YAY!
OKAY. SEE YOU IN THE MORNING. BYE.
BEEP
WILL HE POSTPONE YOUR TEST?
YEAH.
GREAT!

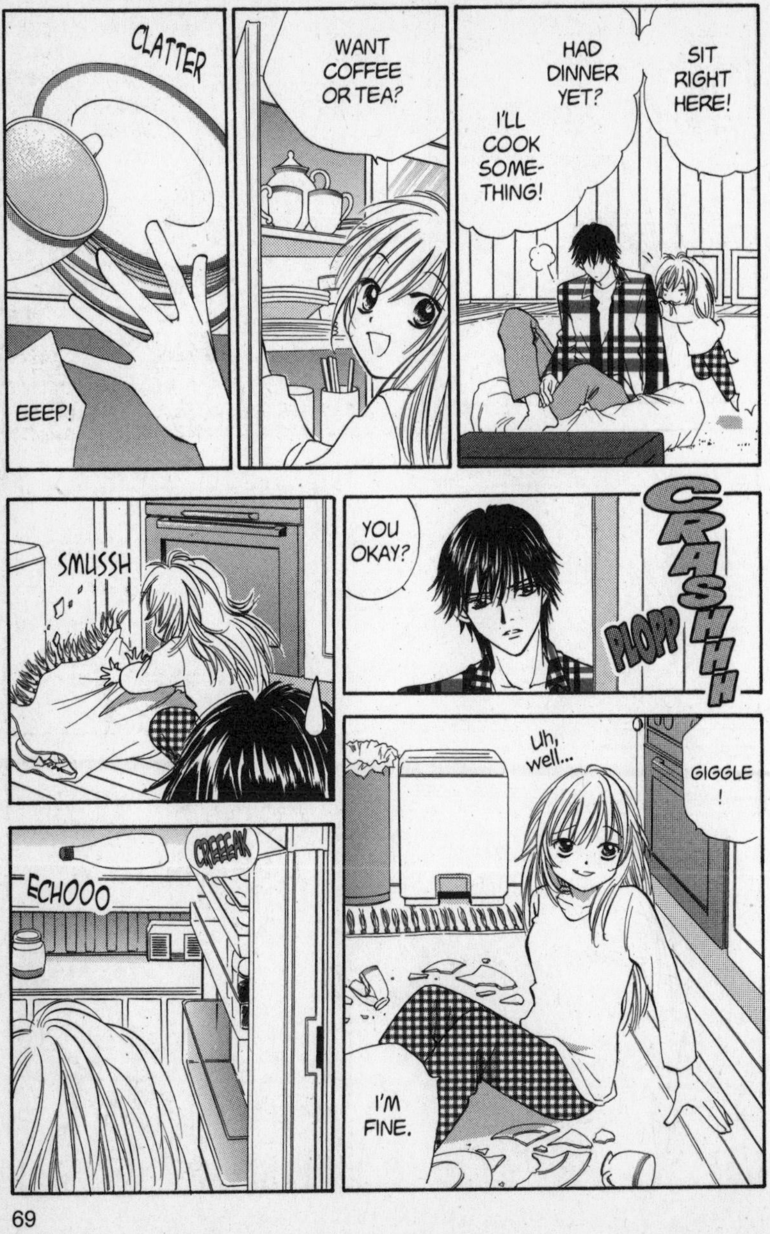
SIT RIGHT HERE!
HAD DINNER YET?
I'LL COOK SOME-THING!
WANT COFFEE OR TEA?
CLATTER
EEEP!
CRASHHH
PLOPP
YOU OKAY?
GIGGLE !
Uh, well...
I'M FINE.
SMUSSH
CREEEAK
ECHOOO

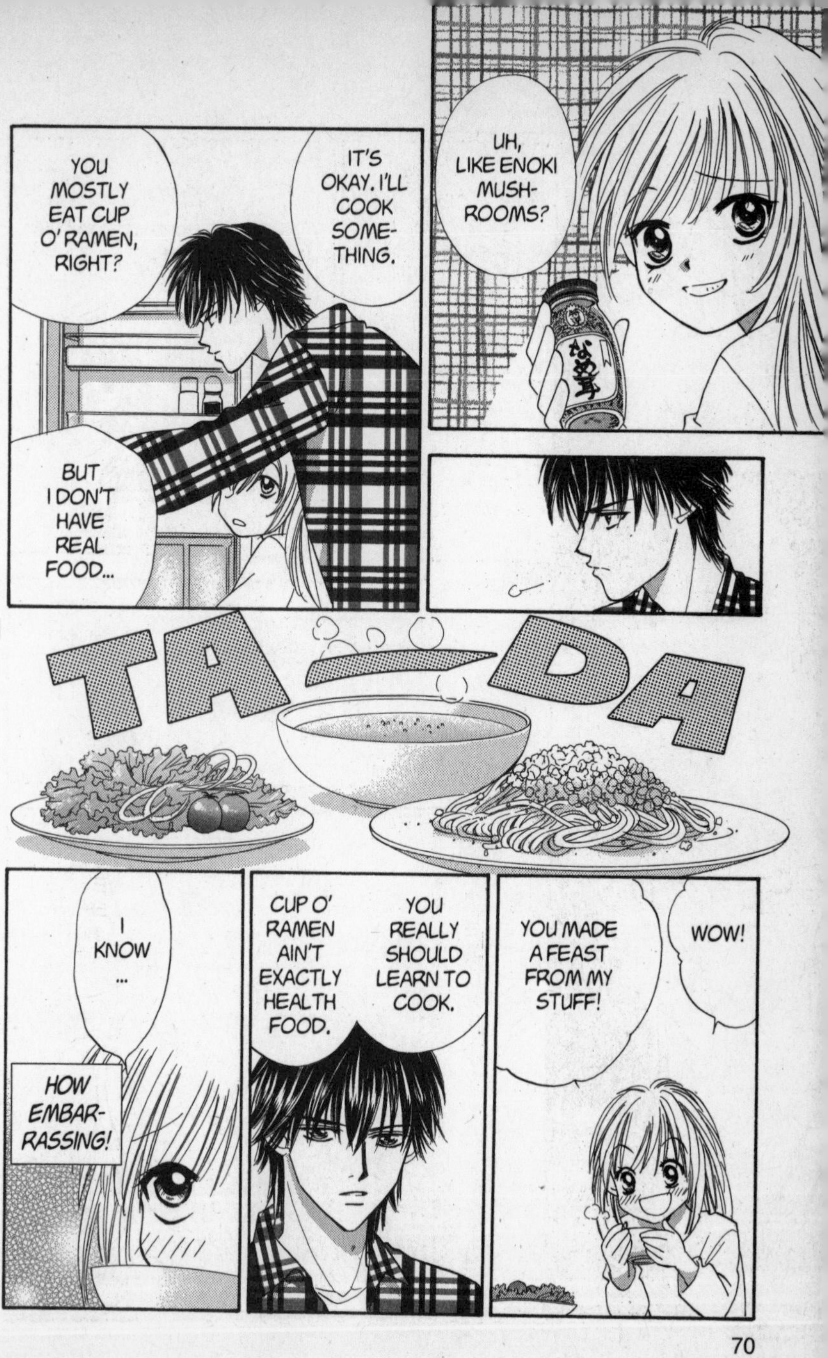
UH, LIKE ENOKI MUSH-ROOMS?
IT'S OKAY. I'LL COOK SOME-THING.
YOU MOSTLY EAT CUP O' RAMEN, RIGHT?
BUT I DON'T HAVE REAL FOOD...
TA—DA
WOW!
YOU MADE A FEAST FROM MY STUFF!
YOU REALLY SHOULD LEARN TO COOK.
CUP O' RAMEN AIN'T EXACTLY HEALTH FOOD.
I KNOW ...
HOW EMBAR-RASSING!

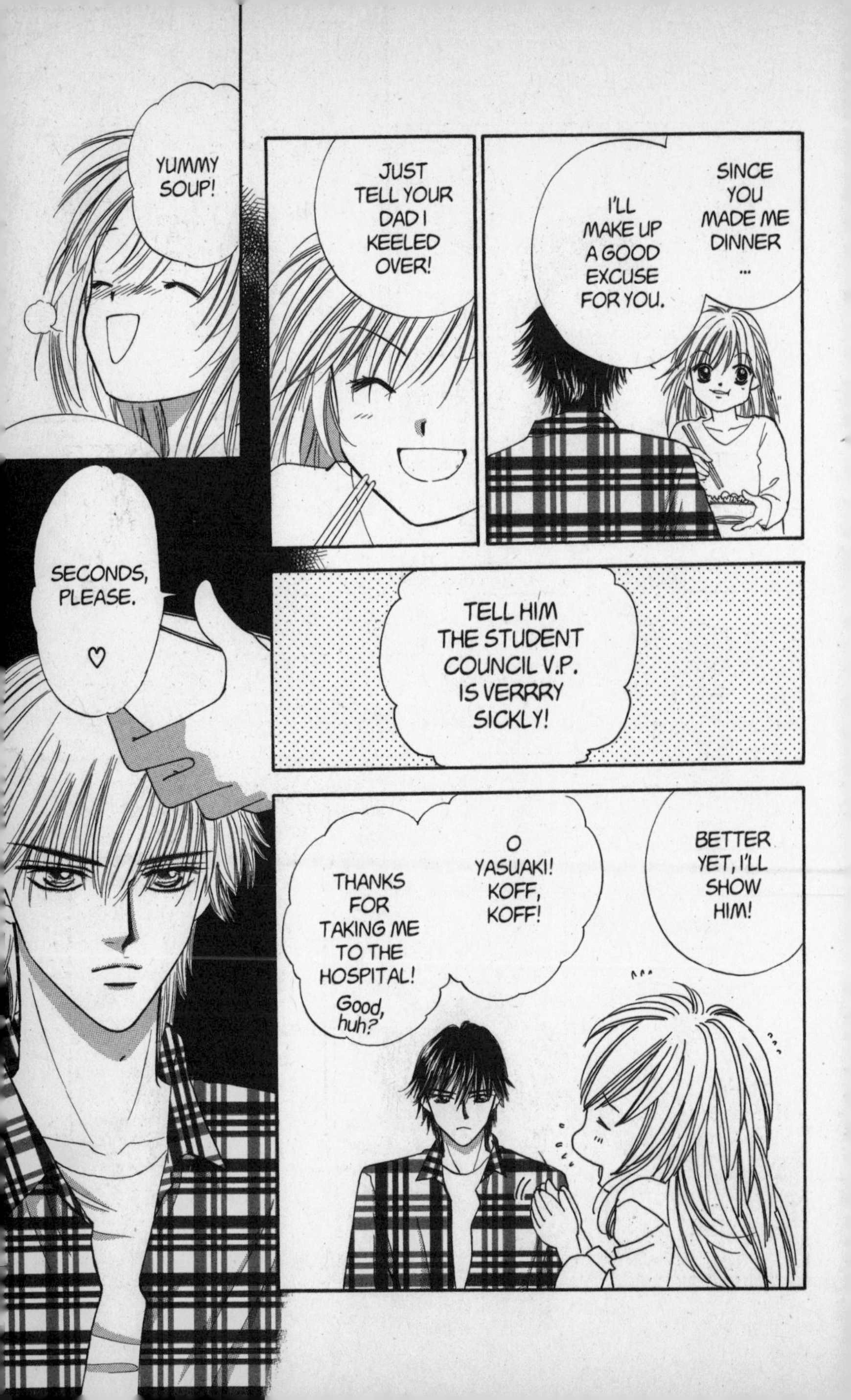
SINCE YOU MADE ME DINNER ...
I'LL MAKE UP A GOOD EXCUSE FOR YOU.
JUST TELL YOUR DAD I KEELED OVER!
YUMMY SOUP!
TELL HIM THE STUDENT COUNCIL V.P. IS VERRRY SICKLY!
BETTER YET, I'LL SHOW HIM!
O YASUAKI! KOFF, KOFF!
THANKS FOR TAKING ME TO THE HOSPITAL!
Good, huh?
SECONDS, PLEASE.
♡

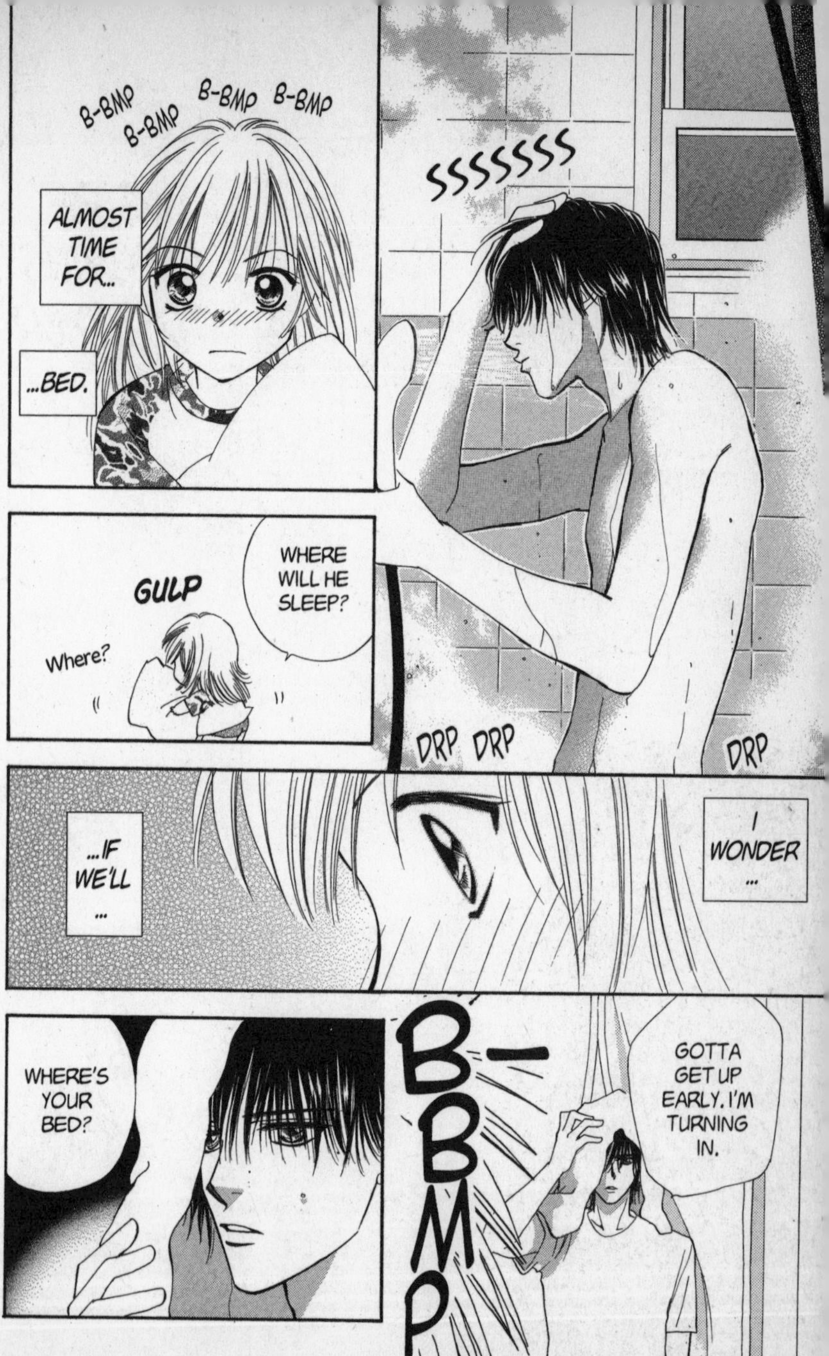
SSSSSSS
DRP DRP
DRP
B-BMP B-BMP B-BMP B-BMP
ALMOST TIME FOR...
...BED.
WHERE WILL HE SLEEP?
GULP
Where?
I WONDER ...
...IF WE'LL ...
GOTTA GET UP EARLY. I'M TURNING IN.
B-BMP
WHERE'S YOUR BED?

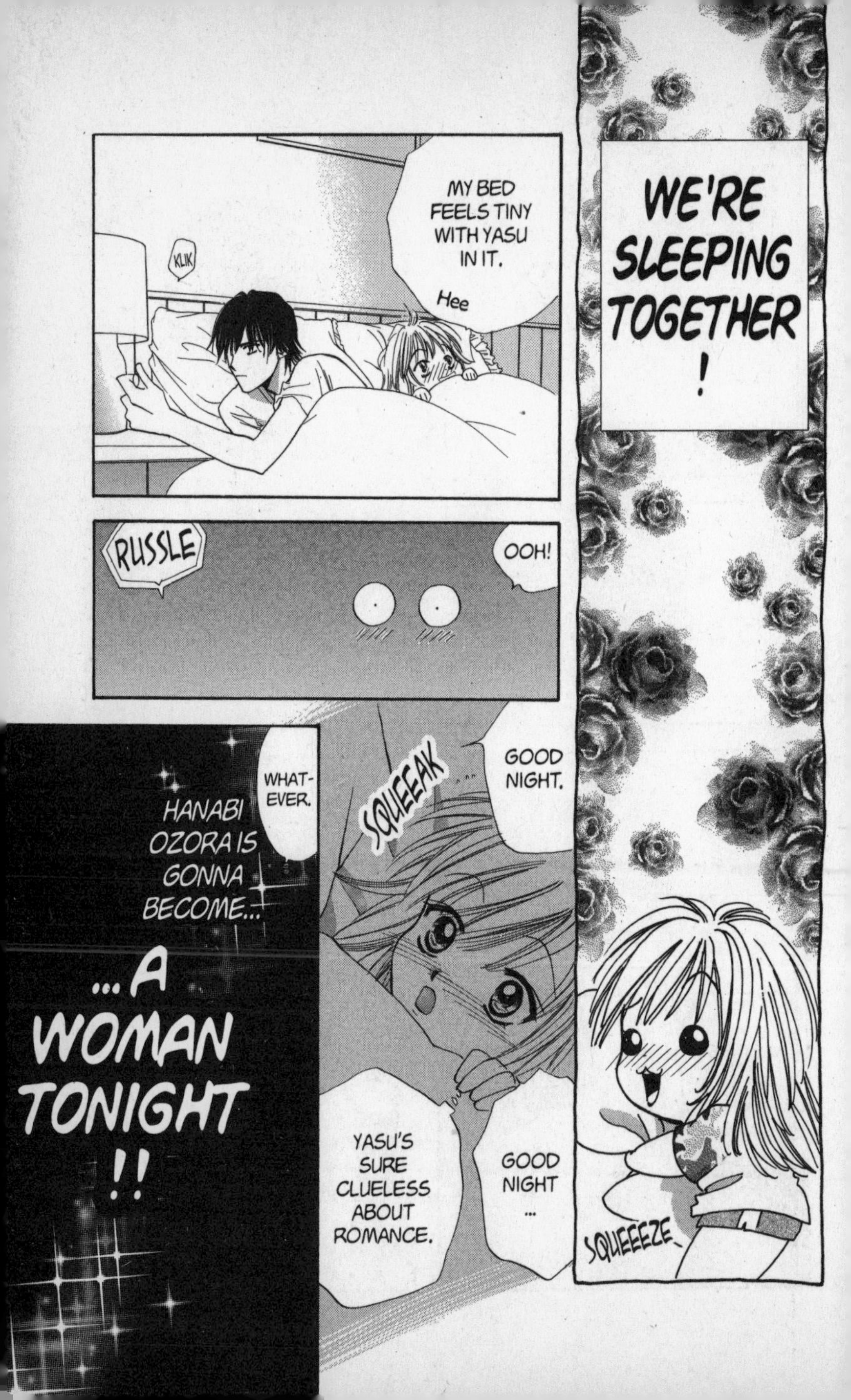
WE'RE SLEEPING TOGETHER !
SQUEEEZE
MY BED FEELS TINY WITH YASU IN IT.
Hee
KLIK
OOH!
RUSSLE
GOOD NIGHT.
...
SQUEEEAK
WHAT-EVER.
GOOD NIGHT ...
YASU'S SURE CLUELESS ABOUT ROMANCE.
HANABI OZORA IS GONNA BECOME...
...A WOMAN TONIGHT !!

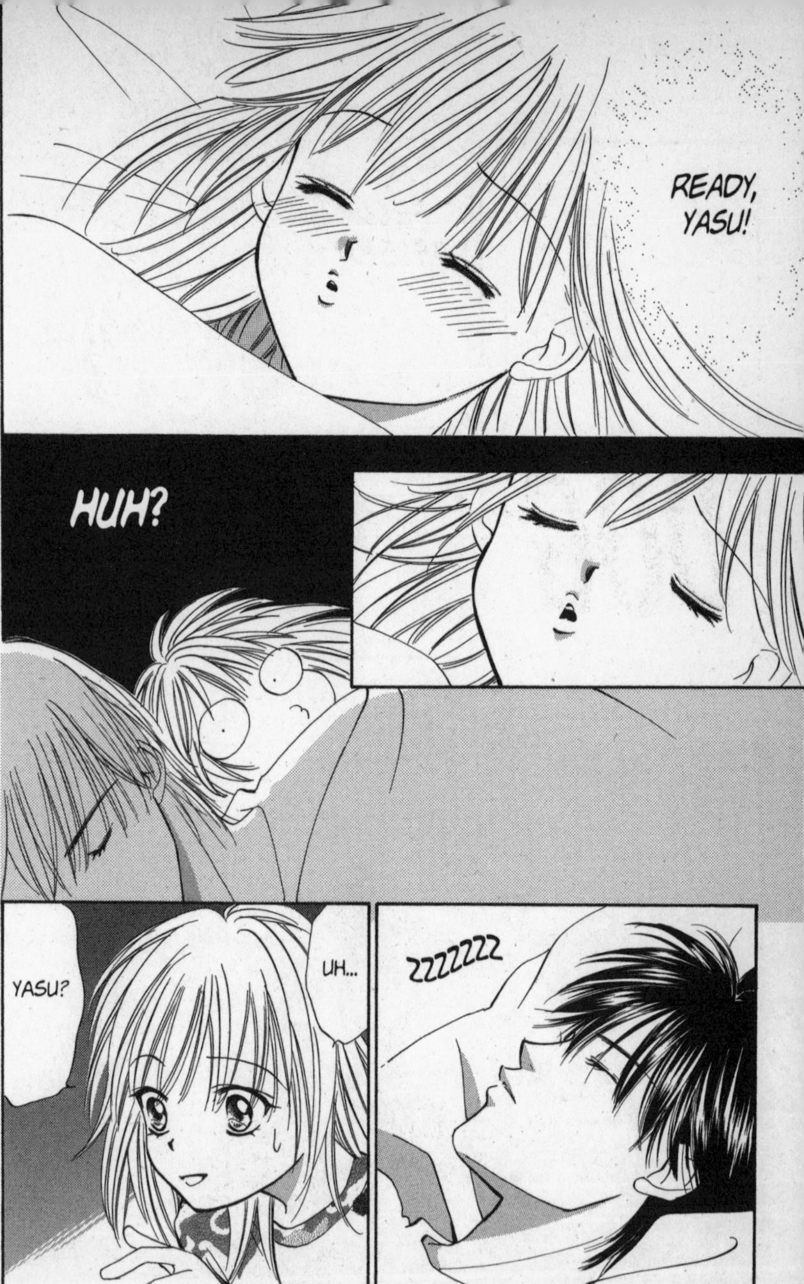
READY, YASU!
HUH?
ZZZZZZZ
UH...
YASU?

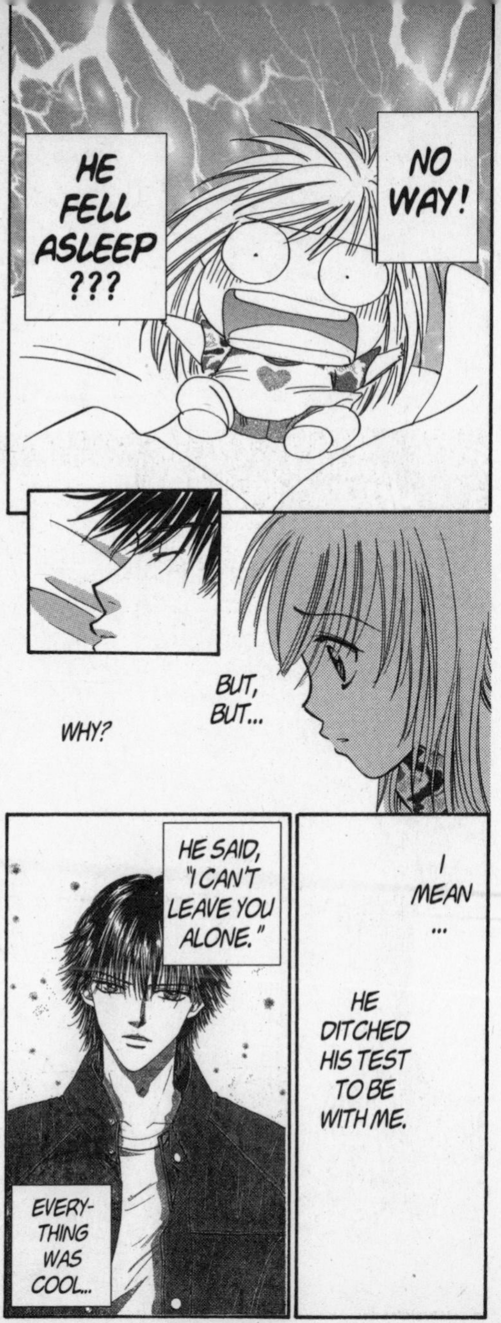
NO WAY!
HE FELL ASLEEP???
BUT, BUT...
WHY?
I MEAN ...
HE DITCHED HIS TEST TO BE WITH ME.
HE SAID, "I CAN'T LEAVE YOU ALONE."
EVERY-THING WAS COOL...

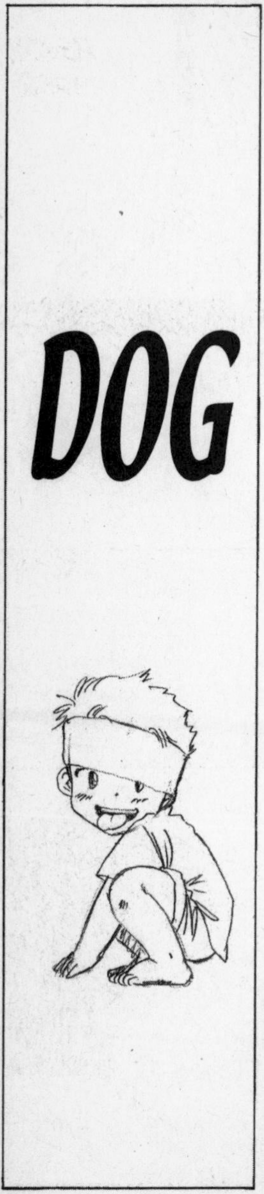
DOG

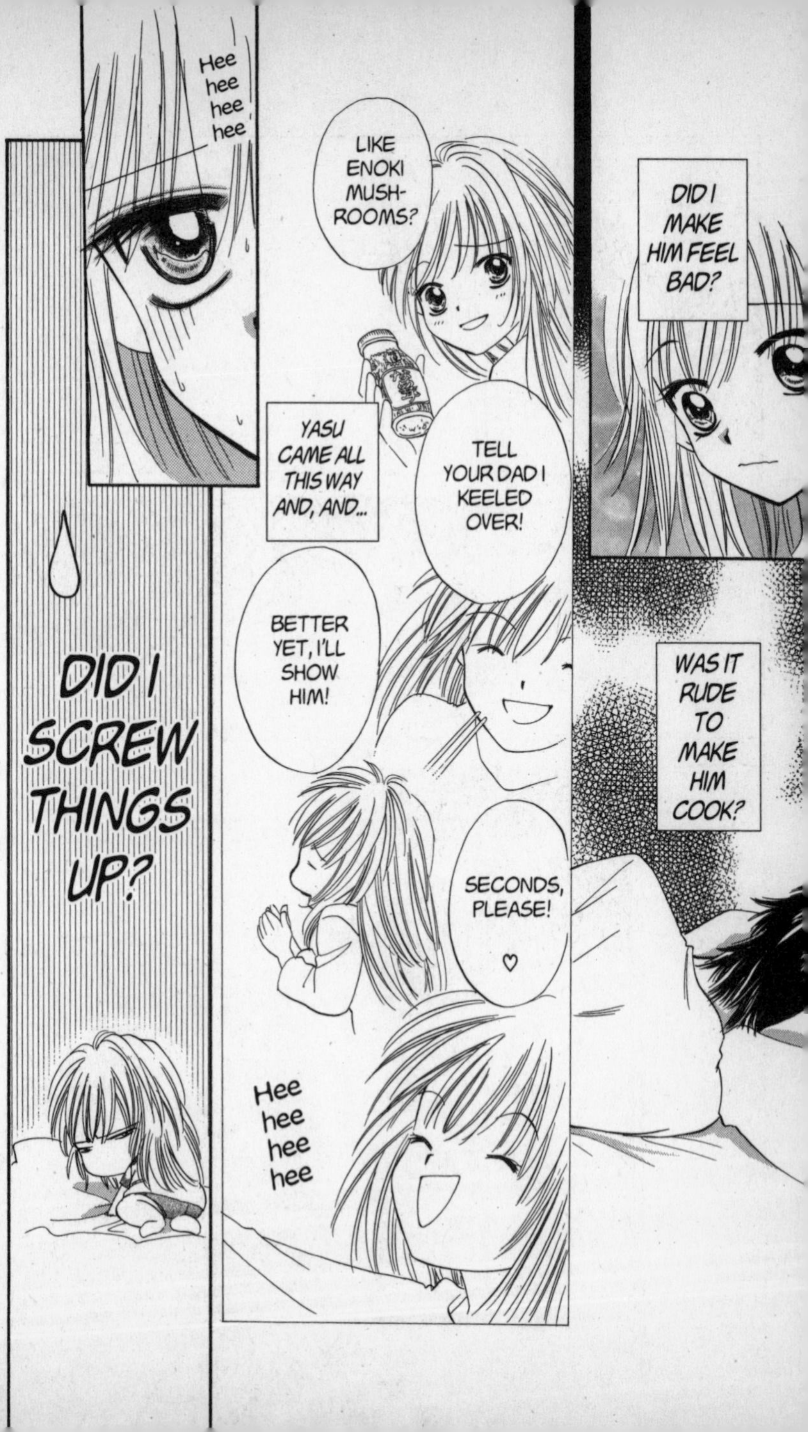
DID I MAKE HIM FEEL BAD?
WAS IT RUDE TO MAKE HIM COOK?
LIKE ENOKI MUSH-ROOMS?
TELL YOUR DAD I KEELED OVER!
YASU CAME ALL THIS WAY AND, AND...
BETTER YET, I'LL SHOW HIM!
SECONDS, PLEASE! ♡
Hee hee hee hee
Hee hee hee hee
DID I SCREW THINGS UP?

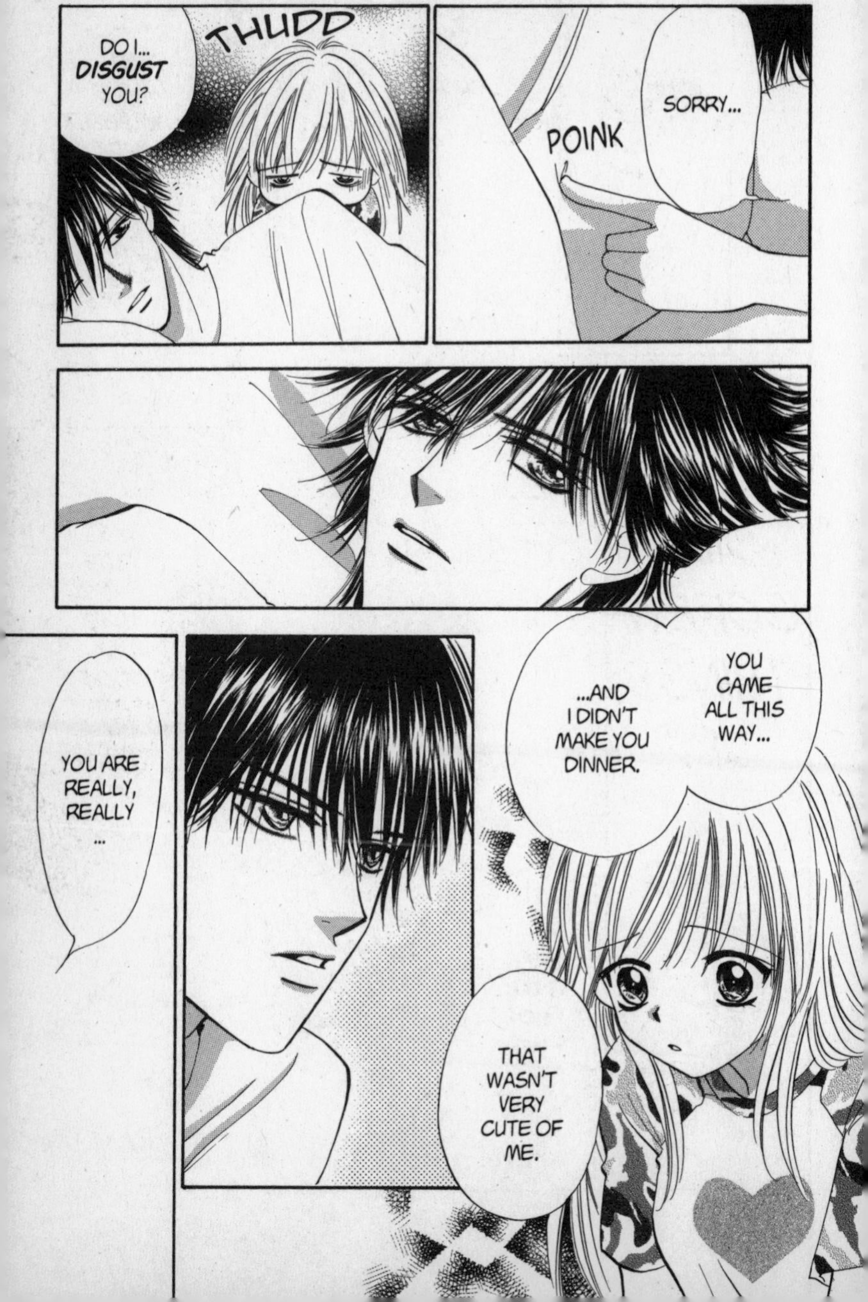
SORRY...
POINK
DO I... **DISGUST** YOU?
THUDD
YOU CAME ALL THIS WAY...
...AND I DIDN'T MAKE YOU DINNER.
THAT WASN'T VERY CUTE OF ME.
YOU ARE REALLY, REALLY ...

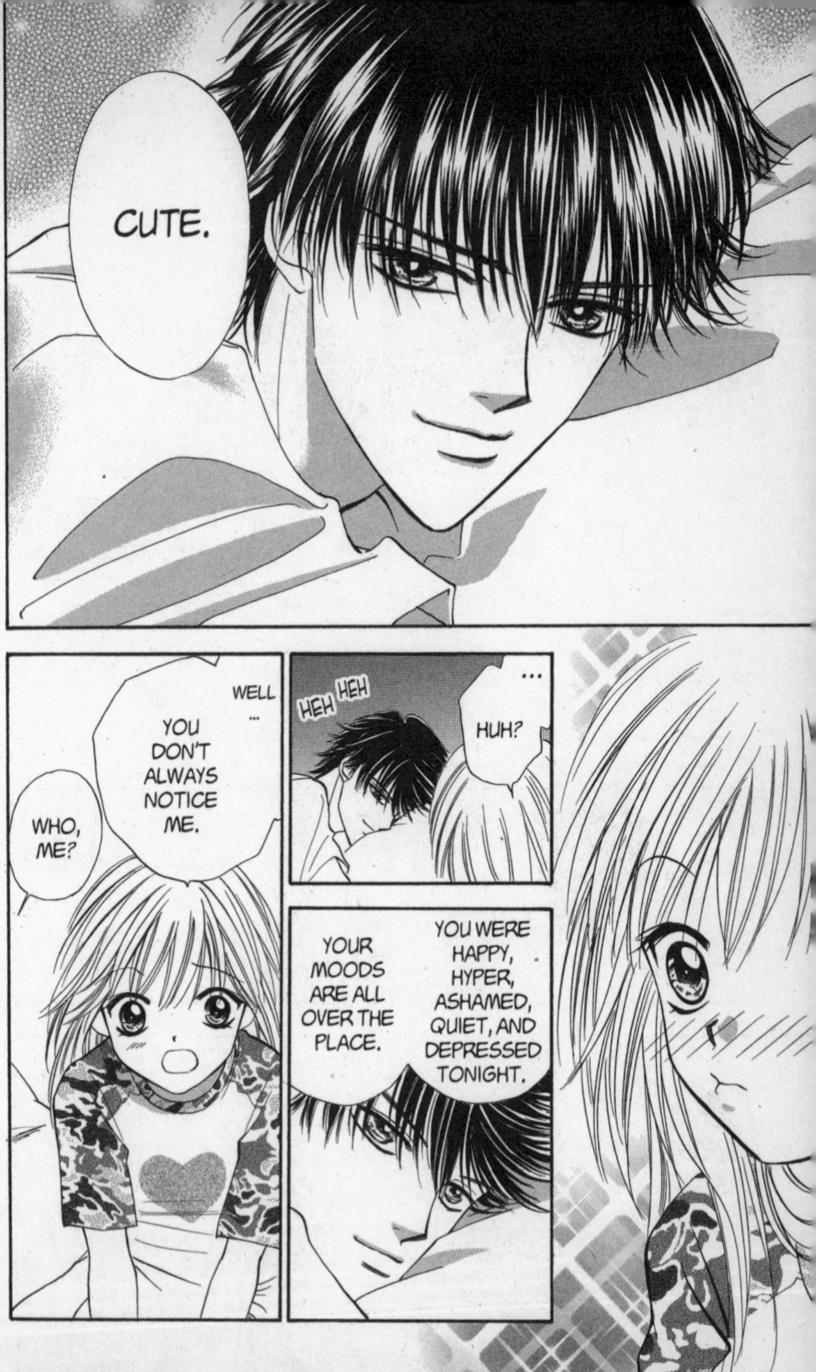
CUTE.
... HUH?
HEH HEH
YOU WERE HAPPY, HYPER, ASHAMED, QUIET, AND DEPRESSED TONIGHT.
YOUR MOODS ARE ALL OVER THE PLACE.
WELL ... YOU DON'T ALWAYS NOTICE ME.
WHO, ME?

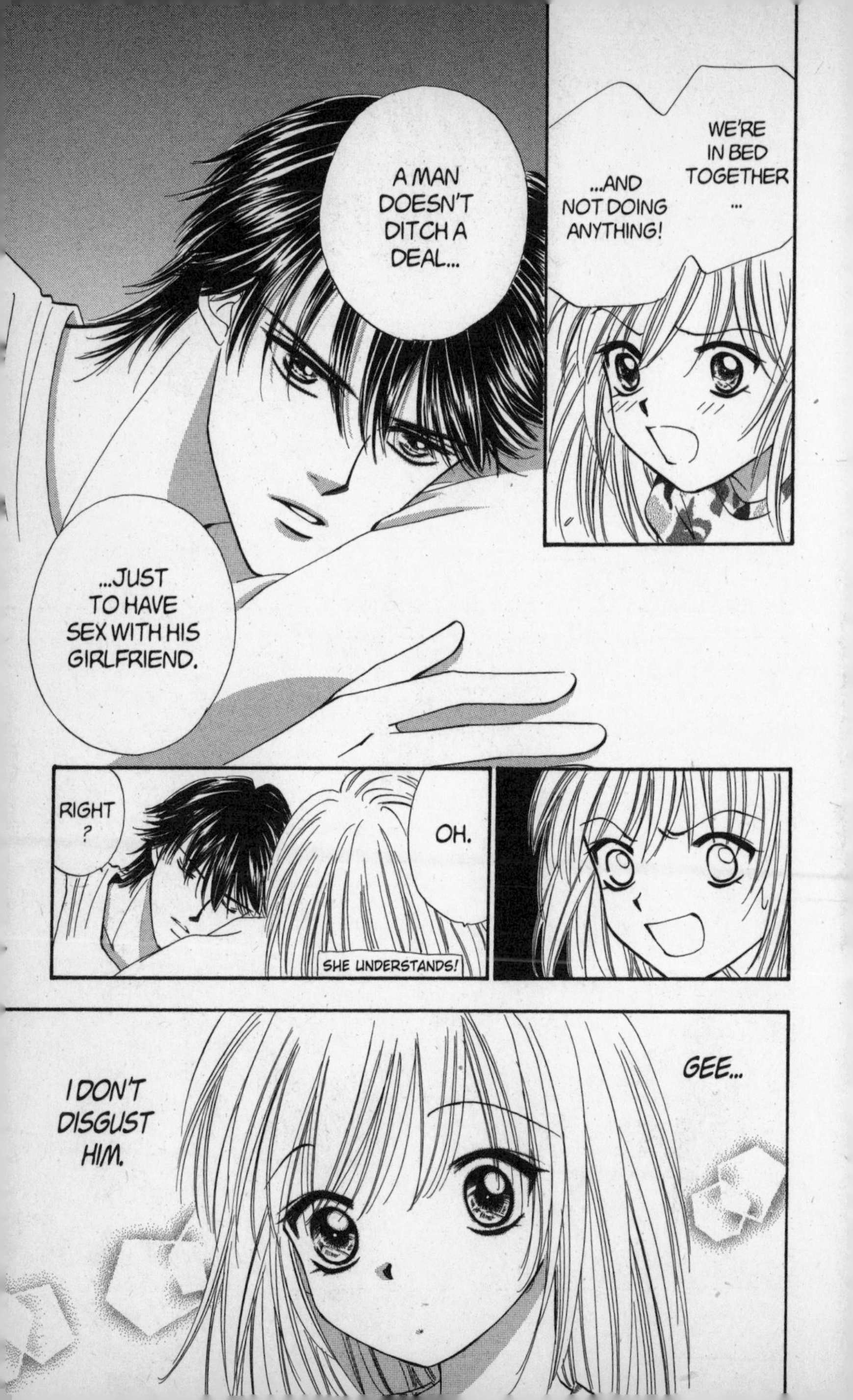
WE'RE IN BED TOGETHER ...
...AND NOT DOING ANYTHING!
A MAN DOESN'T DITCH A DEAL...
...JUST TO HAVE SEX WITH HIS GIRLFRIEND.
RIGHT ?
OH.
SHE UNDERSTANDS!
GEE...
I DON'T DISGUST HIM.

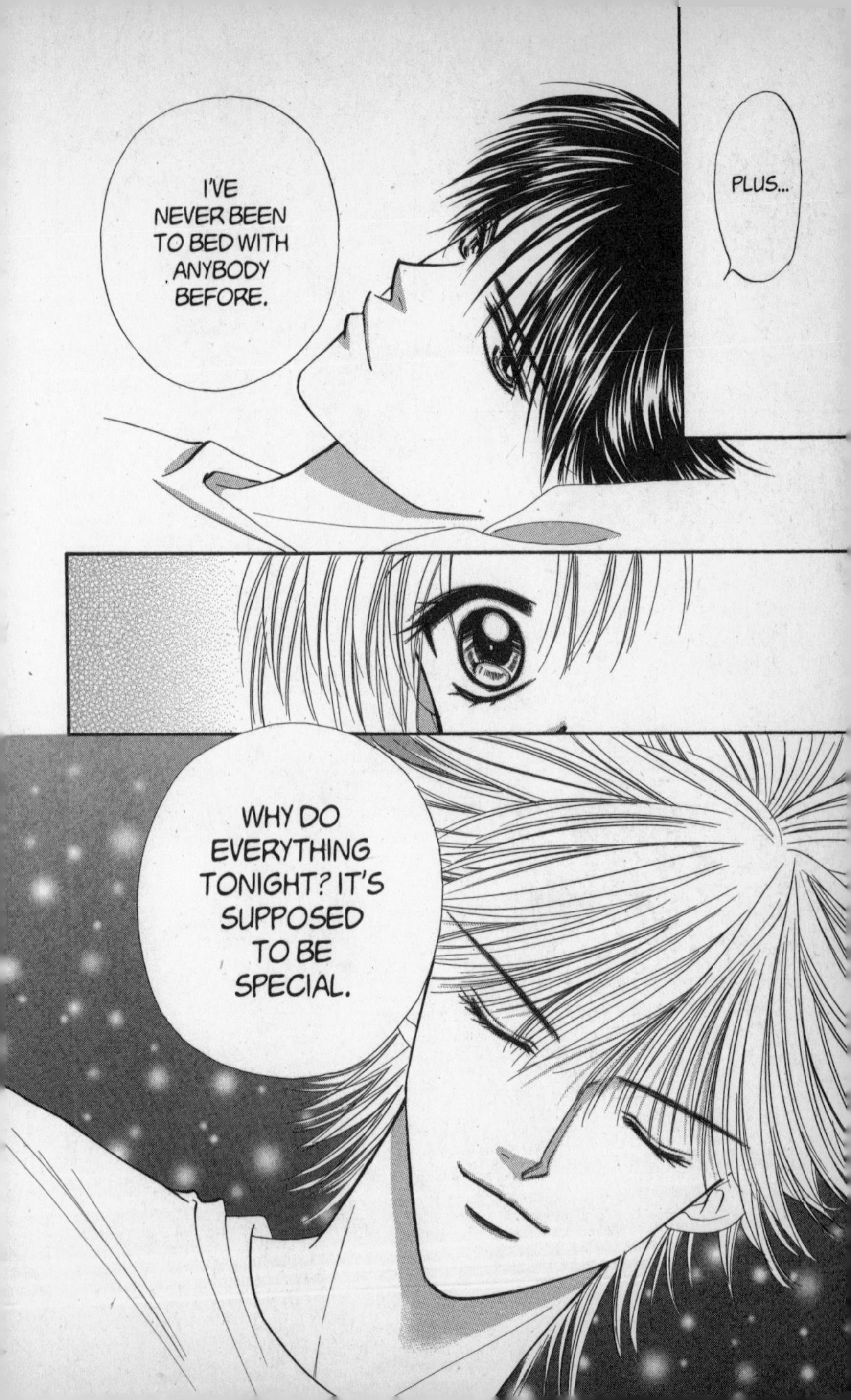
I'VE NEVER BEEN TO BED WITH ANYBODY BEFORE.
PLUS...
WHY DO EVERYTHING TONIGHT? IT'S SUPPOSED TO BE SPECIAL.

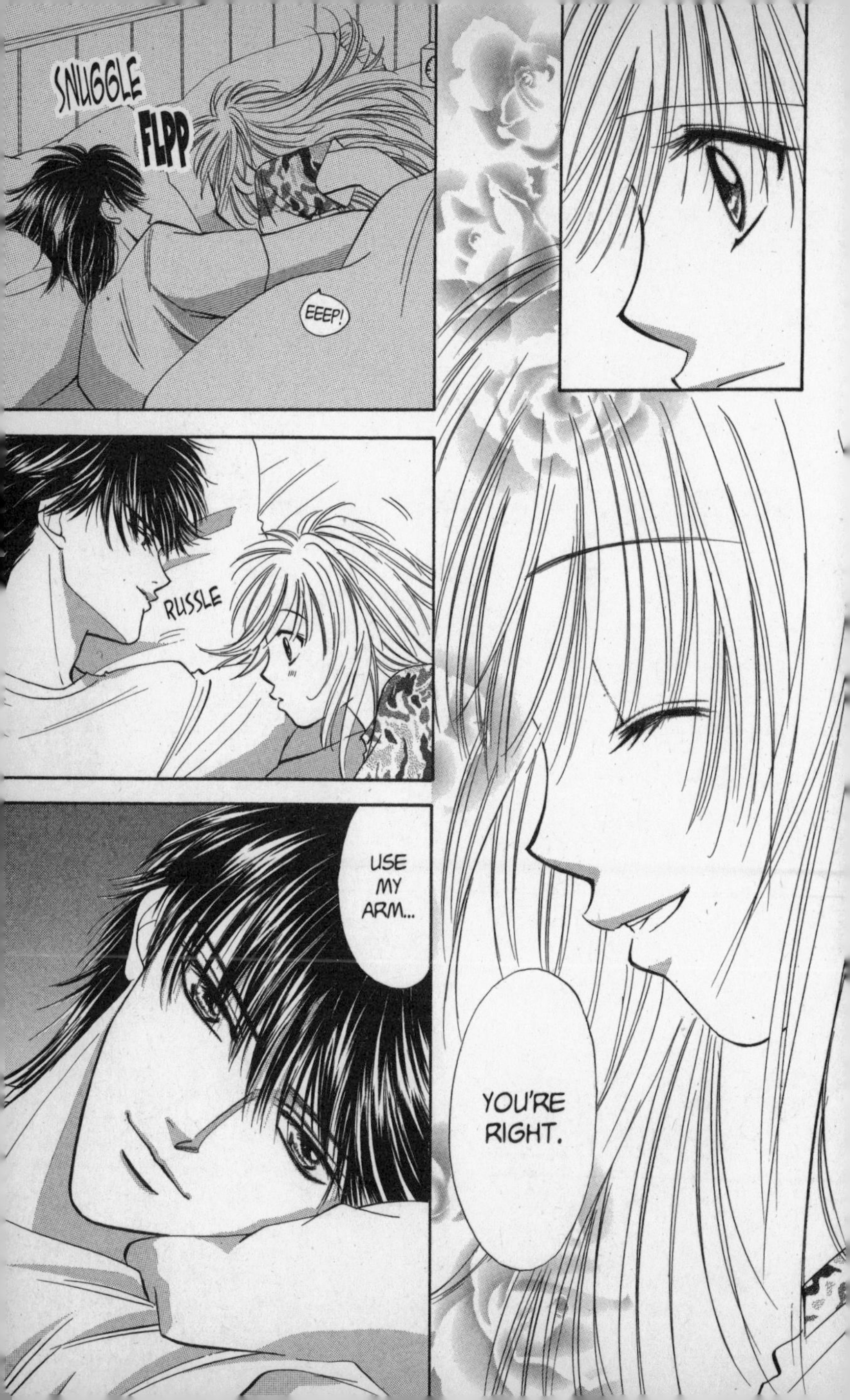
YOU'RE RIGHT.
SNUGGLE
FLPP
EEEP!
RUSSLE
USE MY ARM...

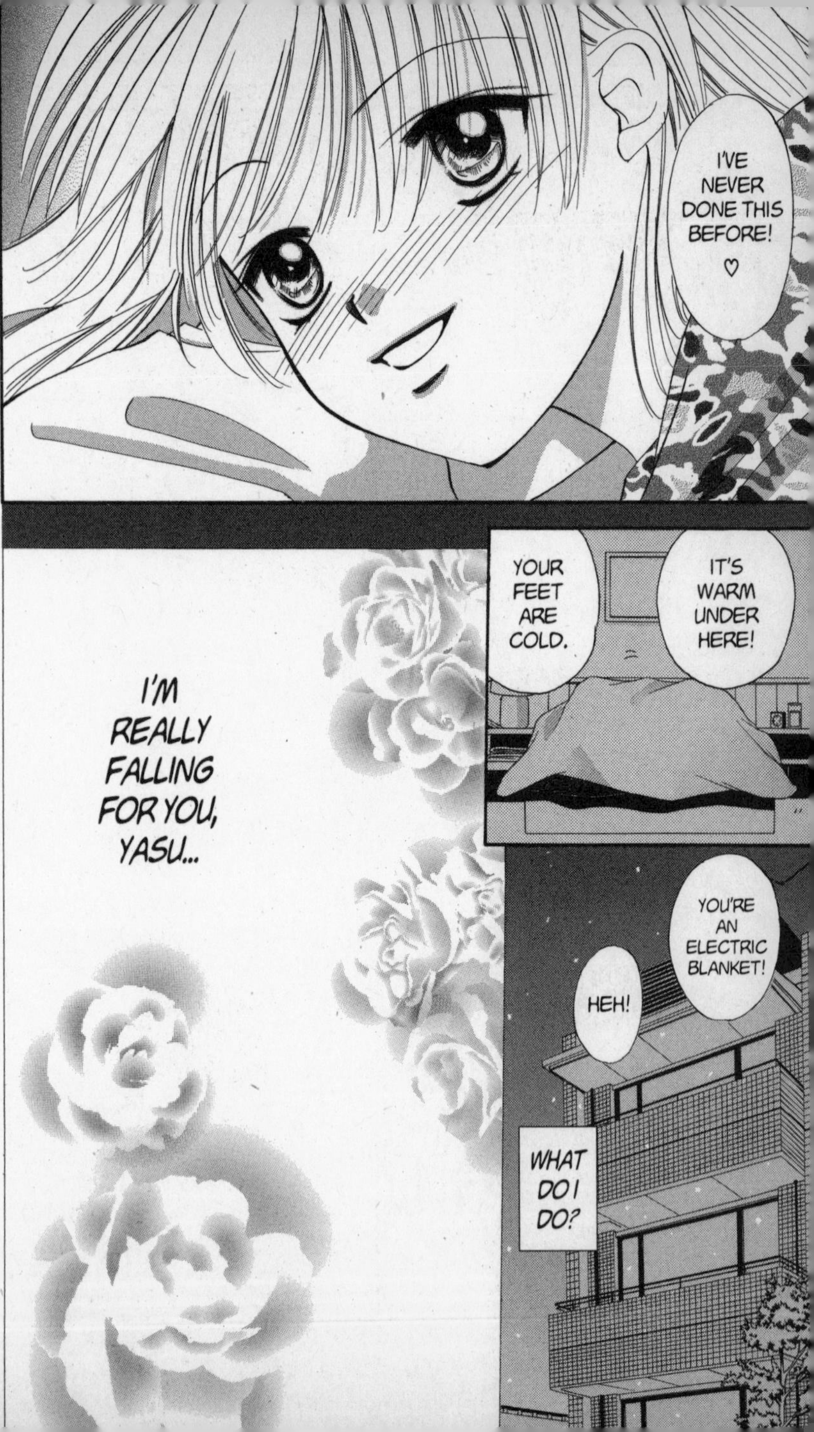
I'VE NEVER DONE THIS BEFORE! ♡
IT'S WARM UNDER HERE!
YOUR FEET ARE COLD.
YOU'RE AN ELECTRIC BLANKET!
HEH!
WHAT DO I DO?
I'M REALLY FALLING FOR YOU, YASU...

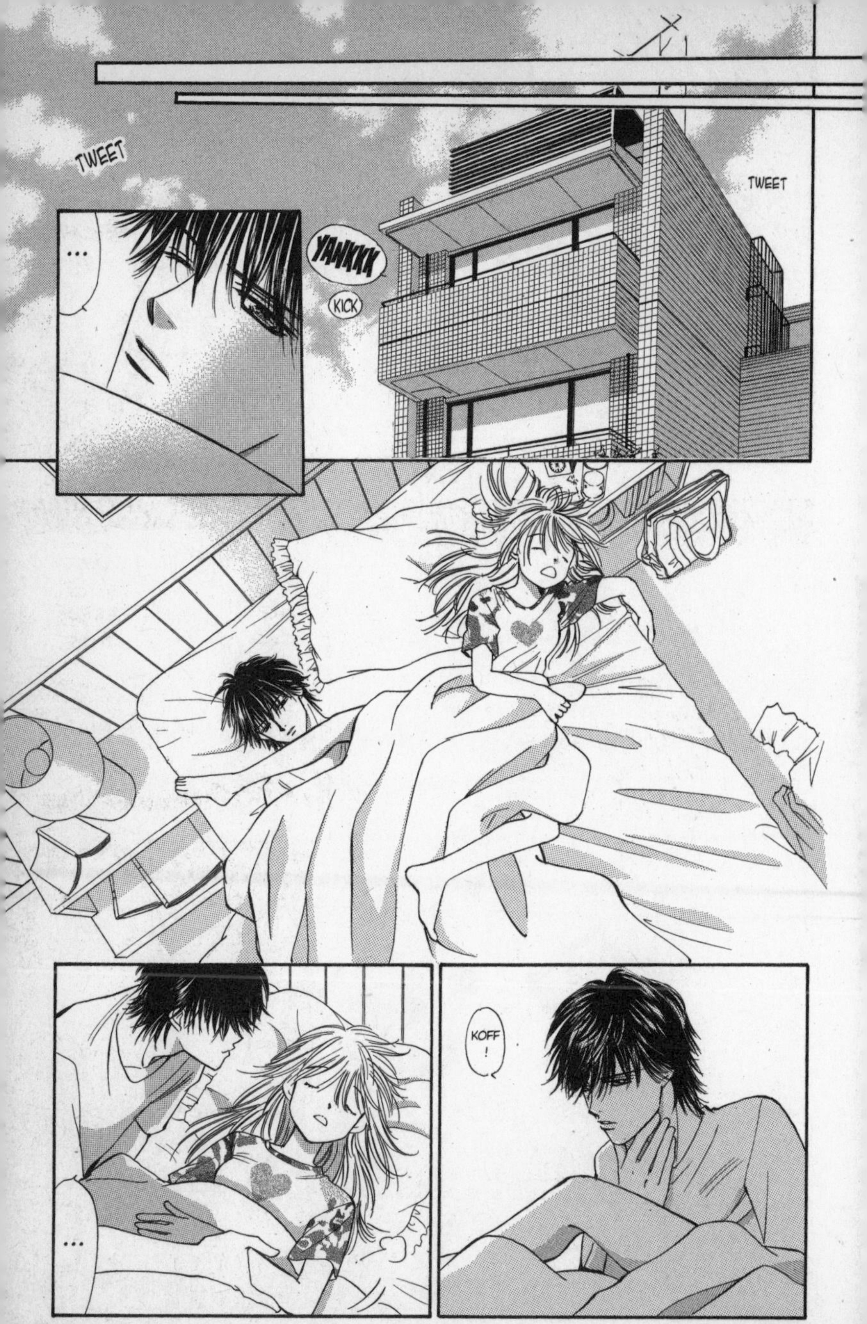
TWEET
TWEET
YANKKK
KICK
...
KOFF !
...

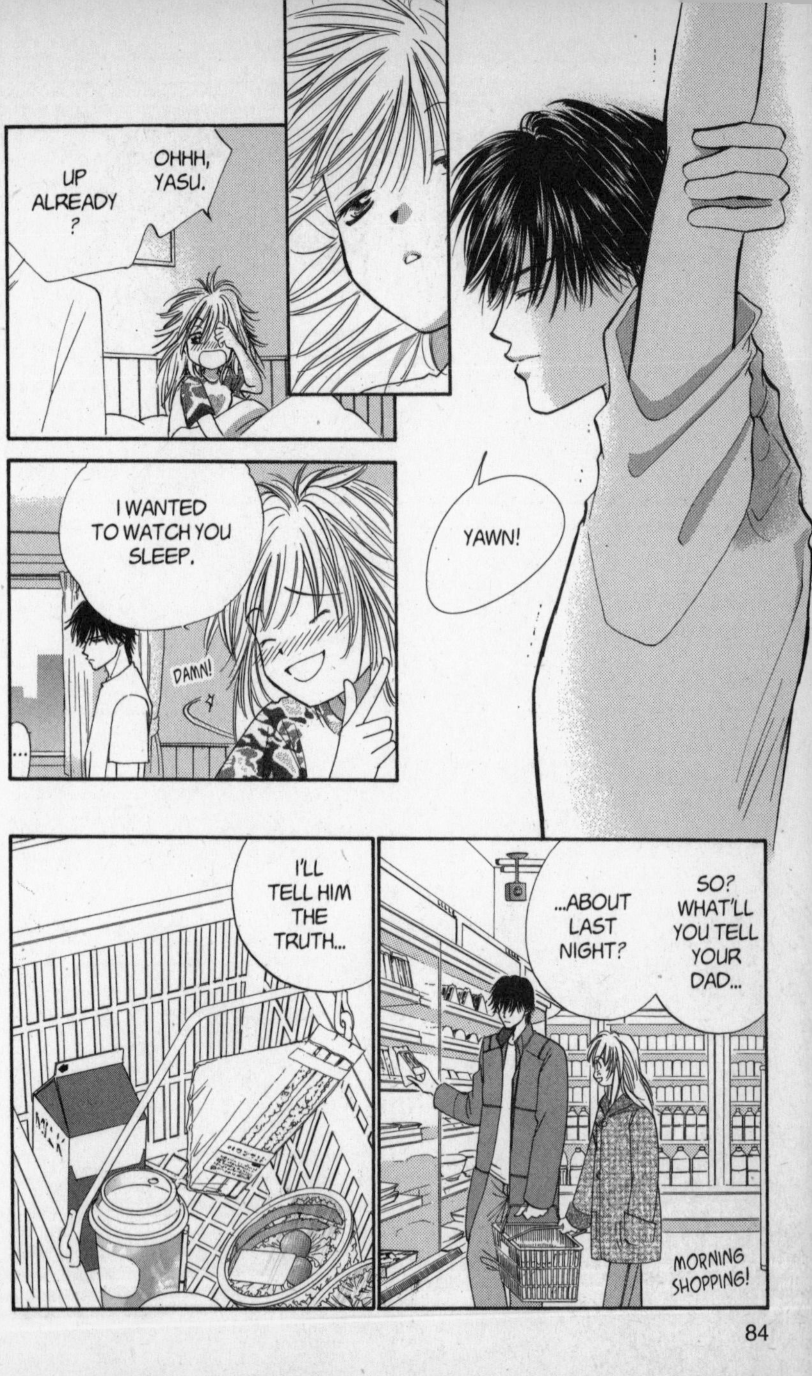
YAWN!
OHHH, YASU.
UP ALREADY?
I WANTED TO WATCH YOU SLEEP.
DAMN!
...
SO? WHAT'LL YOU TELL YOUR DAD...
...ABOUT LAST NIGHT?
MORNING SHOPPING!
I'LL TELL HIM THE TRUTH...

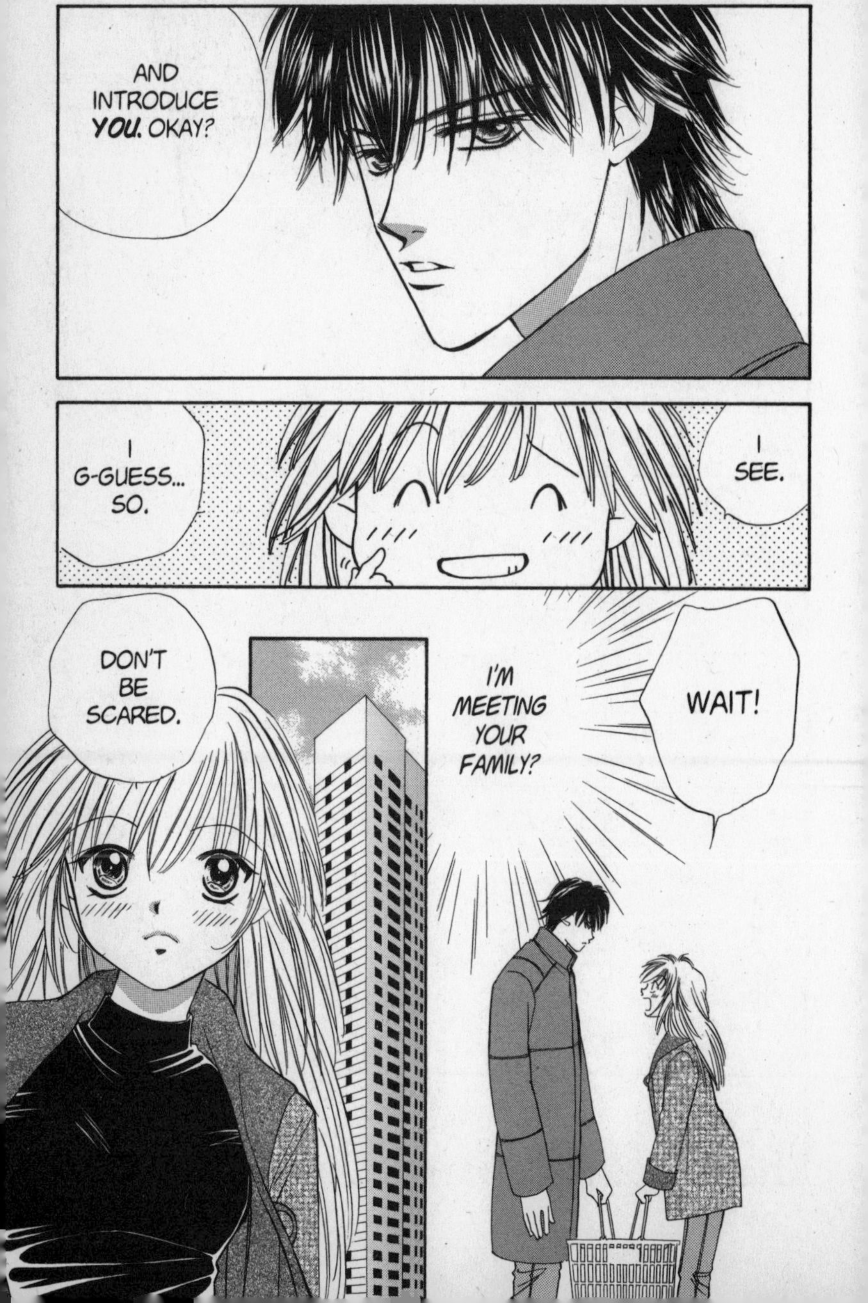
AND INTRODUCE YOU. OKAY?
I SEE.
I G-GUESS... SO.
WAIT!
I'M MEETING YOUR FAMILY?
DON'T BE SCARED.

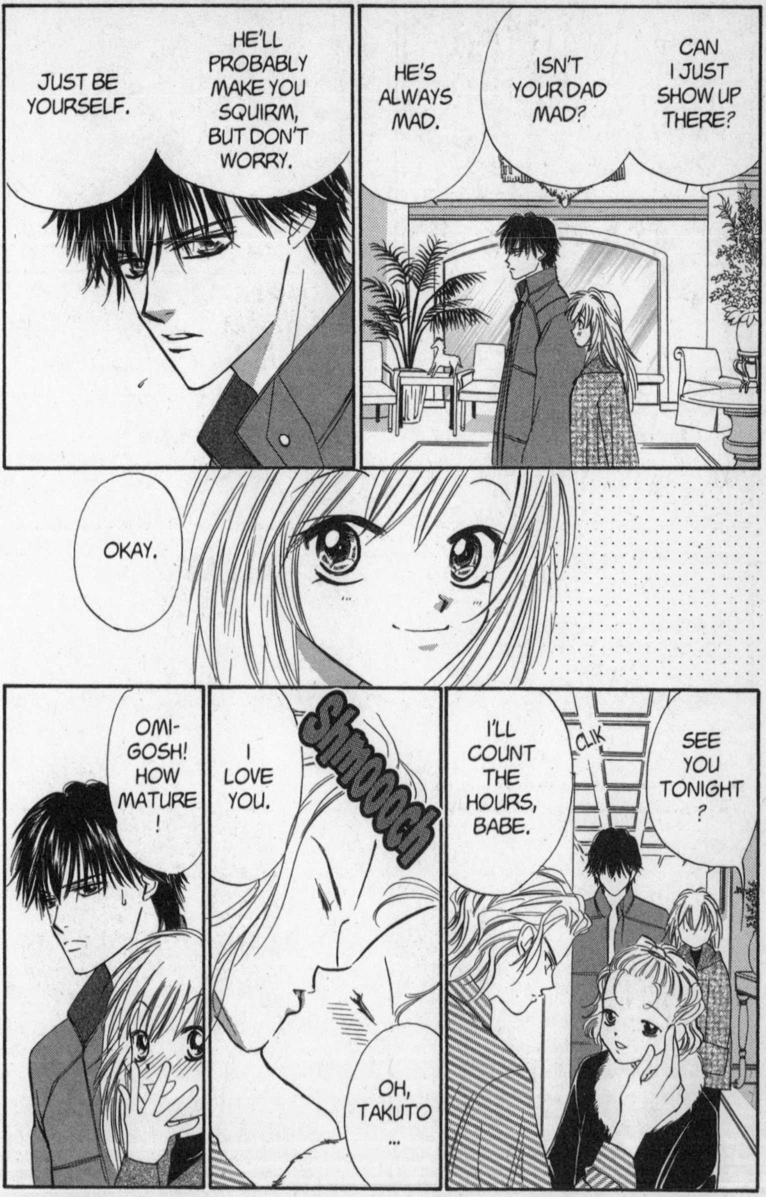
CAN I JUST SHOW UP THERE?
ISN'T YOUR DAD MAD?
HE'S ALWAYS MAD.
HE'LL PROBABLY MAKE YOU SQUIRM, BUT DON'T WORRY.
JUST BE YOURSELF.
OKAY.
SEE YOU TONIGHT?
CLIK
I'LL COUNT THE HOURS, BABE.
Shmoooch
I LOVE YOU.
OH, TAKUTO ...
OMI-GOSH! HOW MATURE!

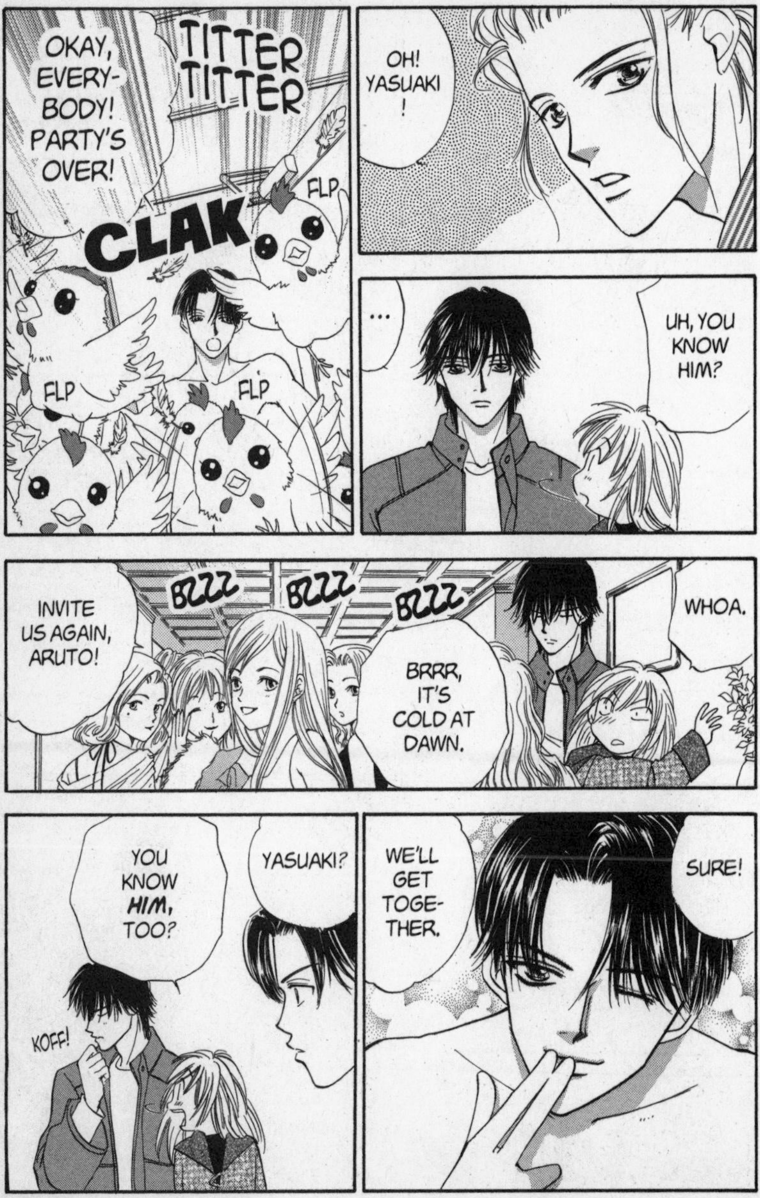
OH! YASUAKI!
UH, YOU KNOW HIM?
...
TITTER TITTER
OKAY, EVERYBODY! PARTY'S OVER!
FLP
CLAK
FLP
FLP
WHOA.
BZZZ
BZZZ
BZZZ
BRRR, IT'S COLD AT DAWN.
INVITE US AGAIN, ARUTO!
SURE!
WE'LL GET TOGETHER.
YASUAKI?
YOU KNOW **HIM**, TOO?
KOFF!

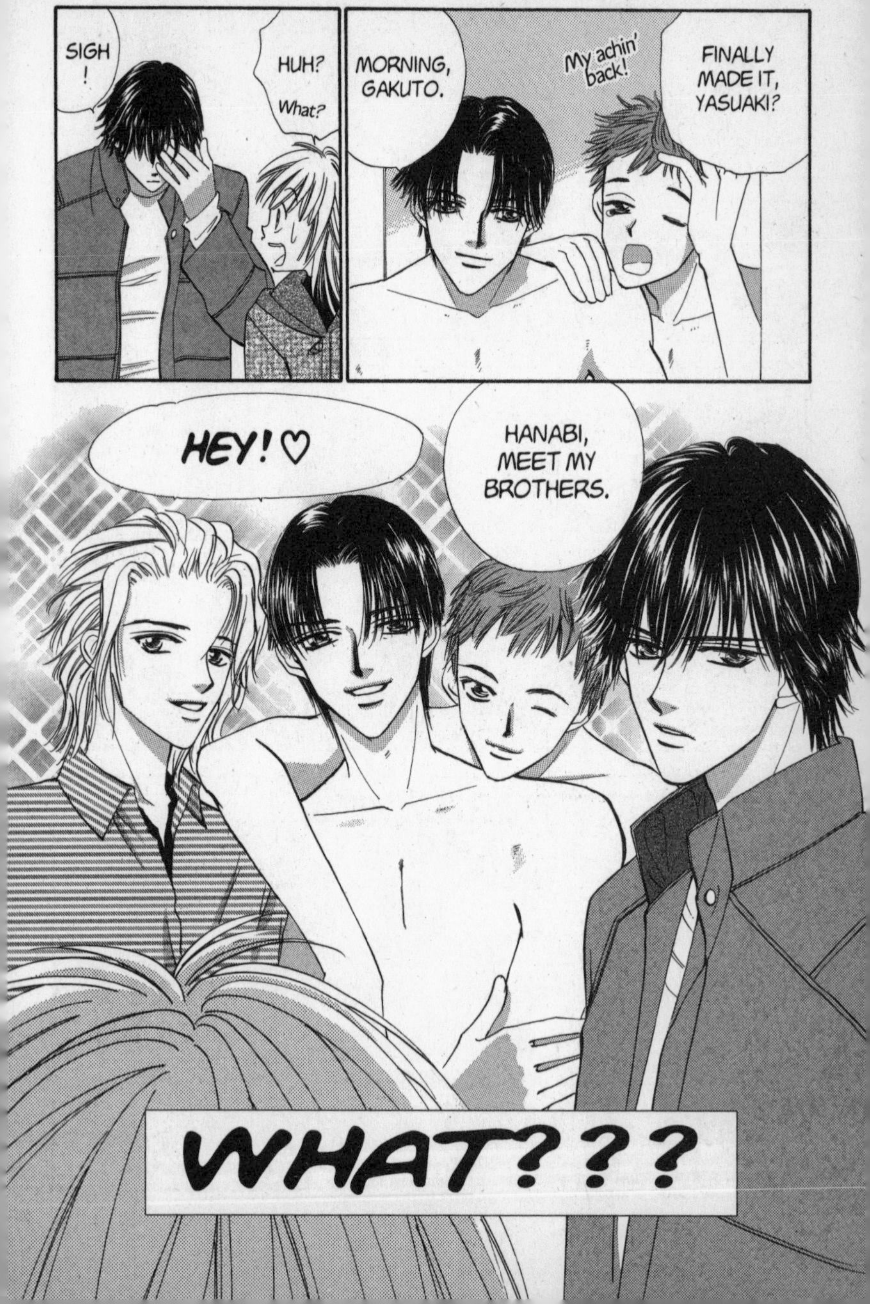
FINALLY MADE IT, YASUAKI?
My achin' back!
MORNING, GAKUTO.
HUH?
What?
SIGH!
HANABI, MEET MY BROTHERS.
HEY! ♡
WHAT???

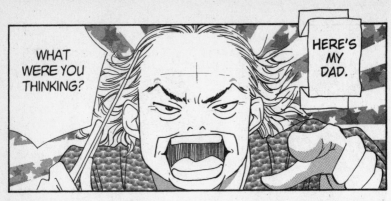

HERE'S MY DAD.
WHAT WERE YOU THINKING?
YASUAKI WAS WITH A GIRL?
THOUGHT HE WAS DIFFERENT THAN US.
GUESS HE'S A GARAKU AFTER ALL!
GARAKU MEN LOVE WOMEN ...
FIRST
SECOND
THIRD
I BOOKED THIS HOTEL AND PIANO JUST FOR YOU.
FOR ME—OR FOR YOURSELF?
YOUNGEST
YASU-AKI'S FAMILY!
I'M DEFINITELY IMPRESSED.
GLAAARE
GASP!
...

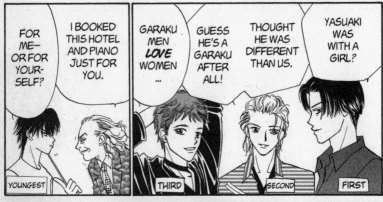

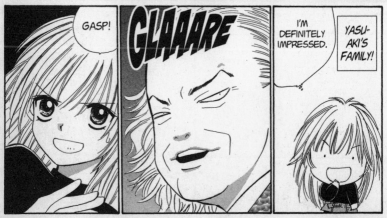

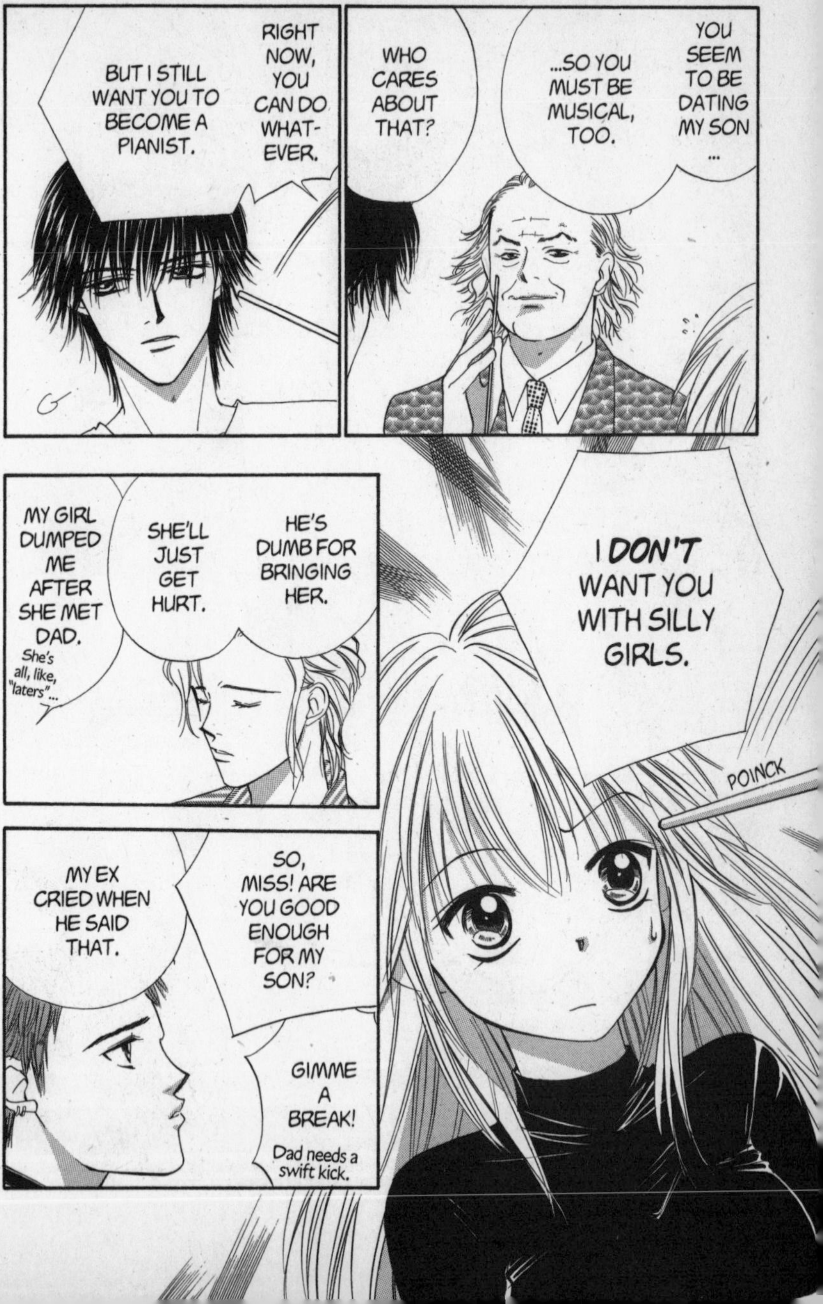
YOU SEEM TO BE DATING MY SON ...
...SO YOU MUST BE MUSICAL, TOO.
WHO CARES ABOUT THAT?
RIGHT NOW, YOU CAN DO WHAT-EVER.
BUT I STILL WANT YOU TO BECOME A PIANIST.
I DON'T WANT YOU WITH SILLY GIRLS.
POINCK
HE'S DUMB FOR BRINGING HER.
SHE'LL JUST GET HURT.
MY GIRL DUMPED ME AFTER SHE MET DAD.
She's all, like, "laters"...
SO, MISS! ARE YOU GOOD ENOUGH FOR MY SON?
MY EX CRIED WHEN HE SAID THAT.
GIMME A BREAK!
Dad needs a swift kick.

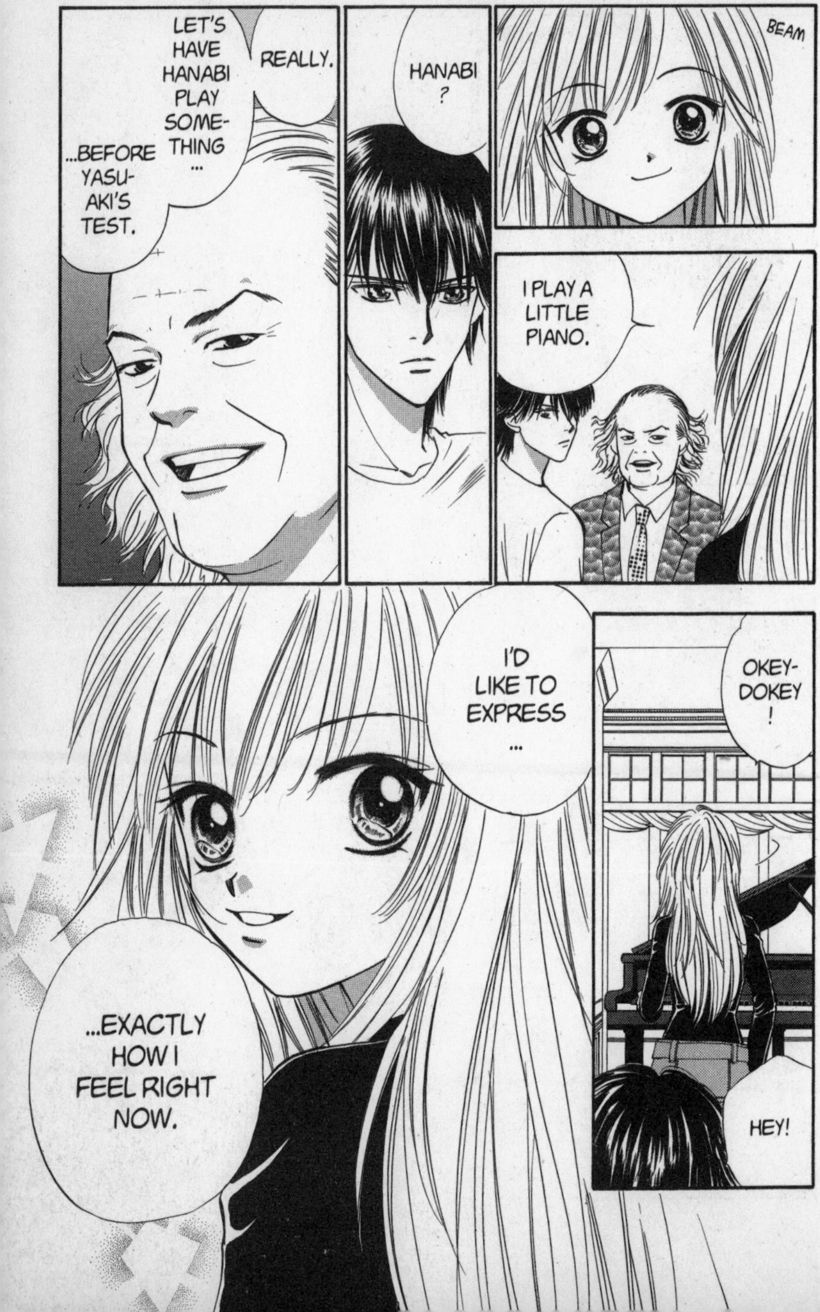
LET'S HAVE HANABI PLAY SOME-THING ...
...BEFORE YASU-AKI'S TEST.
REALLY.
HANABI ?
BEAM
I PLAY A LITTLE PIANO.
I'D LIKE TO EXPRESS ...
...EXACTLY HOW I FEEL RIGHT NOW.
OKEY-DOKEY !
HEY!

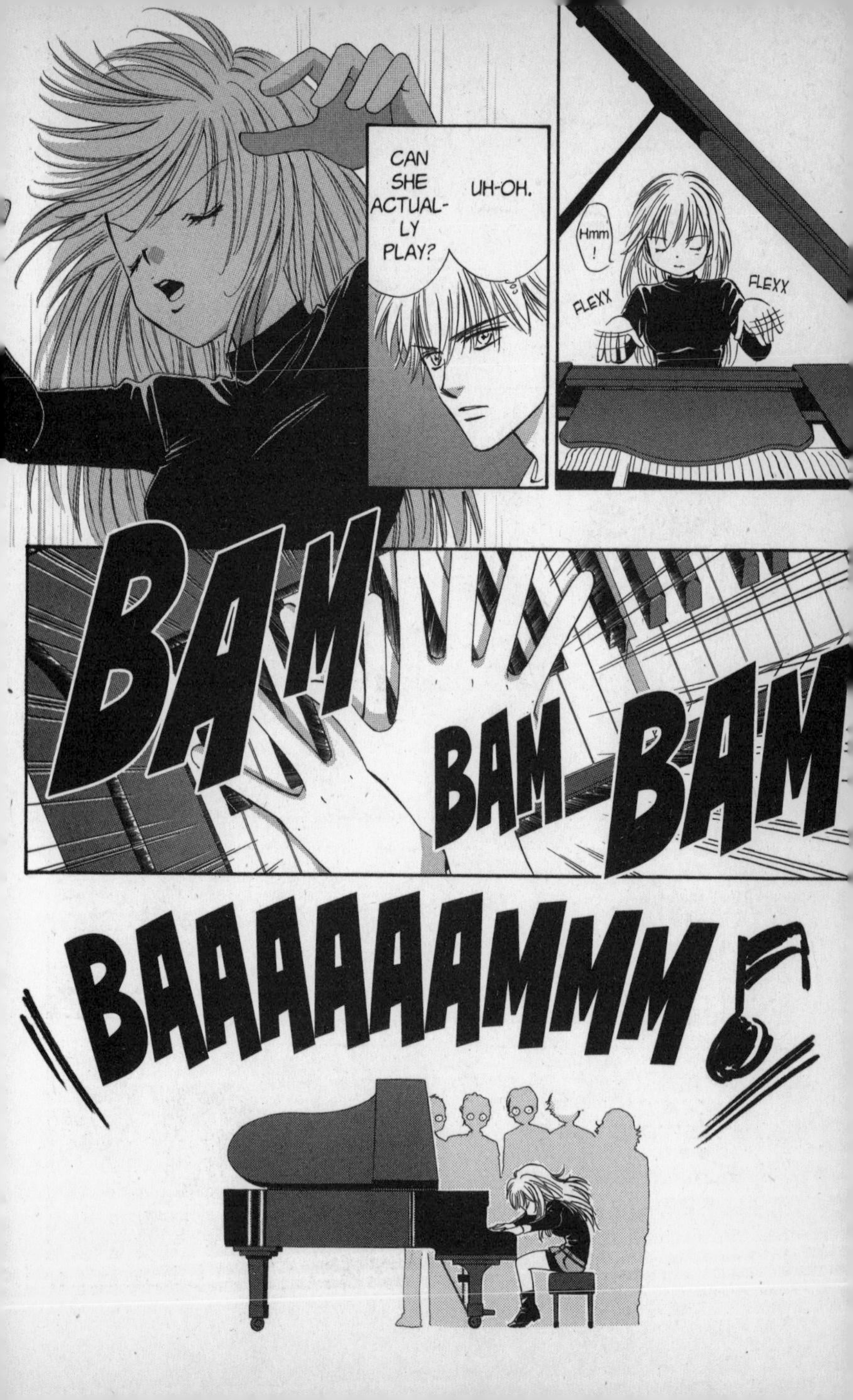
Hmm!
FLEXX
FLEXX
UH-OH.
CAN SHE ACTUAL-LY PLAY?
BAM
BAM BAM BAM
BAAAAAAMMM

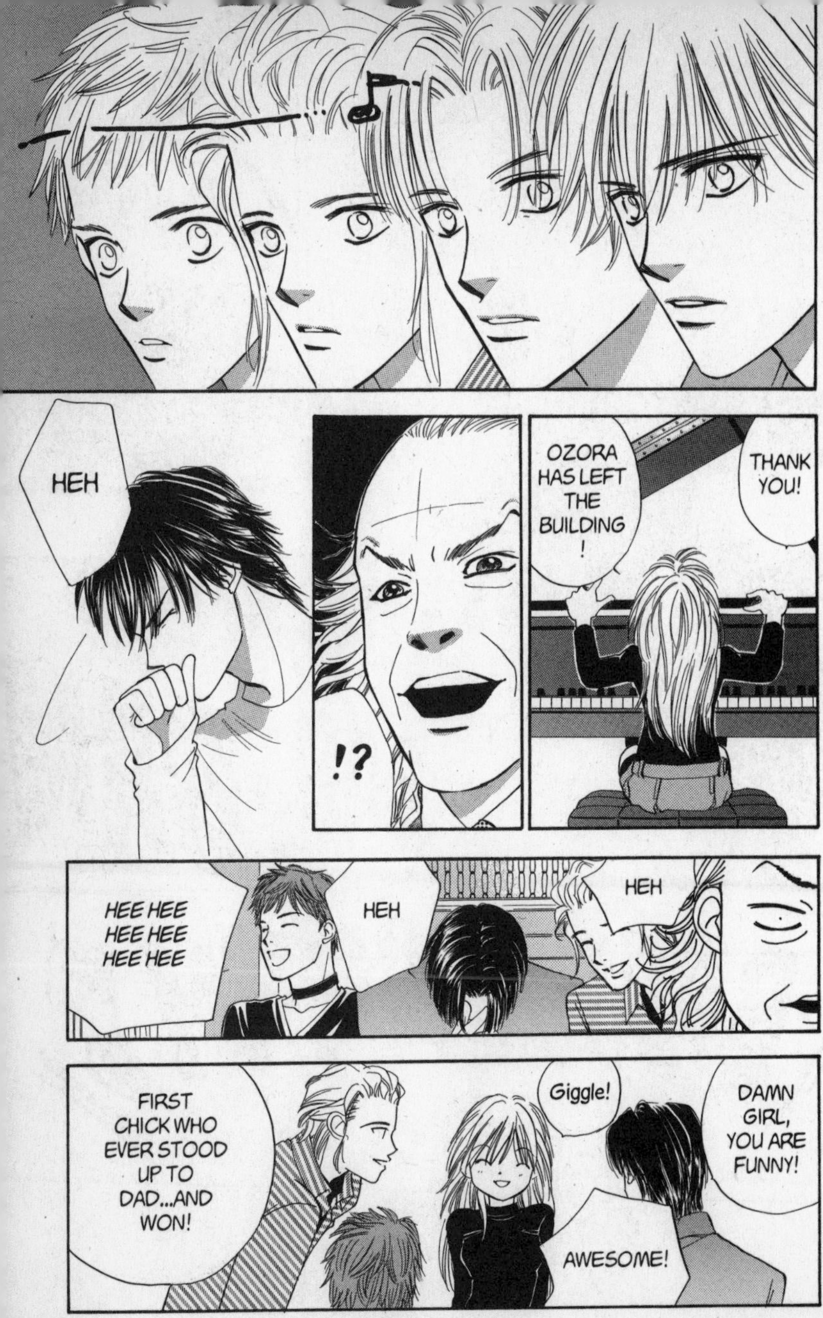
THANK YOU!
OZORA HAS LEFT THE BUILDING!
!?
HEH
HEH
HEH
HEE HEE HEE HEE HEE HEE
DAMN GIRL, YOU ARE FUNNY!
Giggle!
FIRST CHICK WHO EVER STOOD UP TO DAD...AND WON!
AWESOME!

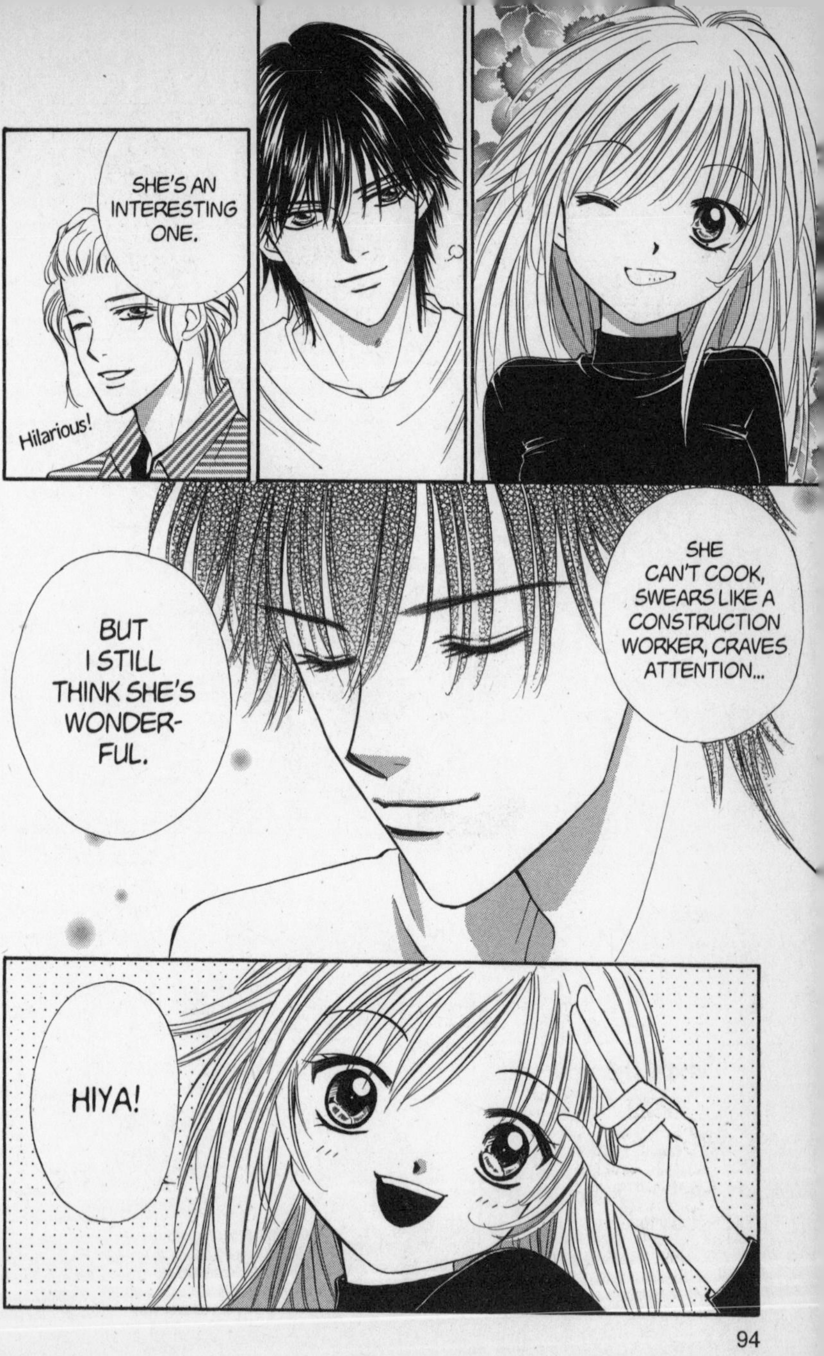
SHE'S AN INTERESTING ONE.
Hilarious!
SHE CAN'T COOK, SWEARS LIKE A CONSTRUCTION WORKER, CRAVES ATTENTION...
BUT I STILL THINK SHE'S WONDER-FUL.
HIYA!

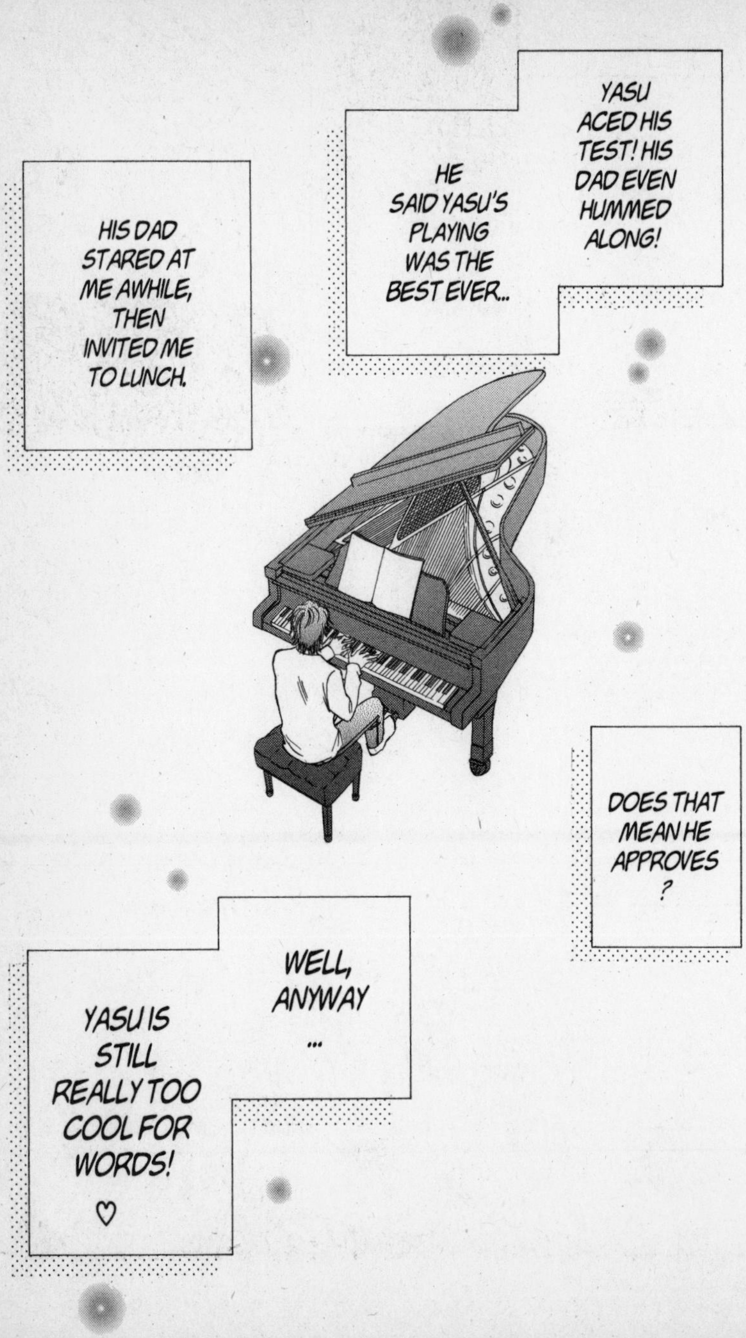
YASU ACED HIS TEST! HIS DAD EVEN HUMMED ALONG!
HE SAID YASU'S PLAYING WAS THE BEST EVER...
HIS DAD STARED AT ME AWHILE, THEN INVITED ME TO LUNCH.
DOES THAT MEAN HE APPROVES?
WELL, ANYWAY...
YASU IS STILL REALLY TOO COOL FOR WORDS! ♡

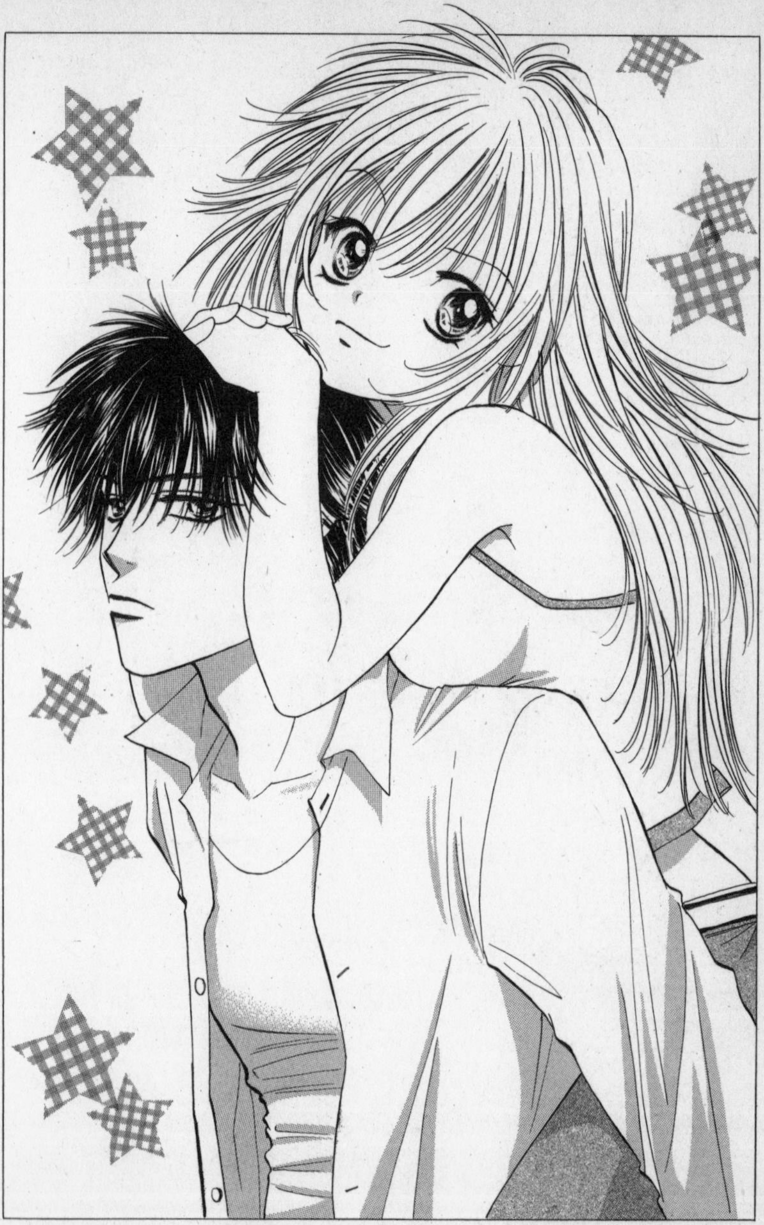

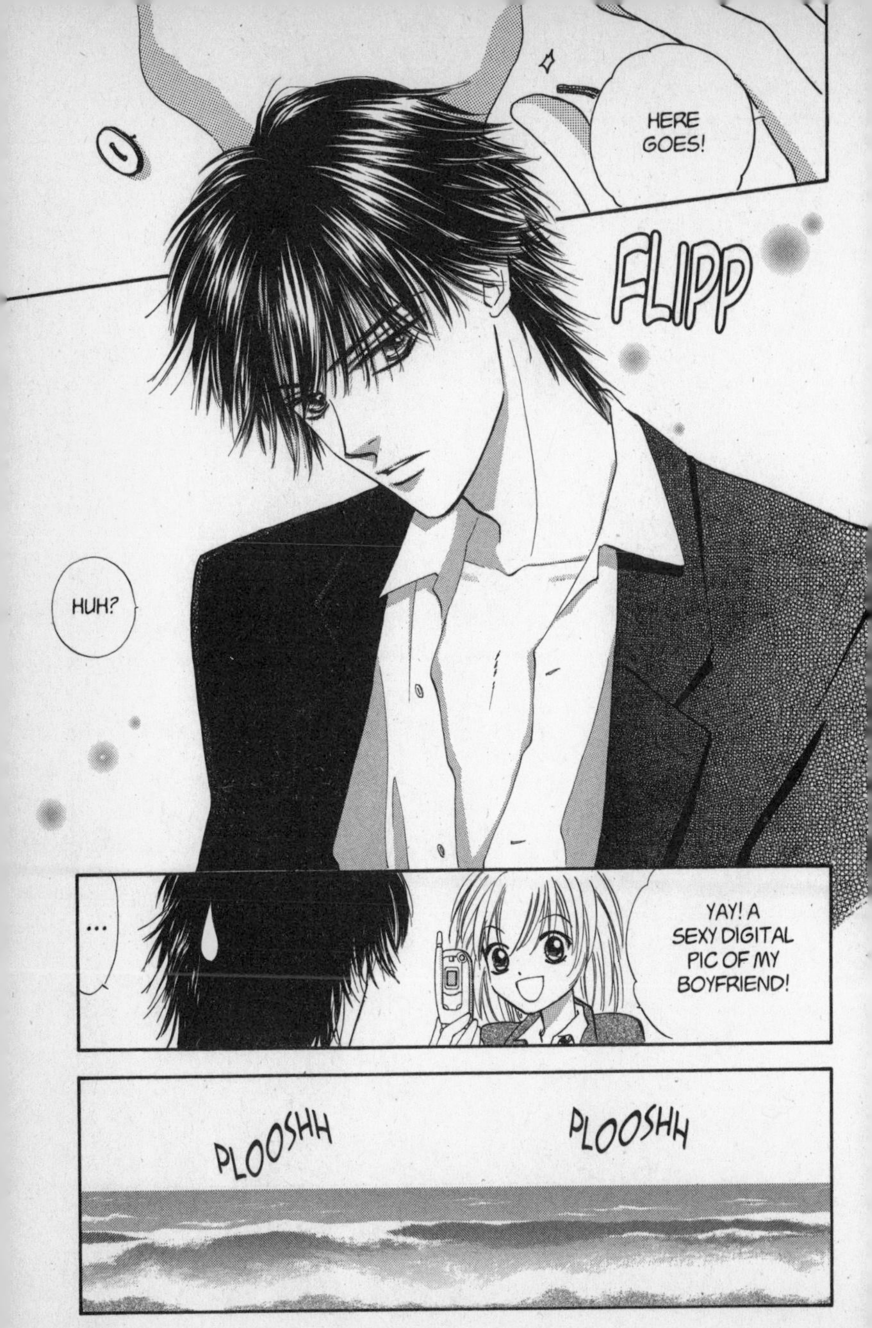
HERE GOES!
FLIPP
HUH?
YAY! A SEXY DIGITAL PIC OF MY BOYFRIEND!
...
PLOOSHH
PLOOSHH

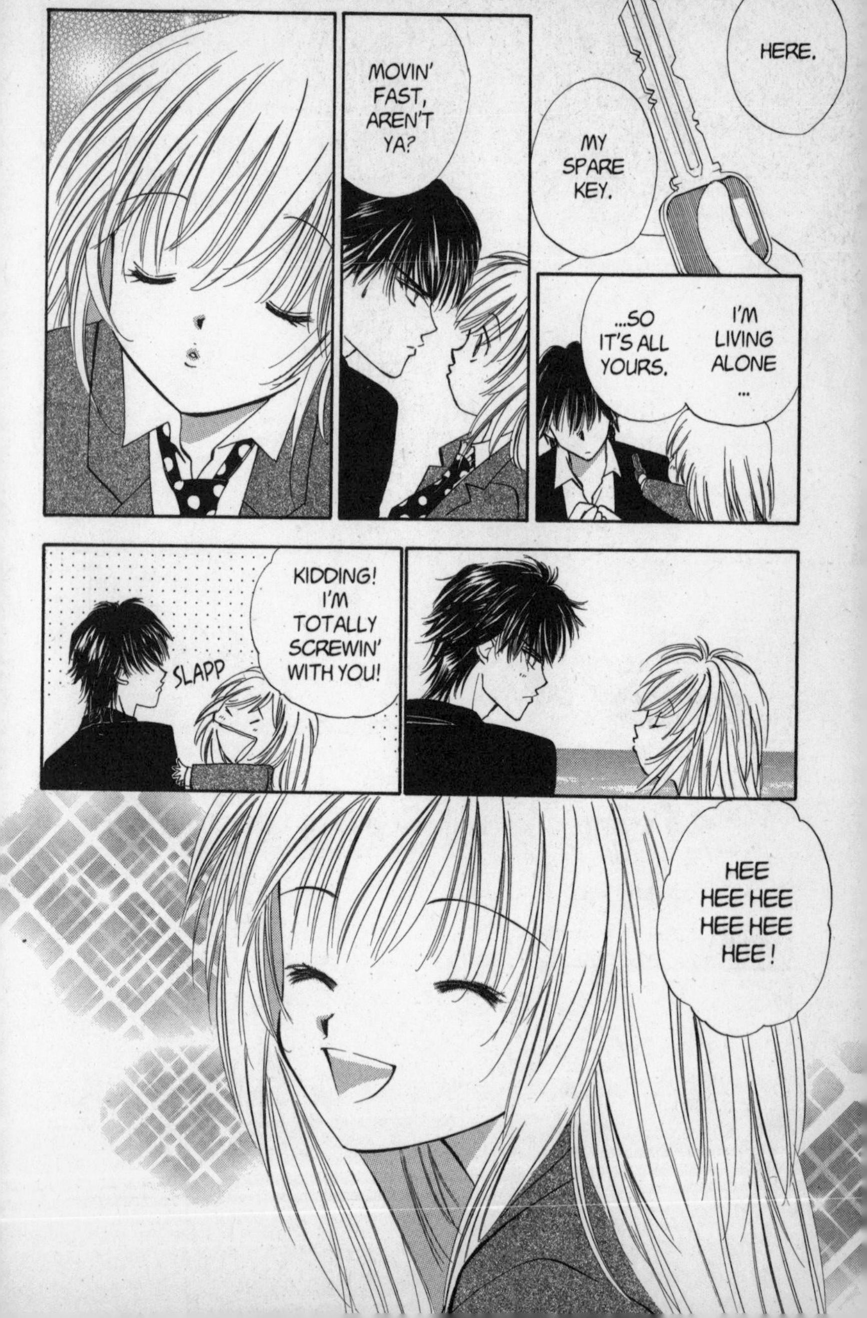
HERE.
MY SPARE KEY.
I'M LIVING ALONE ...
...SO IT'S ALL YOURS.
MOVIN' FAST, AREN'T YA?
KIDDING! I'M TOTALLY SCREWIN' WITH YOU!
SLAPP
HEE HEE HEE HEE HEE HEE!

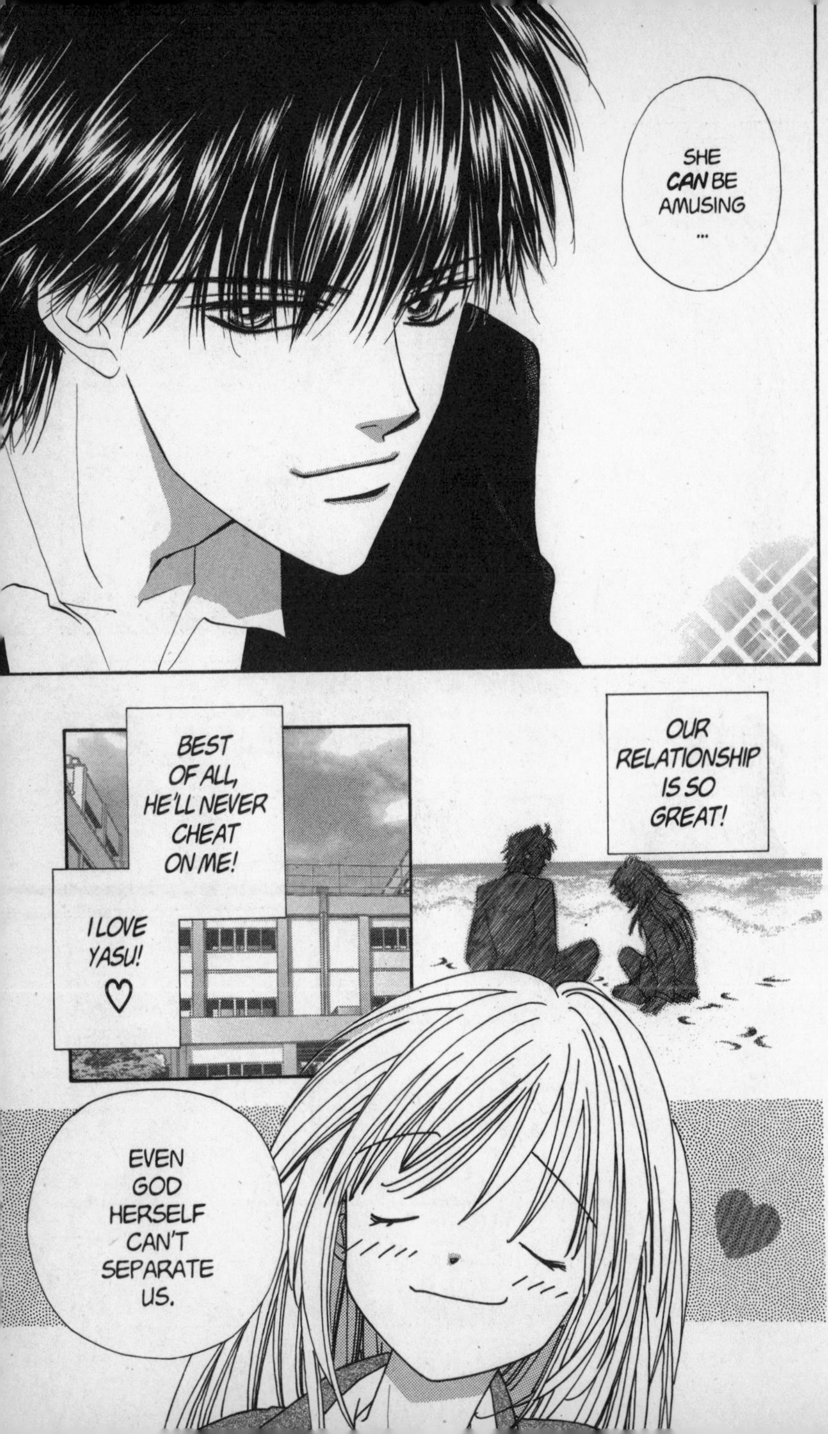
SHE CAN BE AMUSING ...
OUR RELATIONSHIP IS SO GREAT!
BEST OF ALL, HE'LL NEVER CHEAT ON ME!
I LOVE YASU! ♡
EVEN GOD HERSELF CAN'T SEPARATE US.

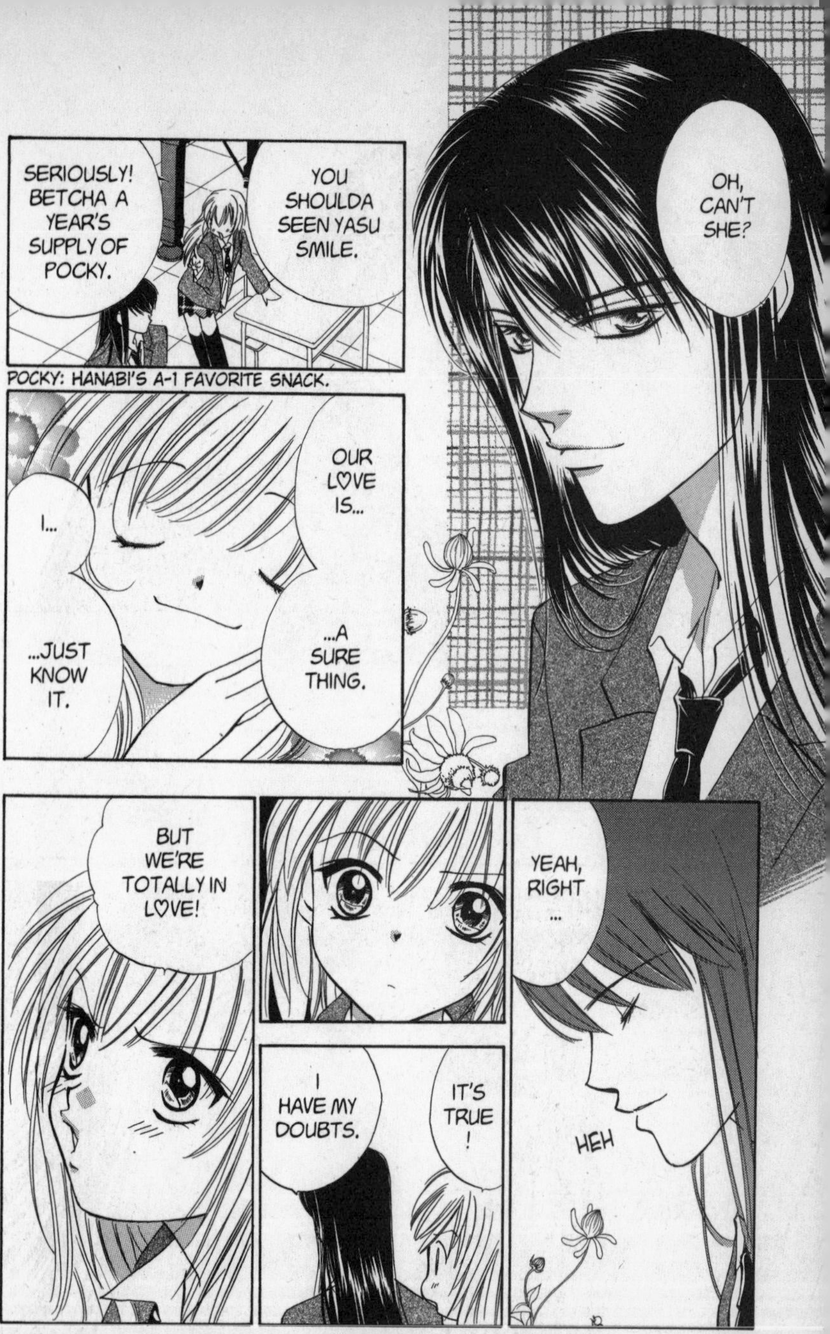
OH, CAN'T SHE?
YOU SHOULDA SEEN YASU SMILE.
SERIOUSLY! BETCHA A YEAR'S SUPPLY OF POCKY.
POCKY: HANABI'S A-1 FAVORITE SNACK.
OUR LOVE IS...
I...
...A SURE THING.
...JUST KNOW IT.
YEAH, RIGHT ...
HEH
IT'S TRUE!
I HAVE MY DOUBTS.
BUT WE'RE TOTALLY IN LOVE!

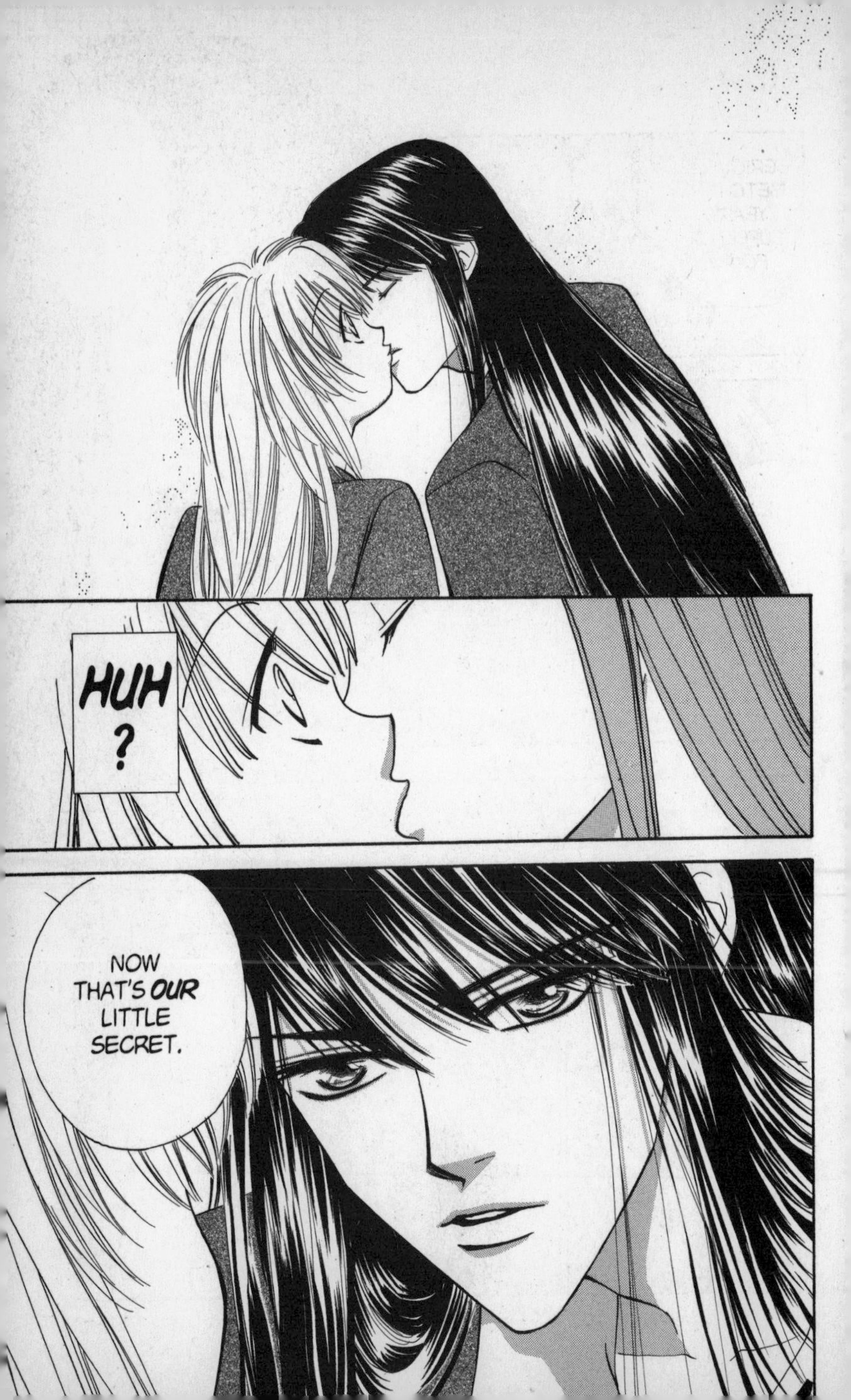
HUH ?
NOW THAT'S OUR LITTLE SECRET.

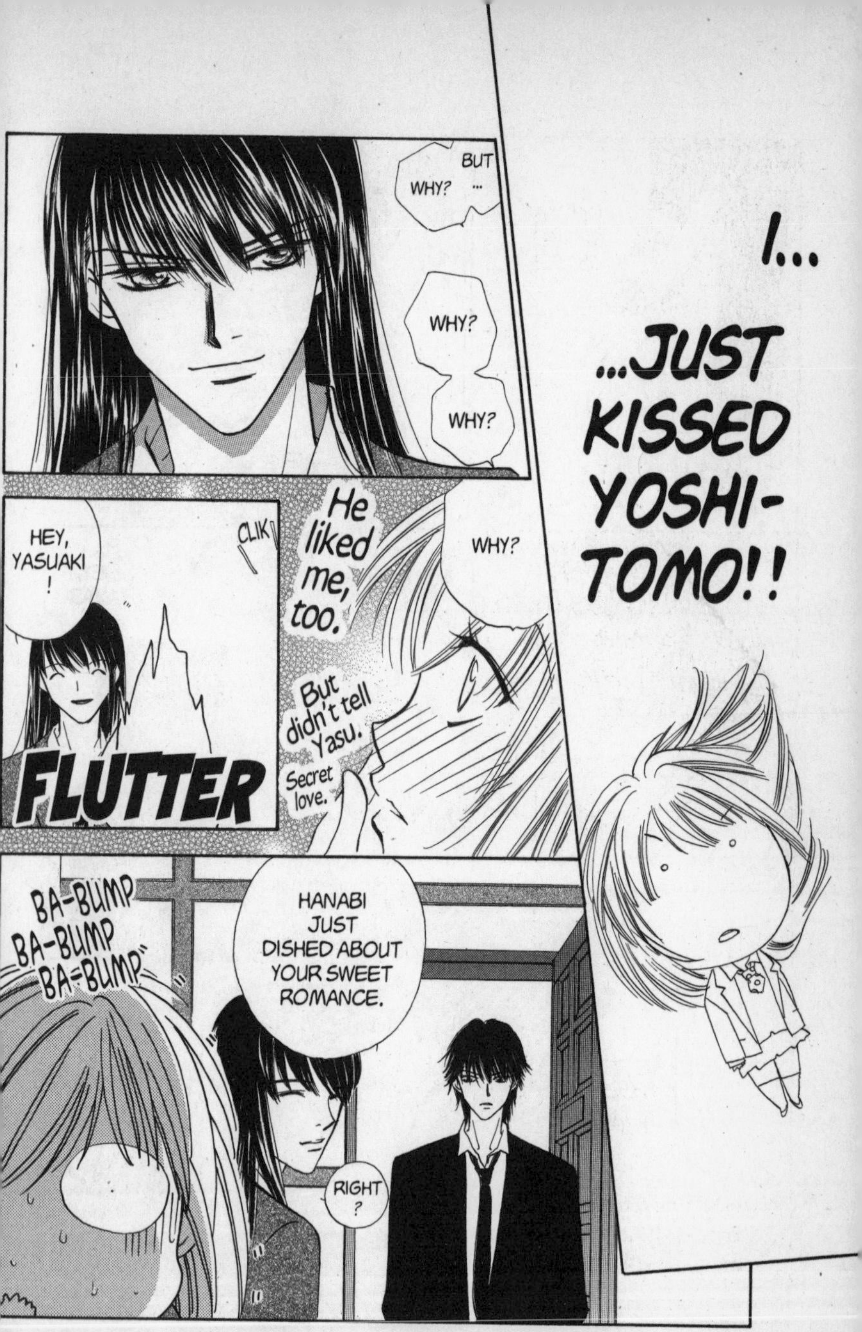
I...
...JUST KISSED YOSHI-TOMO!!
BUT... WHY?
WHY?
WHY?
WHY?
He liked me, too.
But didn't tell Yasu.
Secret love.
CLIK
HEY, YASUAKI!
FLUTTER
HANABI JUST DISHED ABOUT YOUR SWEET ROMANCE.
BA-BUMP BA-BUMP BA-BUMP
RIGHT?

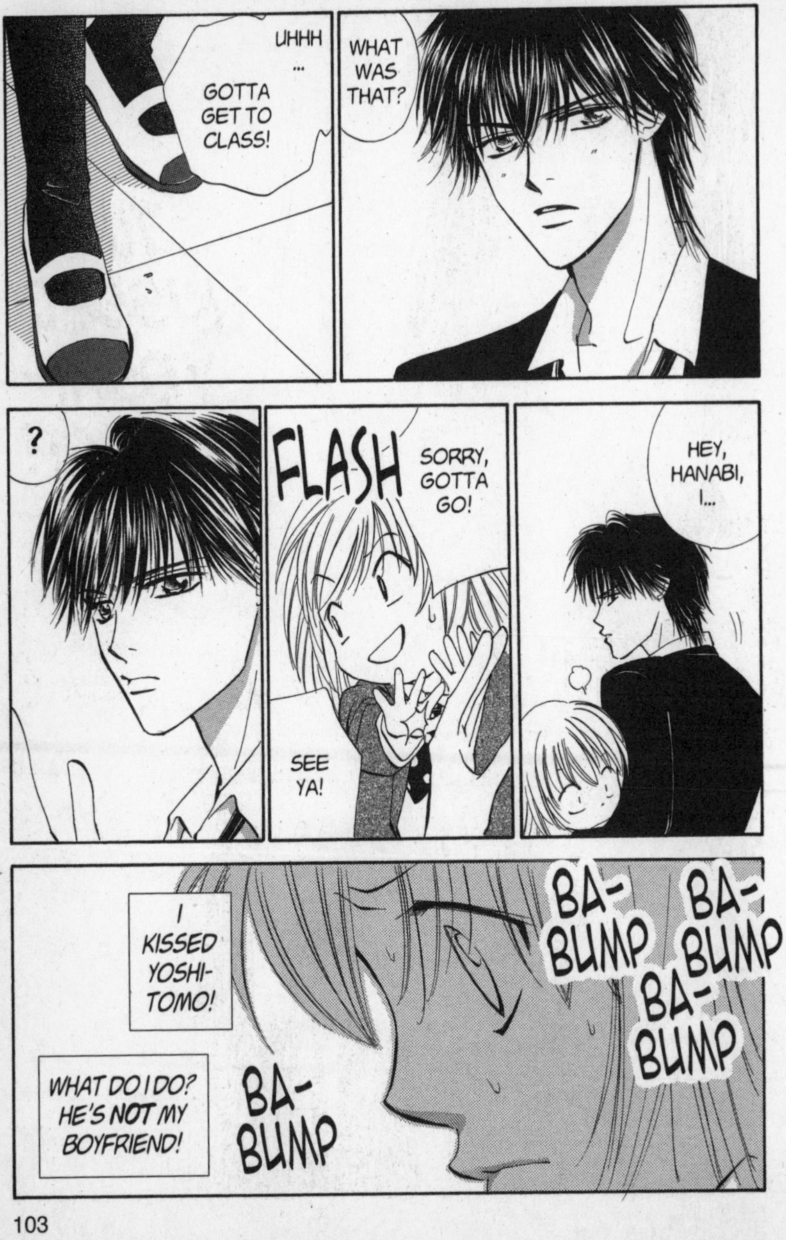
WHAT WAS THAT?
UHHH ... GOTTA GET TO CLASS!
HEY, HANABI, I...
FLASH
SORRY, GOTTA GO!
SEE YA!
?
BA-BUMP
BA-BUMP
BA-BUMP
I KISSED YOSHI-TOMO!
WHAT DO I DO? HE'S NOT MY BOYFRIEND!
BA-BUMP

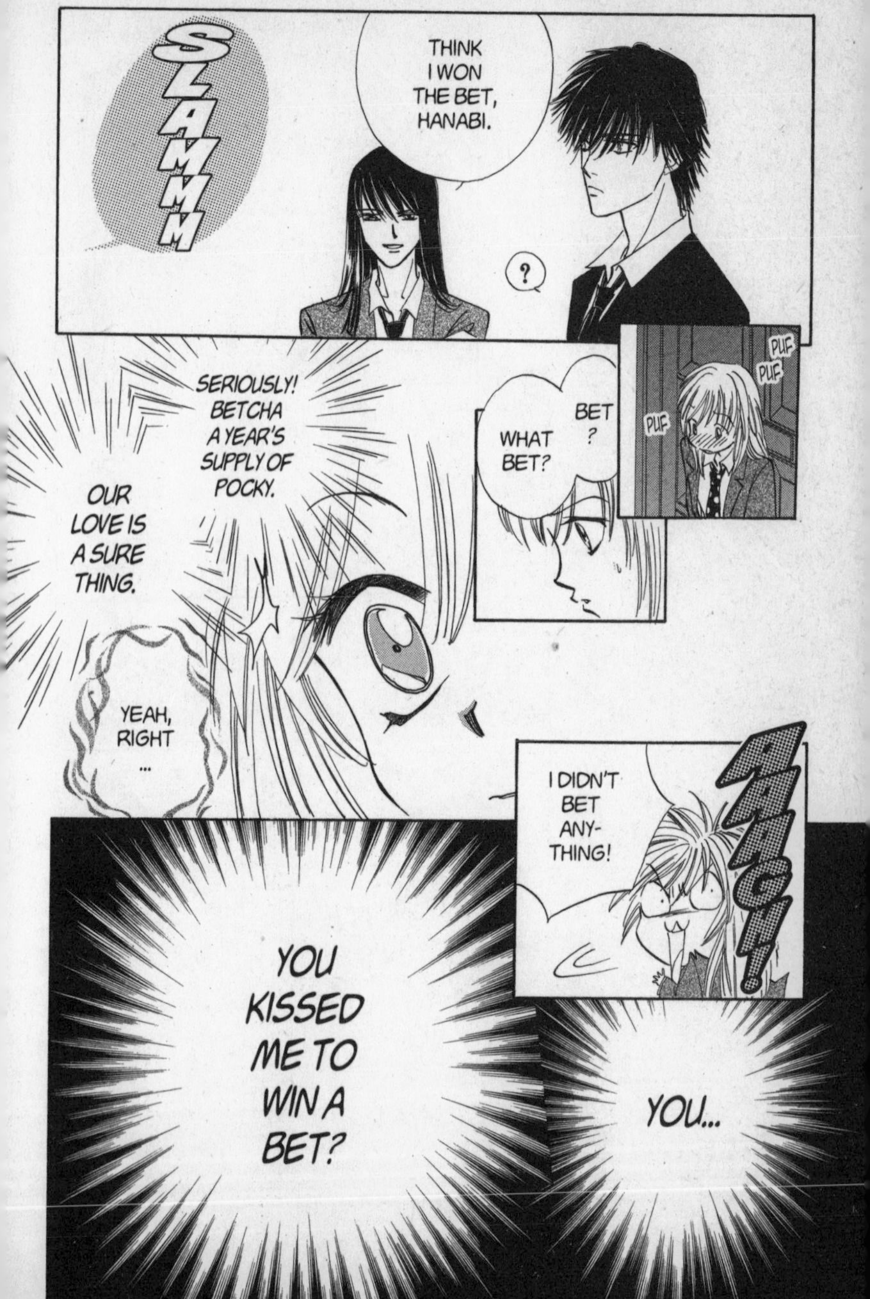
THINK I WON THE BET, HANABI.
SLAMMM
?
PUF
PUF
PUF
BET?
WHAT BET?
SERIOUSLY! BETCHA A YEAR'S SUPPLY OF POCKY.
OUR LOVE IS A SURE THING.
YEAH, RIGHT ...
I DIDN'T BET ANY-THING!
YOU...
YOU KISSED ME TO WIN A BET?

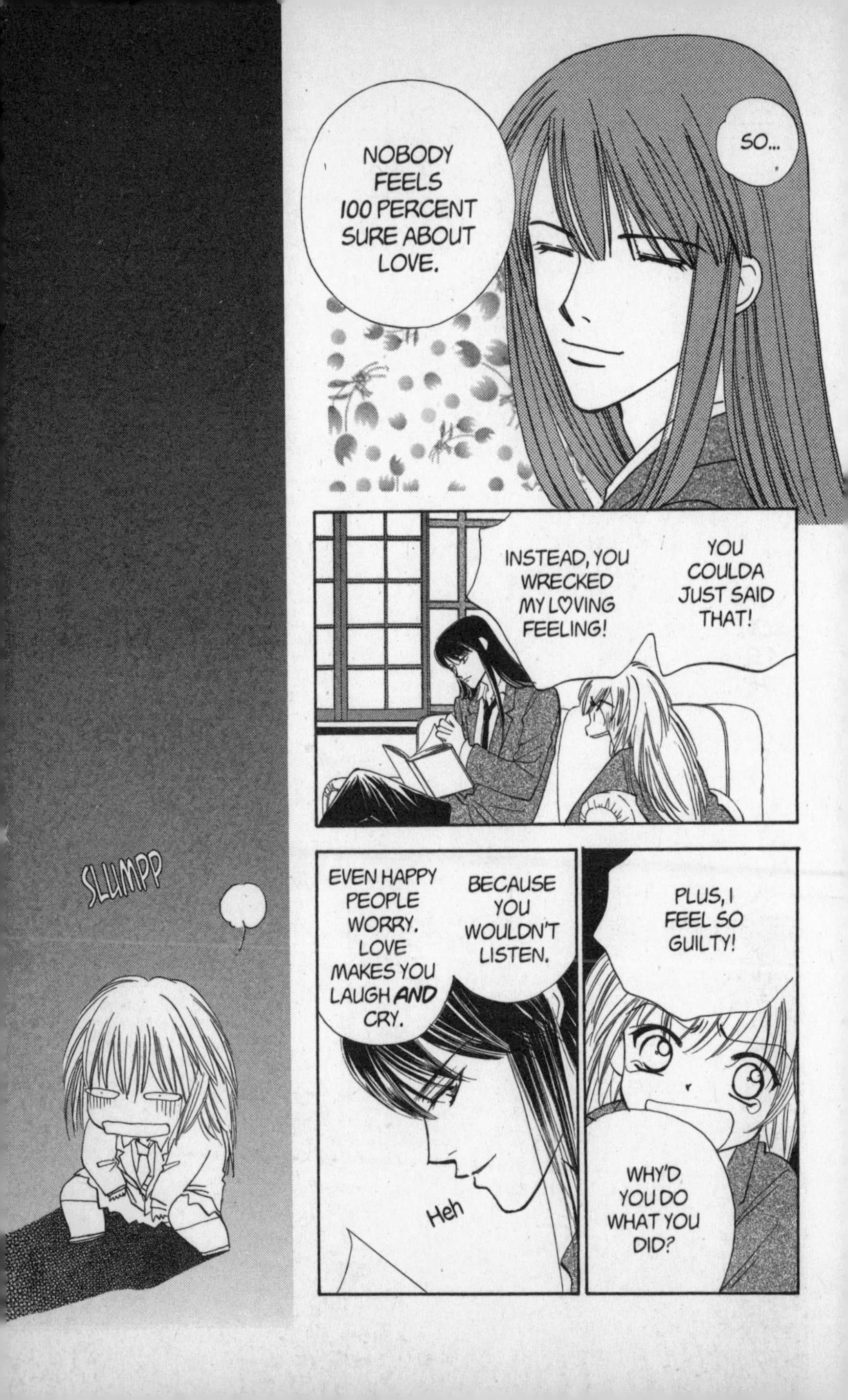
SO...
NOBODY FEELS 100 PERCENT SURE ABOUT LOVE.
YOU COULDA JUST SAID THAT!
INSTEAD, YOU WRECKED MY LOVING FEELING!
PLUS, I FEEL SO GUILTY!
WHY'D YOU DO WHAT YOU DID?
BECAUSE YOU WOULDN'T LISTEN.
EVEN HAPPY PEOPLE WORRY. LOVE MAKES YOU LAUGH **AND** CRY.
Heh
SLUMPP

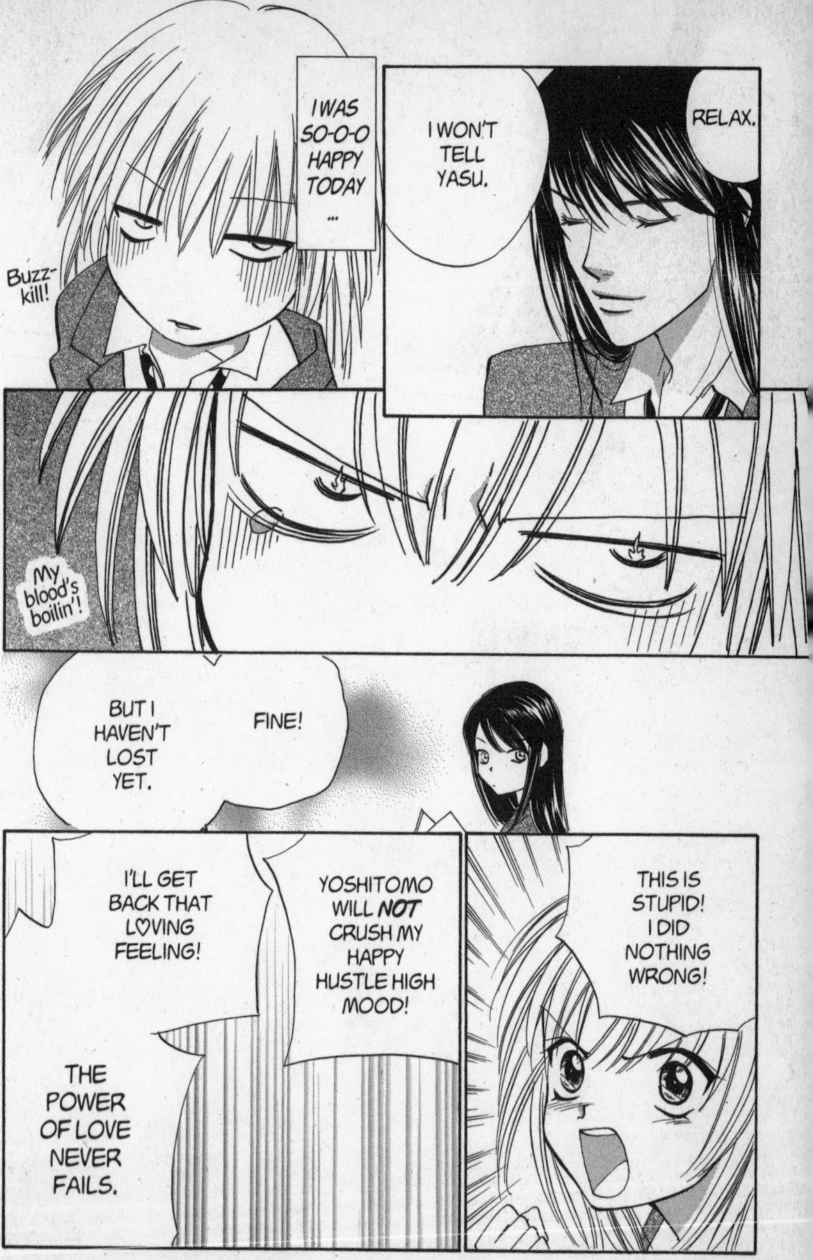
RELAX.
I WON'T TELL YASU.
I WAS SO-O-O HAPPY TODAY ...
Buzz-kill!
My blood's boilin'!
FINE!
BUT I HAVEN'T LOST YET.
THIS IS STUPID! I DID NOTHING WRONG!
YOSHITOMO WILL **NOT** CRUSH MY HAPPY HUSTLE HIGH MOOD!
I'LL GET BACK THAT L♡VING FEELING!
THE POWER OF LOVE NEVER FAILS.

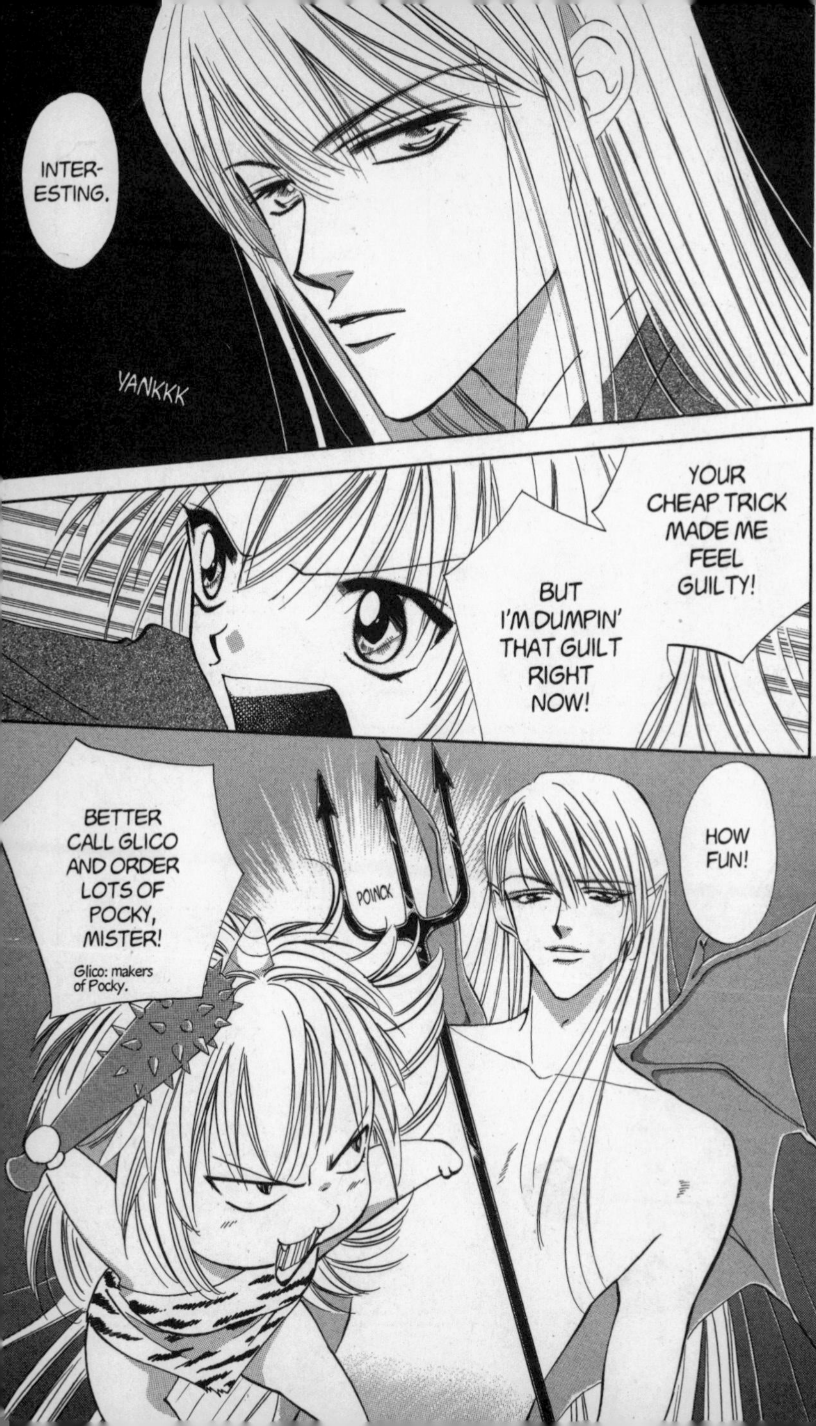
INTER-ESTING.
YANKKK
YOUR CHEAP TRICK MADE ME FEEL GUILTY!
BUT I'M DUMPIN' THAT GUILT RIGHT NOW!
HOW FUN!
POINCK
BETTER CALL GLICO AND ORDER LOTS OF POCKY, MISTER!
Glico: makers of Pocky.

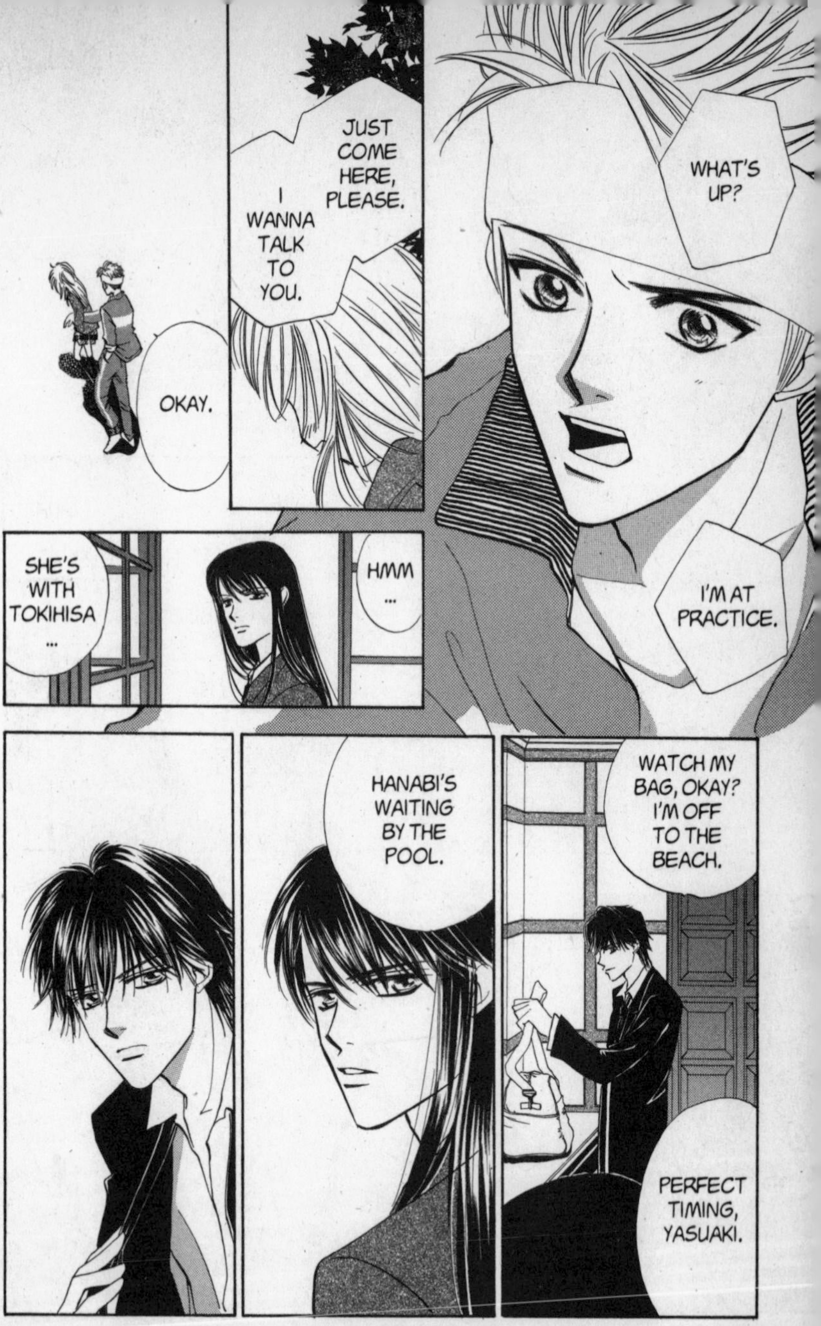
WHAT'S UP?
I'M AT PRACTICE.
JUST COME HERE, PLEASE.
I WANNA TALK TO YOU.
OKAY.
HMM ...
SHE'S WITH TOKIHISA ...
WATCH MY BAG, OKAY? I'M OFF TO THE BEACH.
PERFECT TIMING, YASUAKI.
HANABI'S WAITING BY THE POOL.

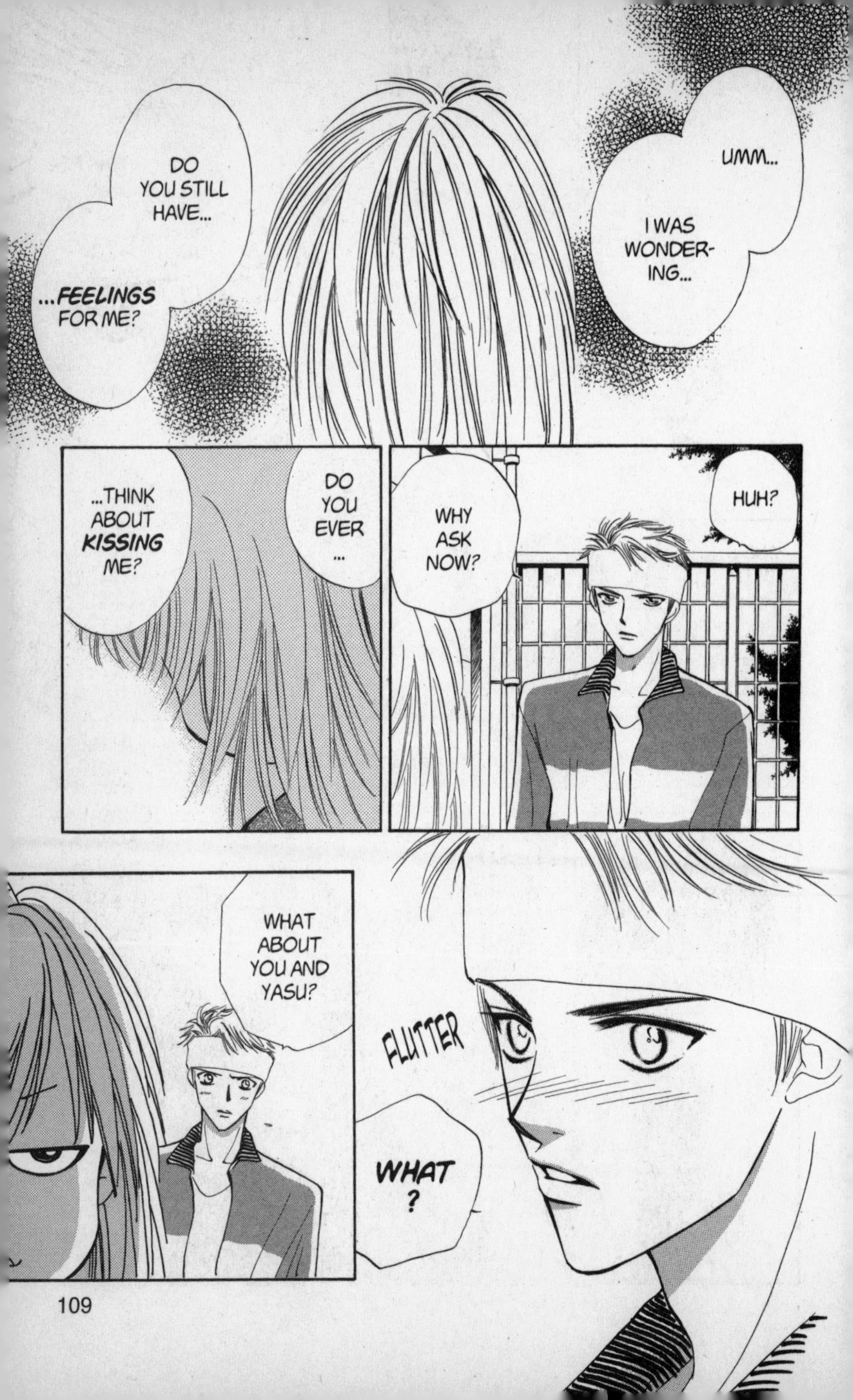
UMM...
I WAS WONDER-ING...
DO YOU STILL HAVE...
...FEELINGS FOR ME?
HUH?
WHY ASK NOW?
DO YOU EVER ...
...THINK ABOUT KISSING ME?
FLUTTER
WHAT ?
WHAT ABOUT YOU AND YASU?

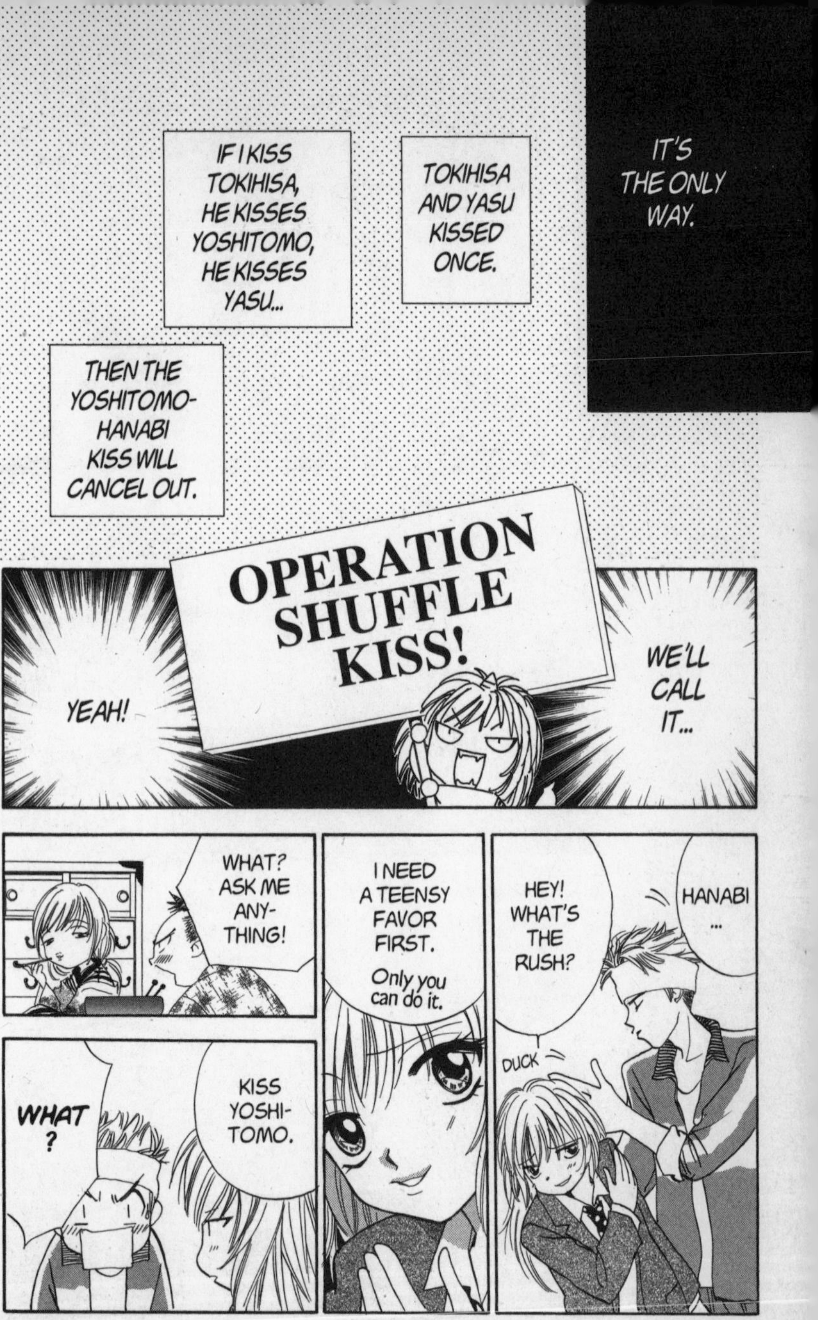
IT'S THE ONLY WAY.
TOKIHISA AND YASU KISSED ONCE.
IF I KISS TOKIHISA, HE KISSES YOSHITOMO, HE KISSES YASU...
THEN THE YOSHITOMO-HANABI KISS WILL CANCEL OUT.
WE'LL CALL IT...
OPERATION SHUFFLE KISS!
YEAH!
HANABI ...
HEY! WHAT'S THE RUSH?
DUCK
I NEED A TEENSY FAVOR FIRST.
Only you can do it.
WHAT? ASK ME ANY-THING!
KISS YOSHI-TOMO.
WHAT ?

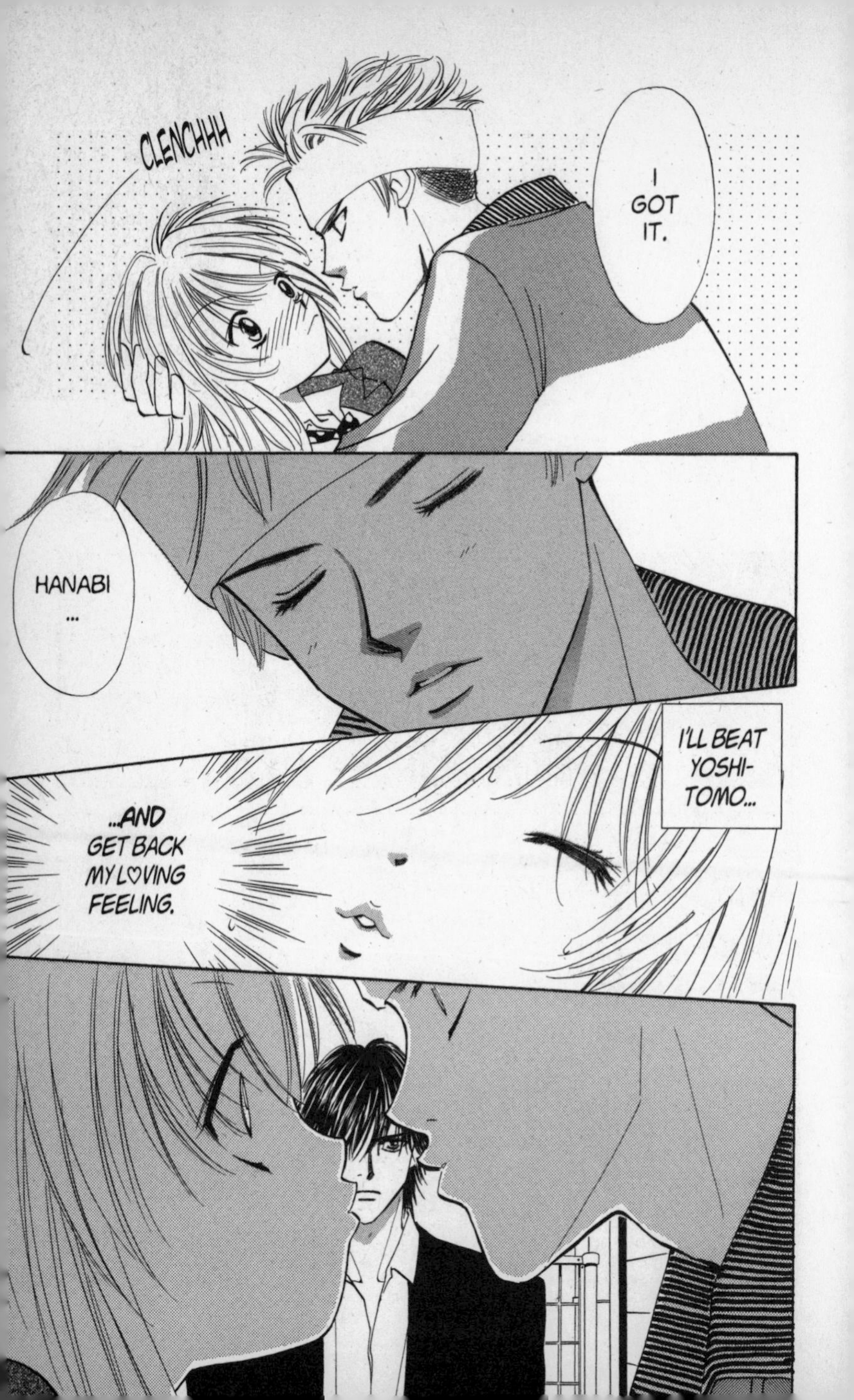
I GOT IT.
CLENCHHH
HANABI ...
I'LL BEAT YOSHI-TOMO...
...AND GET BACK MY L♡VING FEELING.

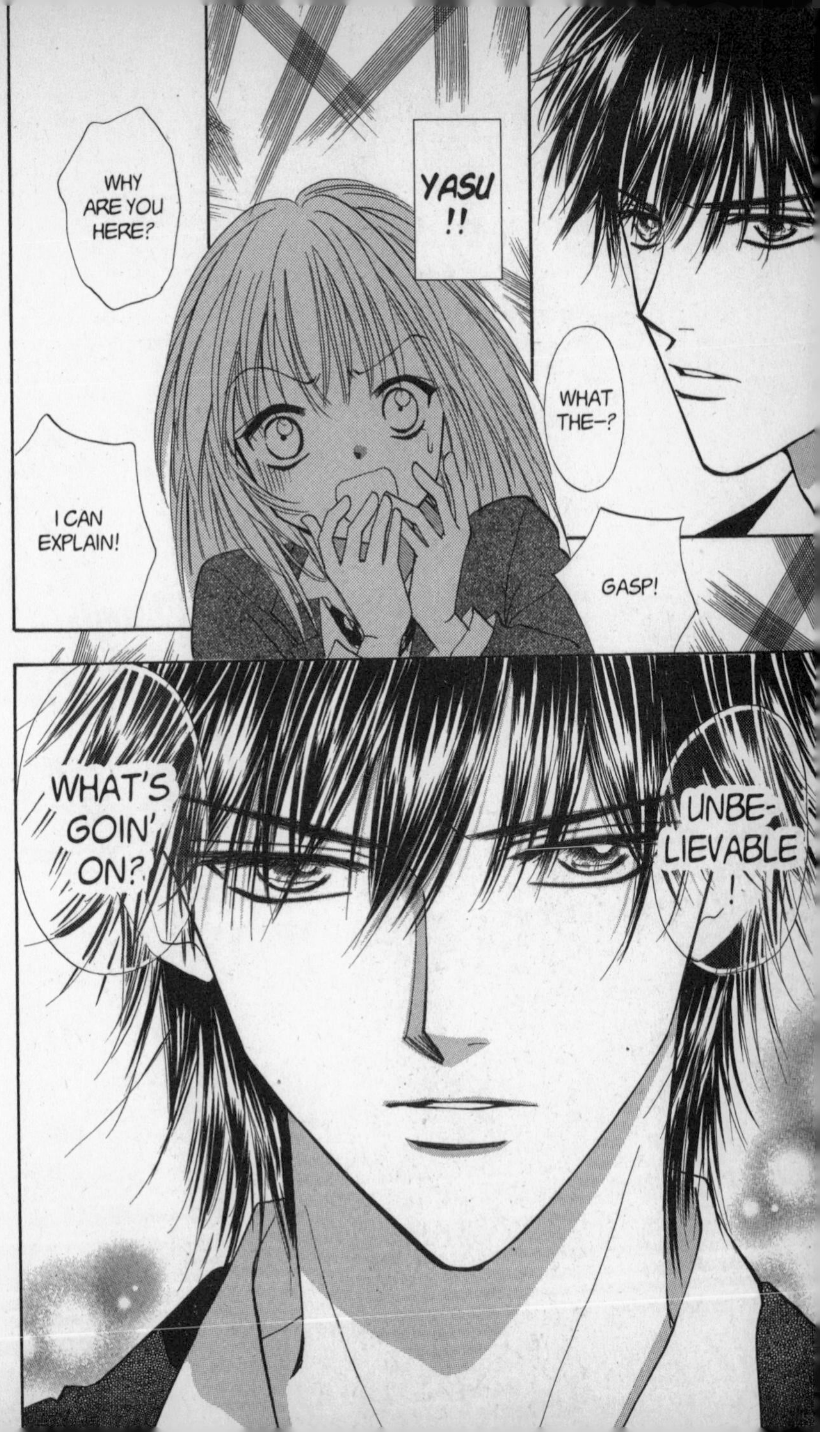
WHAT THE–?
YASU !!
WHY ARE YOU HERE?
GASP!
I CAN EXPLAIN!
UNBE-LIEVABLE !
WHAT'S GOIN' ON?

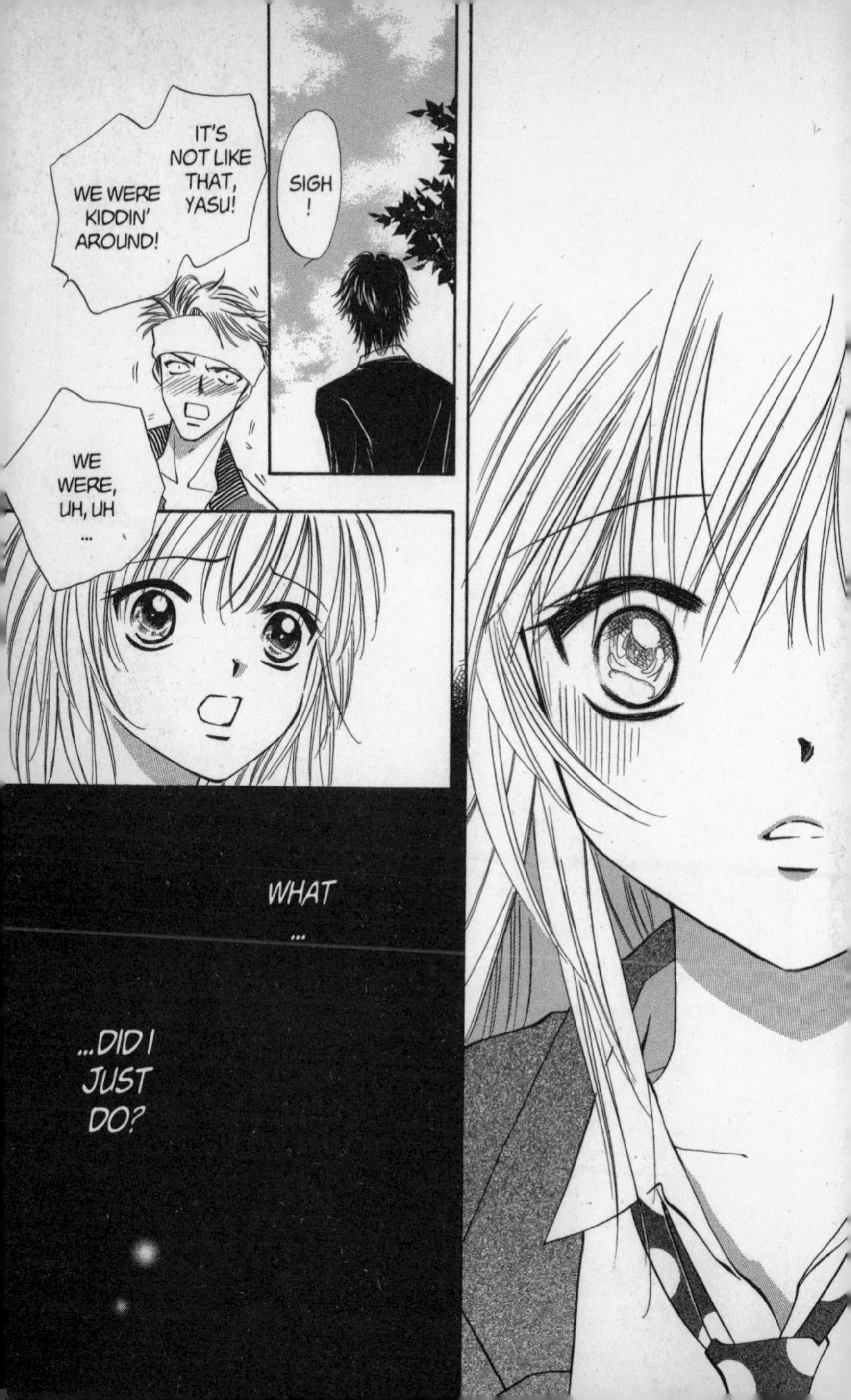
SIGH!
IT'S NOT LIKE THAT, YASU!
WE WERE KIDDIN' AROUND!
WE WERE, UH, UH ...
WHAT ...
...DID I JUST DO?

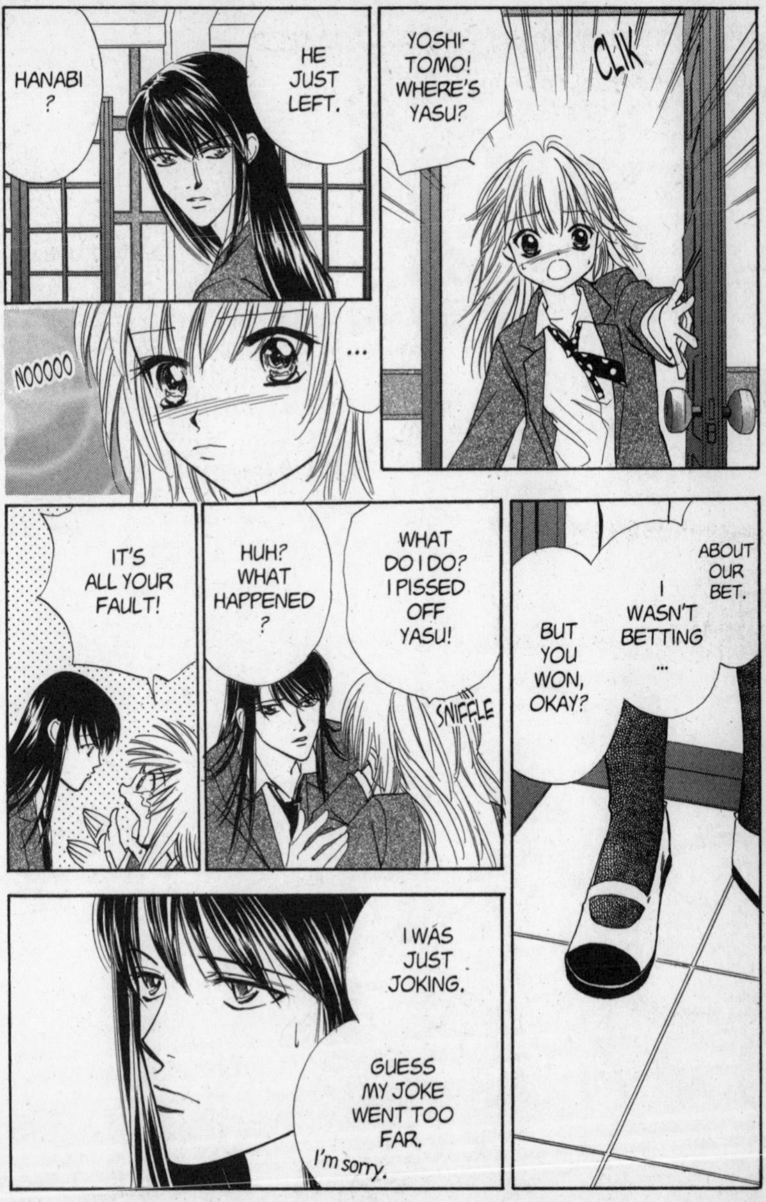
CLIK
YOSHI-TOMO! WHERE'S YASU?
HE JUST LEFT.
HANABI ?
...
NOOOOO
ABOUT OUR BET.
I WASN'T BETTING ...
BUT YOU WON, OKAY?
WHAT DO I DO? I PISSED OFF YASU!
SNIFFLE
HUH? WHAT HAPPENED ?
IT'S ALL YOUR FAULT!
I WAS JUST JOKING.
GUESS MY JOKE WENT TOO FAR.
I'm sorry.

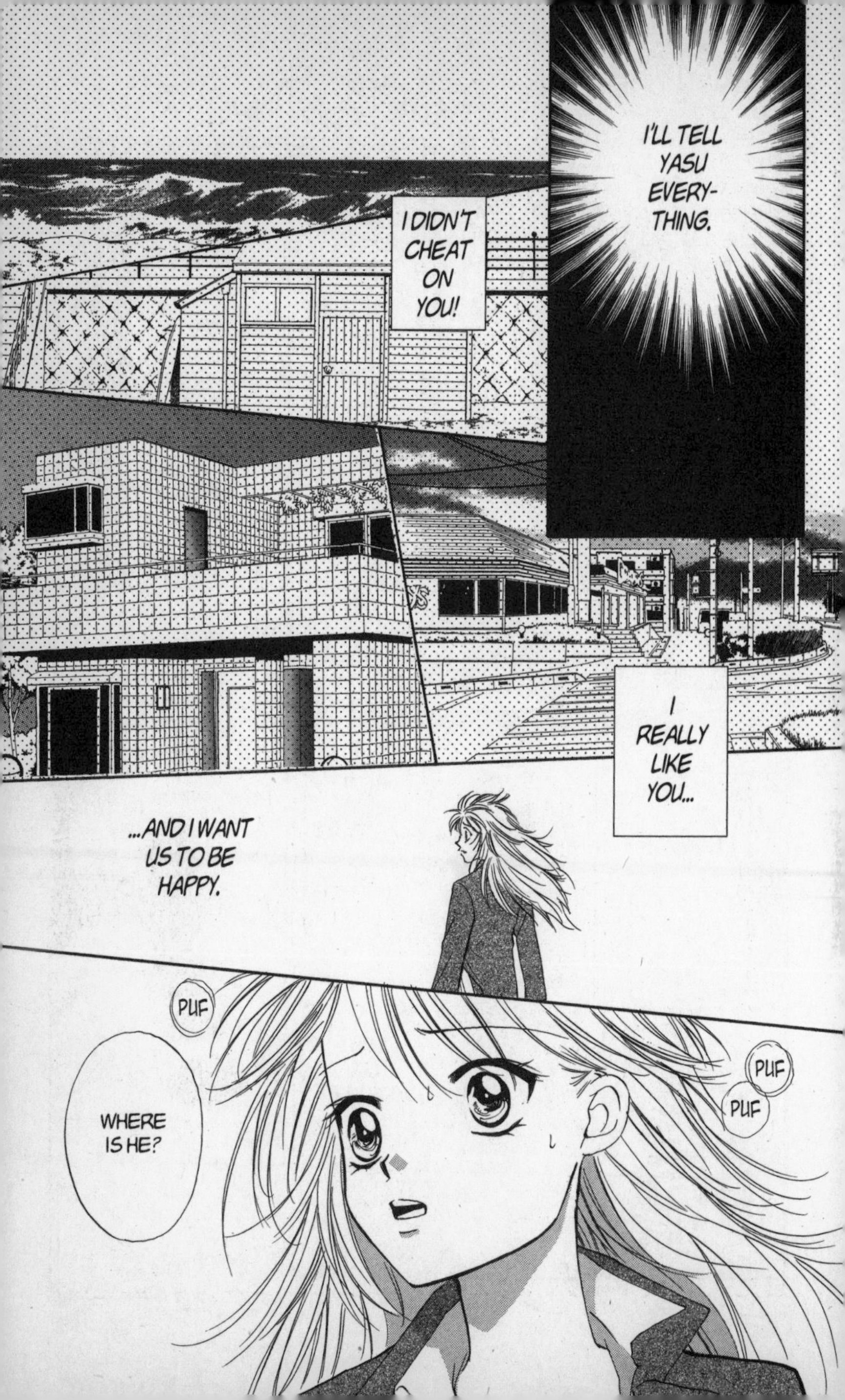

I'LL TELL YASU EVERYTHING.
I DIDN'T CHEAT ON YOU!
I REALLY LIKE YOU...
...AND I WANT US TO BE HAPPY.
PUF
PUF
PUF
WHERE IS HE?

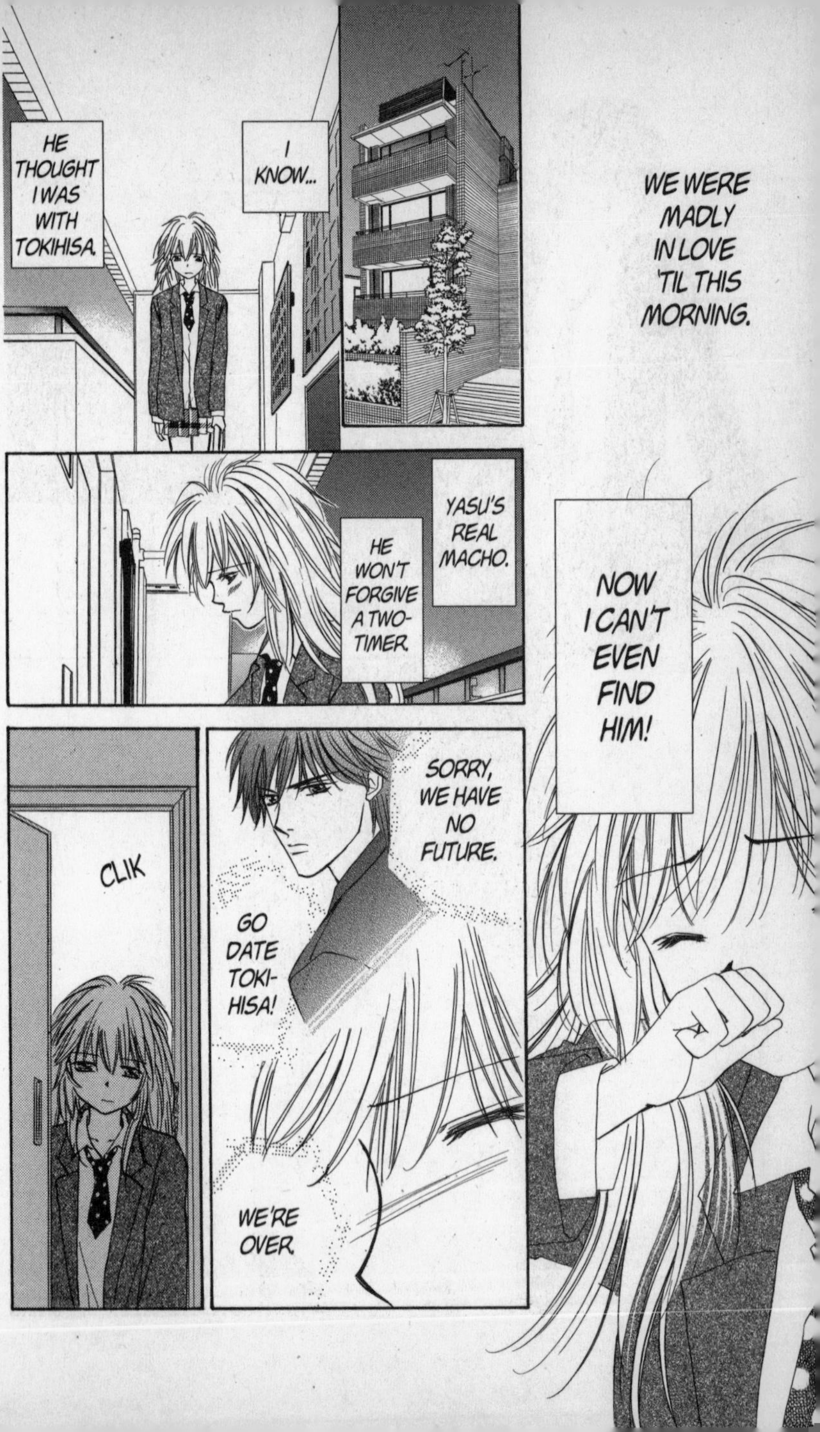
WE WERE MADLY IN LOVE 'TIL THIS MORNING.
NOW I CAN'T EVEN FIND HIM!
I KNOW...
HE THOUGHT I WAS WITH TOKIHISA.
YASU'S REAL MACHO.
HE WON'T FORGIVE A TWO-TIMER.
SORRY, WE HAVE NO FUTURE.
GO DATE TOKI-HISA!
WE'RE OVER.
CLIK

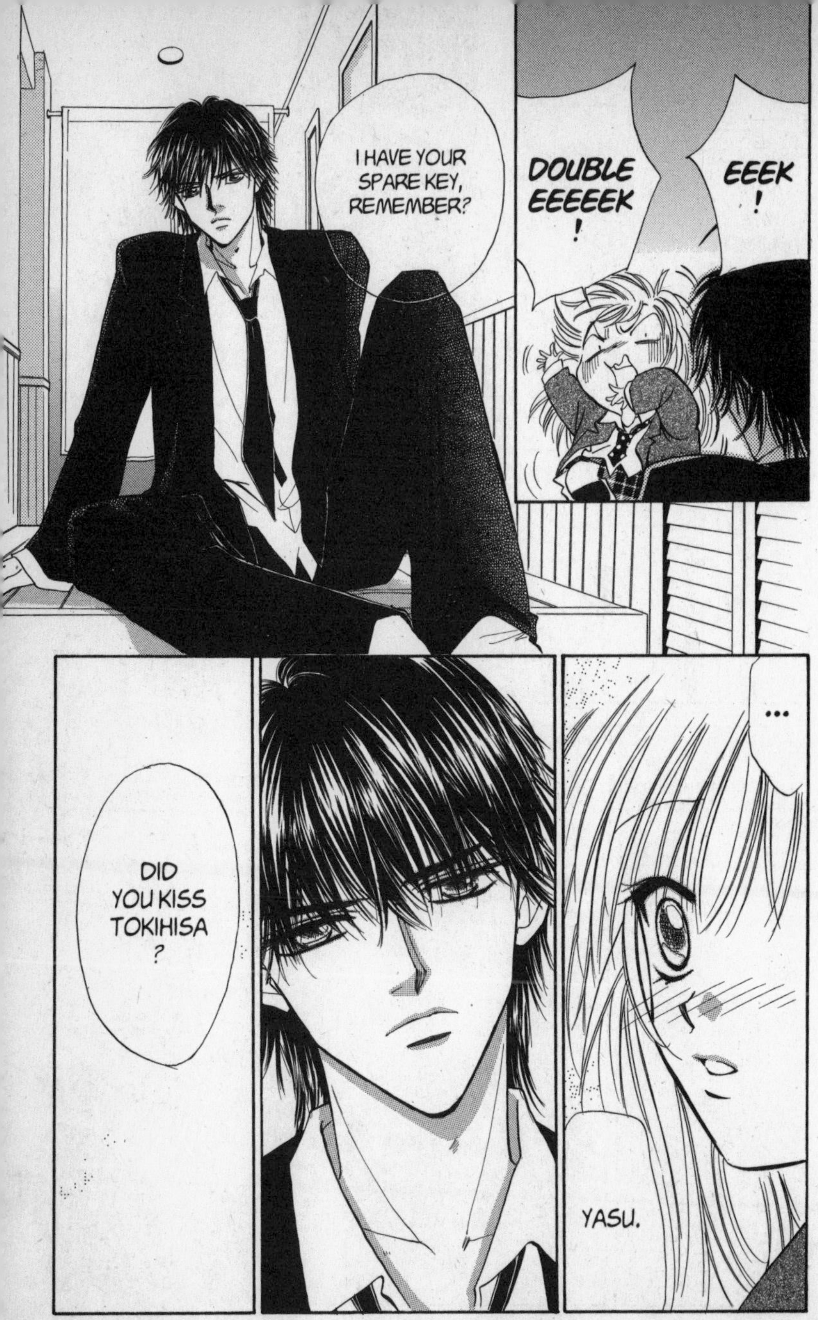
EEEK!
DOUBLE EEEEEK!
I HAVE YOUR SPARE KEY, REMEMBER?
...
YASU.
DID YOU KISS TOKIHISA?

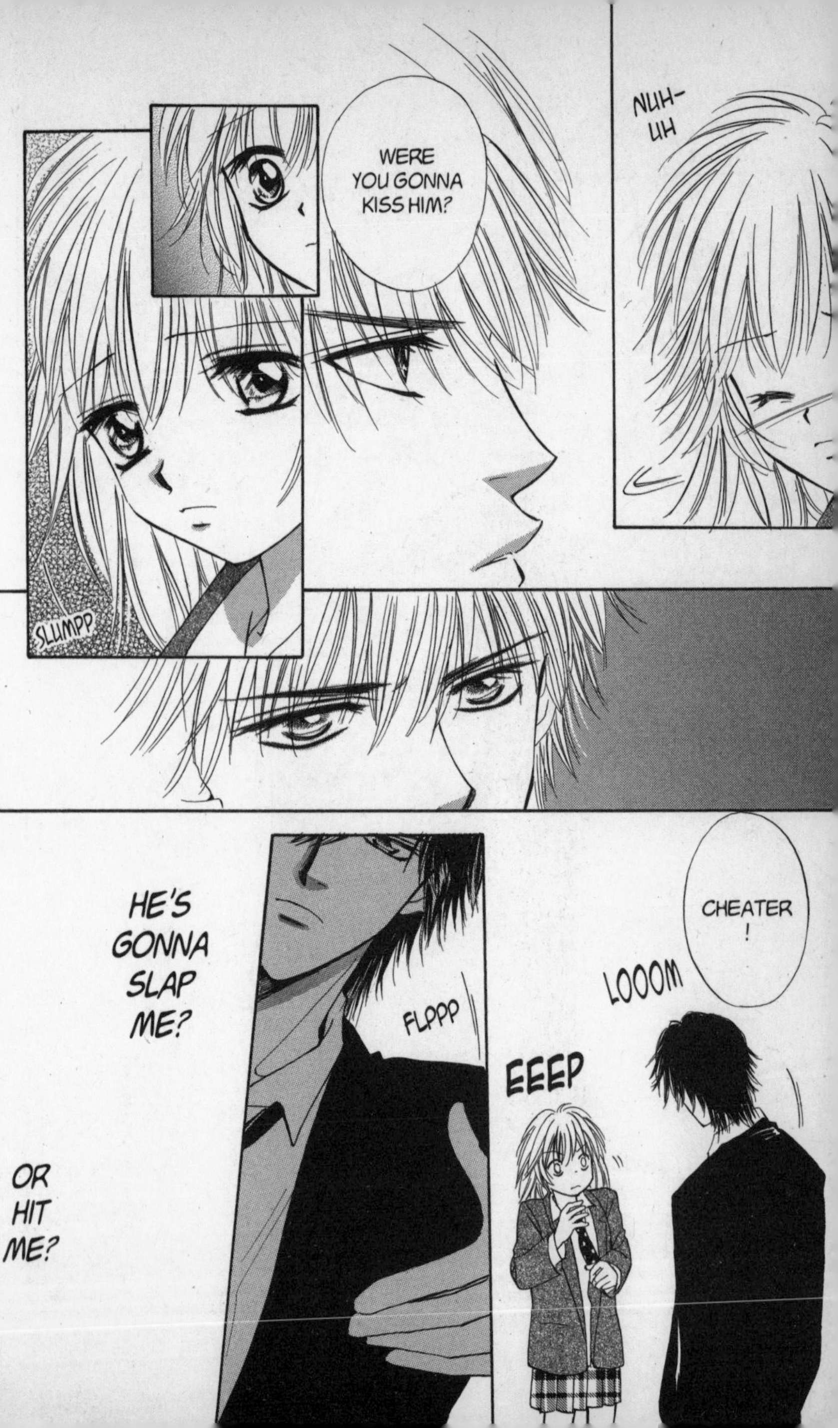
NUH-UH
WERE YOU GONNA KISS HIM?
SLUMPP
CHEATER!
LOOOM
EEEP
FLPPP
HE'S GONNA SLAP ME?
OR HIT ME?

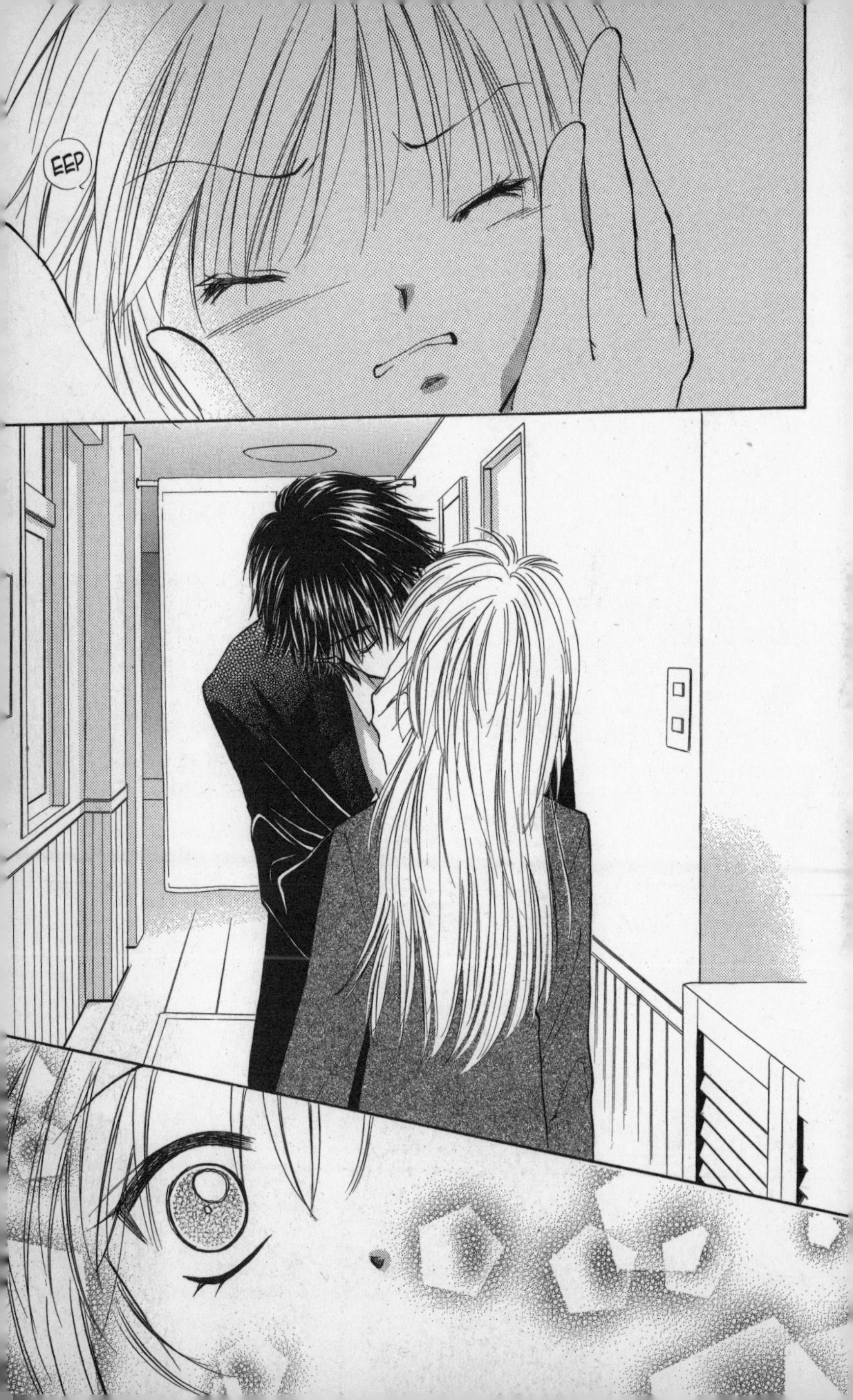
EEP

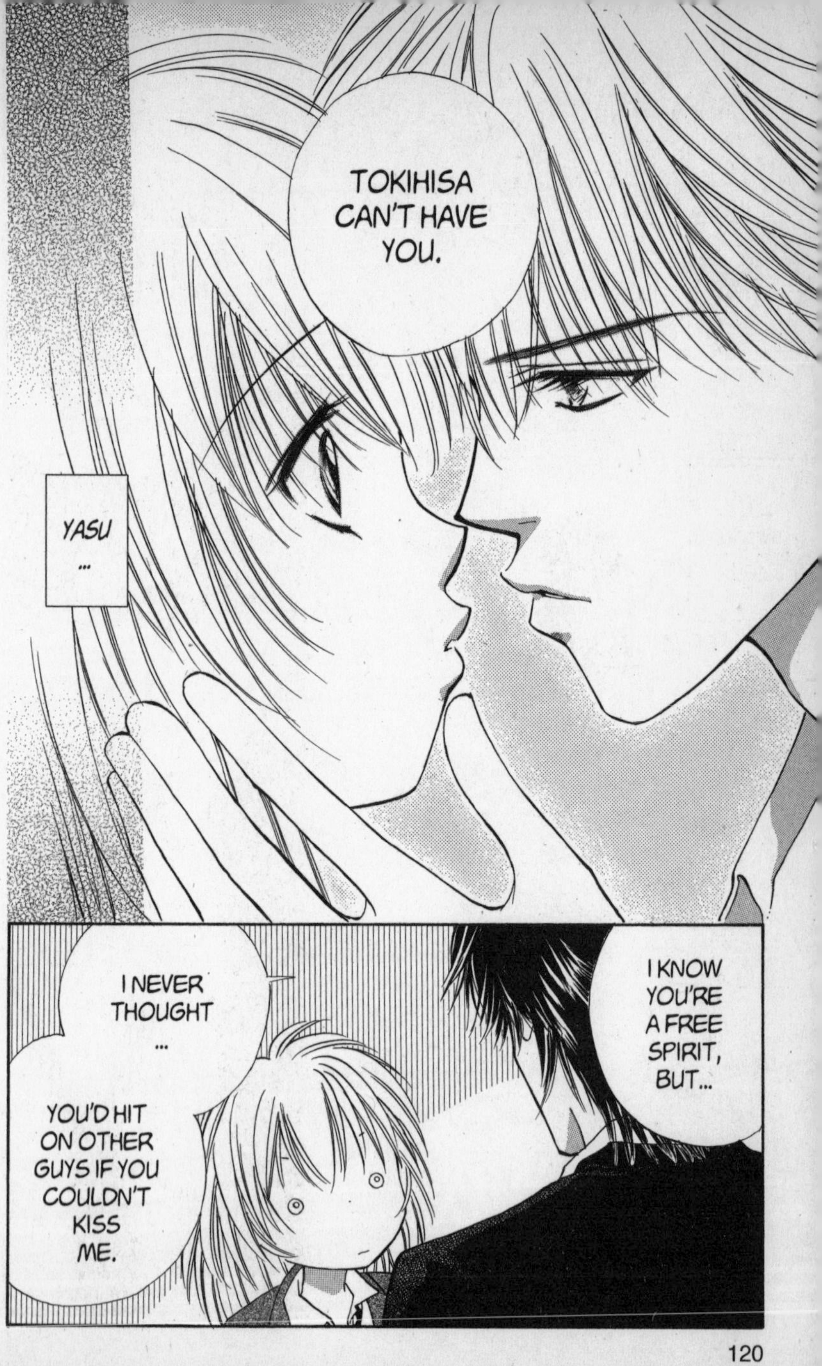
TOKIHISA CAN'T HAVE YOU.
YASU ...
I KNOW YOU'RE A FREE SPIRIT, BUT...
I NEVER THOUGHT ...
YOU'D HIT ON OTHER GUYS IF YOU COULDN'T KISS ME.

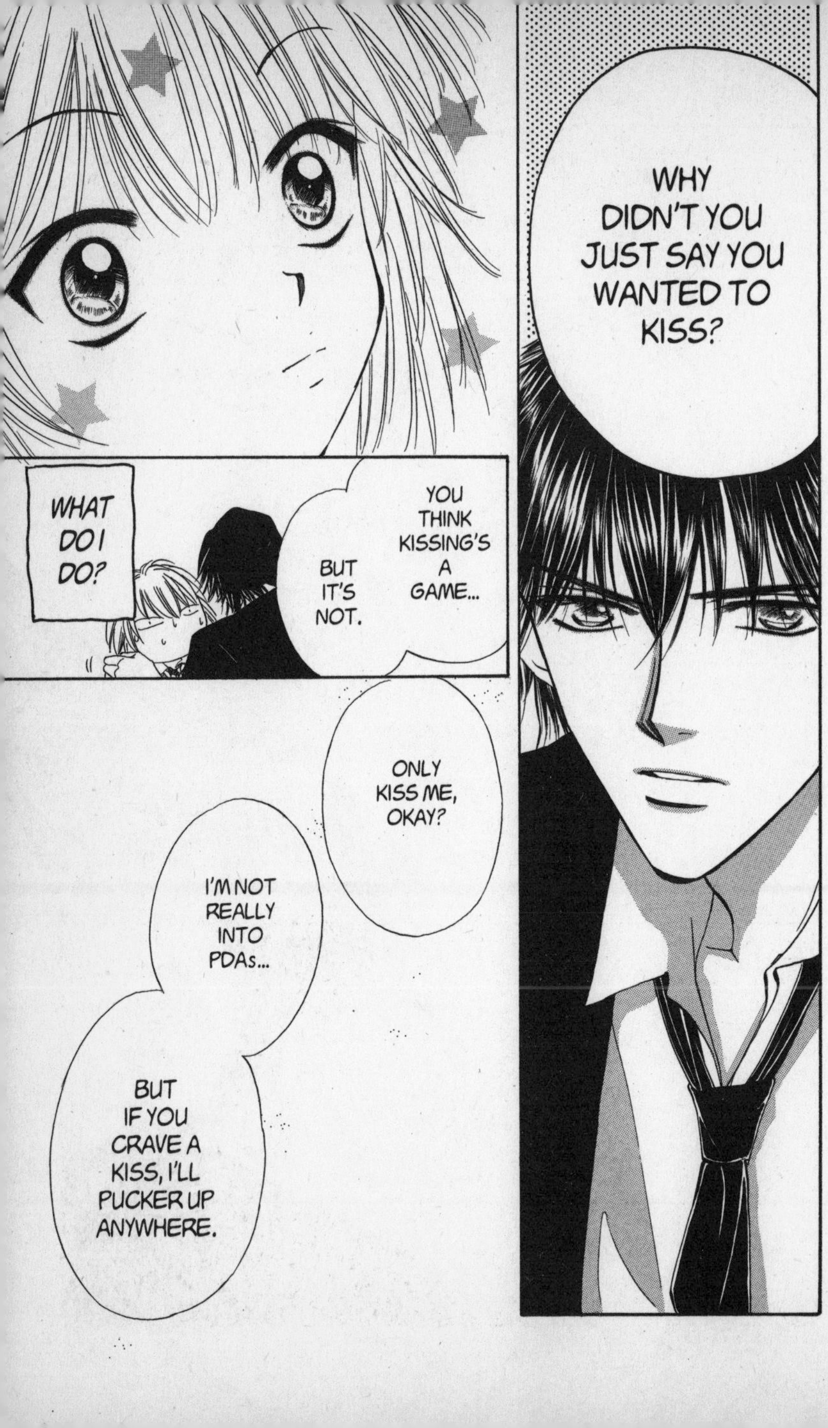
WHY DIDN'T YOU JUST SAY YOU WANTED TO KISS?
YOU THINK KISSING'S A GAME... BUT IT'S NOT.
WHAT DO I DO?
ONLY KISS ME, OKAY?
I'M NOT REALLY INTO PDAs...
BUT IF YOU CRAVE A KISS, I'LL PUCKER UP ANYWHERE.

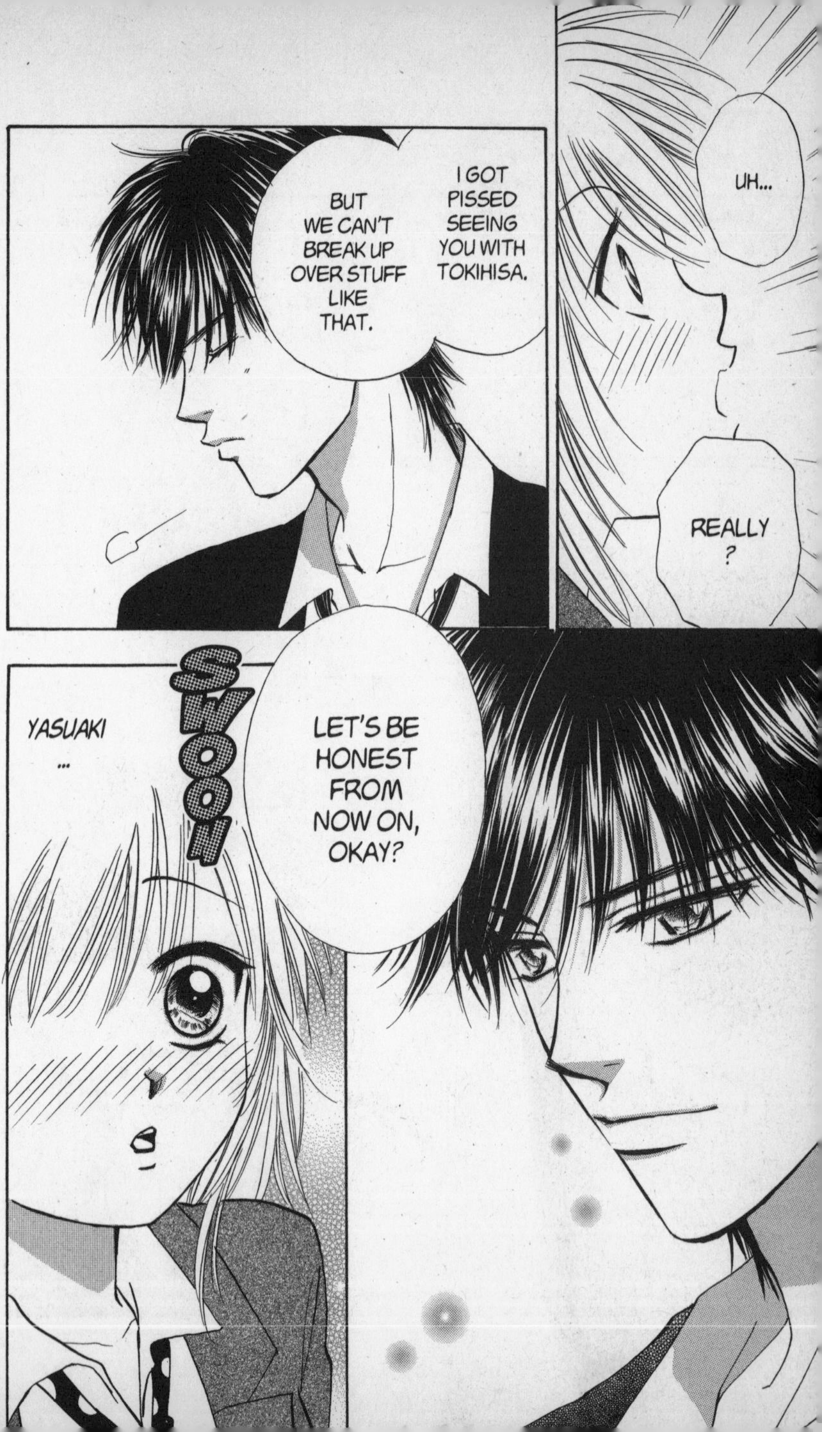
UH...
REALLY ?
I GOT PISSED SEEING YOU WITH TOKIHISA.
BUT WE CAN'T BREAK UP OVER STUFF LIKE THAT.
LET'S BE HONEST FROM NOW ON, OKAY?
SWOON
YASUAKI ...

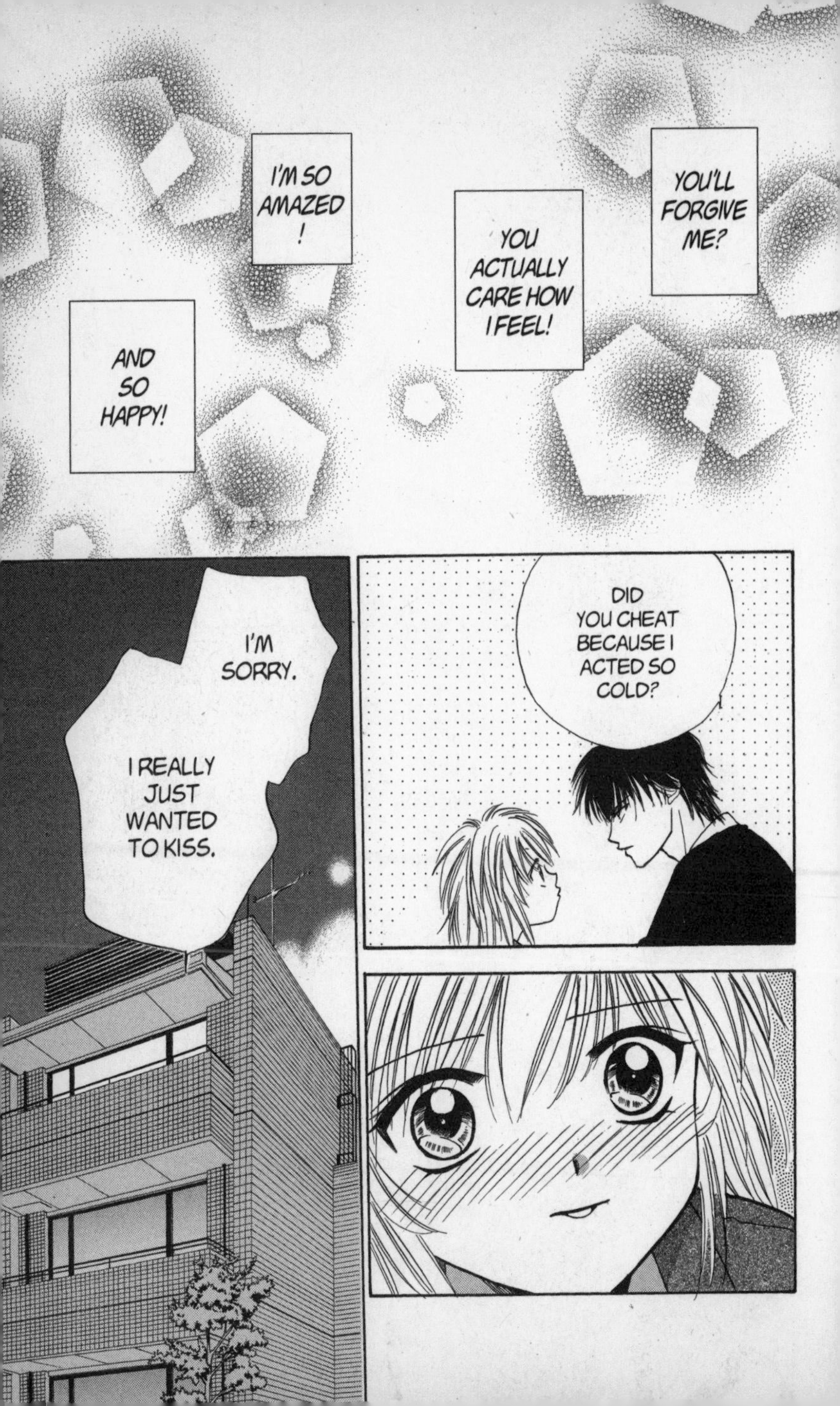
YOU'LL FORGIVE ME?
YOU ACTUALLY CARE HOW I FEEL!
I'M SO AMAZED!
AND SO HAPPY!
DID YOU CHEAT BECAUSE I ACTED SO COLD?
I'M SORRY.
I REALLY JUST WANTED TO KISS.

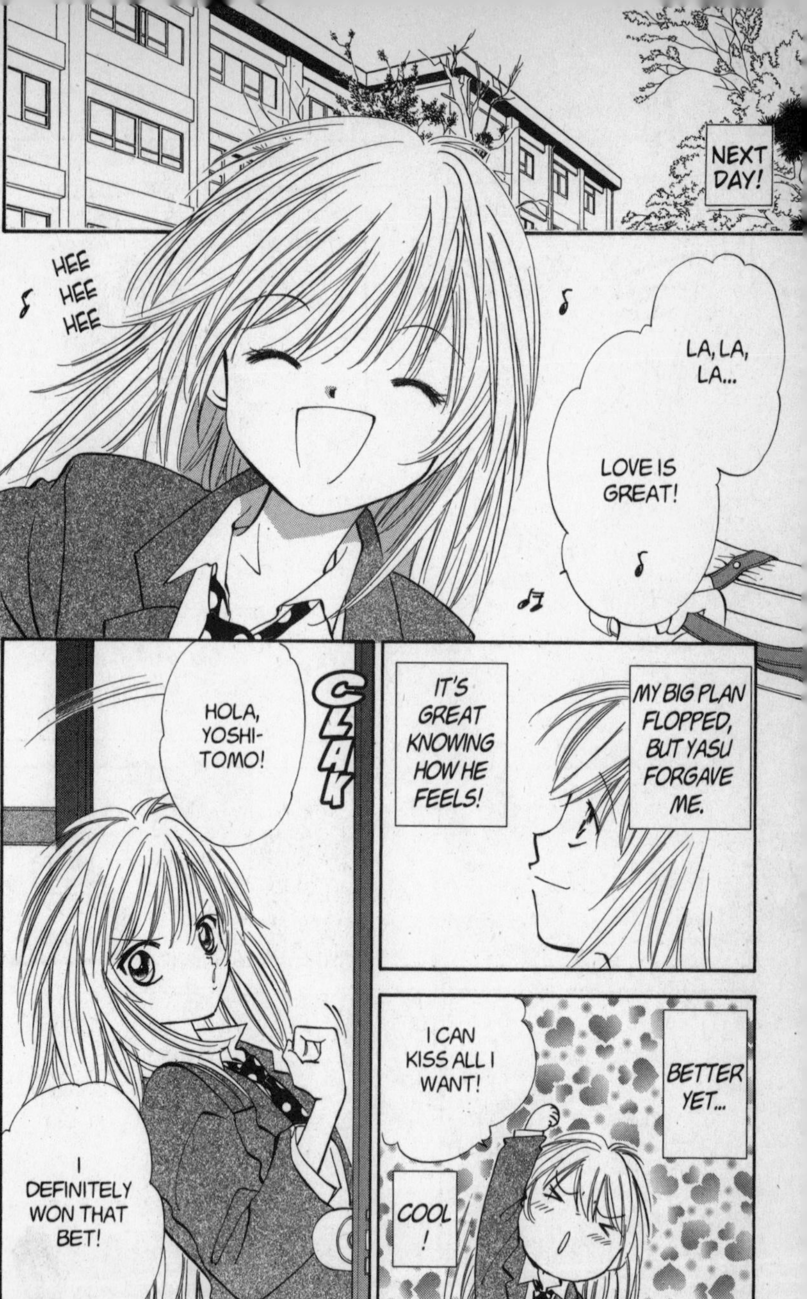
NEXT DAY!
LA, LA, LA...
LOVE IS GREAT!
HEE HEE HEE
MY BIG PLAN FLOPPED, BUT YASU FORGAVE ME.
IT'S GREAT KNOWING HOW HE FEELS!
BETTER YET...
I CAN KISS ALL I WANT!
COOL!
CLAK
HOLA, YOSHI-TOMO!
I DEFINITELY WON THAT BET!

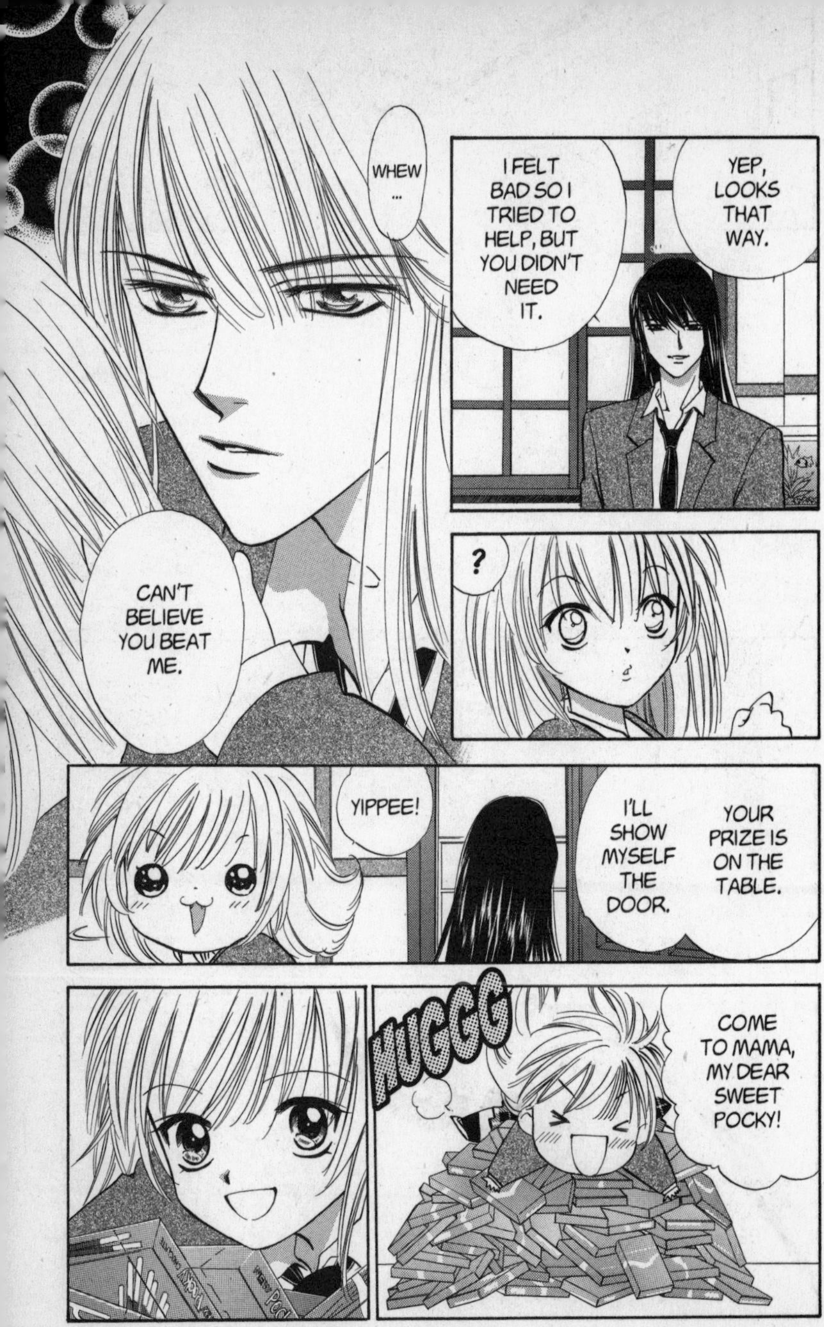
YEP, LOOKS THAT WAY.
I FELT BAD SO I TRIED TO HELP, BUT YOU DIDN'T NEED IT.
?
WHEW ...
CAN'T BELIEVE YOU BEAT ME.
YOUR PRIZE IS ON THE TABLE.
I'LL SHOW MYSELF THE DOOR.
YIPPEE!
COME TO MAMA, MY DEAR SWEET POCKY!
HUGGG

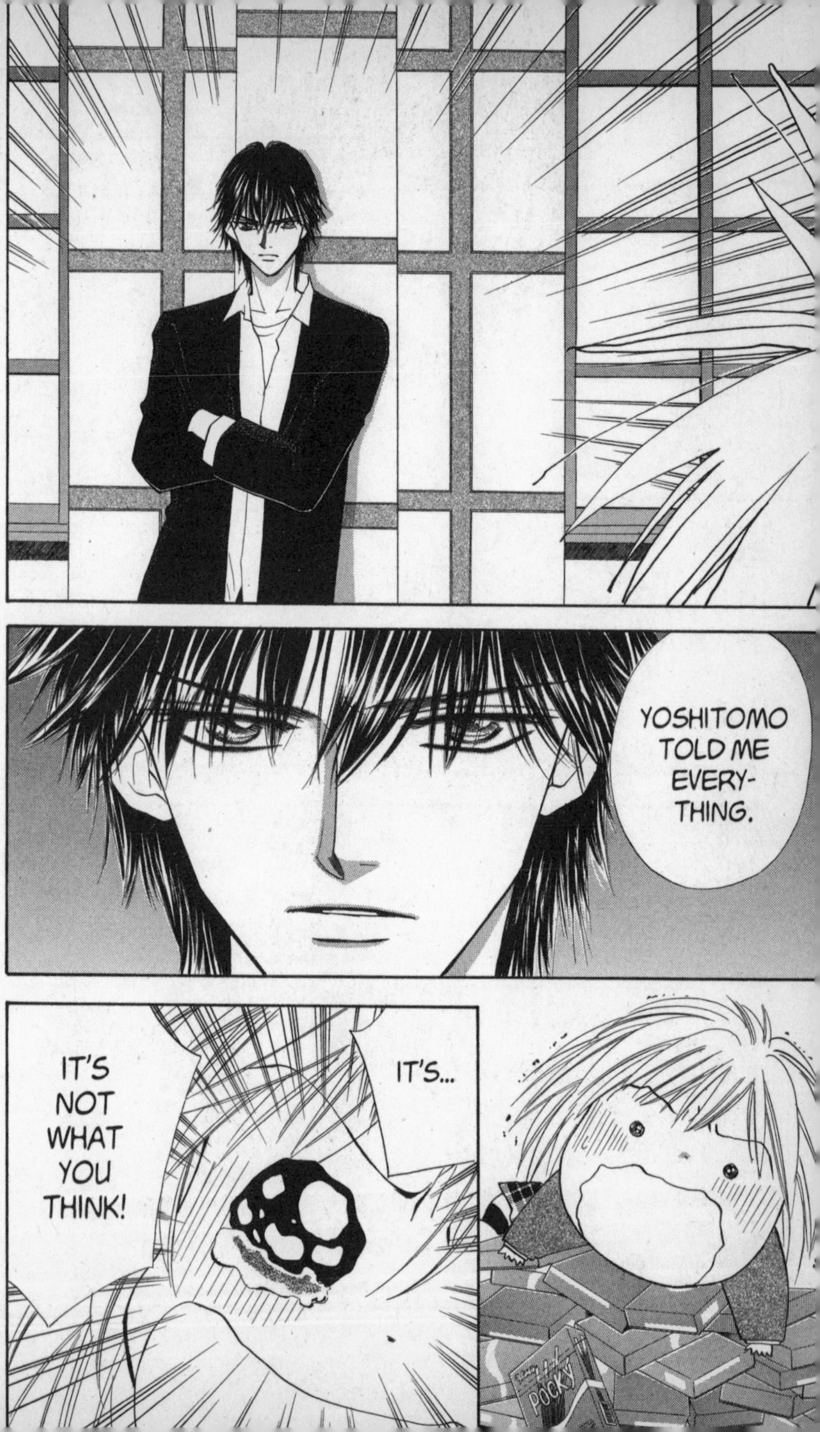
YOSHITOMO TOLD ME EVERY-THING.
IT'S...
IT'S NOT WHAT YOU THINK!

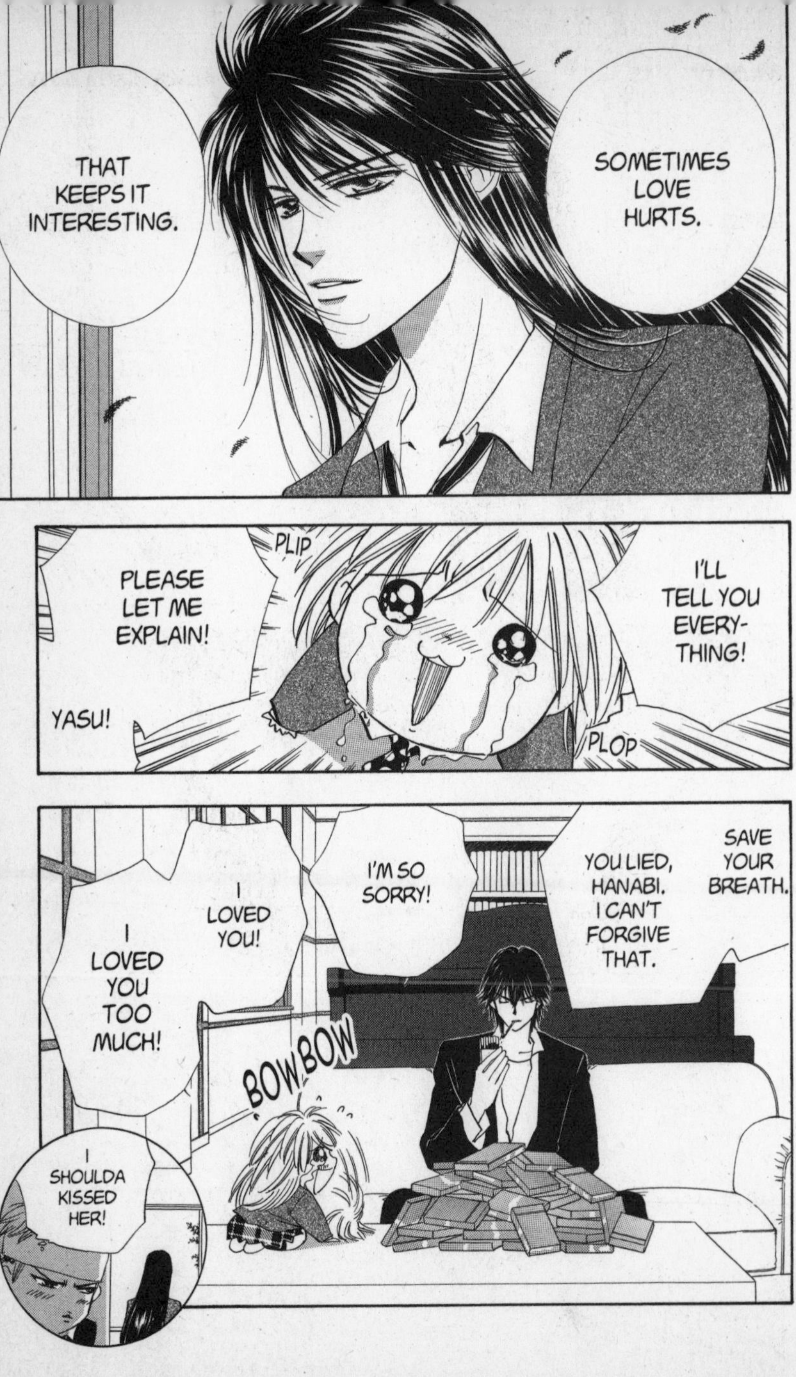
SOMETIMES LOVE HURTS.
THAT KEEPS IT INTERESTING.
I'LL TELL YOU EVERY-THING!
PLIP
PLEASE LET ME EXPLAIN!
PLOP
YASU!
SAVE YOUR BREATH.
YOU LIED, HANABI. I CAN'T FORGIVE THAT.
I'M SO SORRY!
I LOVED YOU!
I LOVED YOU TOO MUCH!
BOW BOW
I SHOULDA KISSED HER!

HAPP
HUSTL
HIGH

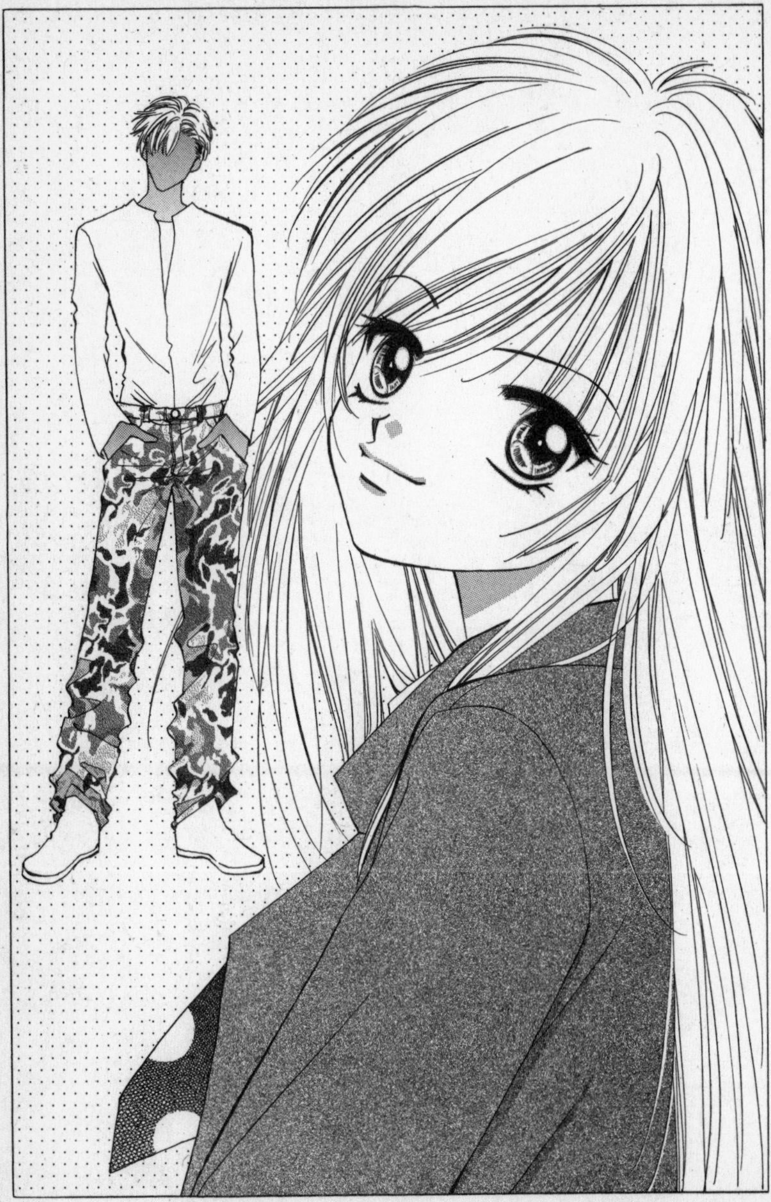

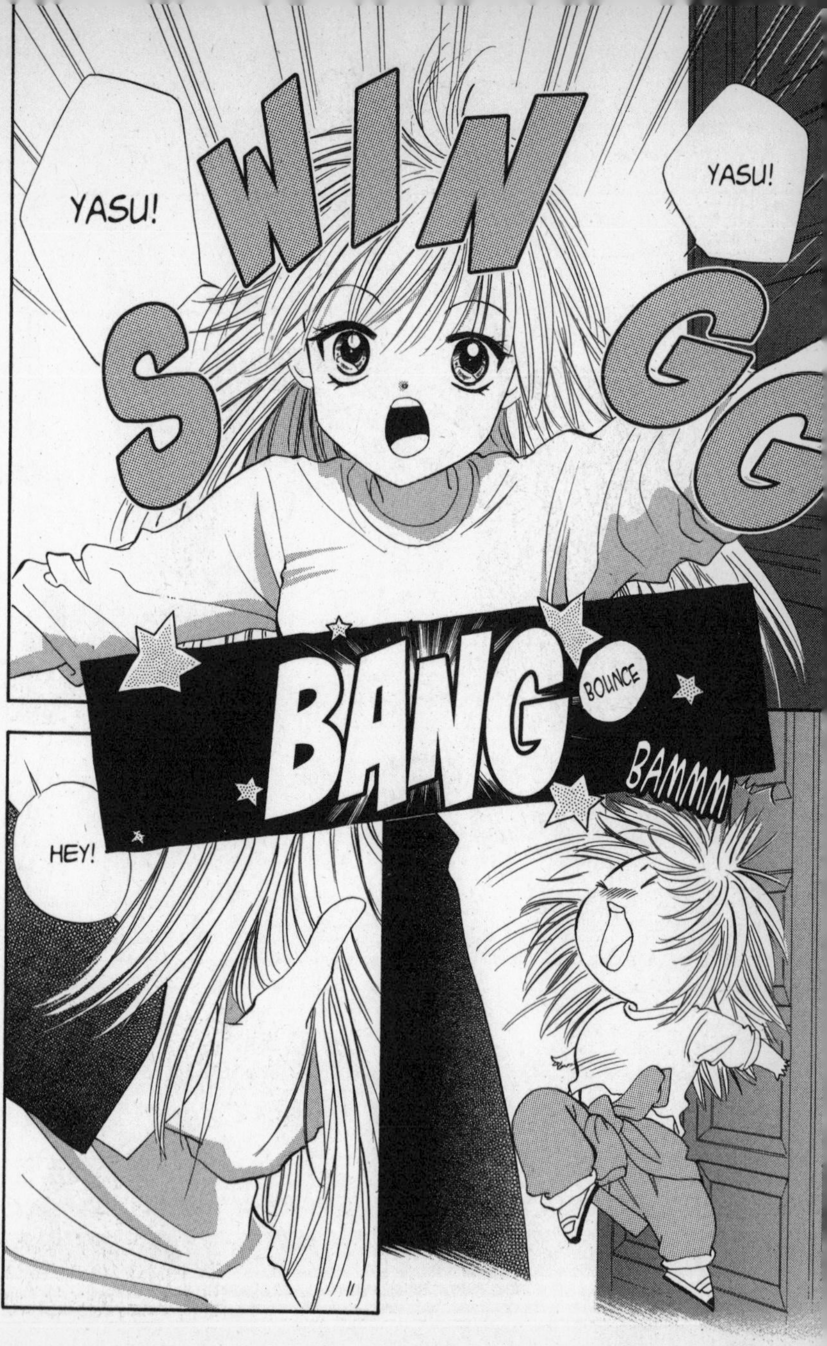
YASU!
YASU!
SWING
BANG
BOUNCE
BAMMM
HEY!

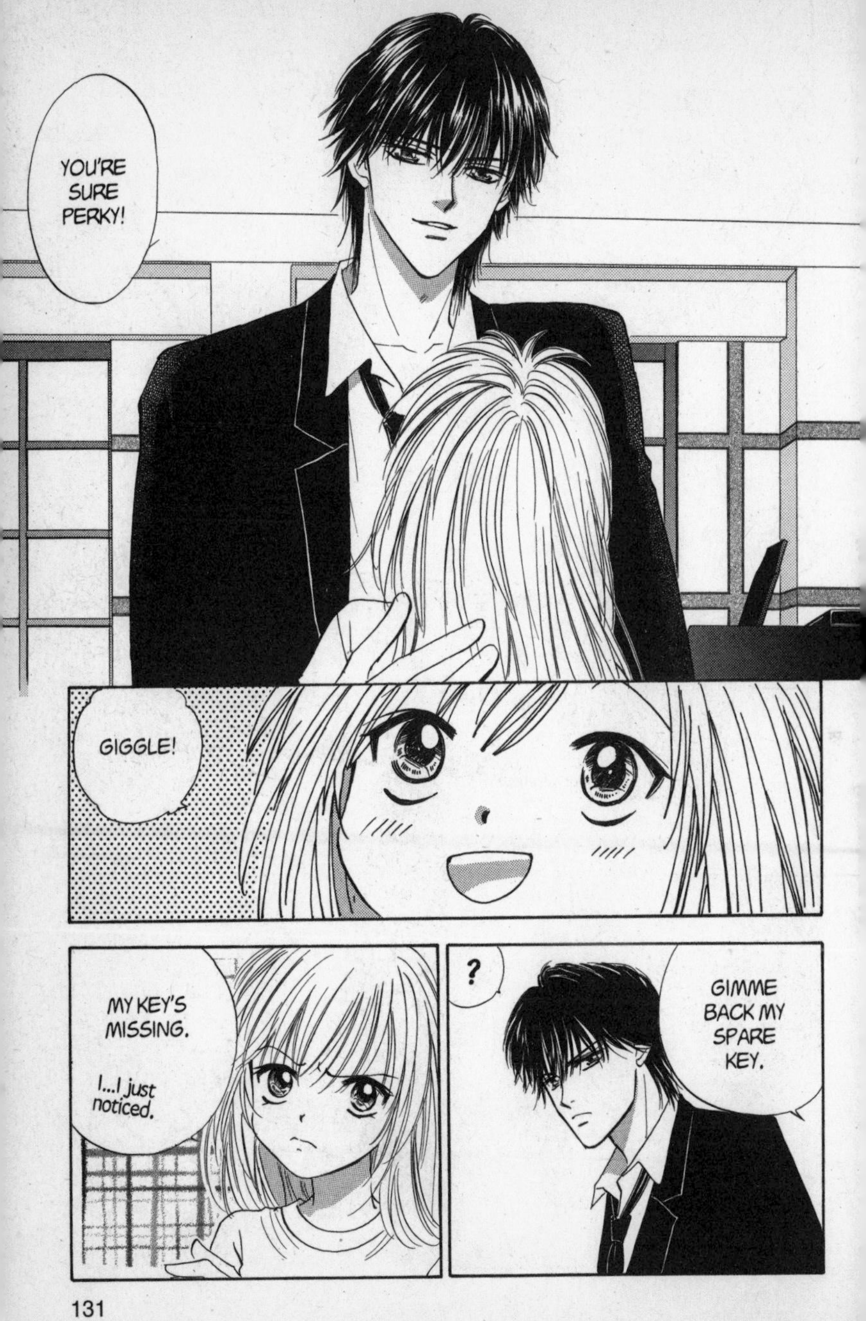
YOU'RE SURE PERKY!
GIGGLE!
GIMME BACK MY SPARE KEY.
?
MY KEY'S MISSING.
I...I just noticed.

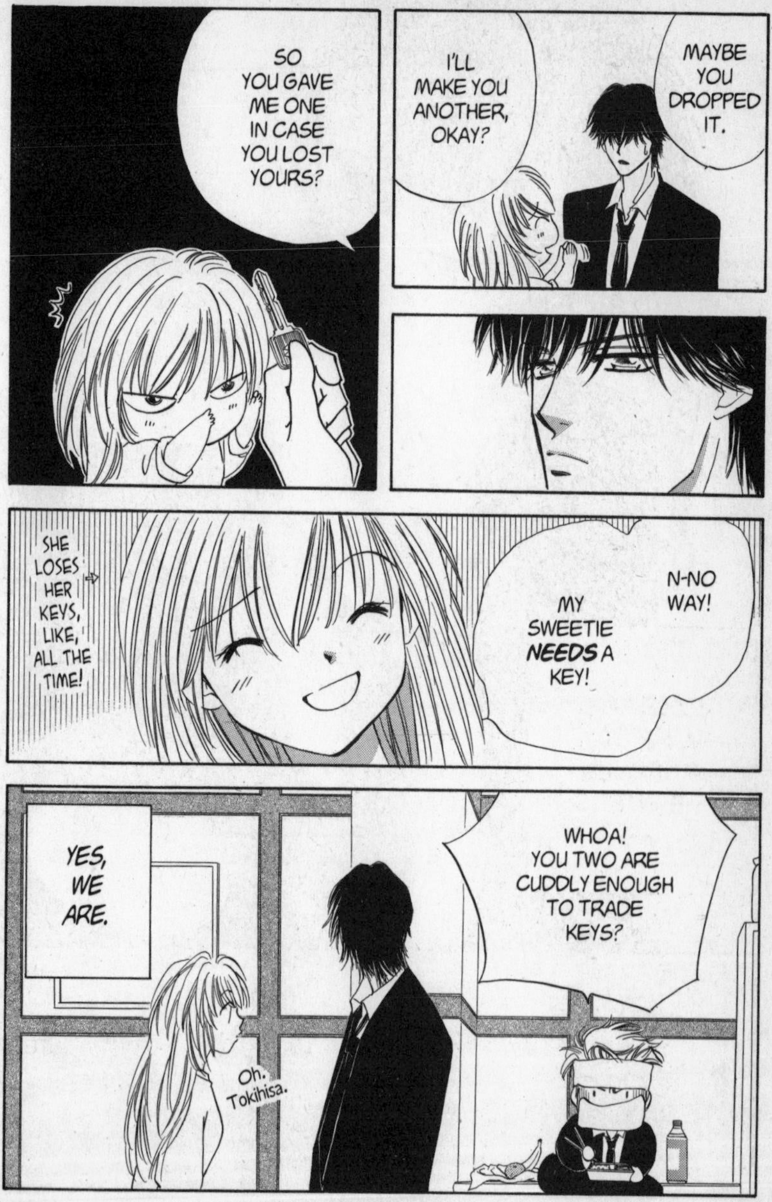
MAYBE YOU DROPPED IT.
I'LL MAKE YOU ANOTHER, OKAY?
SO YOU GAVE ME ONE IN CASE YOU LOST YOURS?
N-NO WAY!
MY SWEETIE **NEEDS** A KEY!
SHE LOSES HER KEYS, LIKE, ALL THE TIME!
WHOA! YOU TWO ARE CUDDLY ENOUGH TO TRADE KEYS?
YES, WE ARE.
Oh. Tokihisa.

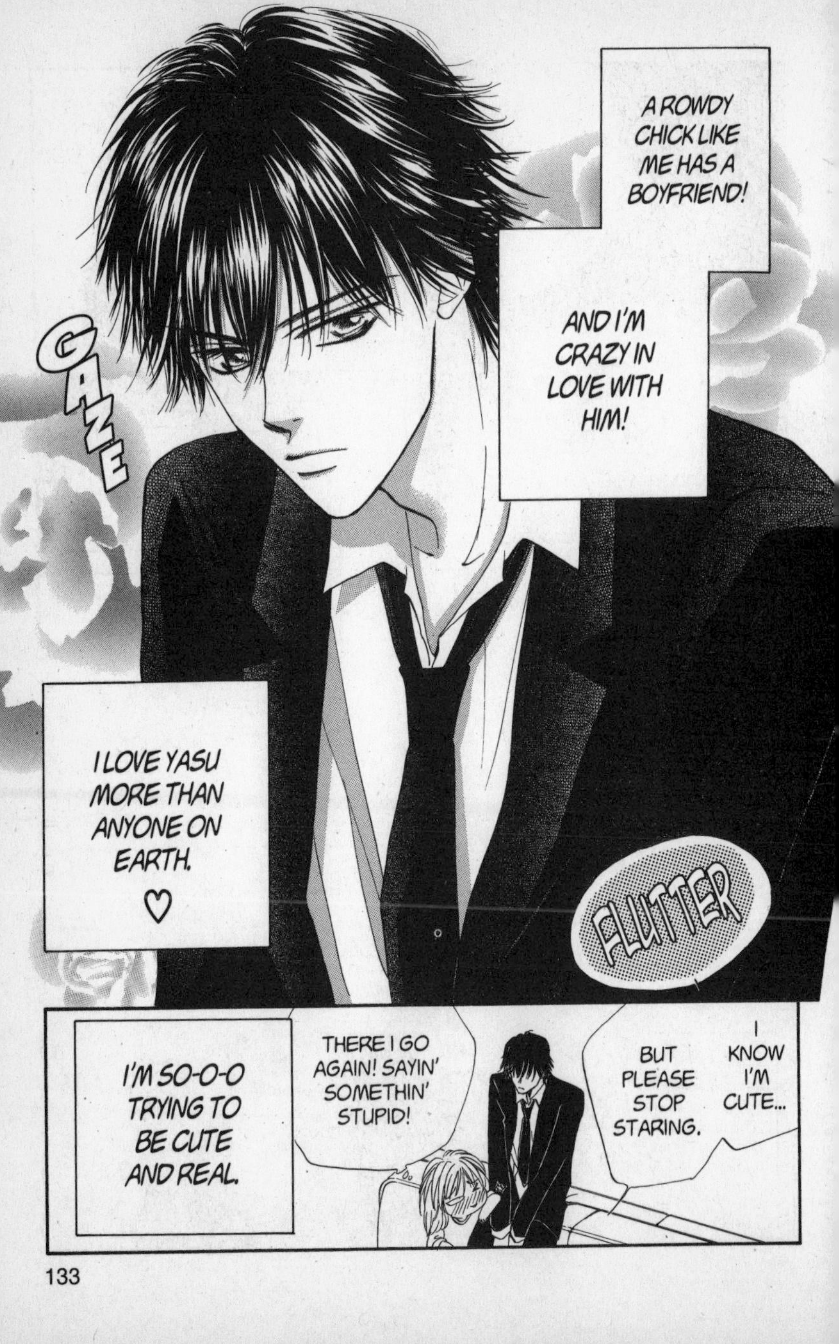
A ROWDY CHICK LIKE ME HAS A BOYFRIEND!
AND I'M CRAZY IN LOVE WITH HIM!
GAZE
I LOVE YASU MORE THAN ANYONE ON EARTH. ♡
FLUTTER
I KNOW I'M CUTE...
BUT PLEASE STOP STARING.
THERE I GO AGAIN! SAYIN' SOMETHIN' STUPID!
I'M SO-O-O TRYING TO BE CUTE AND REAL.

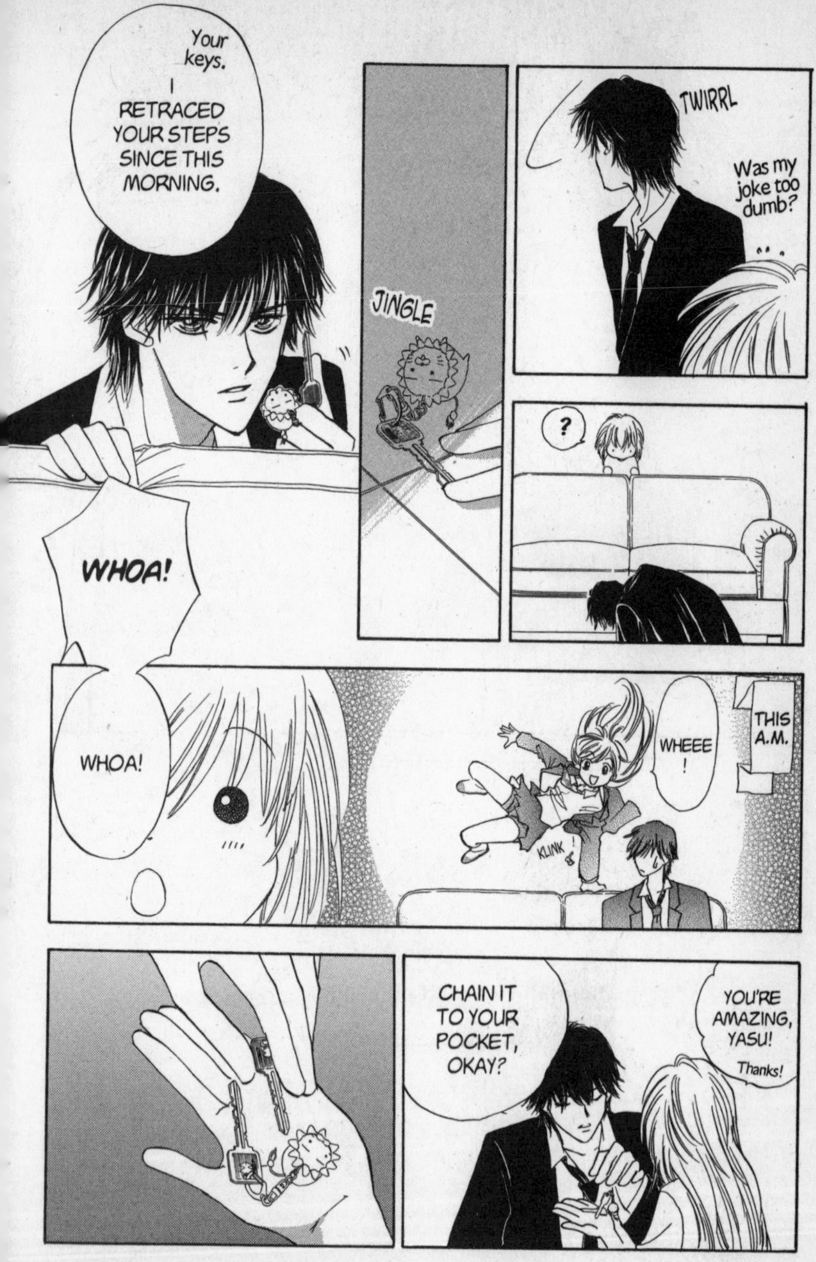
TWIRRL
Was my joke too dumb?
?
JINGLE
Your keys.
I RETRACED YOUR STEPS SINCE THIS MORNING.
WHOA!
THIS A.M.
WHEEE!
KLINK
WHOA!
YOU'RE AMAZING, YASU!
Thanks!
CHAIN IT TO YOUR POCKET, OKAY?

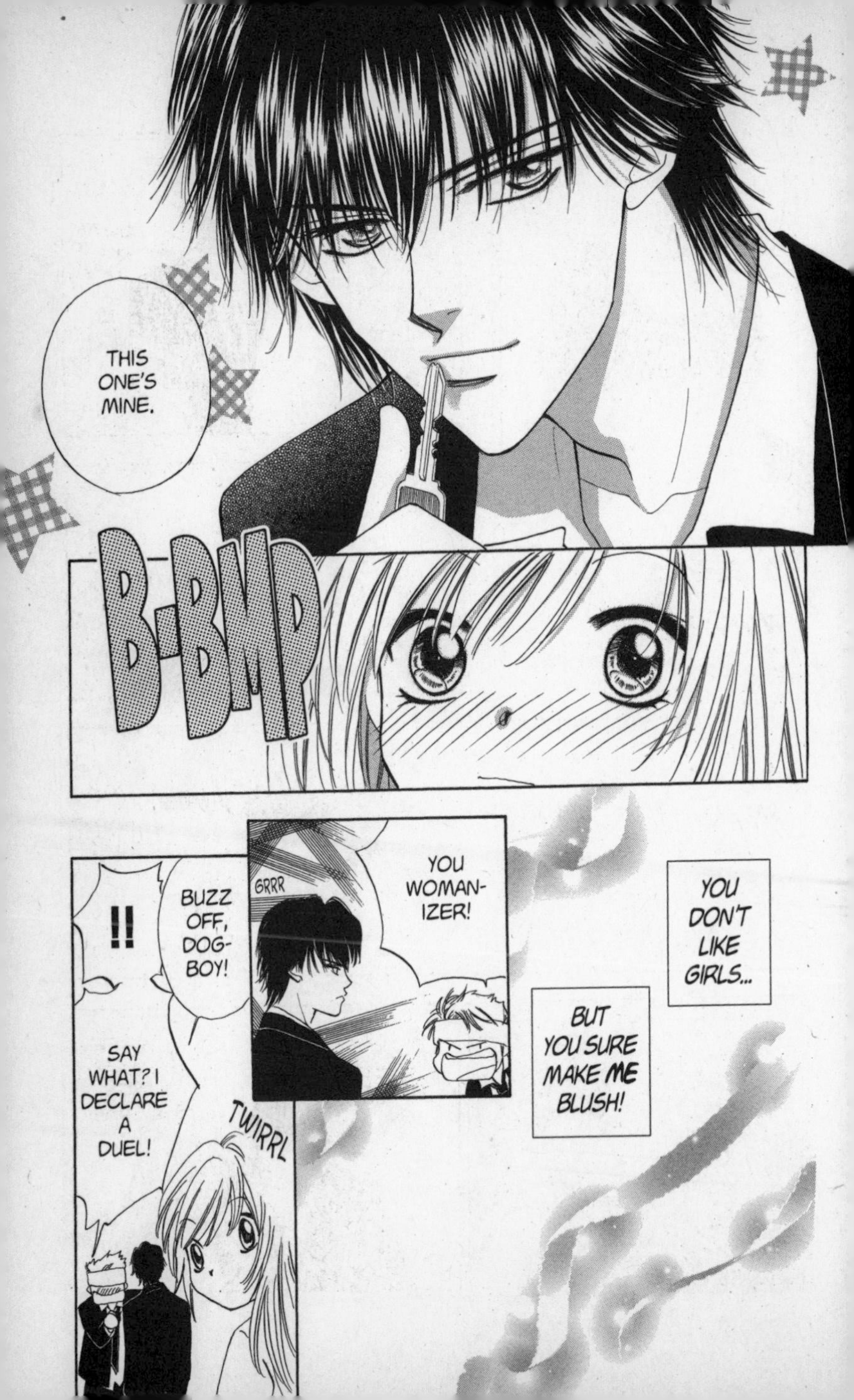
THIS ONE'S MINE.
B-BMP
YOU DON'T LIKE GIRLS...
BUT YOU SURE MAKE ME BLUSH!
YOU WOMAN-IZER!
GRRR
BUZZ OFF, DOG-BOY!
!!
SAY WHAT?! I DECLARE A DUEL!
TWIRRL

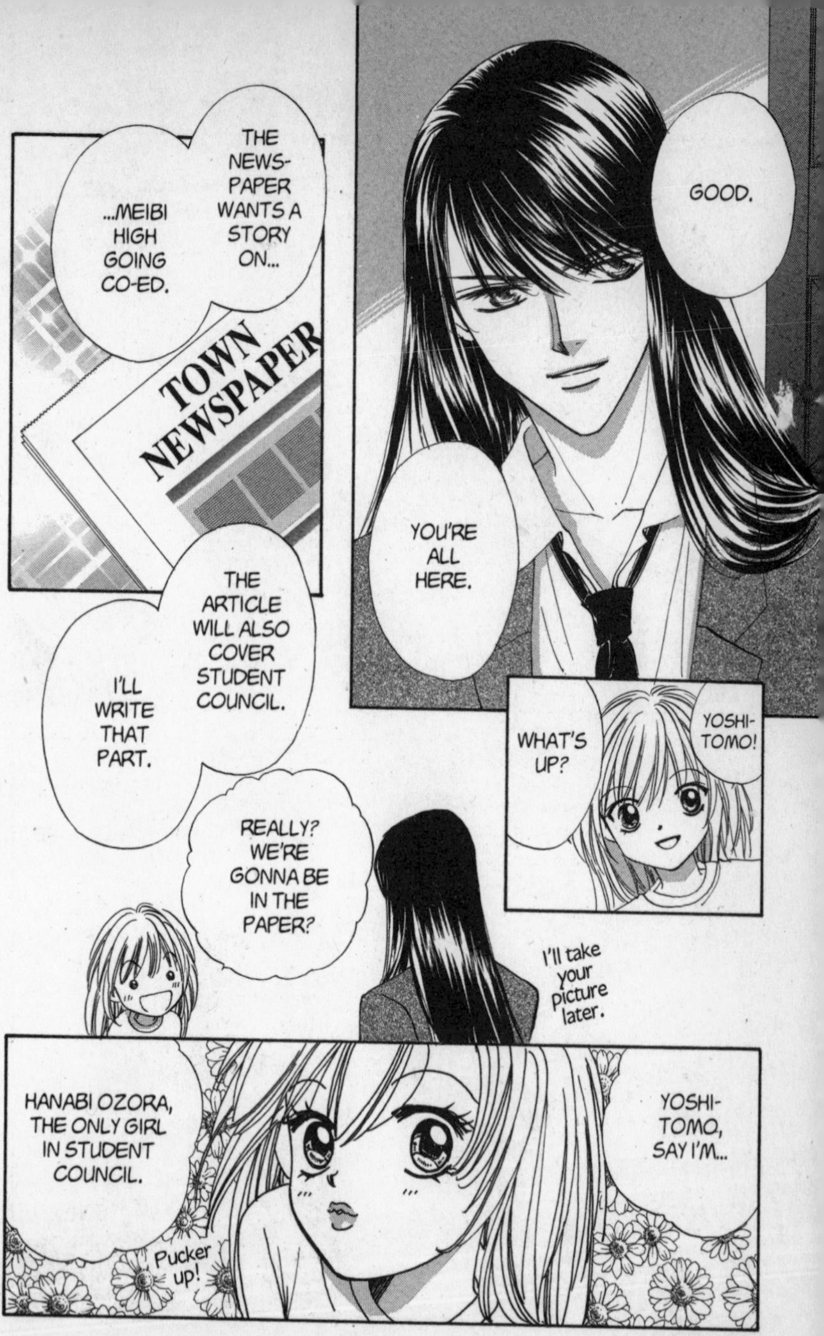
GOOD.
YOU'RE ALL HERE.
THE NEWS-PAPER WANTS A STORY ON...
...MEIBI HIGH GOING CO-ED.
TOWN NEWSPAPER
THE ARTICLE WILL ALSO COVER STUDENT COUNCIL.
I'LL WRITE THAT PART.
REALLY? WE'RE GONNA BE IN THE PAPER?
I'll take your picture later.
YOSHI-TOMO!
WHAT'S UP?
YOSHI-TOMO, SAY I'M...
HANABI OZORA, THE ONLY GIRL IN STUDENT COUNCIL.
Pucker up!

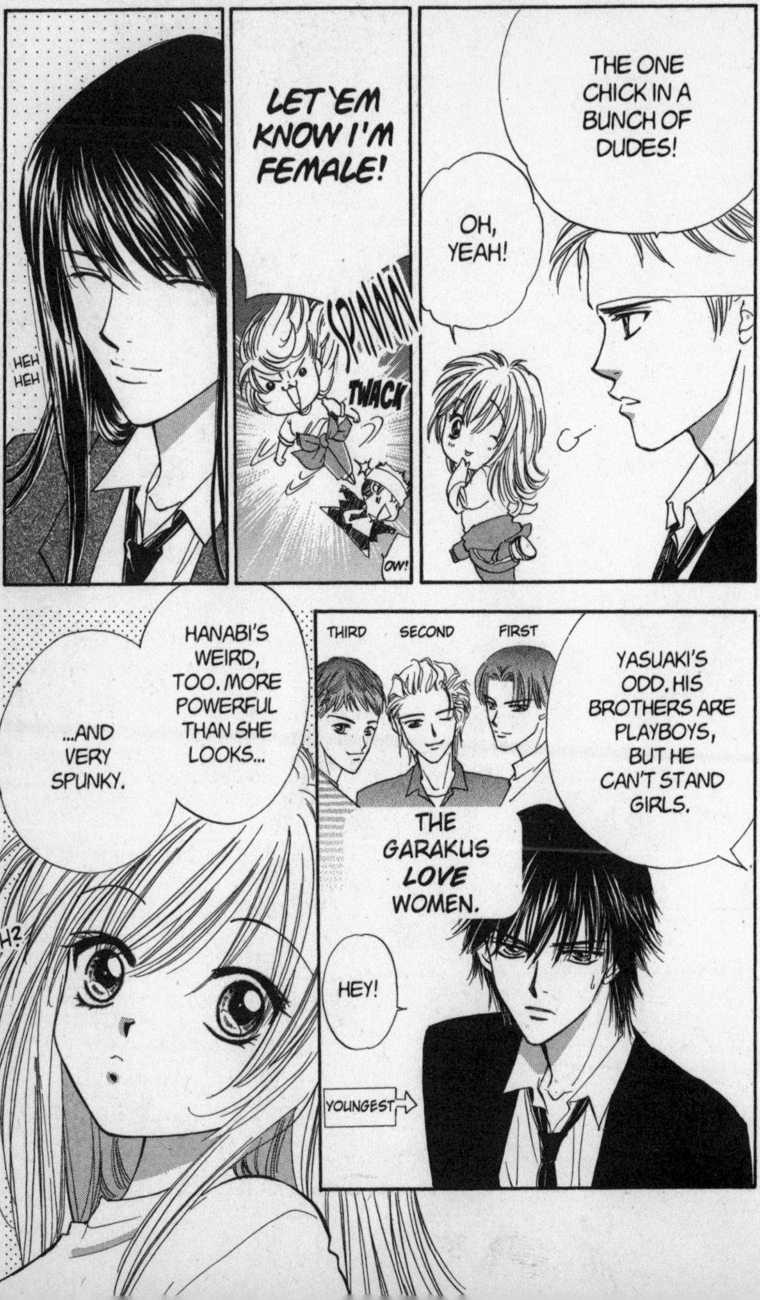
THE ONE CHICK IN A BUNCH OF DUDES!
OH, YEAH!
LET 'EM KNOW I'M FEMALE!
SPINNN
TWACK
OW!
HEH HEH
YASUAKI'S ODD. HIS BROTHERS ARE PLAYBOYS, BUT HE CAN'T STAND GIRLS.
FIRST
SECOND
THIRD
THE GARAKUS *LOVE* WOMEN.
HEY!
YOUNGEST
HANABI'S WEIRD, TOO. MORE POWERFUL THAN SHE LOOKS...
...AND VERY SPUNKY.
HUH?

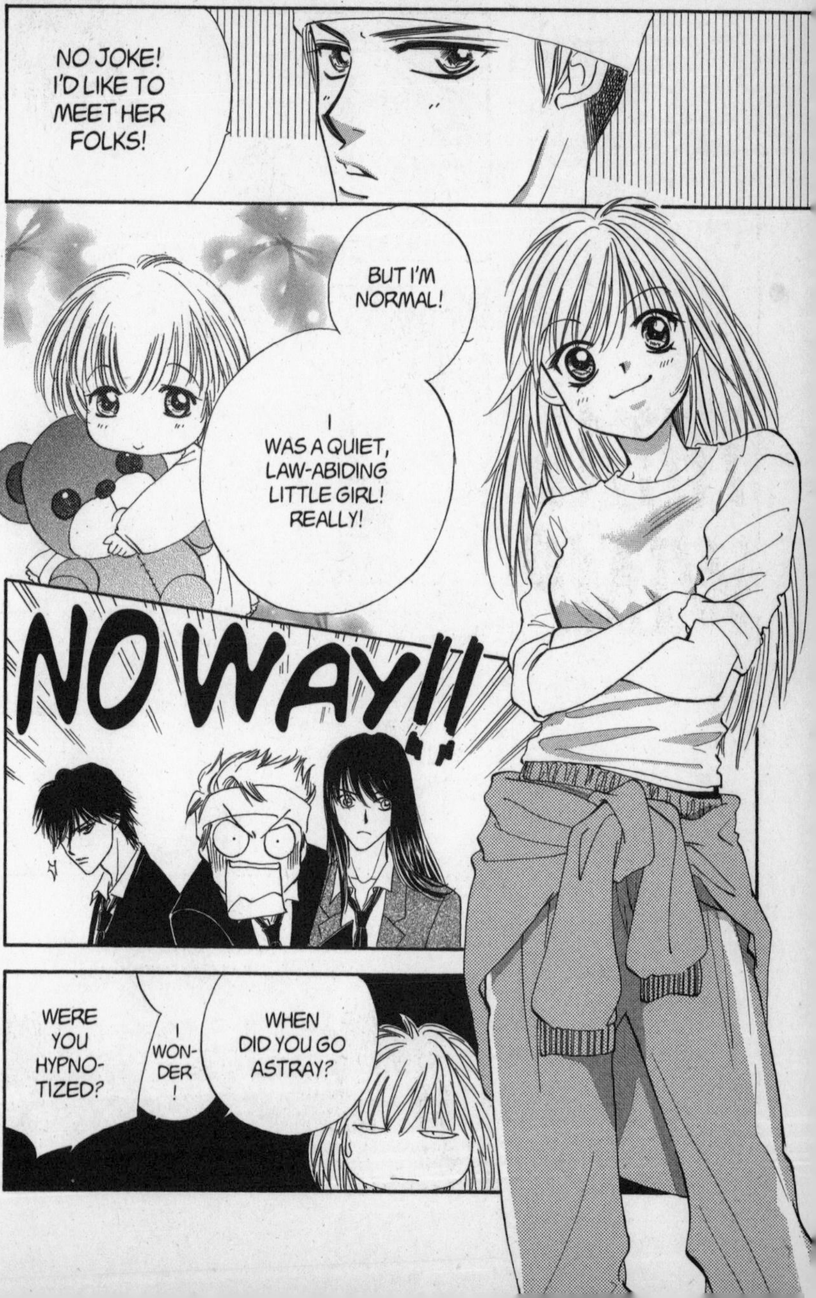
NO JOKE! I'D LIKE TO MEET HER FOLKS!
BUT I'M NORMAL!
I WAS A QUIET, LAW-ABIDING LITTLE GIRL! REALLY!
NO WAY!!
WHEN DID YOU GO ASTRAY?
I WON-DER!
WERE YOU HYPNO-TIZED?

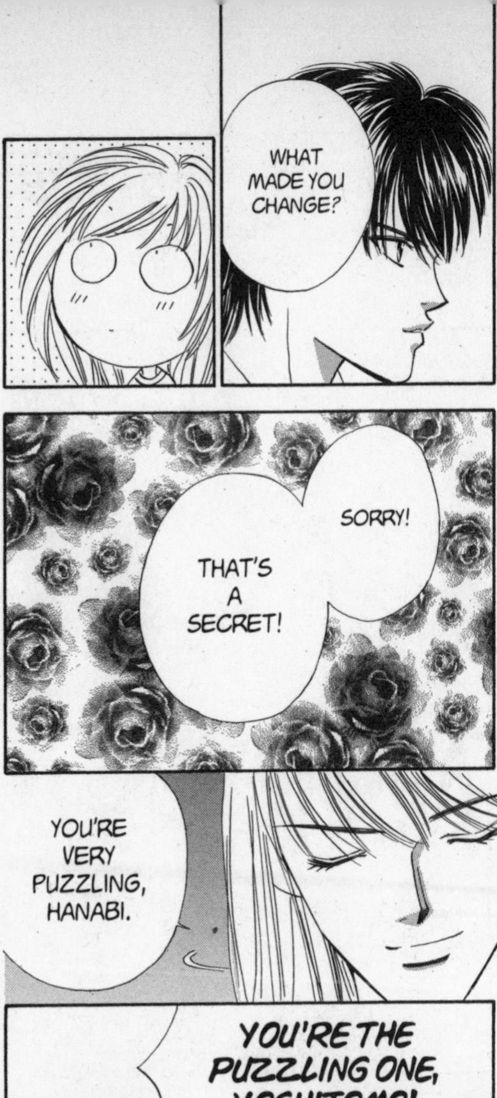
WHAT MADE YOU CHANGE?
SORRY!
THAT'S A SECRET!
YOU'RE VERY PUZZLING, HANABI.
YOU'RE THE PUZZLING ONE, YOSHITOMO!

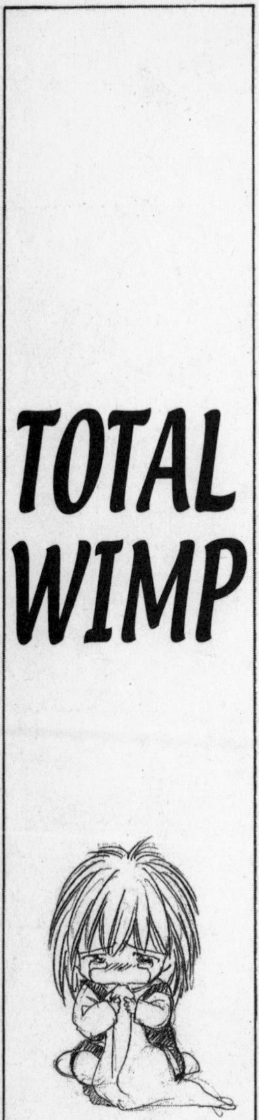
TOTAL WIMP

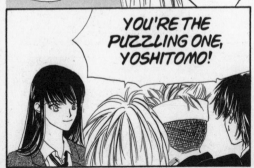

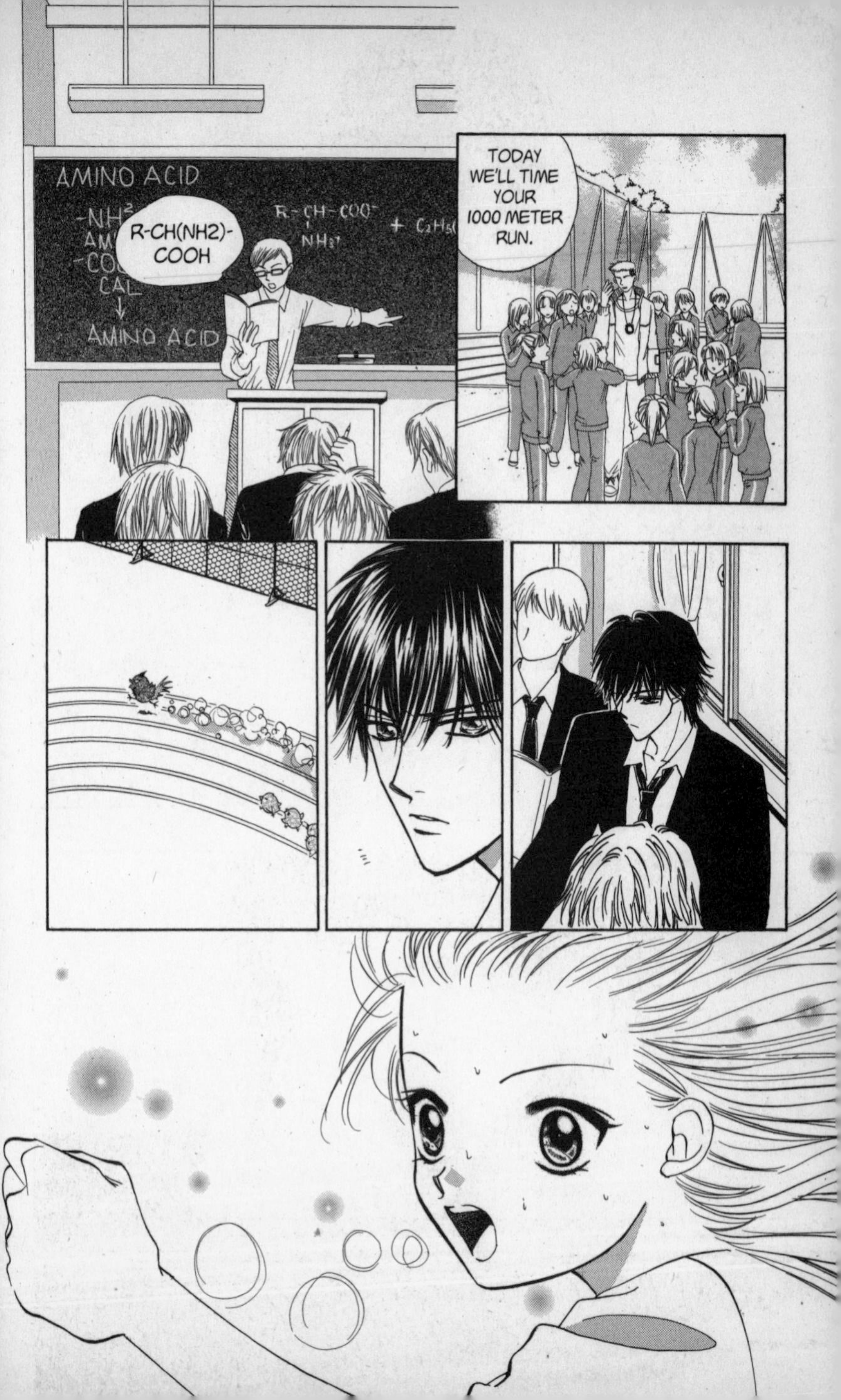
TODAY WE'LL TIME YOUR 1000 METER RUN.
AMINO ACID
R-CH(NH2)-COOH
AMINO ACID

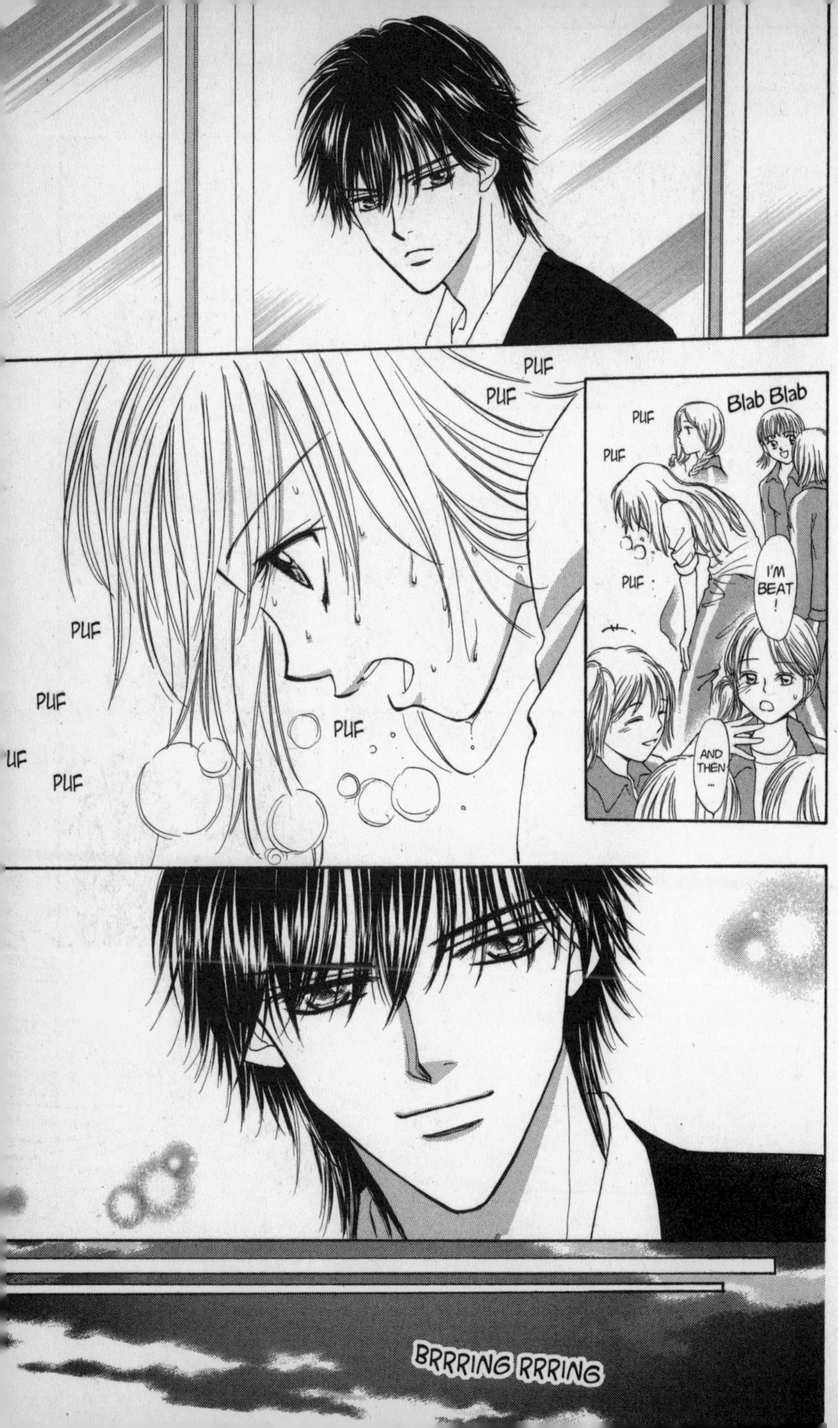
Blab Blab
PUF
PUF
I'M BEAT!
PUF
AND THEN ...
PUF
PUF
PUF
PUF
PUF
UF
PUF
BRRRING RRRING

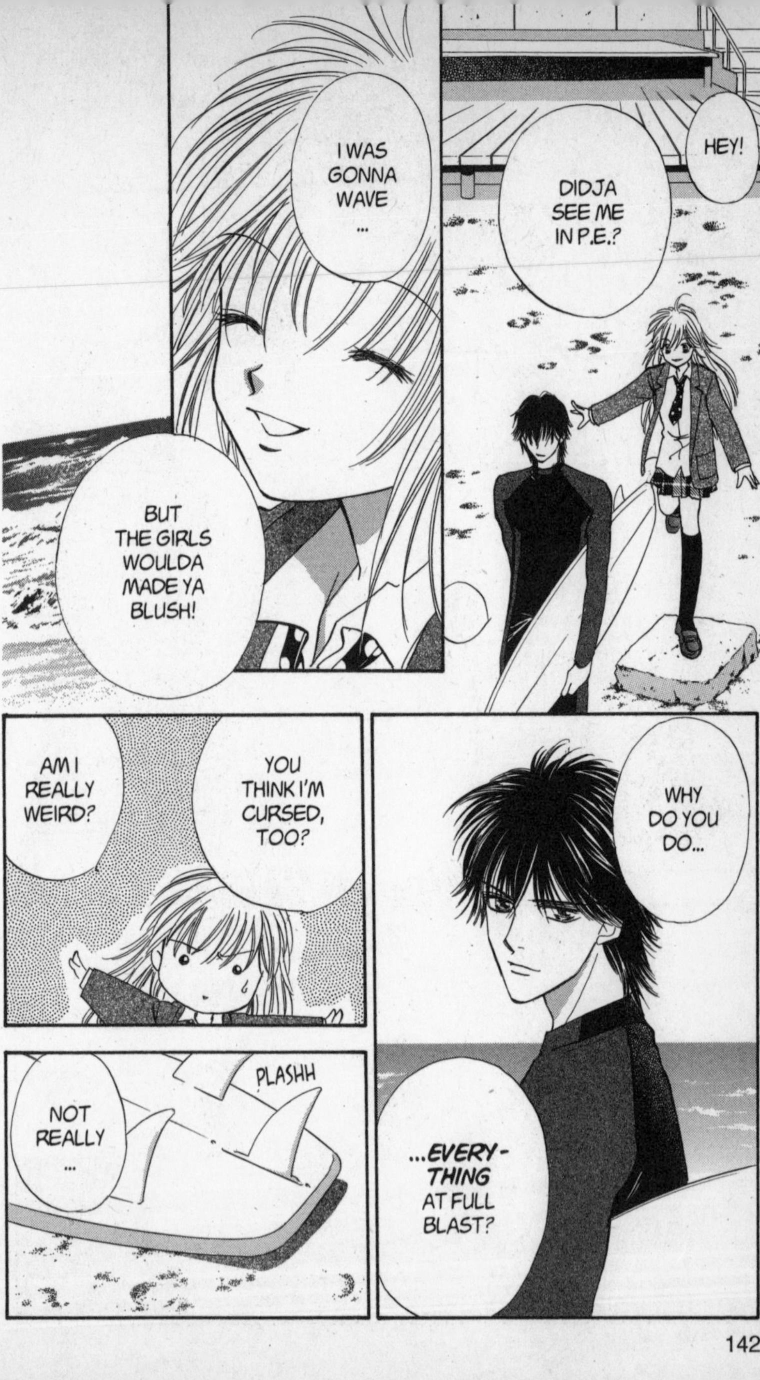
HEY!
DIDJA SEE ME IN P.E.?
I WAS GONNA WAVE ...
BUT THE GIRLS WOULDA MADE YA BLUSH!
WHY DO YOU DO...
...EVERYTHING AT FULL BLAST?
YOU THINK I'M CURSED, TOO?
AM I REALLY WEIRD?
PLASHH
NOT REALLY ...

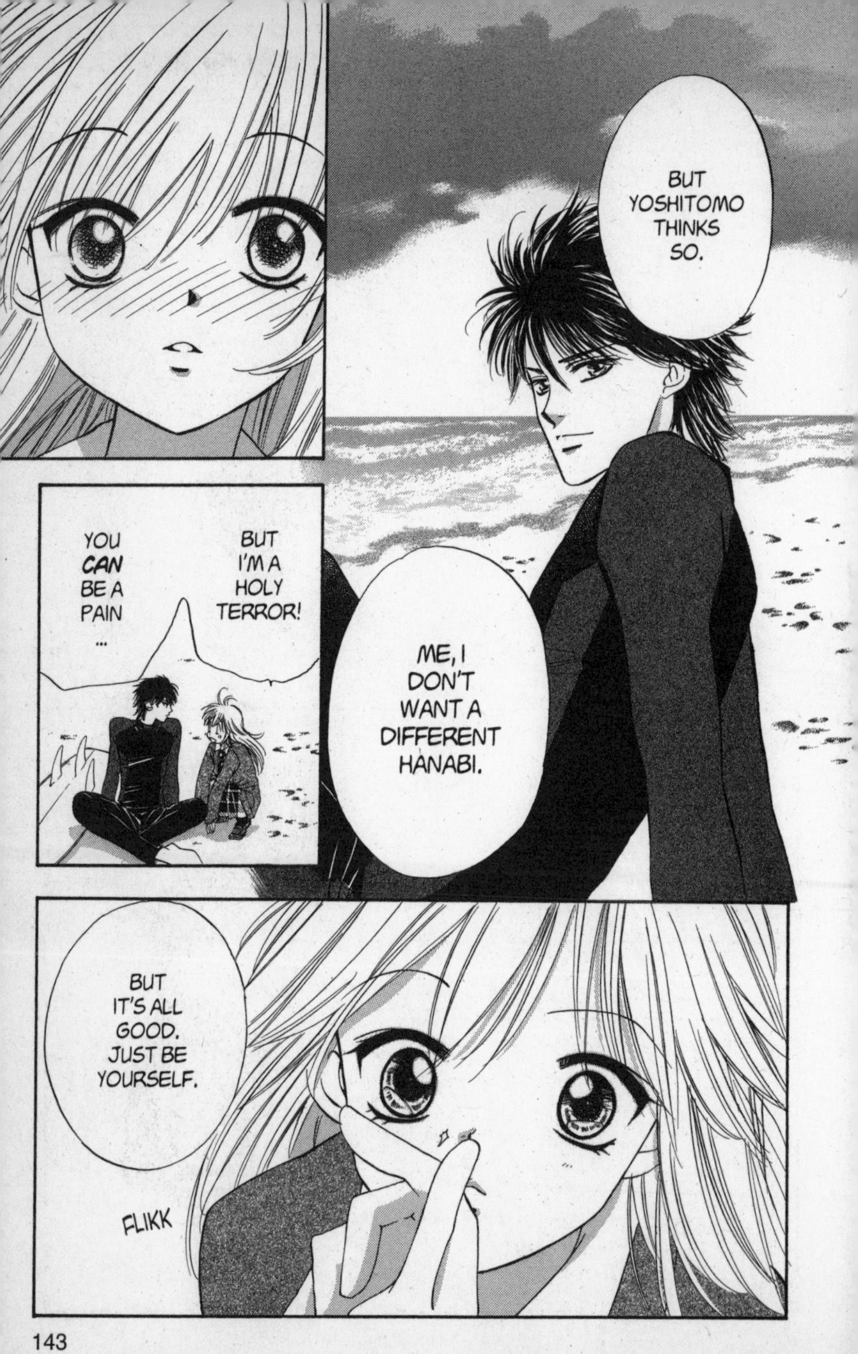
BUT YOSHITOMO THINKS SO.
ME, I DON'T WANT A DIFFERENT HANABI.
BUT I'M A HOLY TERROR!
YOU **CAN** BE A PAIN ...
BUT IT'S ALL GOOD. JUST BE YOURSELF.
FLIKK

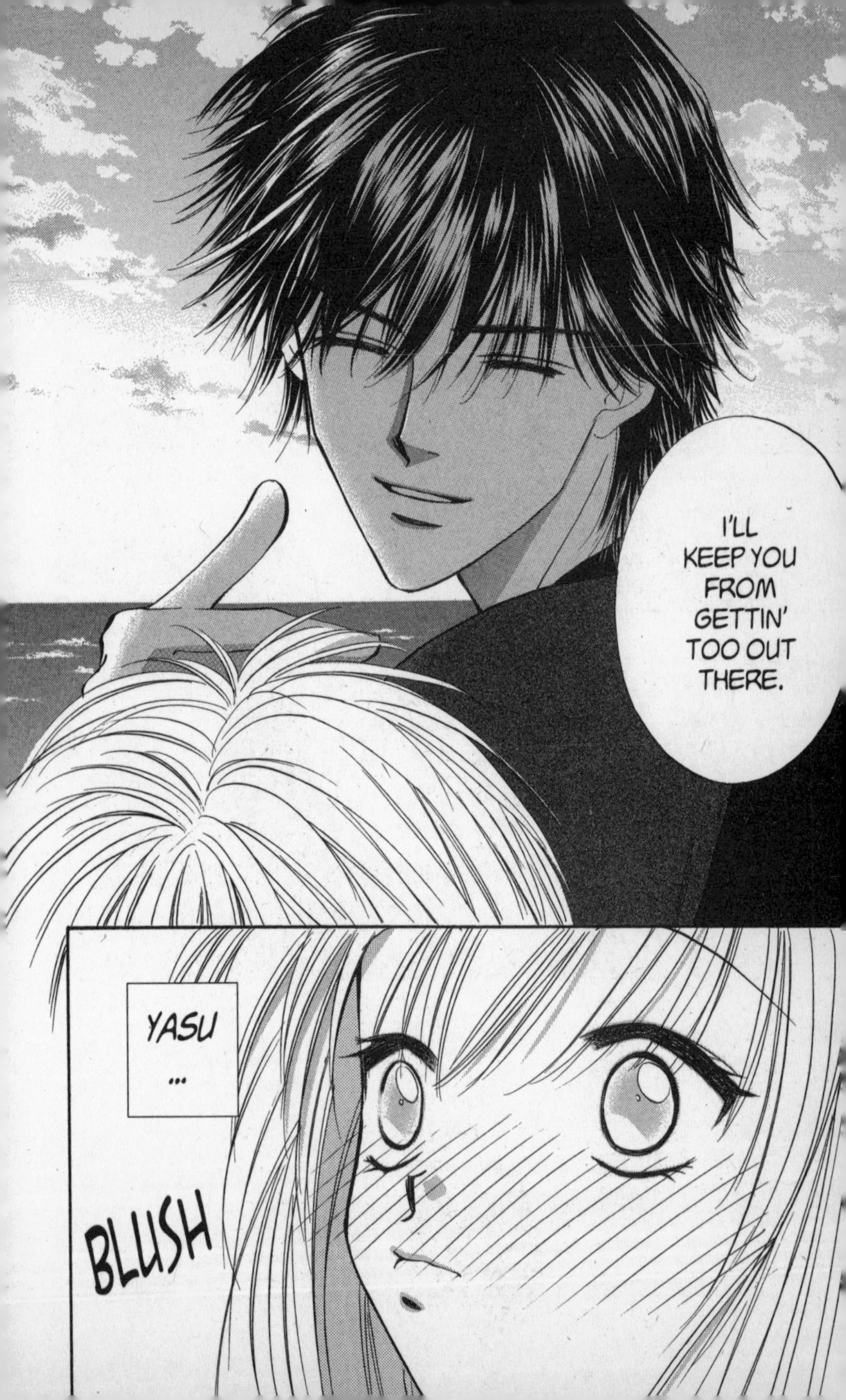
I'LL KEEP YOU FROM GETTIN' TOO OUT THERE.
YASU ...
BLUSH

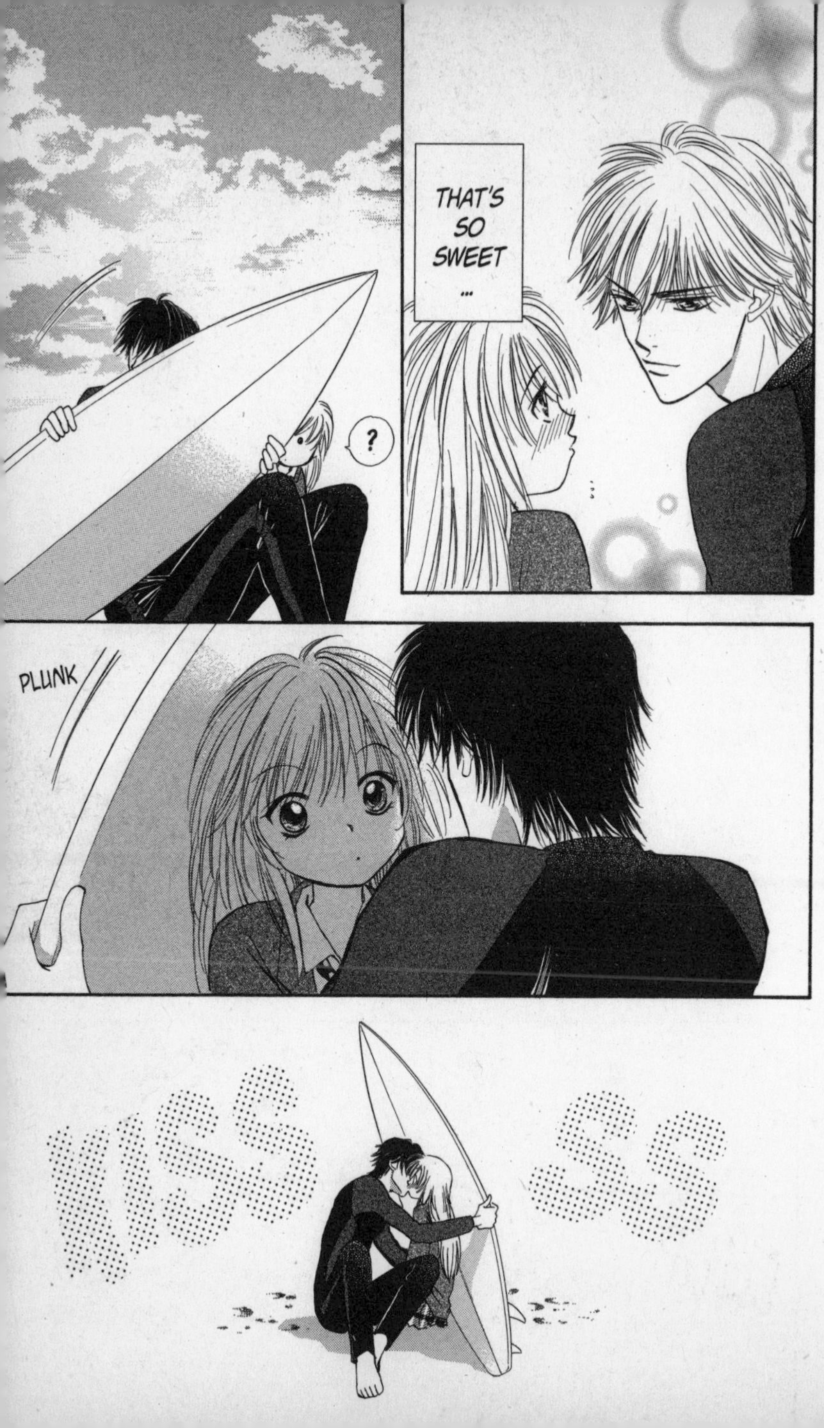
THAT'S SO SWEET ...
?
PLUNK

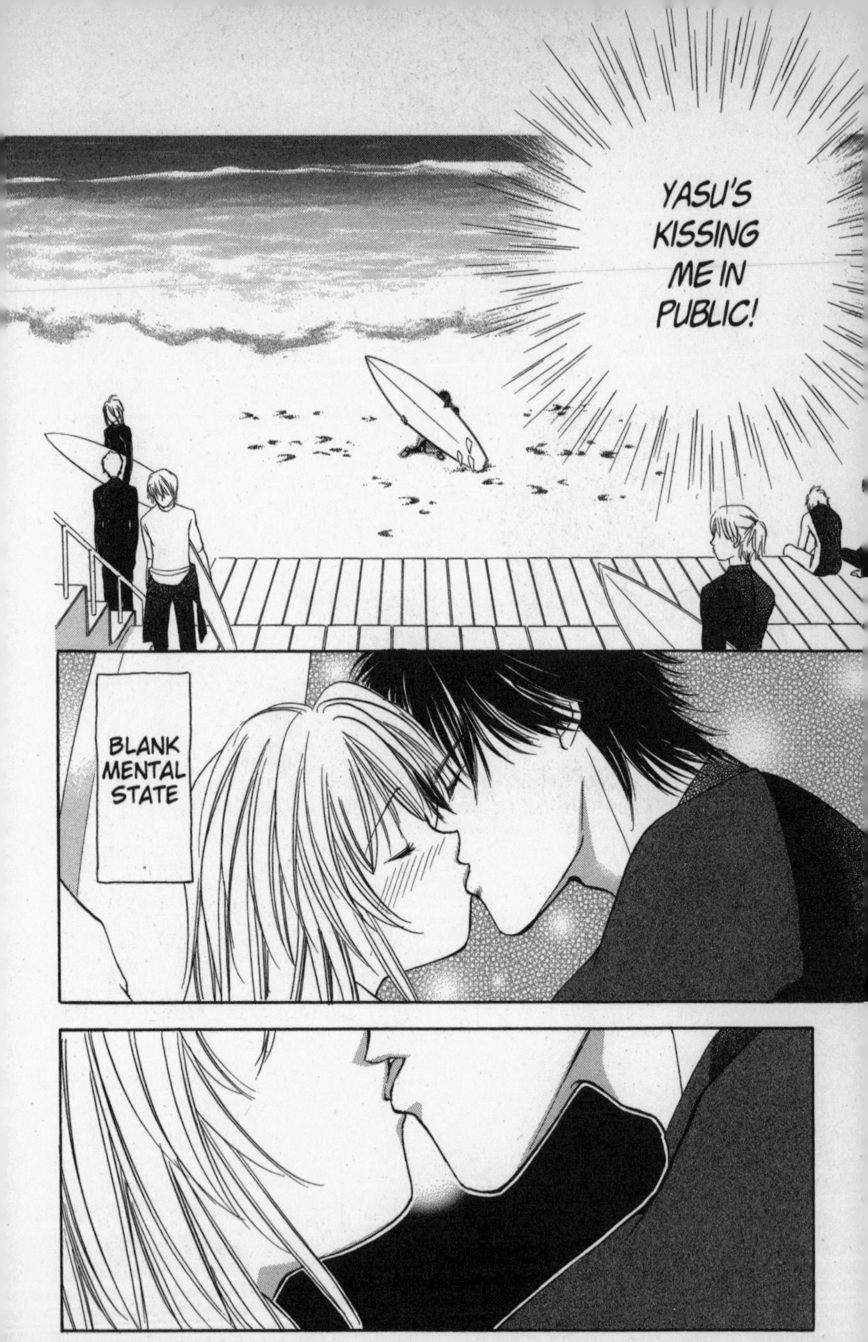
YASU'S KISSING ME IN PUBLIC!
BLANK MENTAL STATE

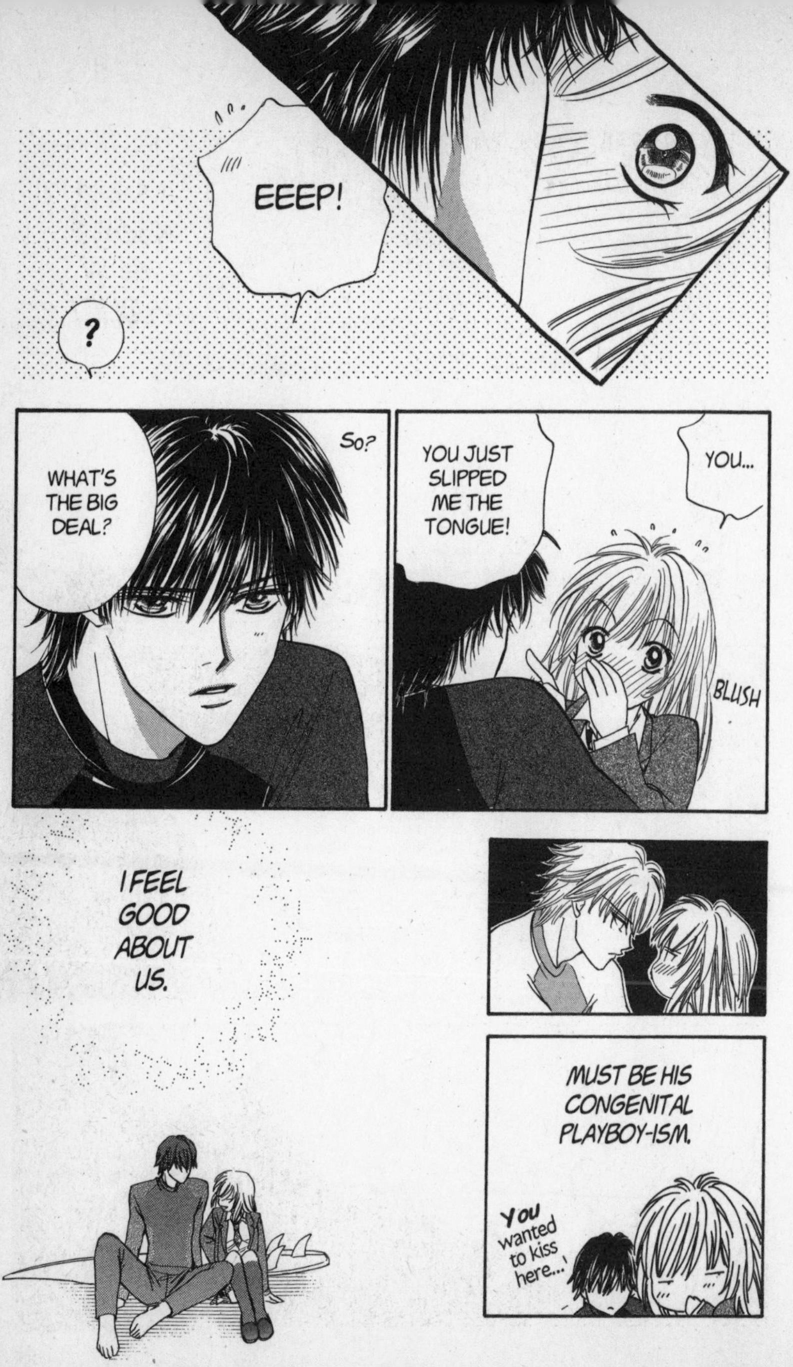
EEEP!
?
YOU...
YOU JUST SLIPPED ME THE TONGUE!
BLUSH
So?
WHAT'S THE BIG DEAL?
MUST BE HIS CONGENITAL PLAYBOY-ISM.
You wanted to kiss here...!
I FEEL GOOD ABOUT US.

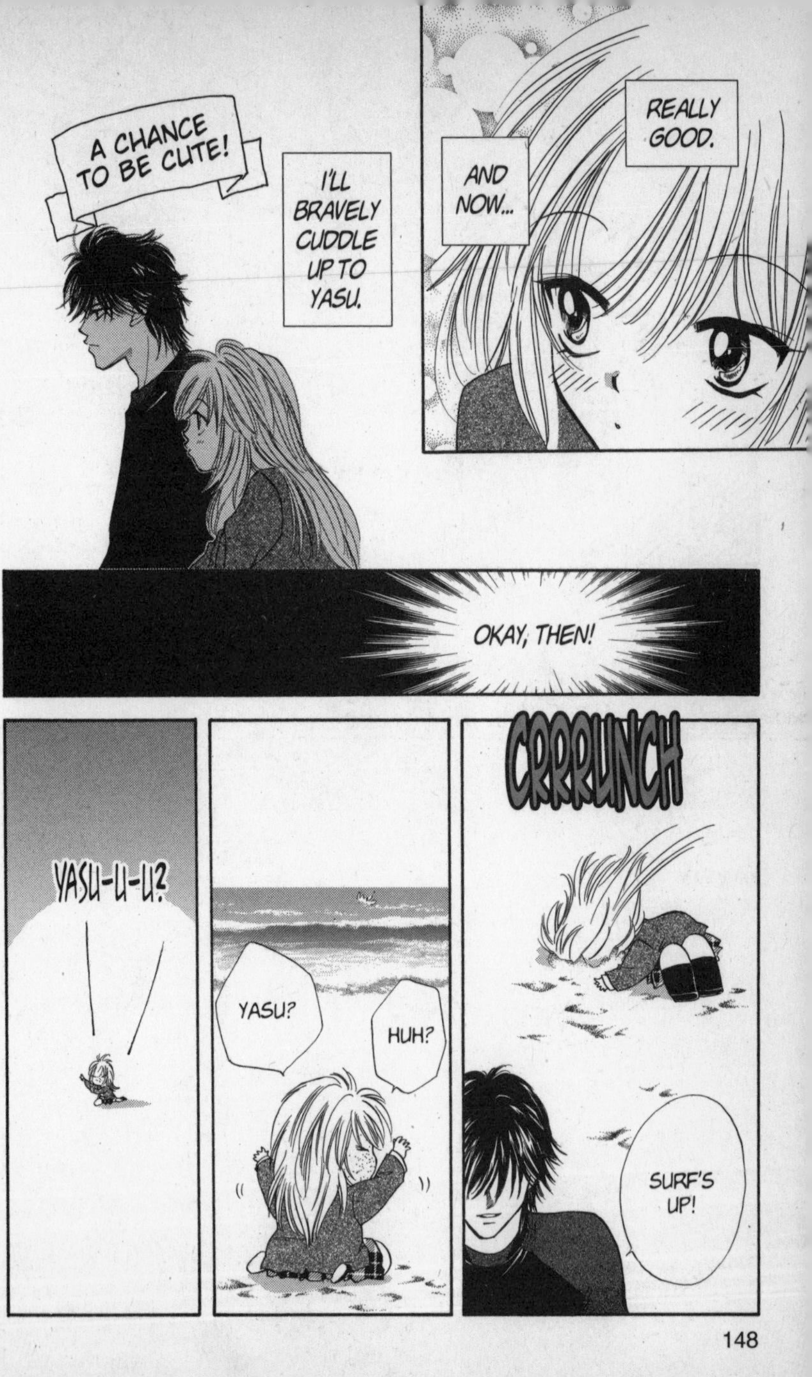
REALLY GOOD.
AND NOW...
I'LL BRAVELY CUDDLE UP TO YASU.
A CHANCE TO BE CUTE!
OKAY, THEN!
CRRRUNCH
SURF'S UP!
HUH?
YASU?
YASU-U-U?

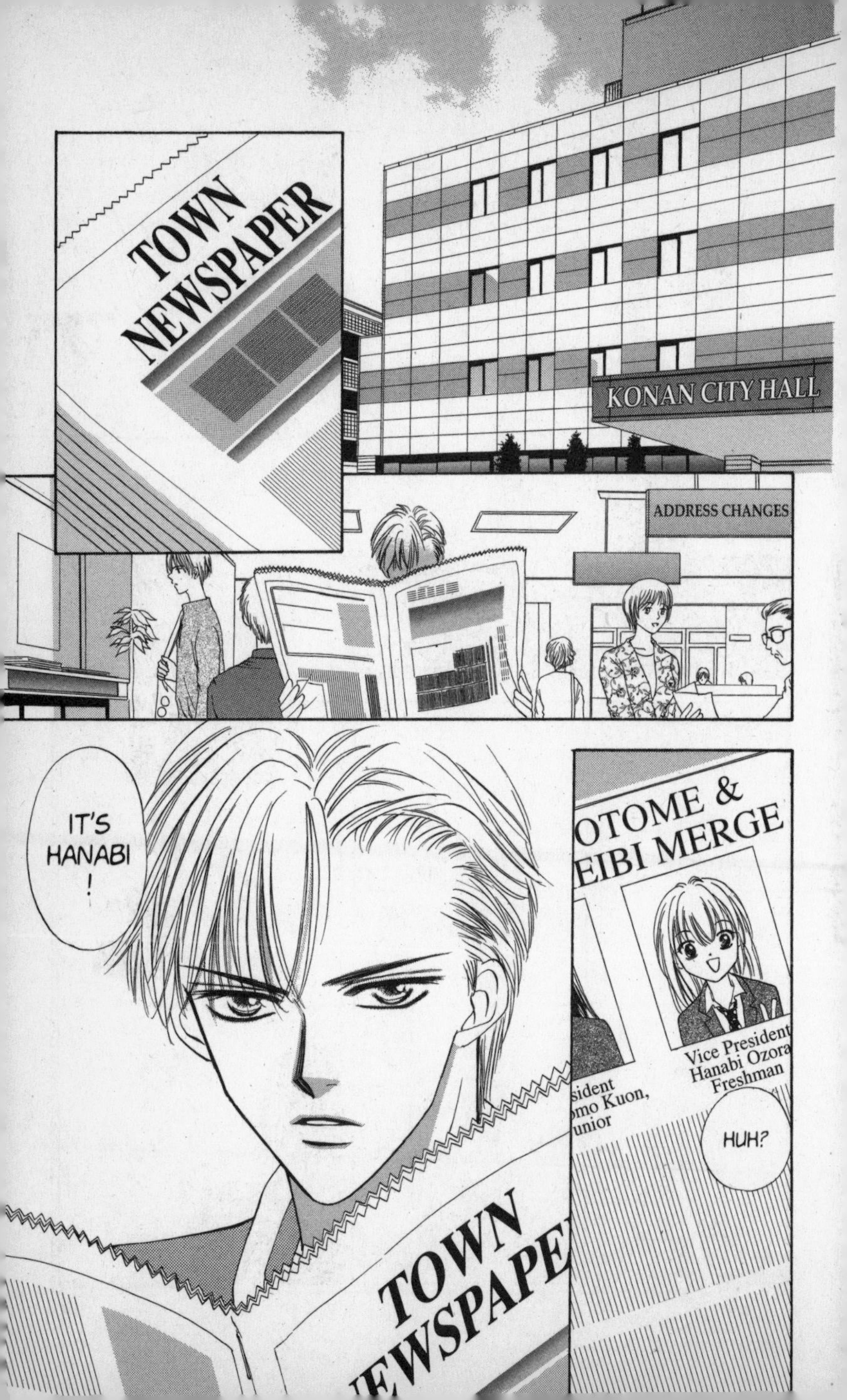
KONAN CITY HALL
TOWN NEWSPAPER
ADDRESS CHANGES
OTOME & EIBI MERGE
Vice President Hanabi Ozora Freshman
sident omo Kuon, unior
HUH?
IT'S HANABI!
TOWN NEWSPAPE

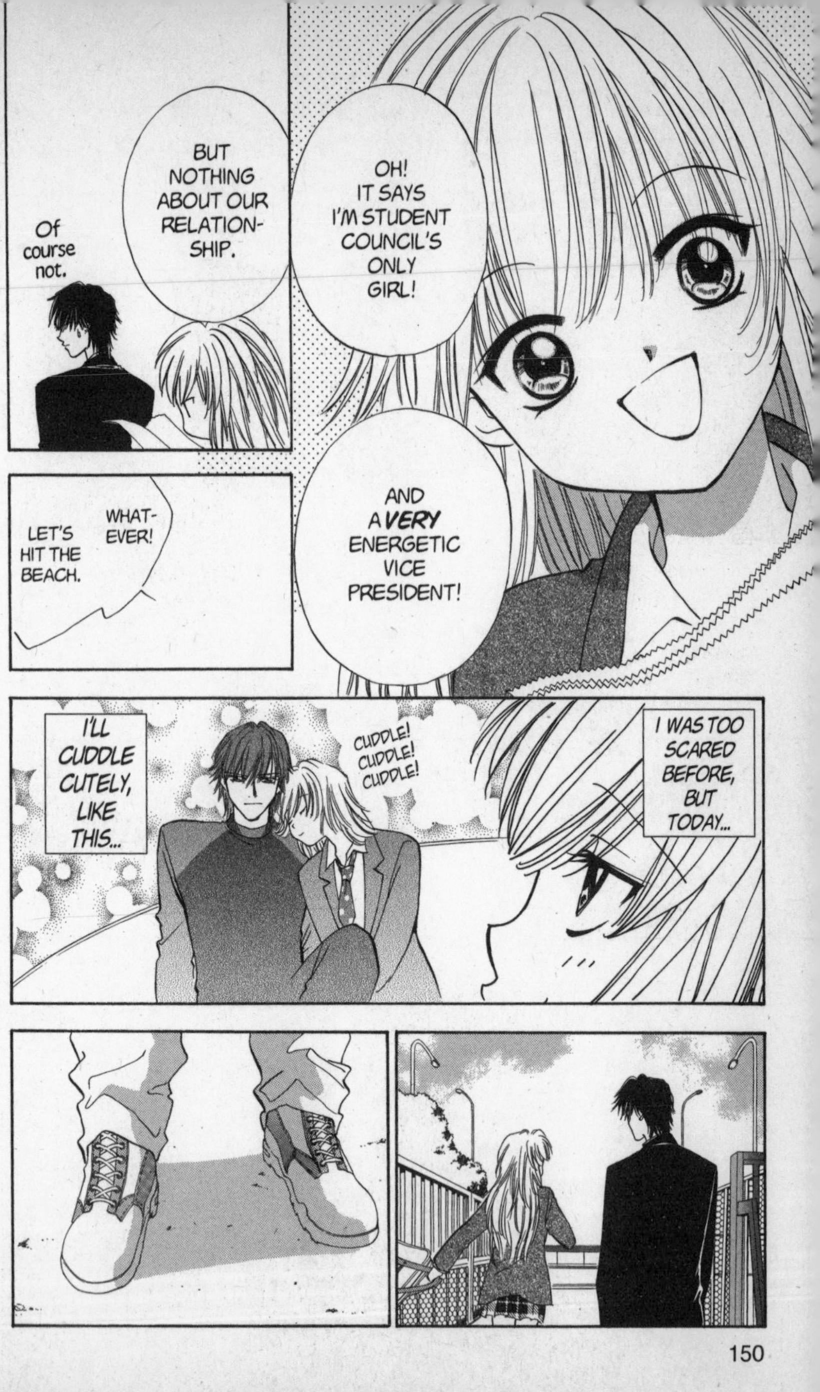
OH! IT SAYS I'M STUDENT COUNCIL'S ONLY GIRL!
AND A **VERY** ENERGETIC VICE PRESIDENT!
BUT NOTHING ABOUT OUR RELATION-SHIP.
Of course not.
WHAT-EVER!
LET'S HIT THE BEACH.
I WAS TOO SCARED BEFORE, BUT TODAY...
CUDDLE! CUDDLE! CUDDLE!
I'LL CUDDLE CUTELY, LIKE THIS...

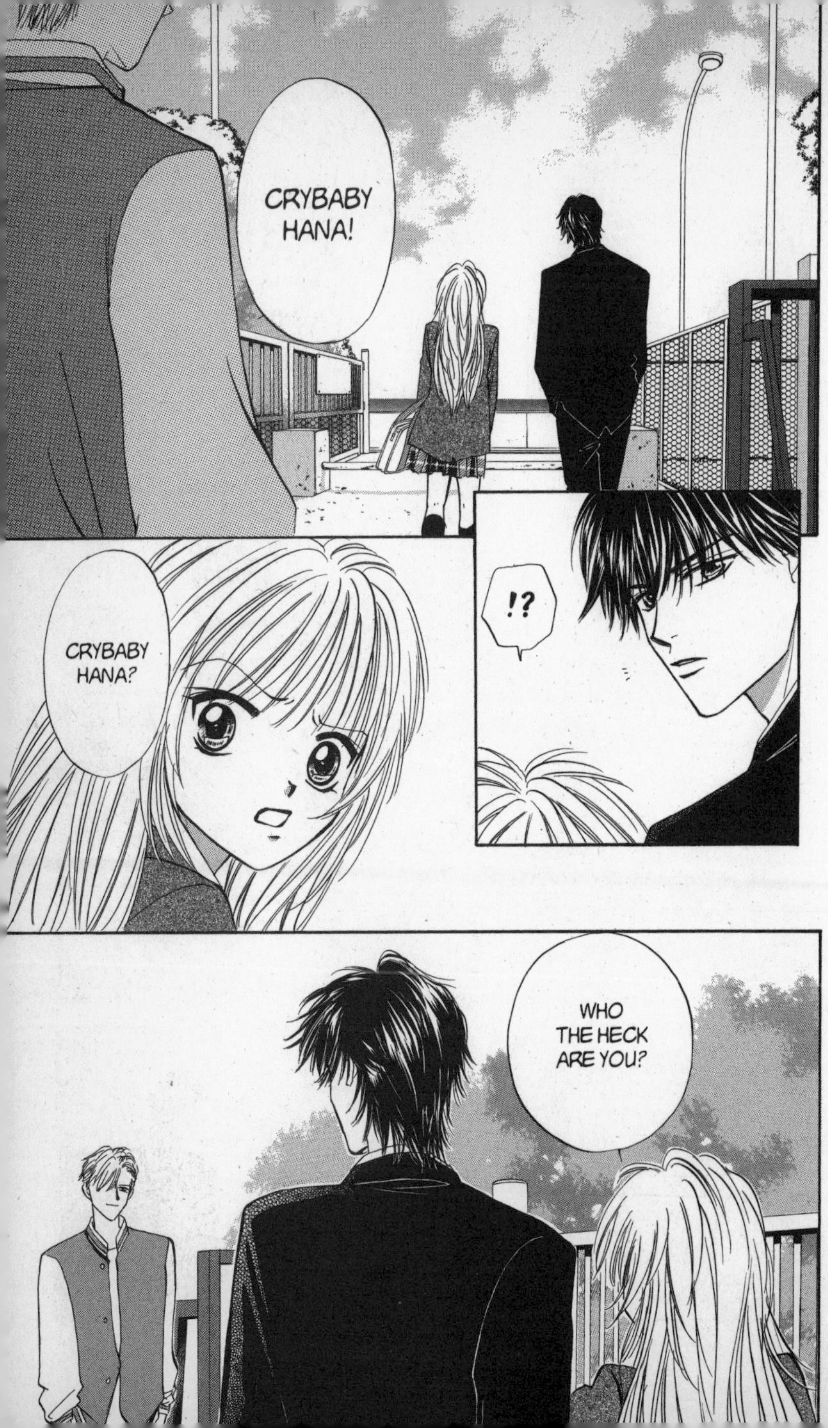
CRYBABY HANA!
!?
CRYBABY HANA?
WHO THE HECK ARE YOU?

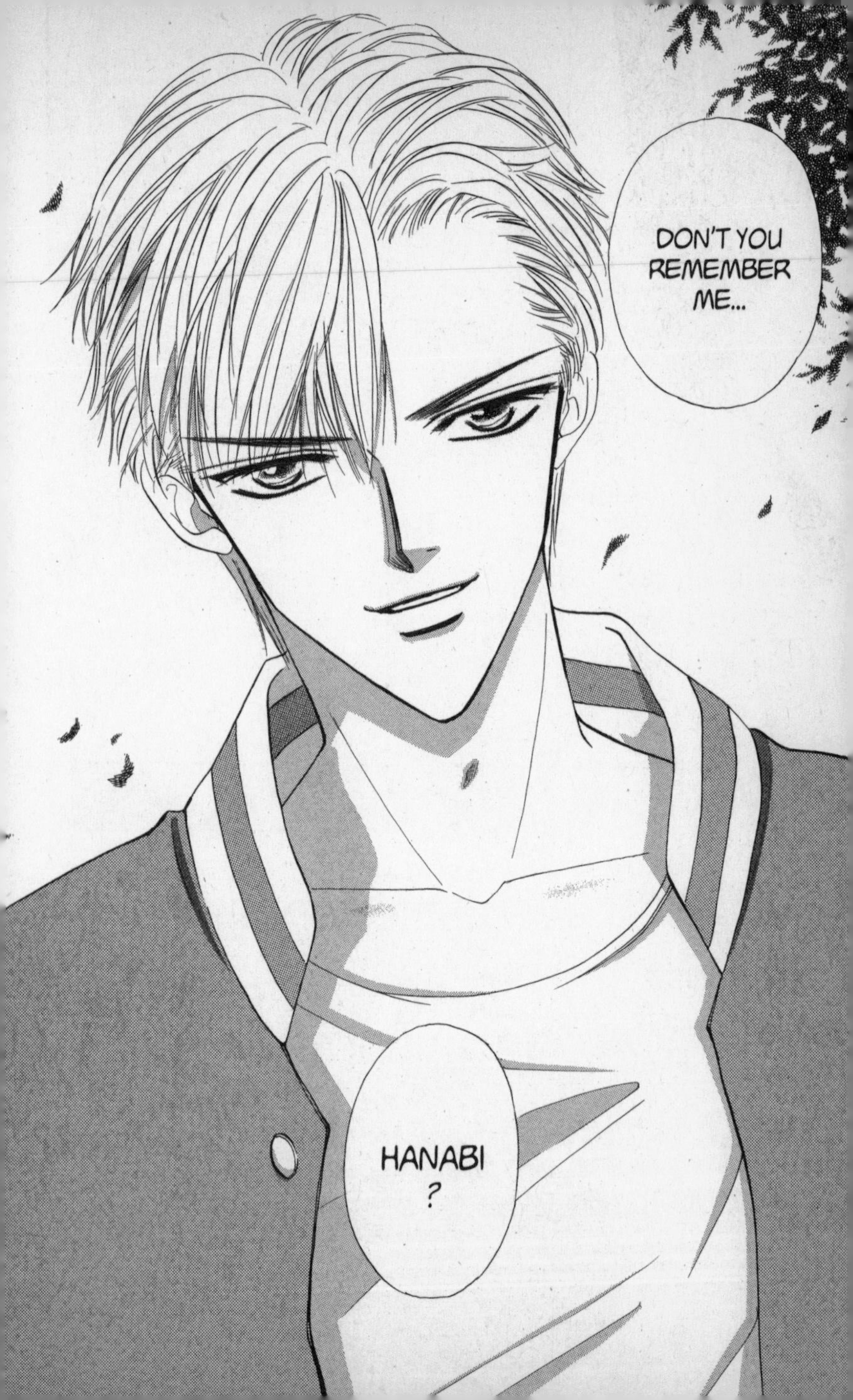
DON'T YOU REMEMBER ME...
HANABI ?

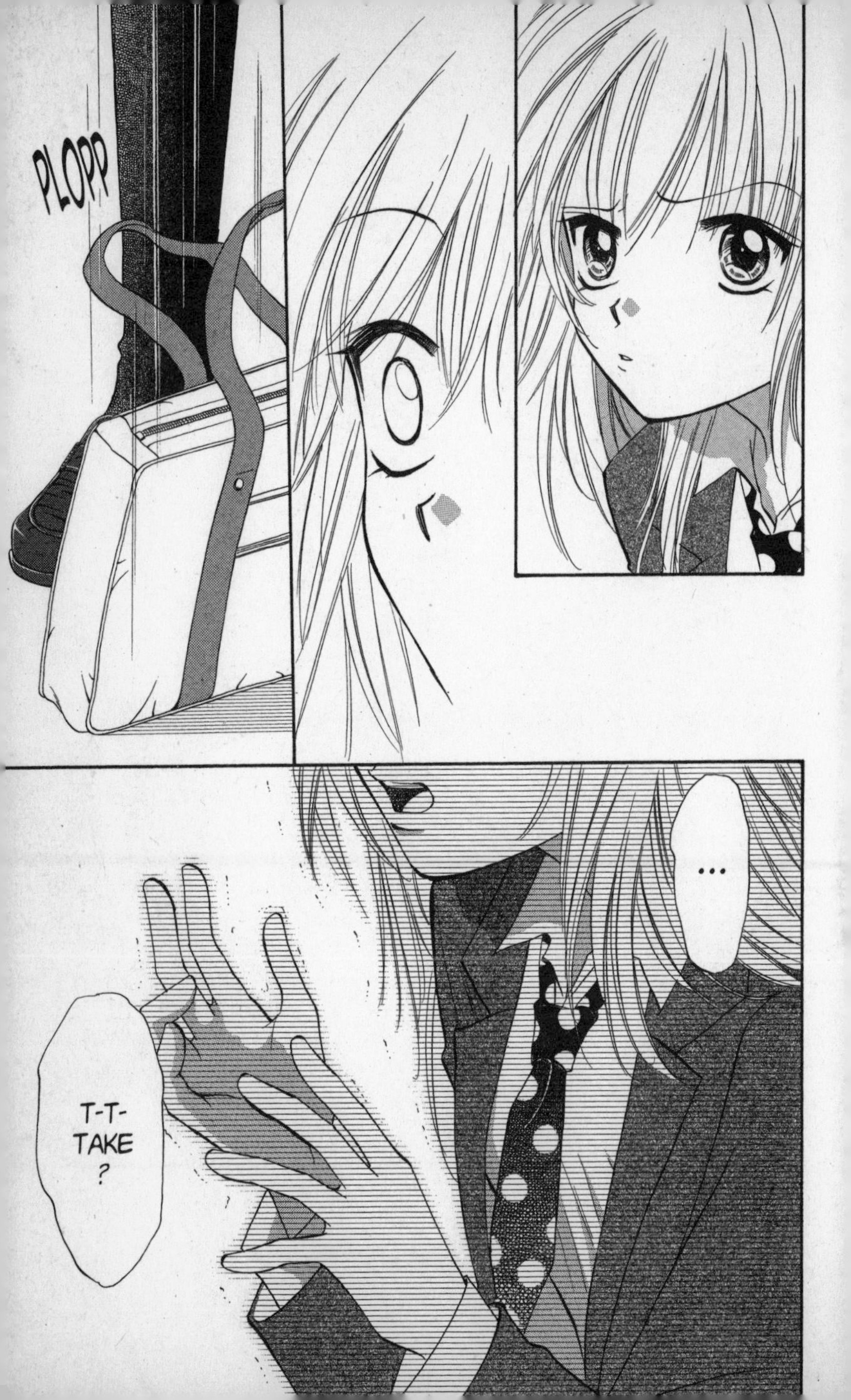
PLOPP
...
T-T-TAKE?

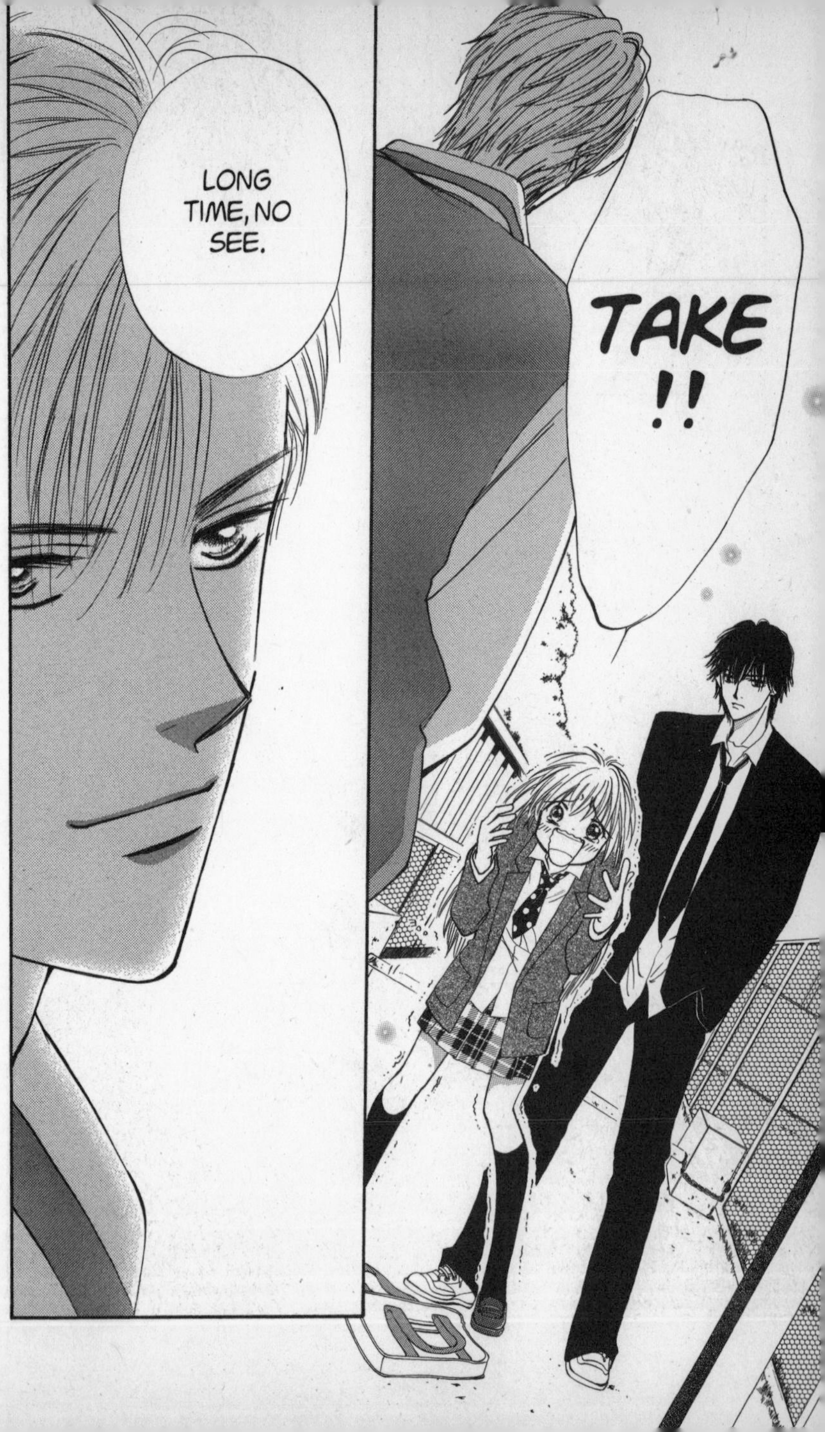
TAKE !!
LONG TIME, NO SEE.

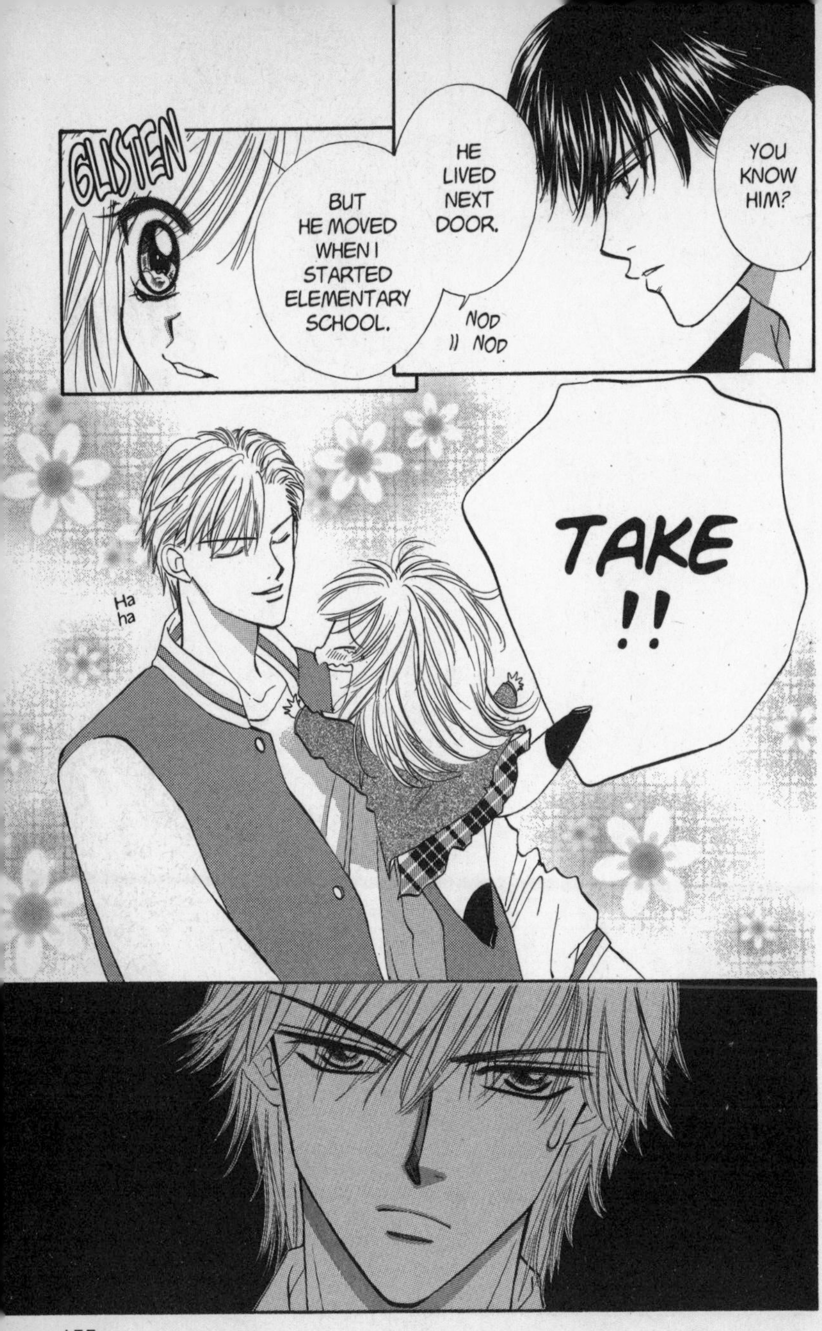
YOU KNOW HIM?
HE LIVED NEXT DOOR.
NOD NOD
BUT HE MOVED WHEN I STARTED ELEMENTARY SCHOOL.
GLISTEN
TAKE !!
Ha ha

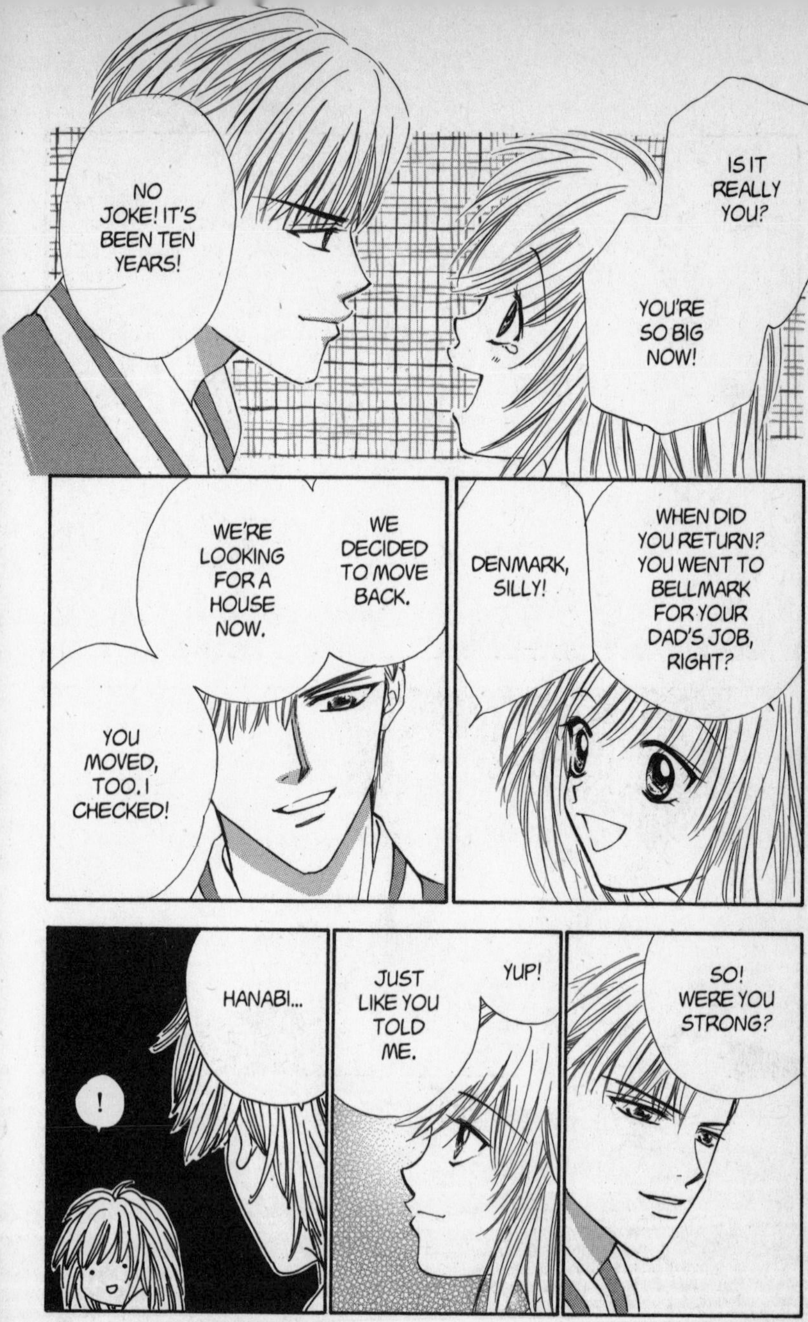
IS IT REALLY YOU?
YOU'RE SO BIG NOW!
NO JOKE! IT'S BEEN TEN YEARS!
WHEN DID YOU RETURN? YOU WENT TO BELLMARK FOR YOUR DAD'S JOB, RIGHT?
DENMARK, SILLY!
WE DECIDED TO MOVE BACK.
WE'RE LOOKING FOR A HOUSE NOW.
YOU MOVED, TOO. I CHECKED!
SO! WERE YOU STRONG?
YUP!
JUST LIKE YOU TOLD ME.
HANABI...
!

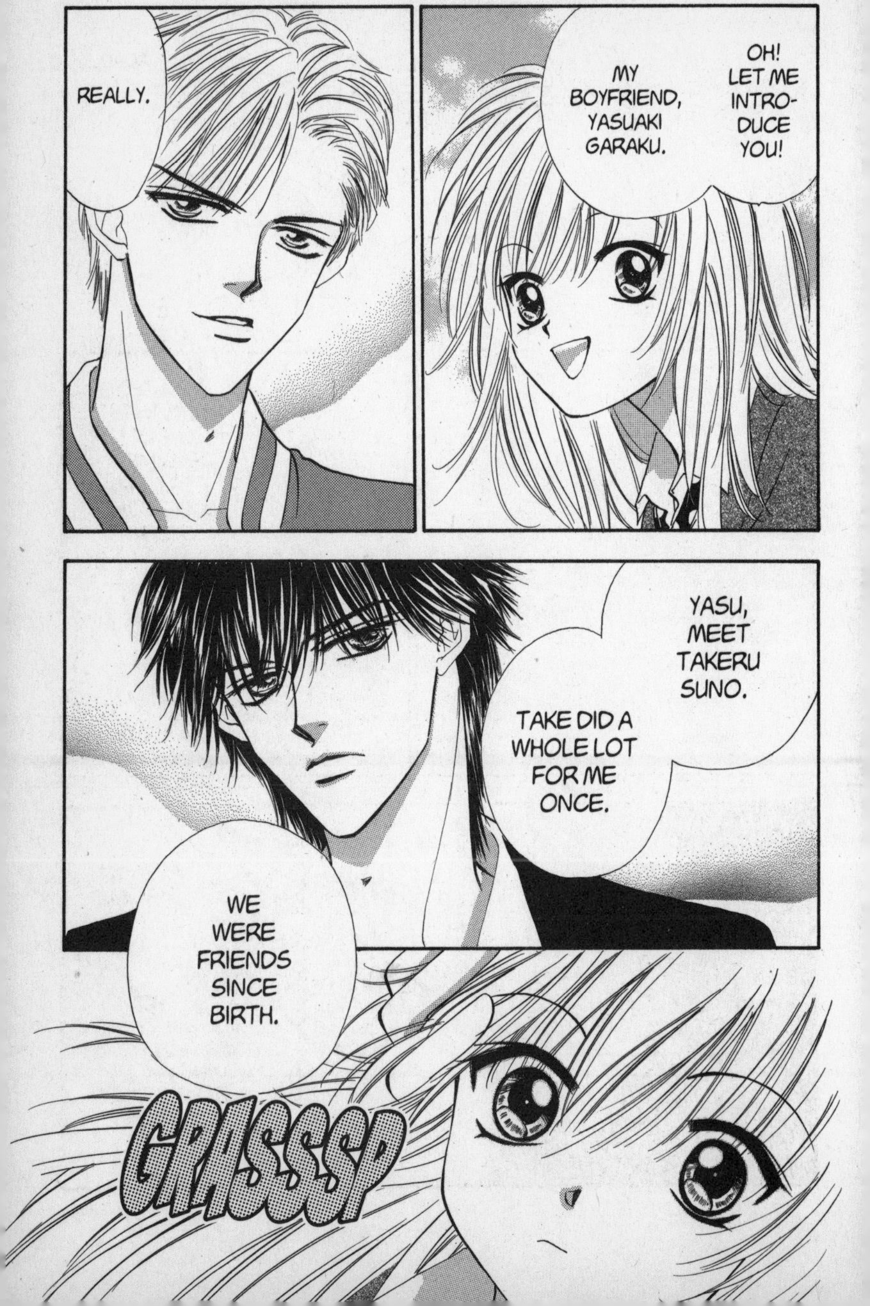
OH! LET ME INTRO-DUCE YOU!
MY BOYFRIEND, YASUAKI GARAKU.
REALLY.
YASU, MEET TAKERU SUNO.
TAKE DID A WHOLE LOT FOR ME ONCE.
WE WERE FRIENDS SINCE BIRTH.
GRASSSP

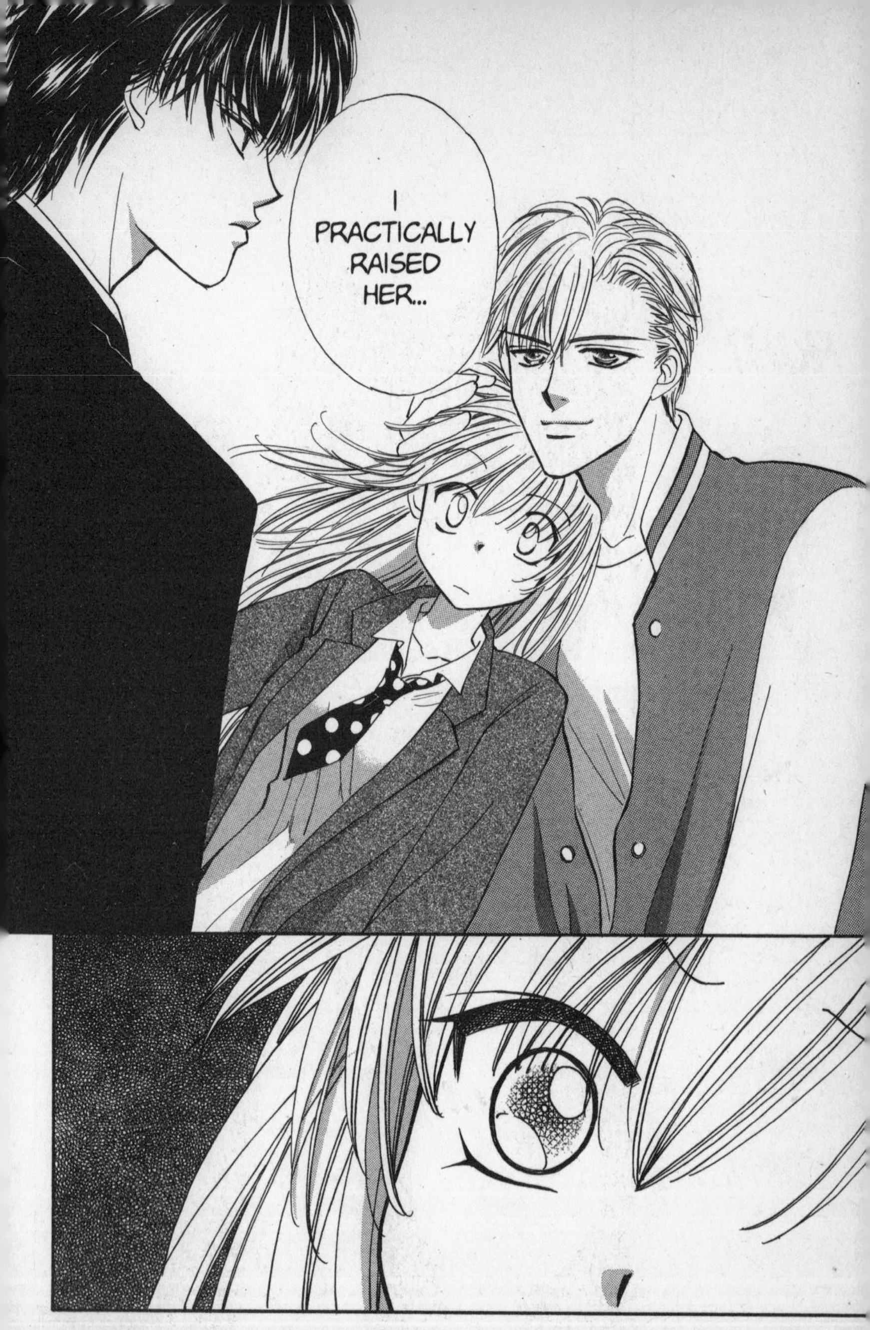
I PRACTICALLY RAISED HER...

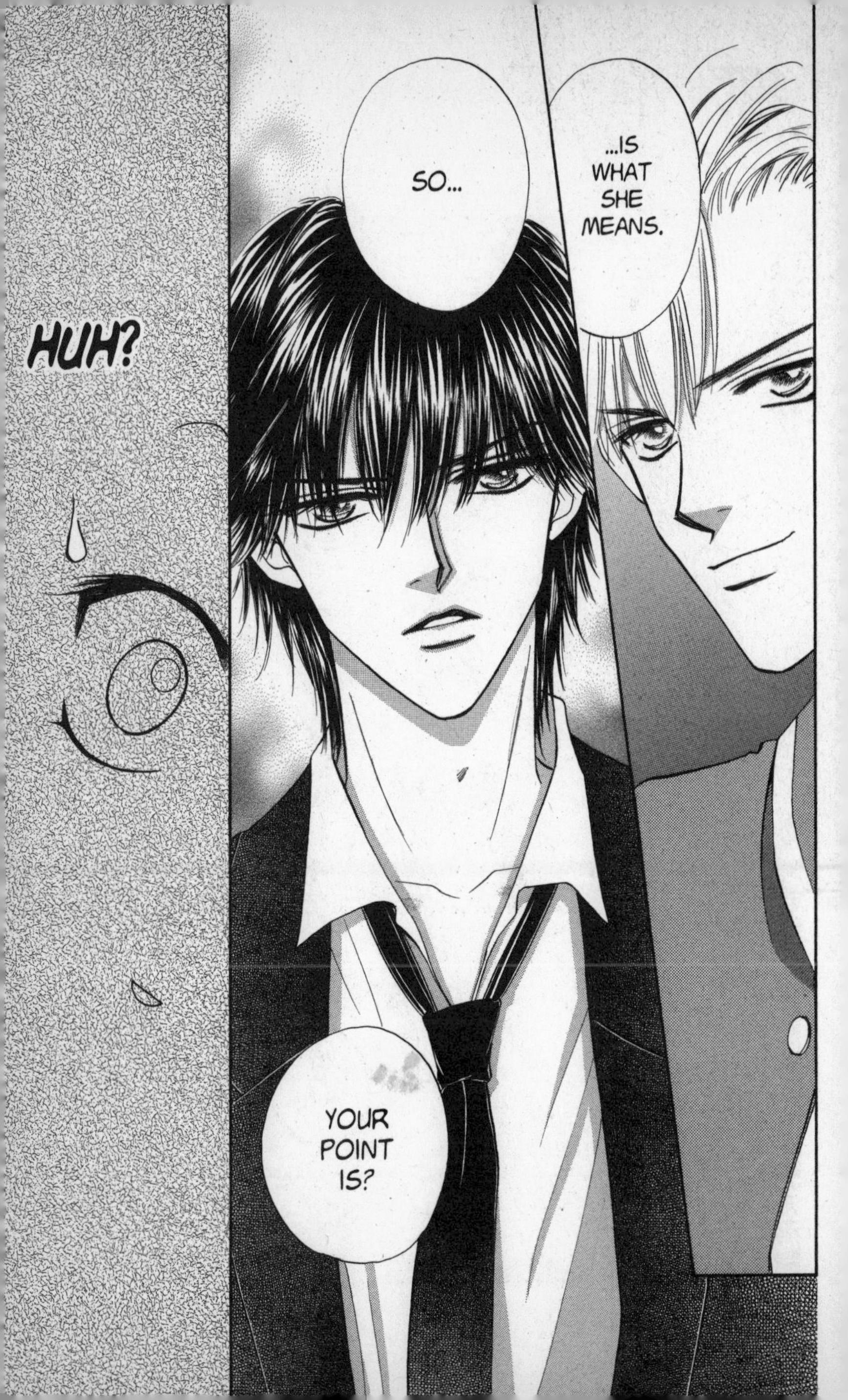
...IS WHAT SHE MEANS.
SO...
HUH?
YOUR POINT IS?

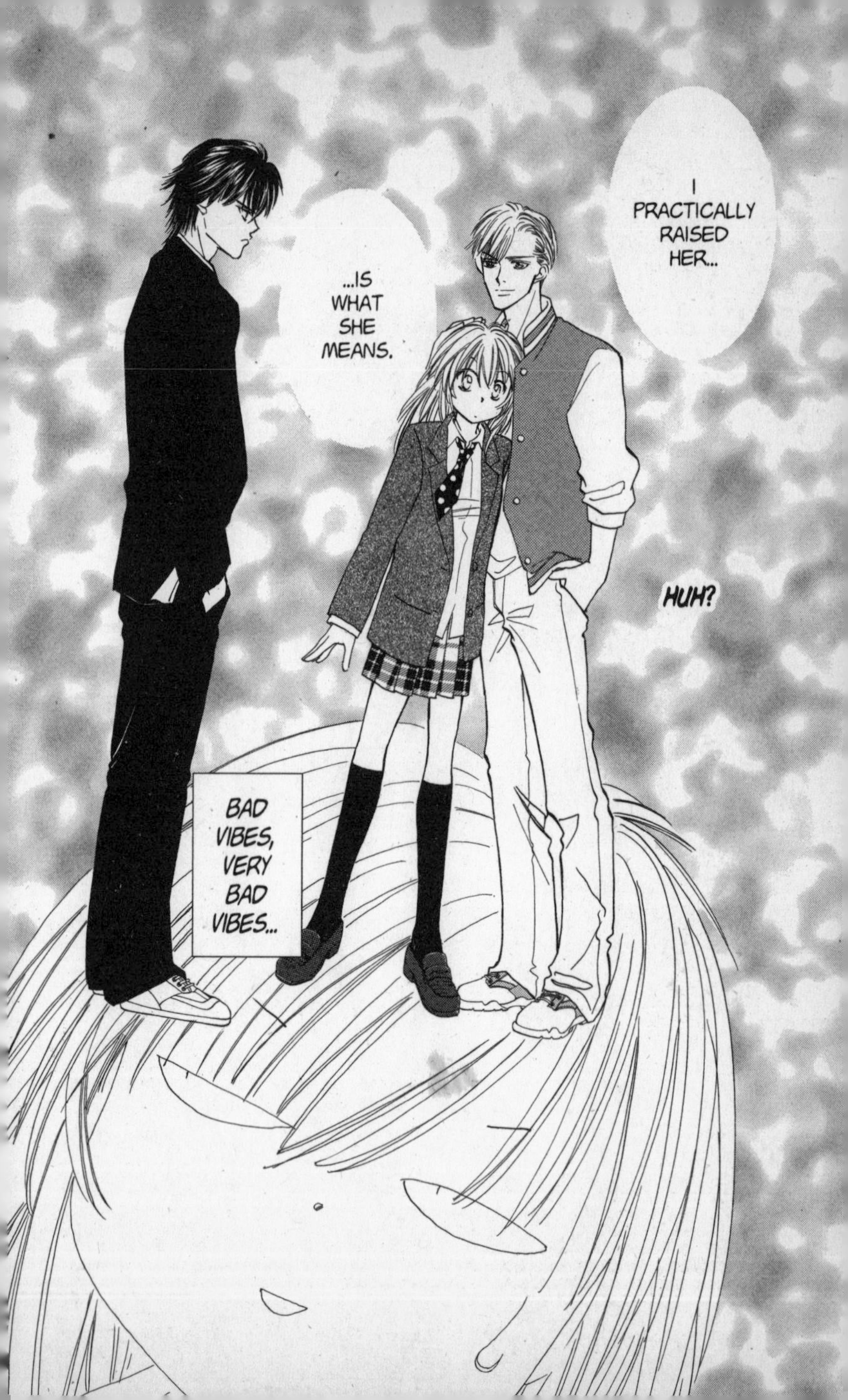
I PRACTICALLY RAISED HER...
...IS WHAT SHE MEANS.
HUH?
BAD VIBES, VERY BAD VIBES...

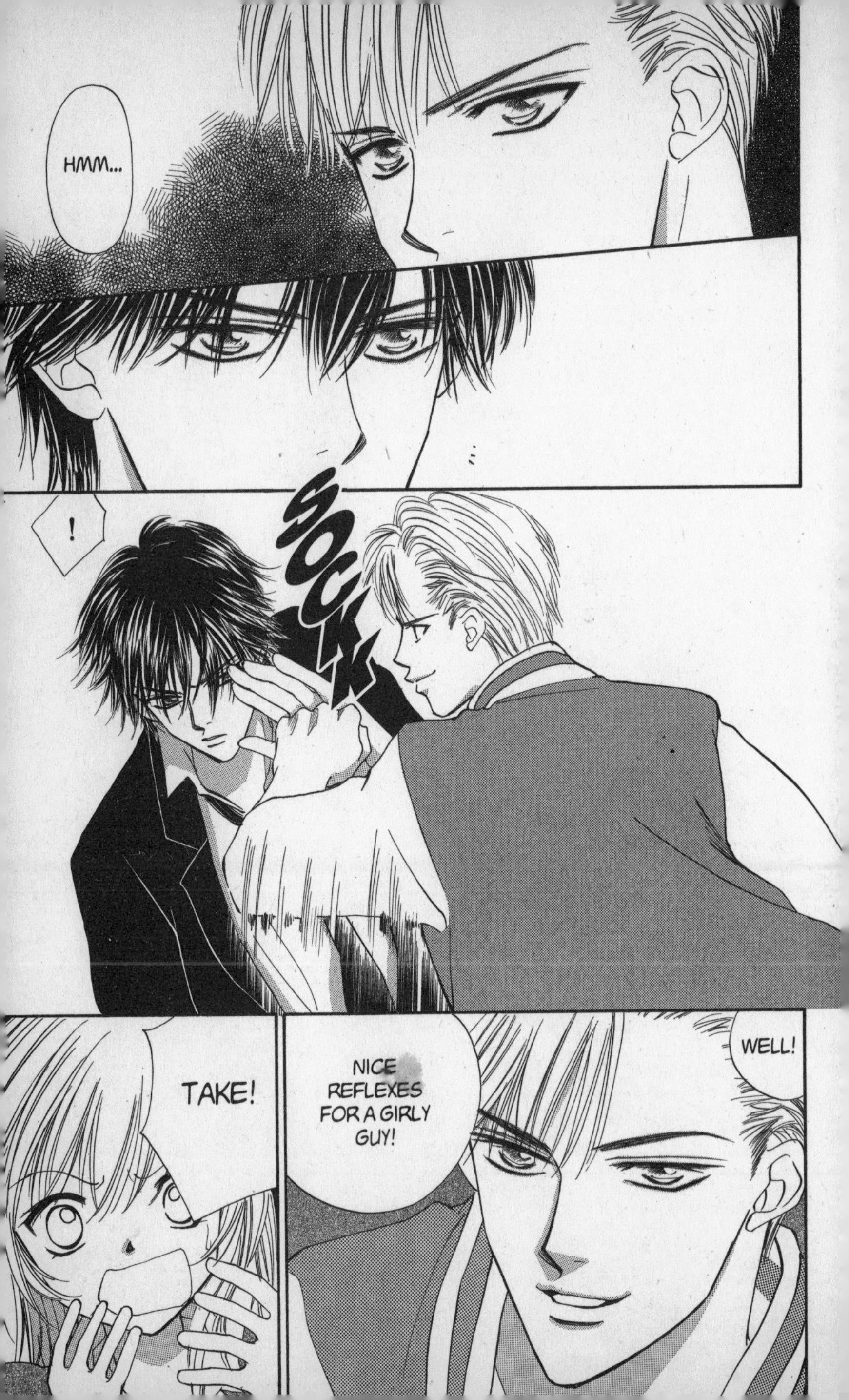
HMM...
SOCK!
!
WELL!
NICE REFLEXES FOR A GIRLY GUY!
TAKE!

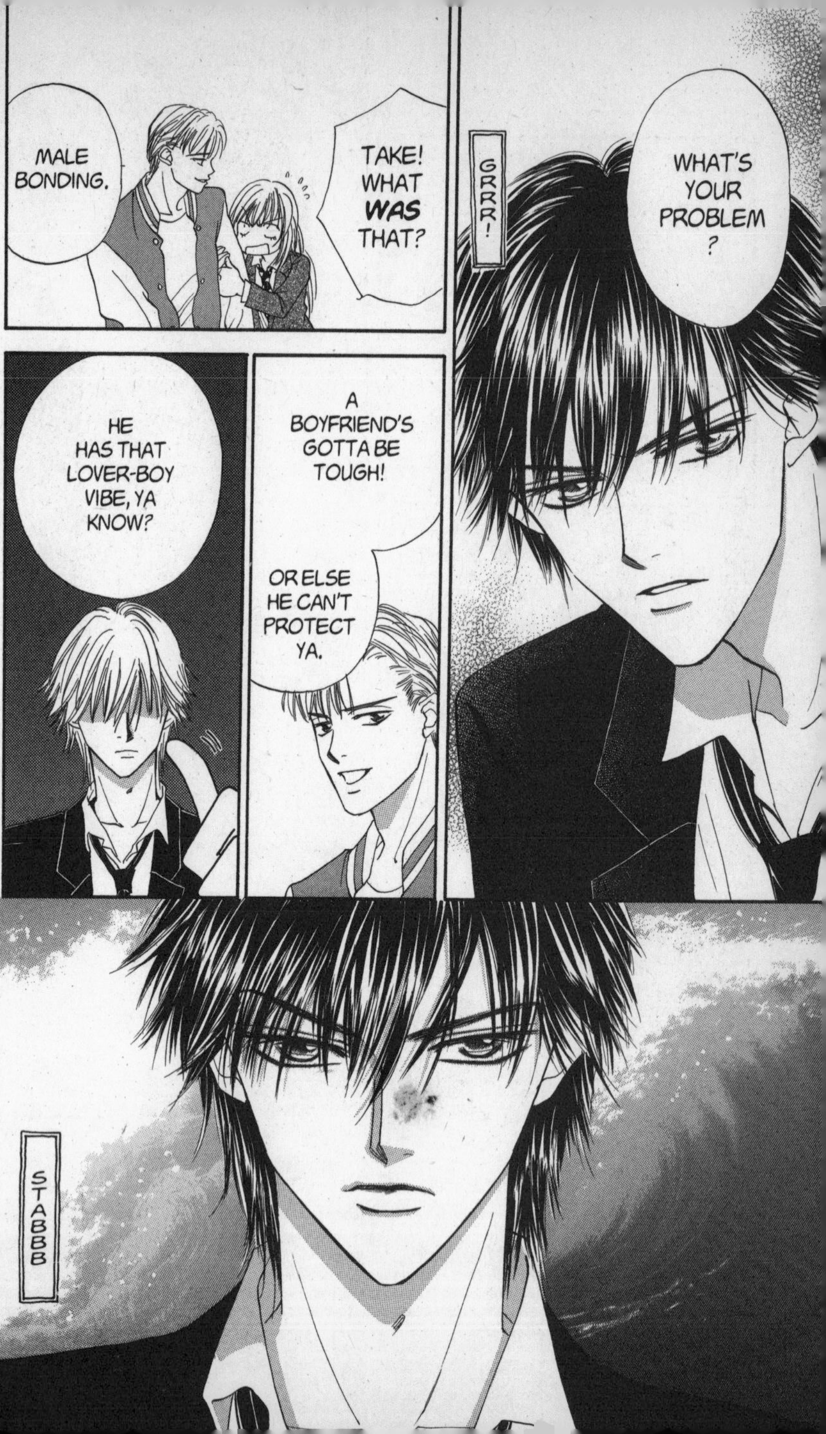
GRRR!
WHAT'S YOUR PROBLEM?
TAKE! WHAT **WAS** THAT?
MALE BONDING.
A BOYFRIEND'S GOTTA BE TOUGH!
OR ELSE HE CAN'T PROTECT YA.
HE HAS THAT LOVER-BOY VIBE, YA KNOW?
STABBB

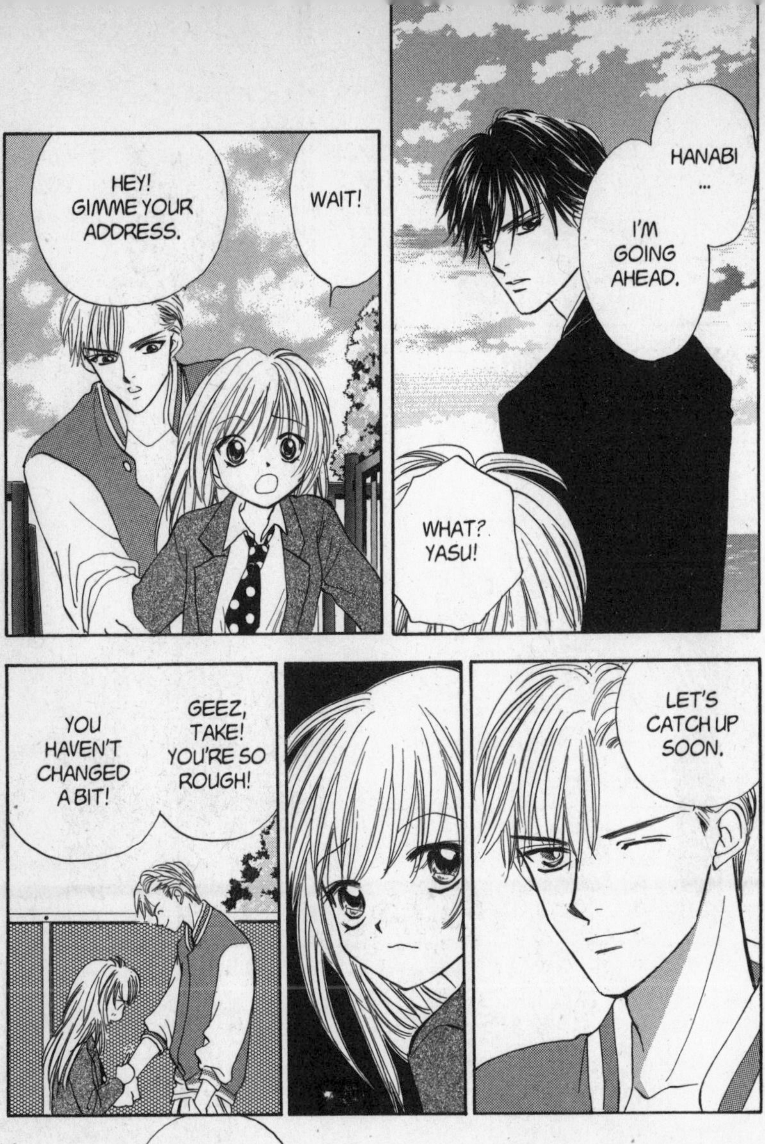
HANABI ... I'M GOING AHEAD.
WHAT? YASU!
WAIT!
HEY! GIMME YOUR ADDRESS.
LET'S CATCH UP SOON.
GEEZ, TAKE! YOU'RE SO ROUGH!
YOU HAVEN'T CHANGED A BIT!
YOU HAVE CHANGED.

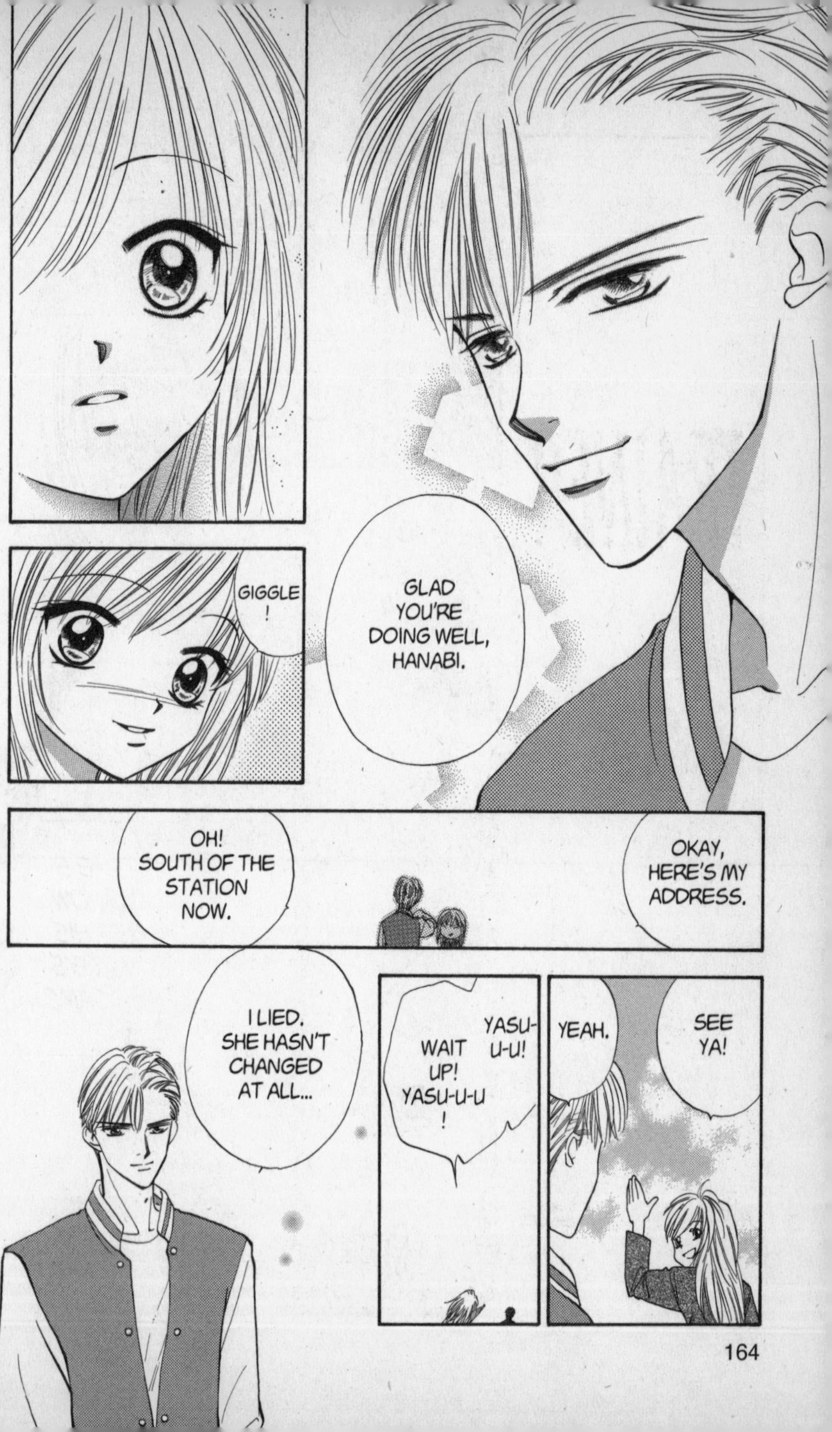
GLAD YOU'RE DOING WELL, HANABI.
GIGGLE !
OKAY, HERE'S MY ADDRESS.
OH! SOUTH OF THE STATION NOW.
SEE YA!
YEAH.
YASU-U-U!
WAIT UP! YASU-U-U !
I LIED. SHE HASN'T CHANGED AT ALL...

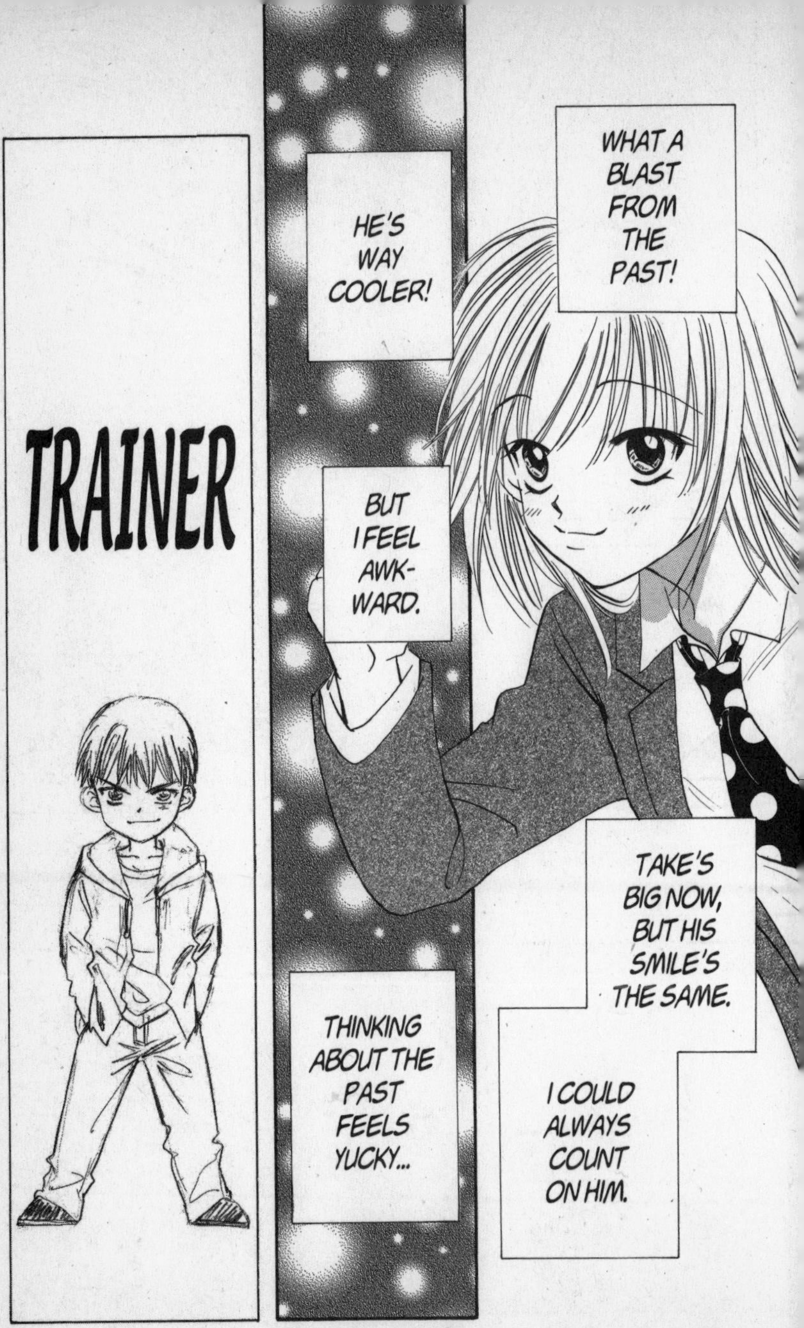
WHAT A BLAST FROM THE PAST!
HE'S WAY COOLER!
BUT I FEEL AWK-WARD.
TAKE'S BIG NOW, BUT HIS SMILE'S THE SAME.
I COULD ALWAYS COUNT ON HIM.
THINKING ABOUT THE PAST FEELS YUCKY...
TRAINER

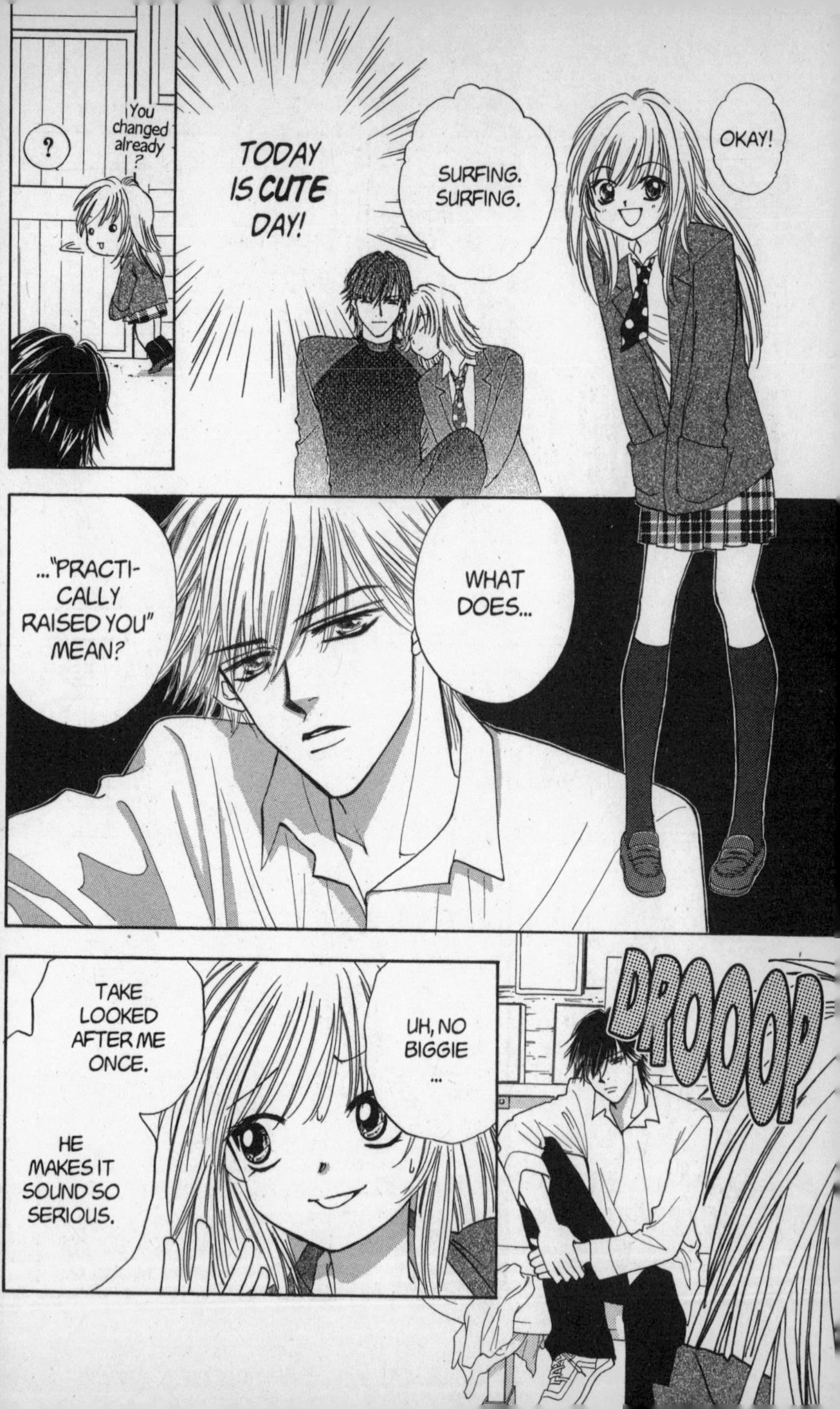
OKAY!
SURFING. SURFING.
TODAY IS CUTE DAY!
You changed already?
?
WHAT DOES...
..."PRACTICALLY RAISED YOU" MEAN?
DROOOP
UH, NO BIGGIE ...
TAKE LOOKED AFTER ME ONCE.
HE MAKES IT SOUND SO SERIOUS.

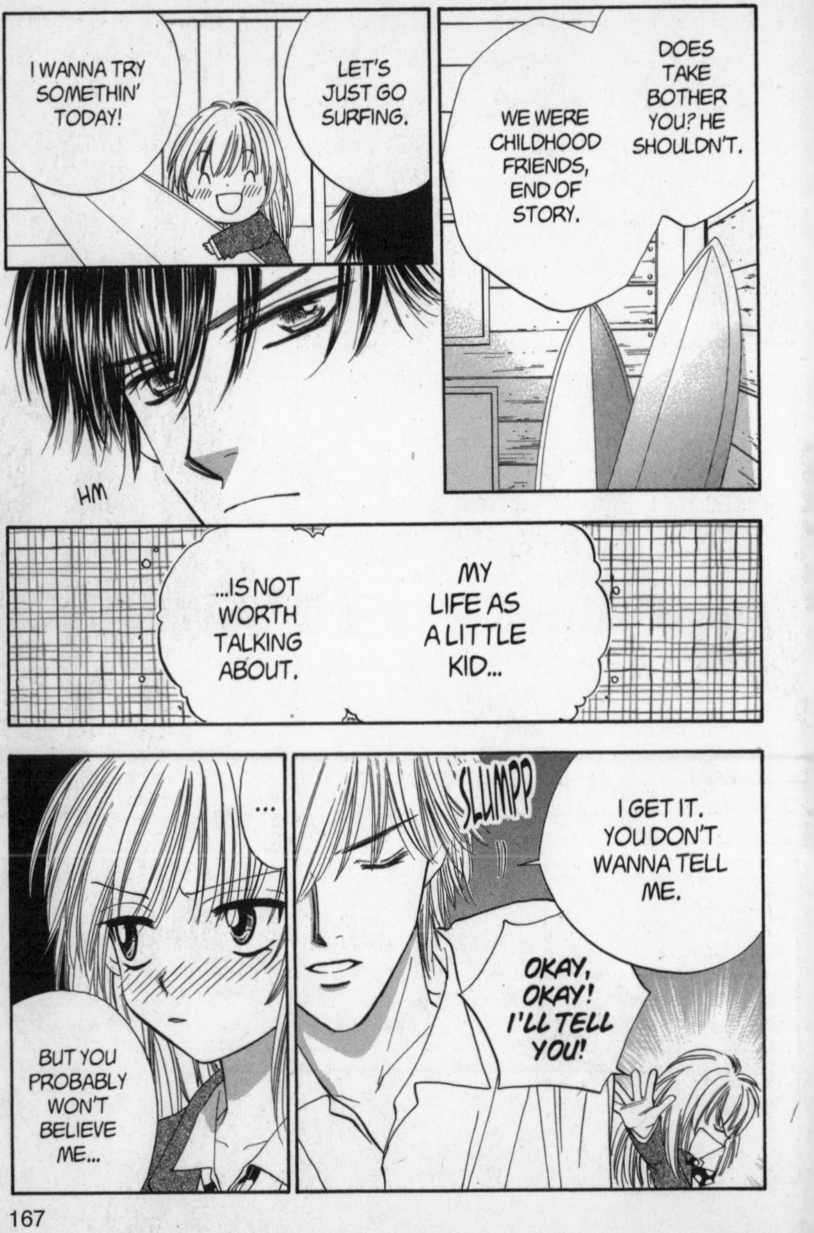
DOES TAKE BOTHER YOU? HE SHOULDN'T.
WE WERE CHILDHOOD FRIENDS, END OF STORY.
LET'S JUST GO SURFING.
I WANNA TRY SOMETHIN' TODAY!
HM
MY LIFE AS A LITTLE KID...
...IS NOT WORTH TALKING ABOUT.
SLUMPP
I GET IT. YOU DON'T WANNA TELL ME.
OKAY, OKAY! I'LL TELL YOU!
...
BUT YOU PROBABLY WON'T BELIEVE ME...

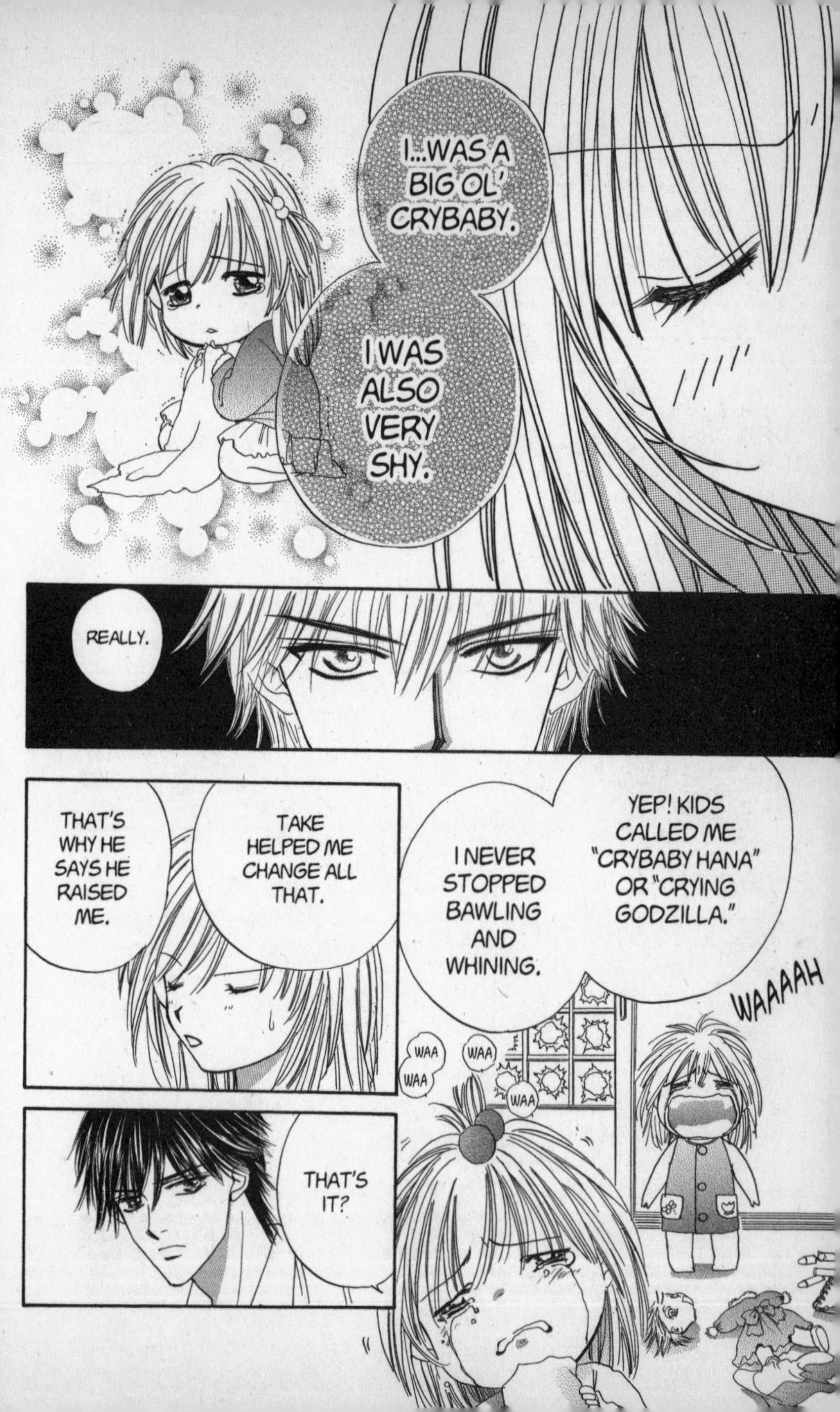
I...WAS A BIG OL' CRYBABY.
I WAS ALSO VERY SHY.
REALLY.
YEP! KIDS CALLED ME "CRYBABY HANA" OR "CRYING GODZILLA."
I NEVER STOPPED BAWLING AND WHINING.
WAAAAH
WAA
WAA
WAA
WAA
TAKE HELPED ME CHANGE ALL THAT.
THAT'S WHY HE SAYS HE RAISED ME.
THAT'S IT?

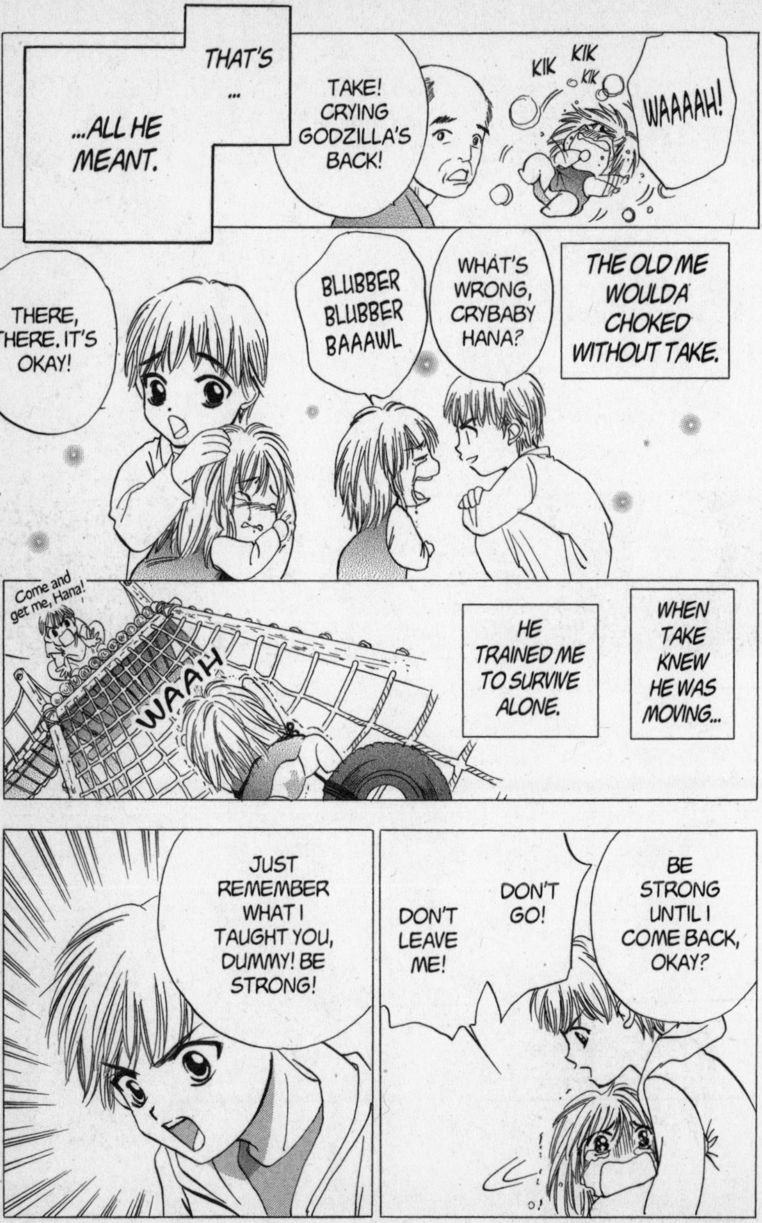
WAAAAH!
KIK KIK KIK
TAKE! CRYING GODZILLA'S BACK!
THAT'S ...
...ALL HE MEANT.
THE OLD ME WOULDA CHOKED WITHOUT TAKE.
WHAT'S WRONG, CRYBABY HANA?
BLUBBER BLUBBER BAAAWL
THERE, THERE. IT'S OKAY!
WHEN TAKE KNEW HE WAS MOVING...
HE TRAINED ME TO SURVIVE ALONE.
WAAH
Come and get me, Hana!
BE STRONG UNTIL I COME BACK, OKAY?
DON'T GO!
DON'T LEAVE ME!
JUST REMEMBER WHAT I TAUGHT YOU, DUMMY! BE STRONG!

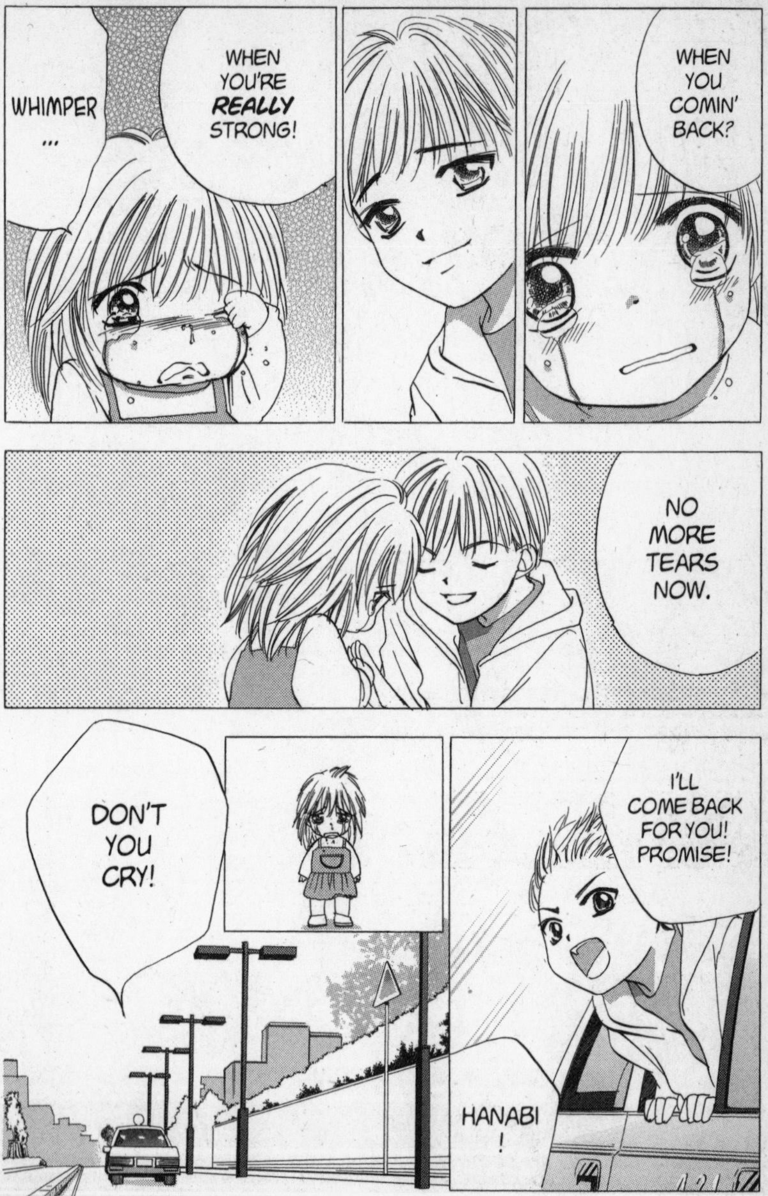
WHEN YOU COMIN' BACK?
WHEN YOU'RE REALLY STRONG!
WHIMPER...
NO MORE TEARS NOW.
I'LL COME BACK FOR YOU! PROMISE!
HANABI!
DON'T YOU CRY!

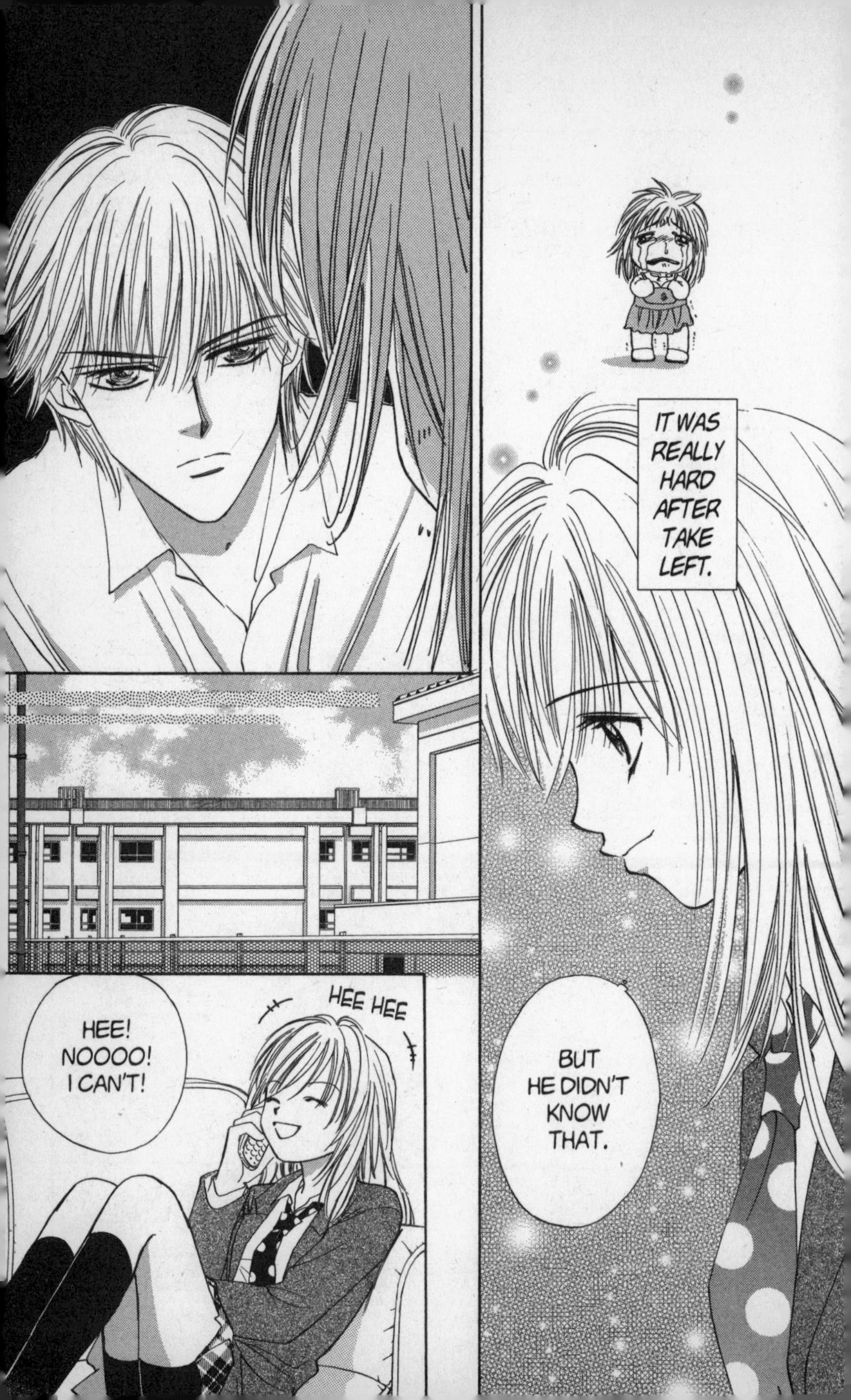
IT WAS REALLY HARD AFTER TAKE LEFT.
BUT HE DIDN'T KNOW THAT.
HEE HEE
HEE! NOOOO! I CAN'T!

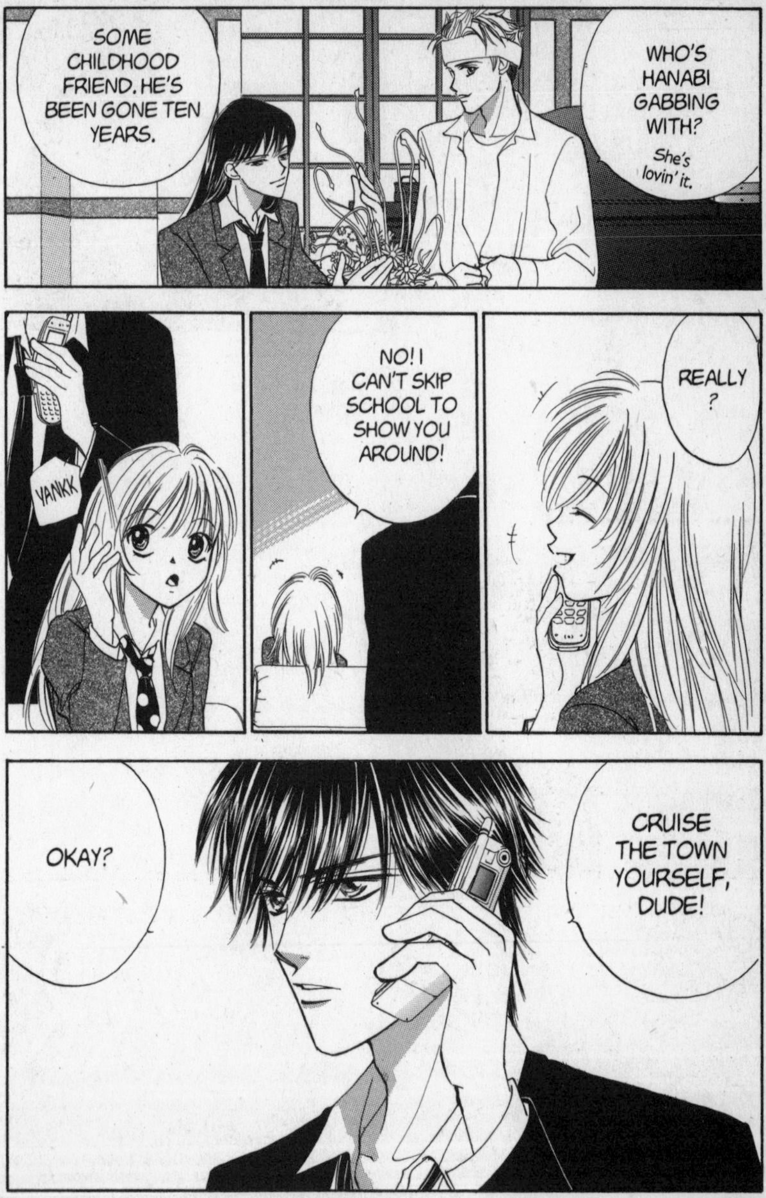
WHO'S HANABI GABBING WITH?
She's lovin' it.
SOME CHILDHOOD FRIEND. HE'S BEEN GONE TEN YEARS.
REALLY ?
NO! I CAN'T SKIP SCHOOL TO SHOW YOU AROUND!
YANKK
CRUISE THE TOWN YOURSELF, DUDE!
OKAY?

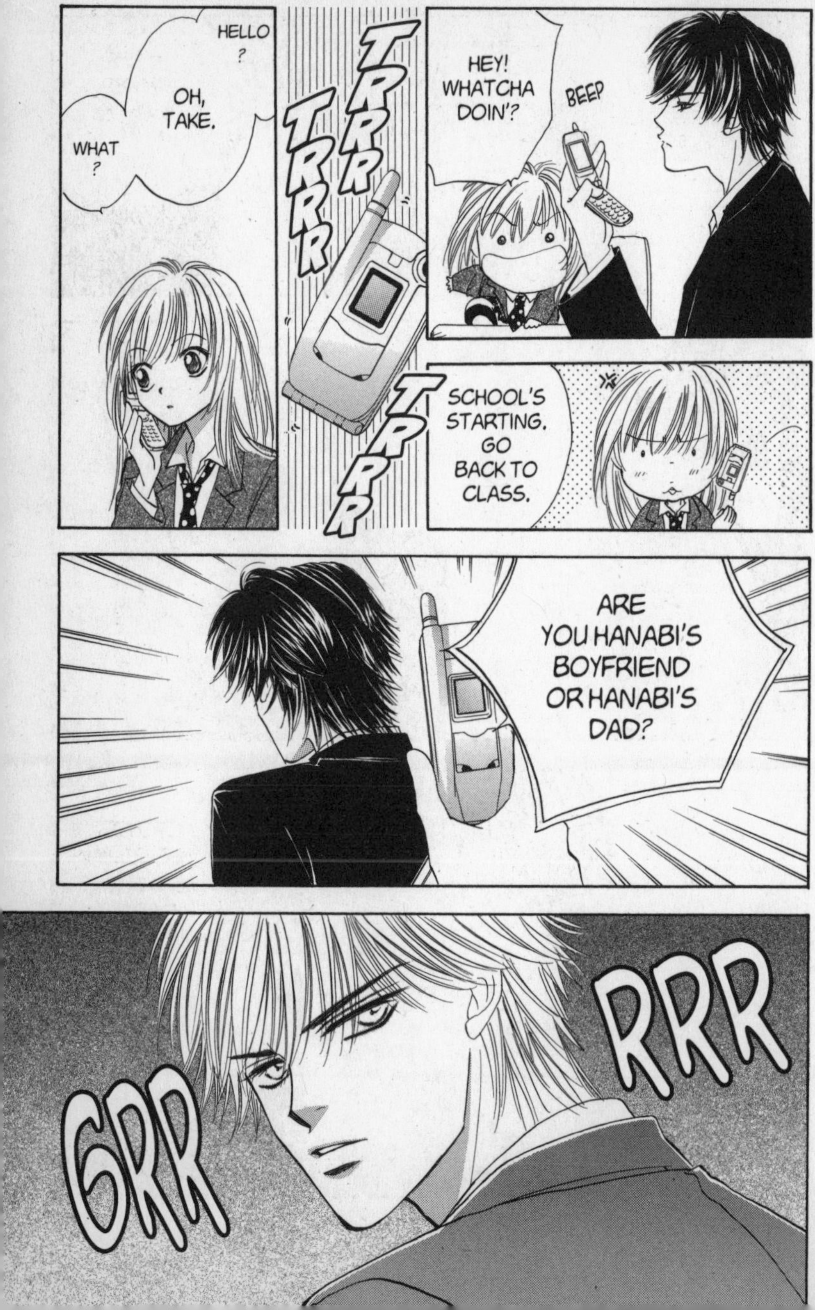
HEY! WHATCHA DOIN'?
BEEP
SCHOOL'S STARTING. GO BACK TO CLASS.
TRRRR
TRRRR
TRRRR
HELLO?
OH, TAKE.
WHAT?
ARE YOU HANABI'S BOYFRIEND OR HANABI'S DAD?
RRR
GRR

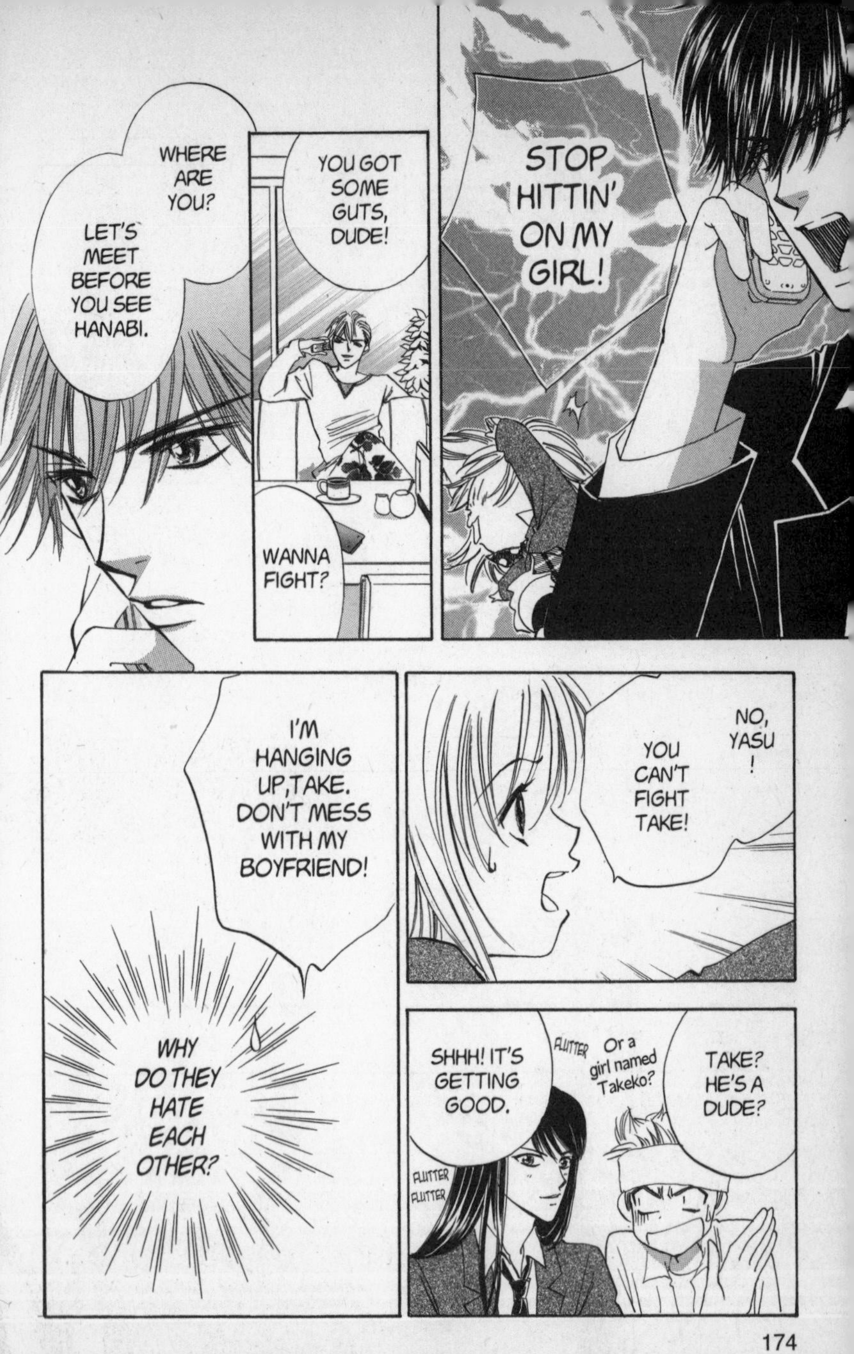
STOP HITTIN' ON MY GIRL!
YOU GOT SOME GUTS, DUDE!
WANNA FIGHT?
WHERE ARE YOU?
LET'S MEET BEFORE YOU SEE HANABI.
NO, YASU!
YOU CAN'T FIGHT TAKE!
TAKE? HE'S A DUDE?
Or a girl named Takeko?
FLUTTER
SHHH! IT'S GETTING GOOD.
FLUTTER FLUTTER
I'M HANGING UP,TAKE. DON'T MESS WITH MY BOYFRIEND!
WHY DO THEY HATE EACH OTHER?

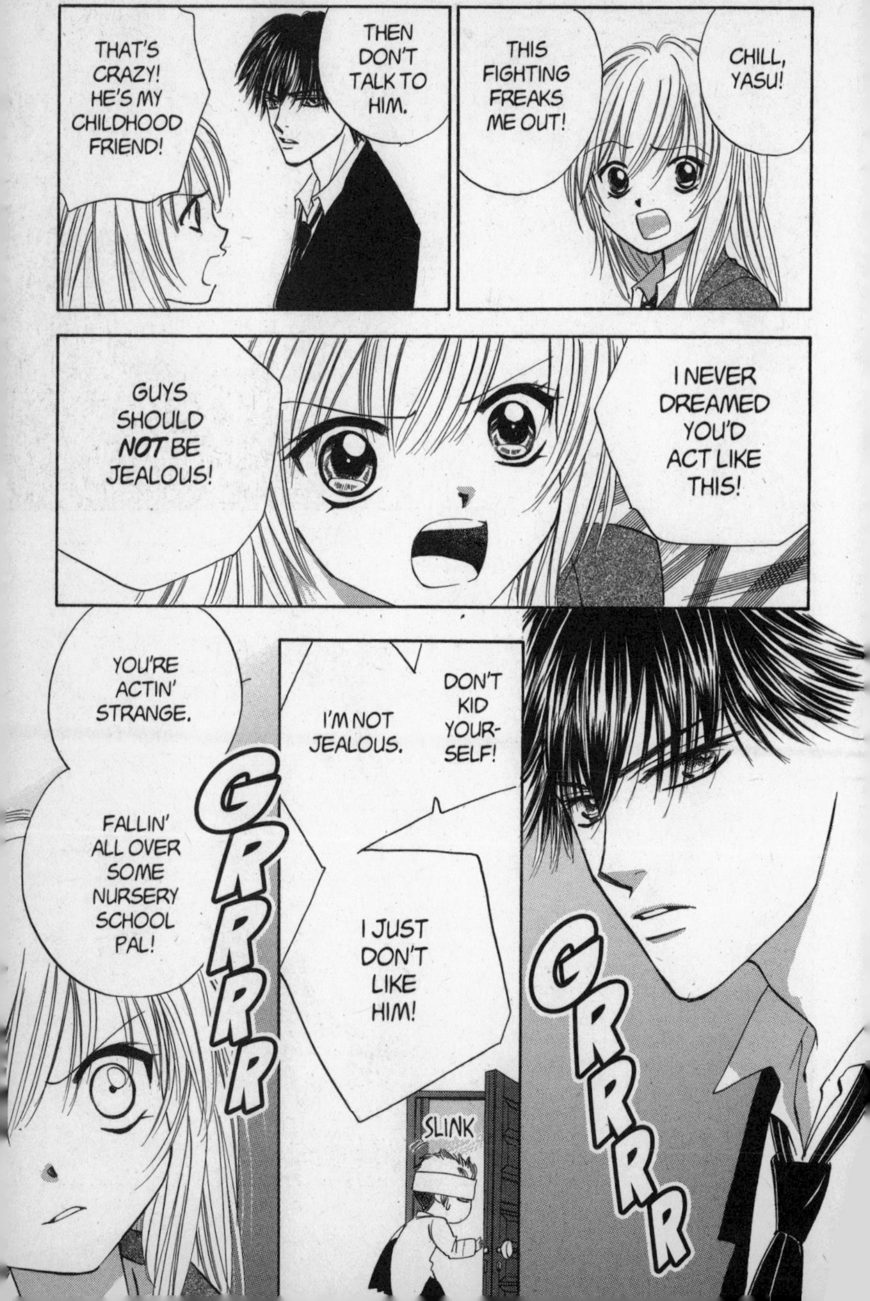
CHILL, YASU!
THIS FIGHTING FREAKS ME OUT!
THEN DON'T TALK TO HIM.
THAT'S CRAZY! HE'S MY CHILDHOOD FRIEND!
I NEVER DREAMED YOU'D ACT LIKE THIS!
GUYS SHOULD **NOT** BE JEALOUS!
GRRRR
DON'T KID YOUR-SELF!
I'M NOT JEALOUS.
I JUST DON'T LIKE HIM!
SLINK
YOU'RE ACTIN' STRANGE.
FALLIN' ALL OVER SOME NURSERY SCHOOL PAL!
GRRRR

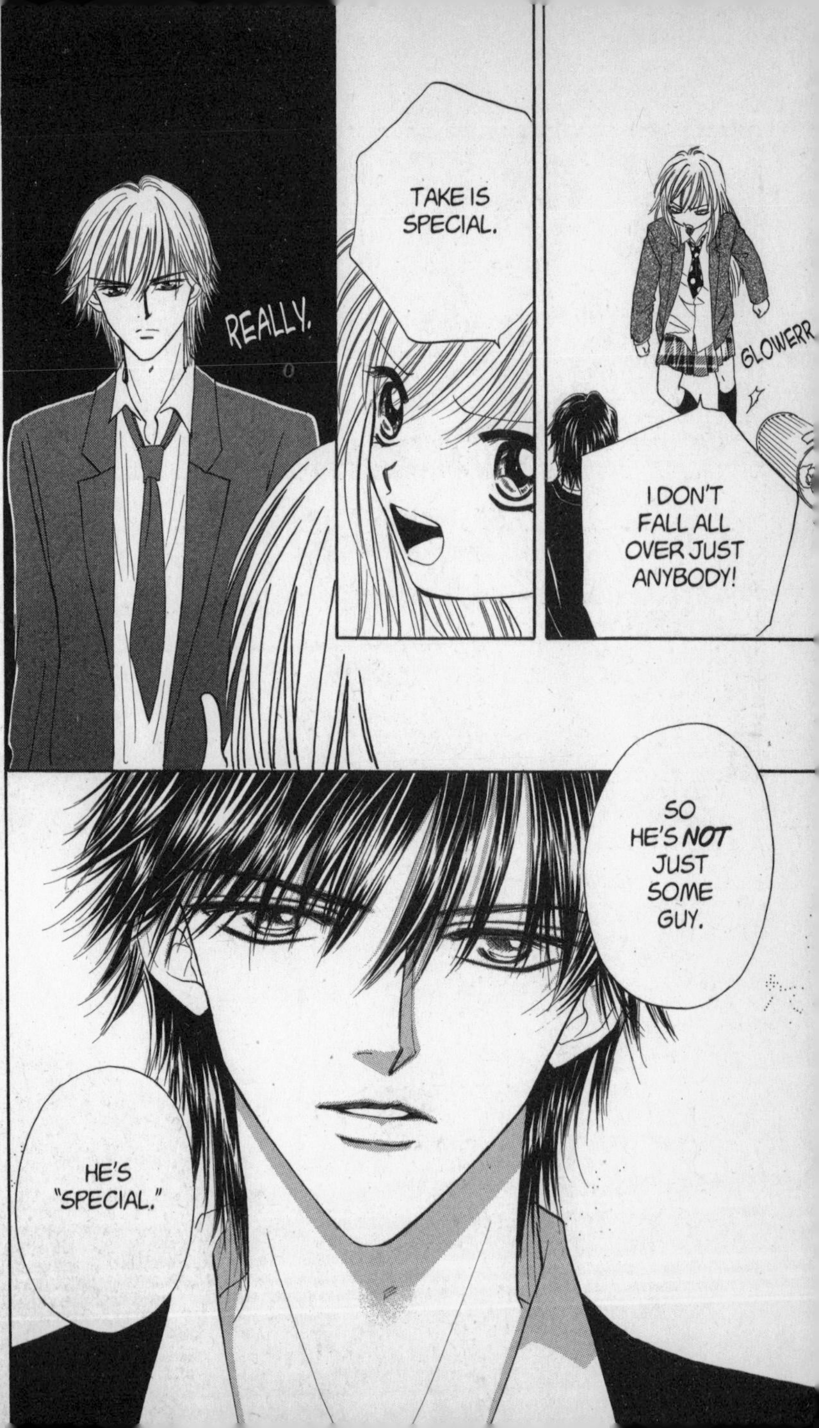
GLOWERR
I DON'T FALL ALL OVER JUST ANYBODY!
TAKE IS SPECIAL.
REALLY.
SO HE'S **NOT** JUST SOME GUY.
HE'S "SPECIAL."

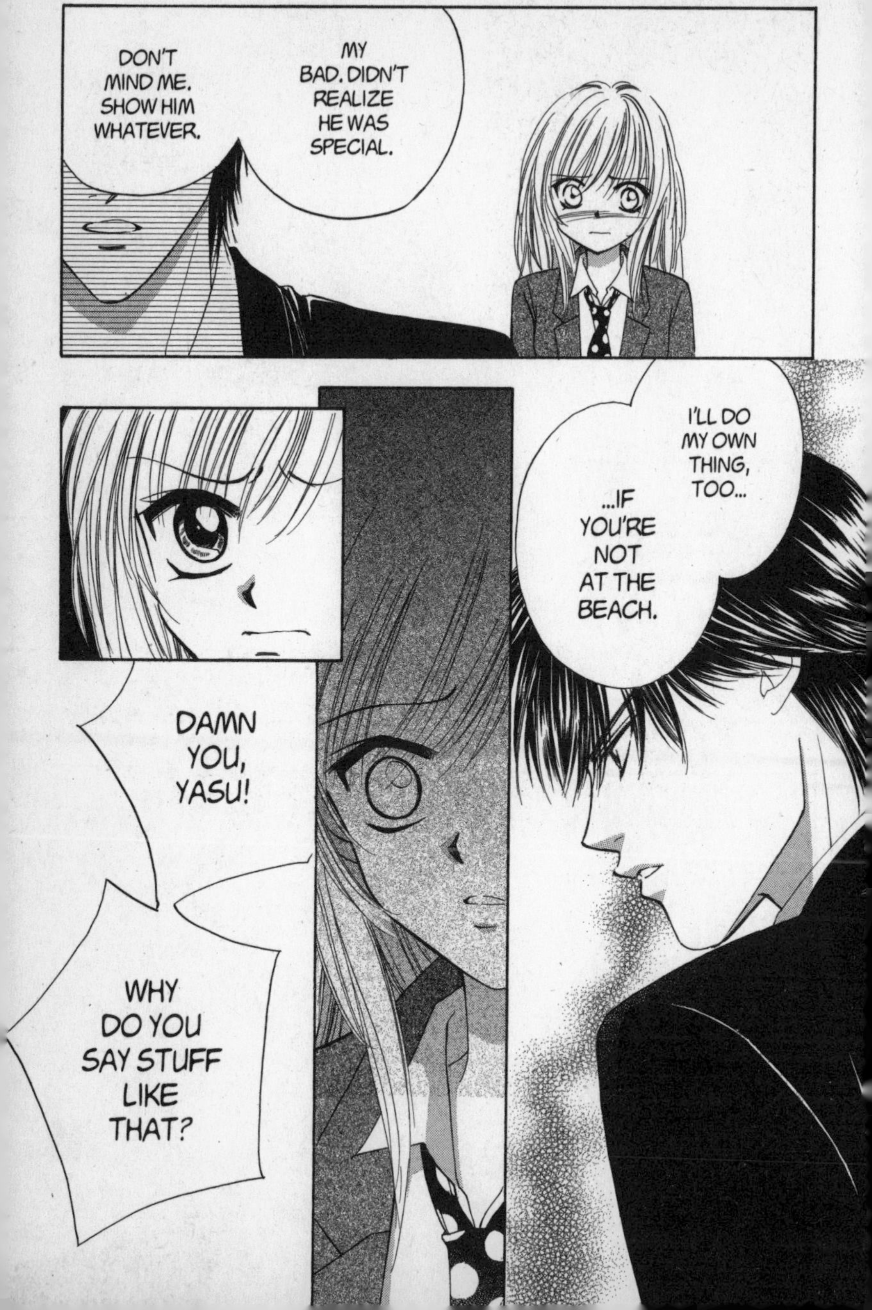
MY BAD. DIDN'T REALIZE HE WAS SPECIAL.
DON'T MIND ME. SHOW HIM WHATEVER.
I'LL DO MY OWN THING, TOO...
...IF YOU'RE NOT AT THE BEACH.
DAMN YOU, YASU!
WHY DO YOU SAY STUFF LIKE THAT?

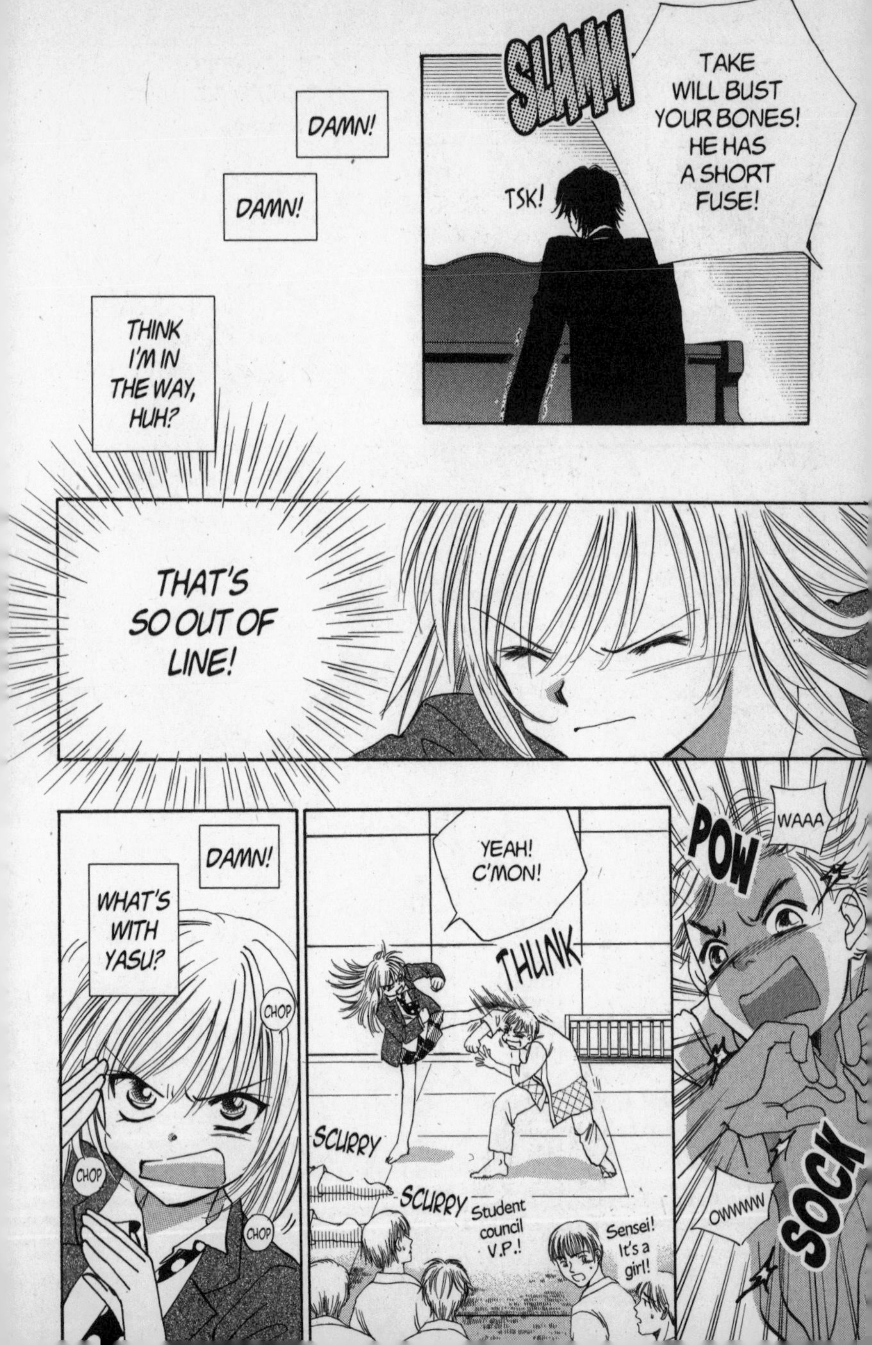
SLAMM
TAKE WILL BUST YOUR BONES! HE HAS A SHORT FUSE!
TSK!
DAMN!
DAMN!
THINK I'M IN THE WAY, HUH?
THAT'S SO OUT OF LINE!
POW
WAAA
SOCK
OWWWW
YEAH! C'MON!
THUNK
SCURRY
SCURRY
Sensei! It's a girl!
Student council V.P.!
DAMN!
WHAT'S WITH YASU?
CHOP
CHOP
CHOP

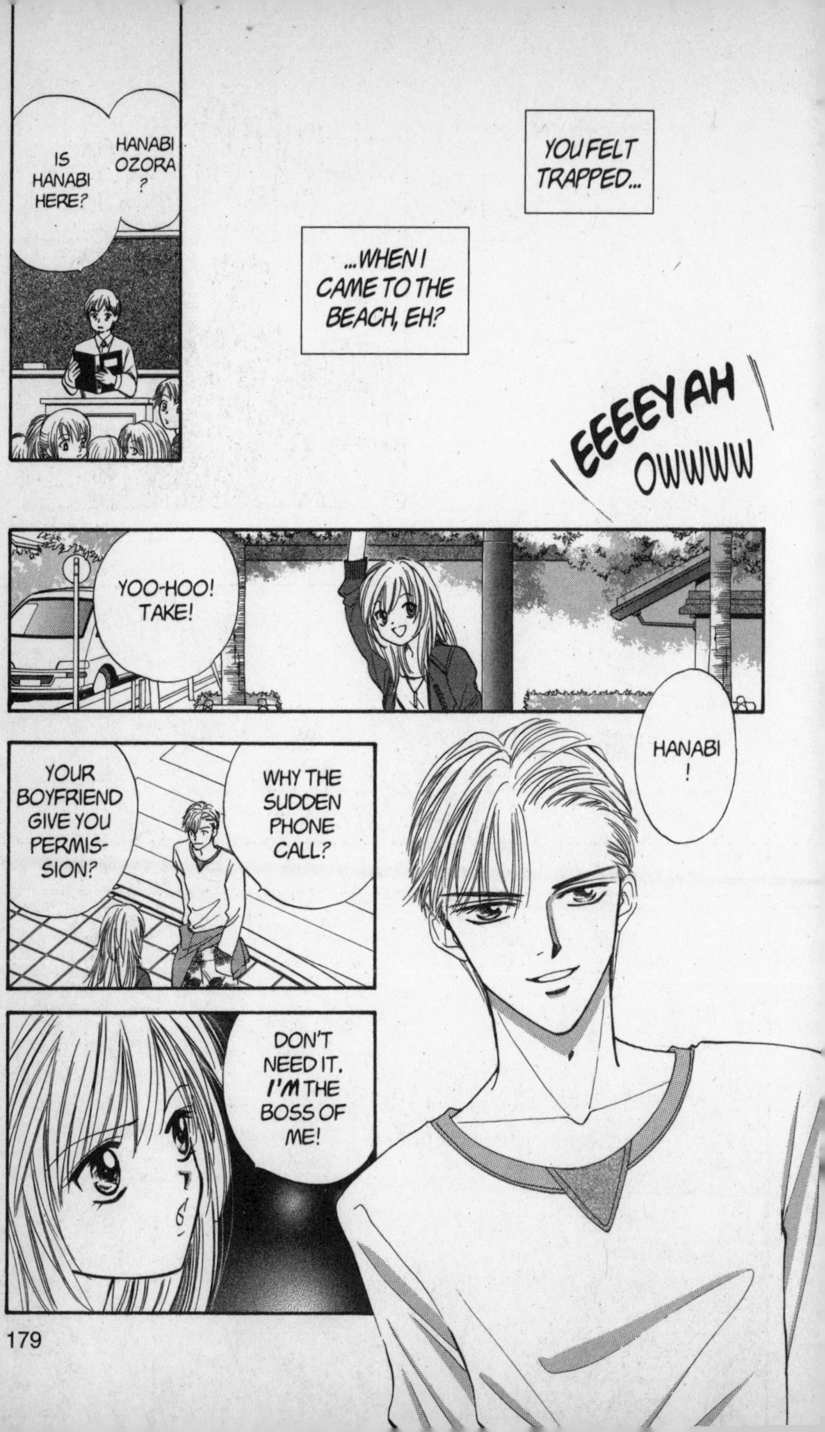
YOU FELT TRAPPED...
...WHEN I CAME TO THE BEACH, EH?
HANABI OZORA?
IS HANABI HERE?
EEEEYAH OWWWW
YOO-HOO! TAKE!
HANABI!
WHY THE SUDDEN PHONE CALL?
YOUR BOYFRIEND GIVE YOU PERMISSION?
DON'T NEED IT. *I'M* THE BOSS OF ME!

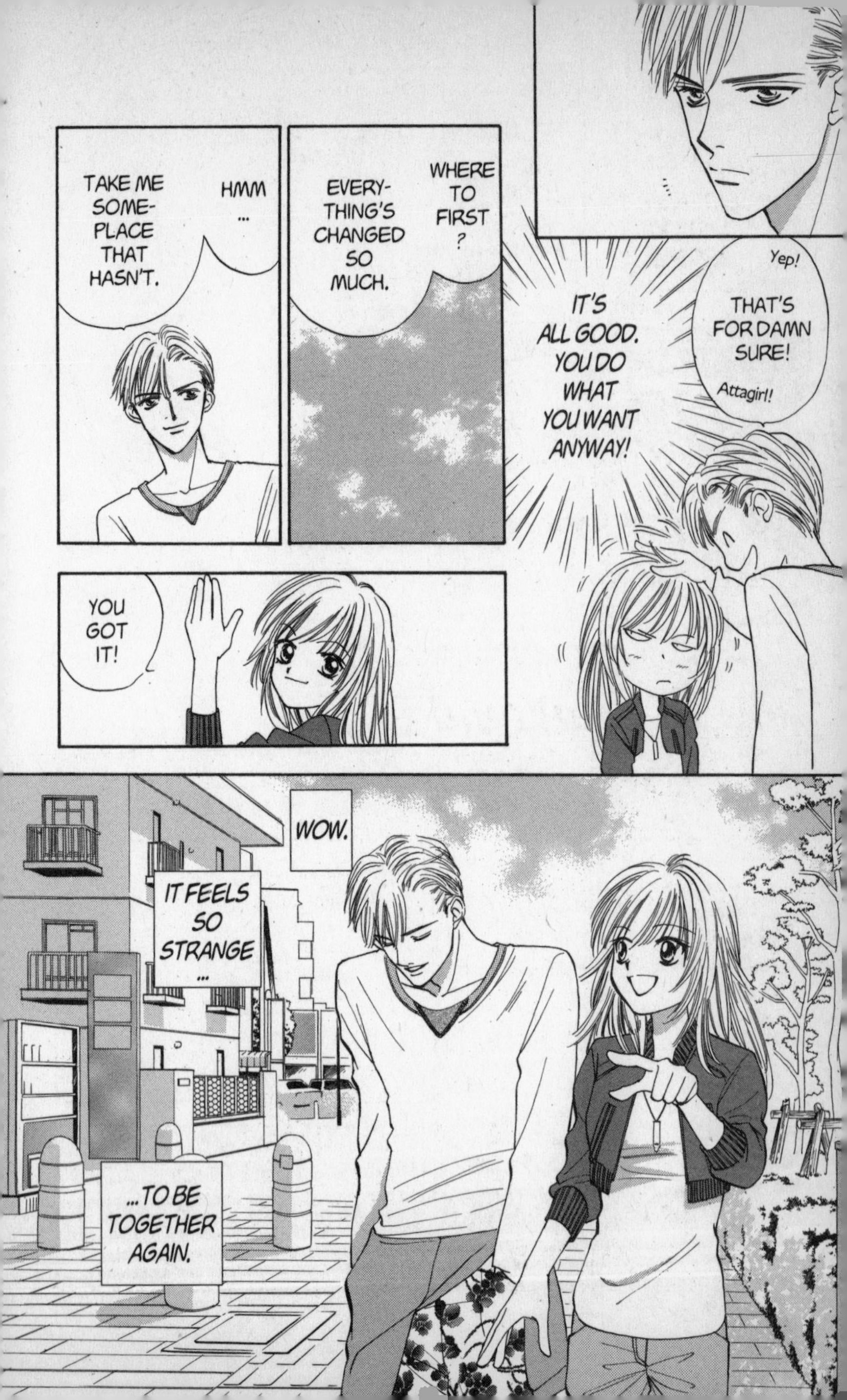
Yep!
THAT'S FOR DAMN SURE!
Attagirl!
IT'S ALL GOOD. YOU DO WHAT YOU WANT ANYWAY!
WHERE TO FIRST?
EVERY-THING'S CHANGED SO MUCH.
HMM...
TAKE ME SOME-PLACE THAT HASN'T.
YOU GOT IT!
WOW.
IT FEELS SO STRANGE...
...TO BE TOGETHER AGAIN.

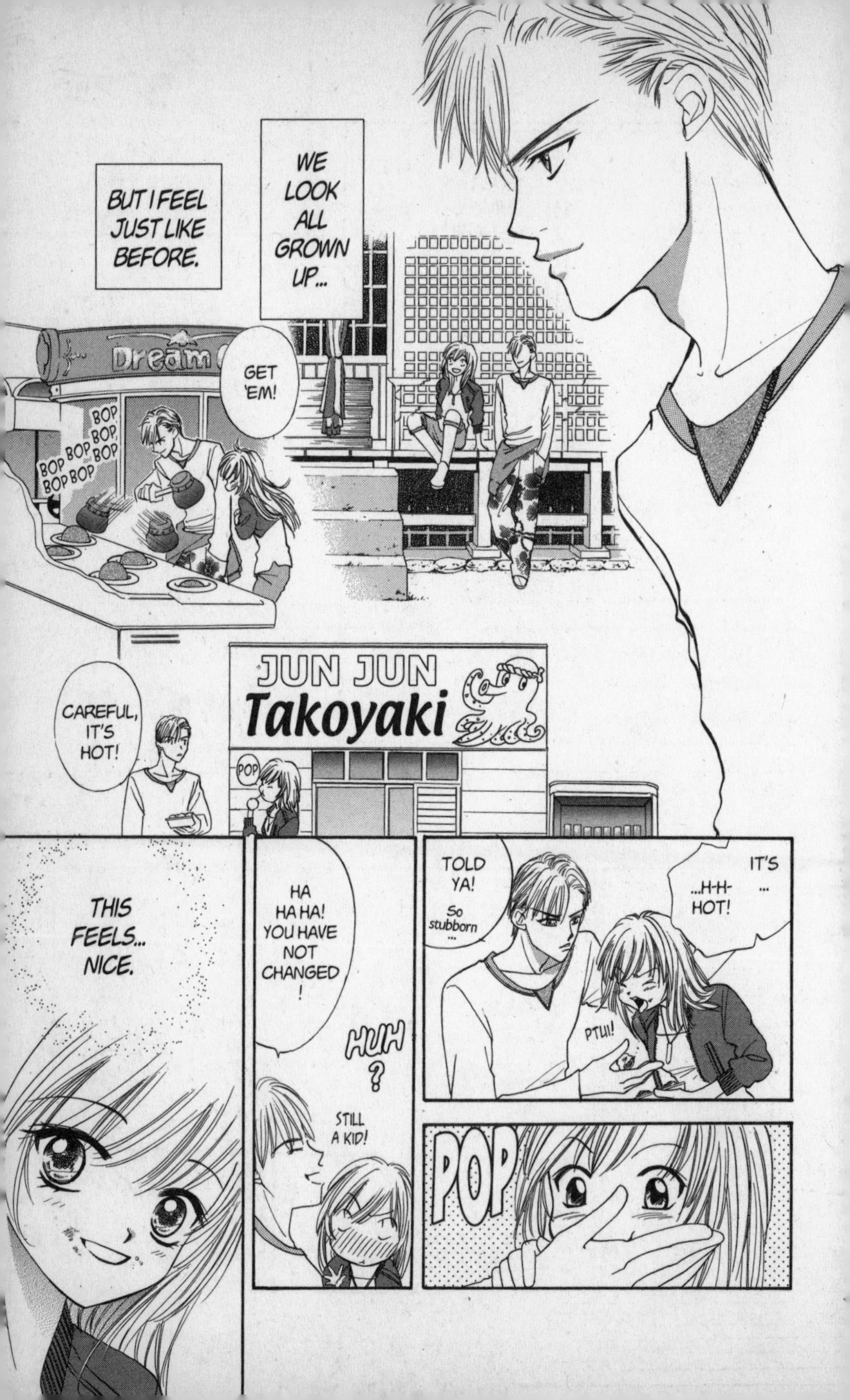
WE LOOK ALL GROWN UP...
BUT I FEEL JUST LIKE BEFORE.
GET 'EM!
BOP BOP, BOP BOP and BOP BOP BOP
JUN JUN Takoyaki
CAREFUL, IT'S HOT!
POP
IT'S ... ...H-H-HOT!
TOLD YA!
So stubborn ...
PTUI!
POP
HA HA HA! YOU HAVE NOT CHANGED!
HUH?
STILL A KID!
THIS FEELS... NICE.

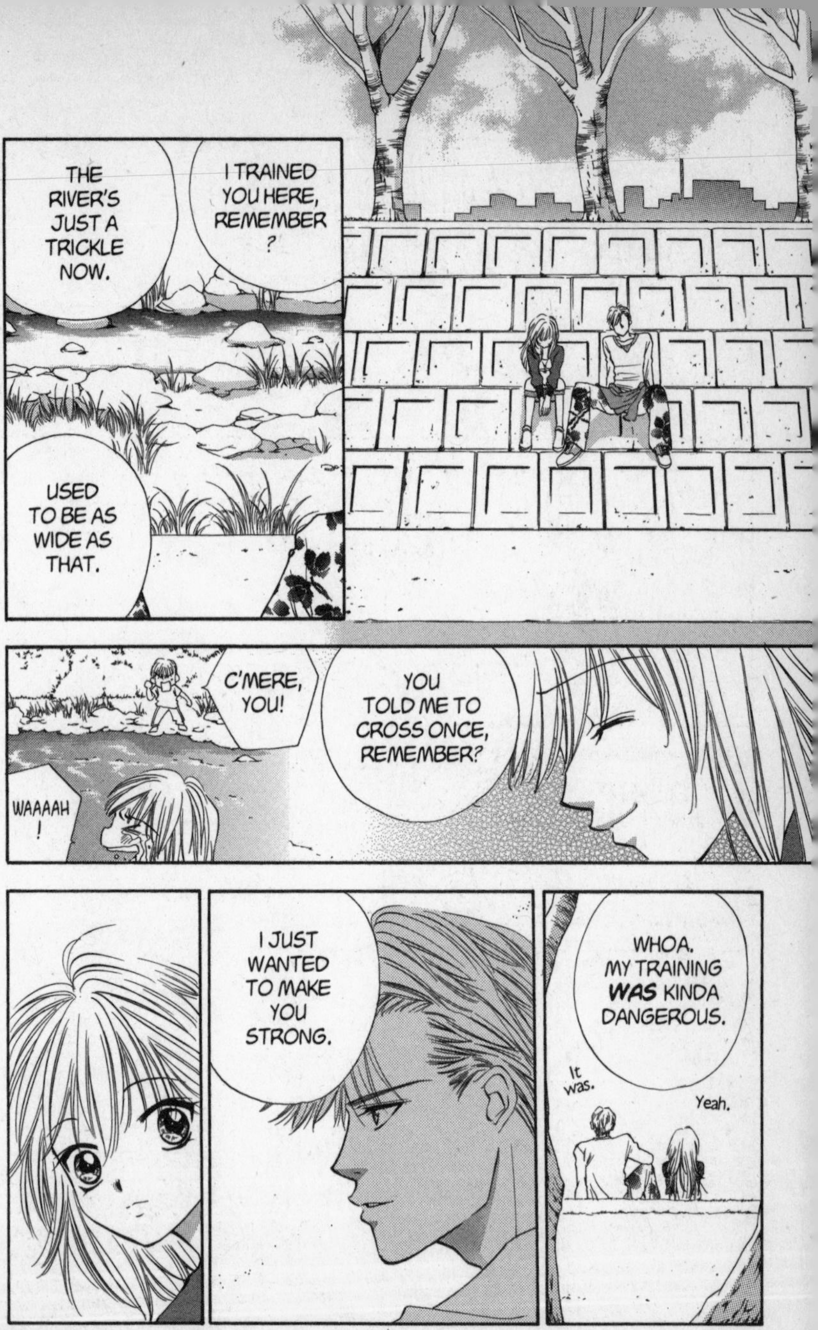
I TRAINED YOU HERE, REMEMBER?
THE RIVER'S JUST A TRICKLE NOW.
USED TO BE AS WIDE AS THAT.
YOU TOLD ME TO CROSS ONCE, REMEMBER?
C'MERE, YOU!
WAAAAH!
WHOA. MY TRAINING **WAS** KINDA DANGEROUS.
It was.
Yeah.
I JUST WANTED TO MAKE YOU STRONG.

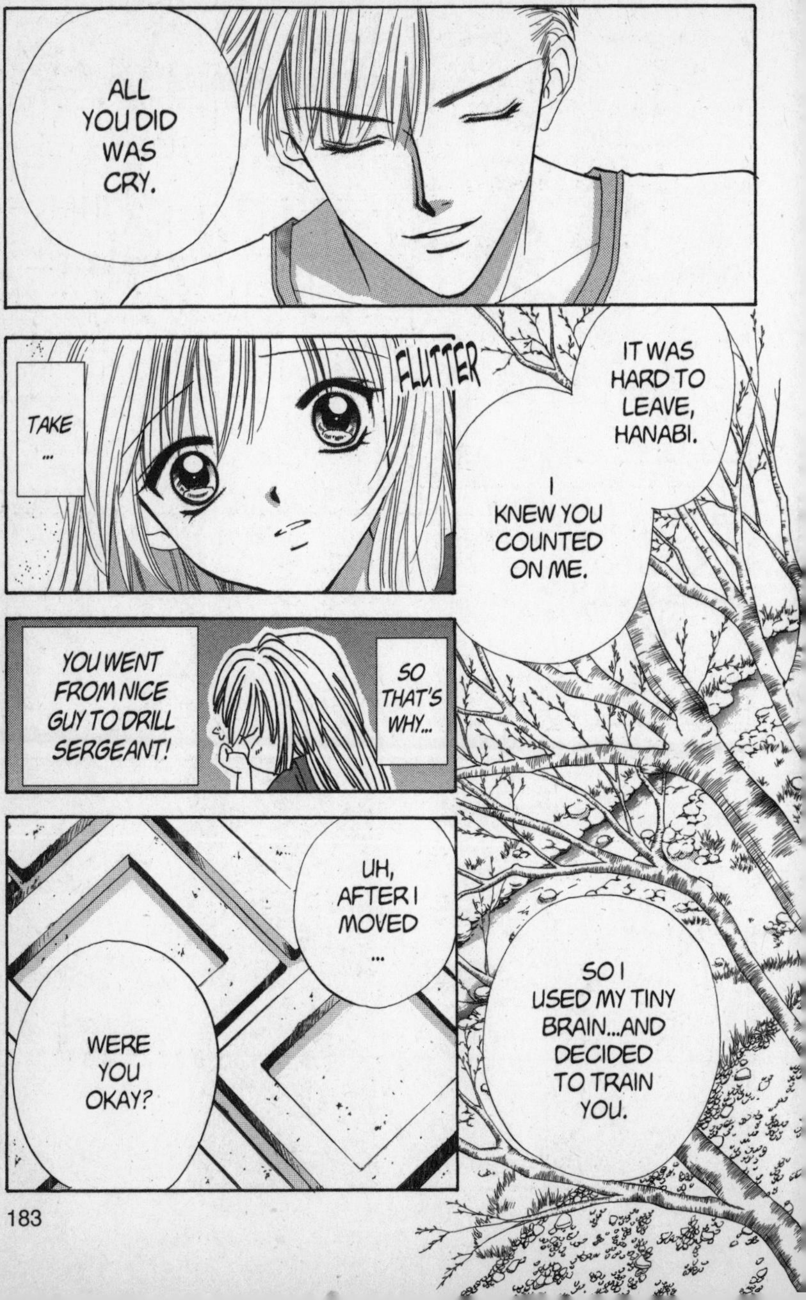
ALL YOU DID WAS CRY.
IT WAS HARD TO LEAVE, HANABI.
I KNEW YOU COUNTED ON ME.
SO I USED MY TINY BRAIN...AND DECIDED TO TRAIN YOU.
FLUTTER
TAKE ...
SO THAT'S WHY...
YOU WENT FROM NICE GUY TO DRILL SERGEANT!
UH, AFTER I MOVED ...
WERE YOU OKAY?

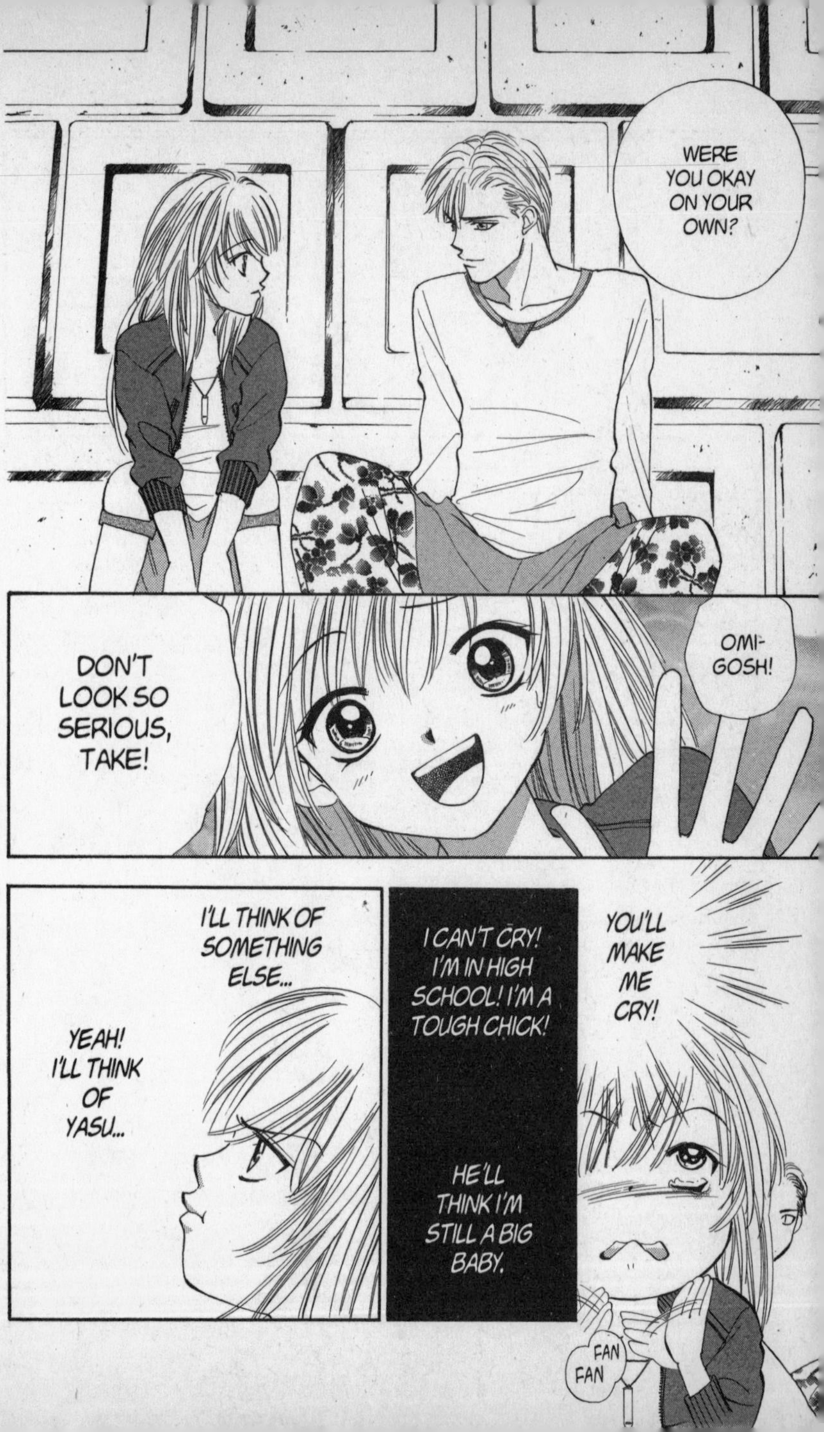
WERE YOU OKAY ON YOUR OWN?
OMI-GOSH!
DON'T LOOK SO SERIOUS, TAKE!
YOU'LL MAKE ME CRY!
FAN FAN
I CAN'T CRY! I'M IN HIGH SCHOOL! I'M A TOUGH CHICK!
HE'LL THINK I'M STILL A BIG BABY.
I'LL THINK OF SOMETHING ELSE...
YEAH! I'LL THINK OF YASU...

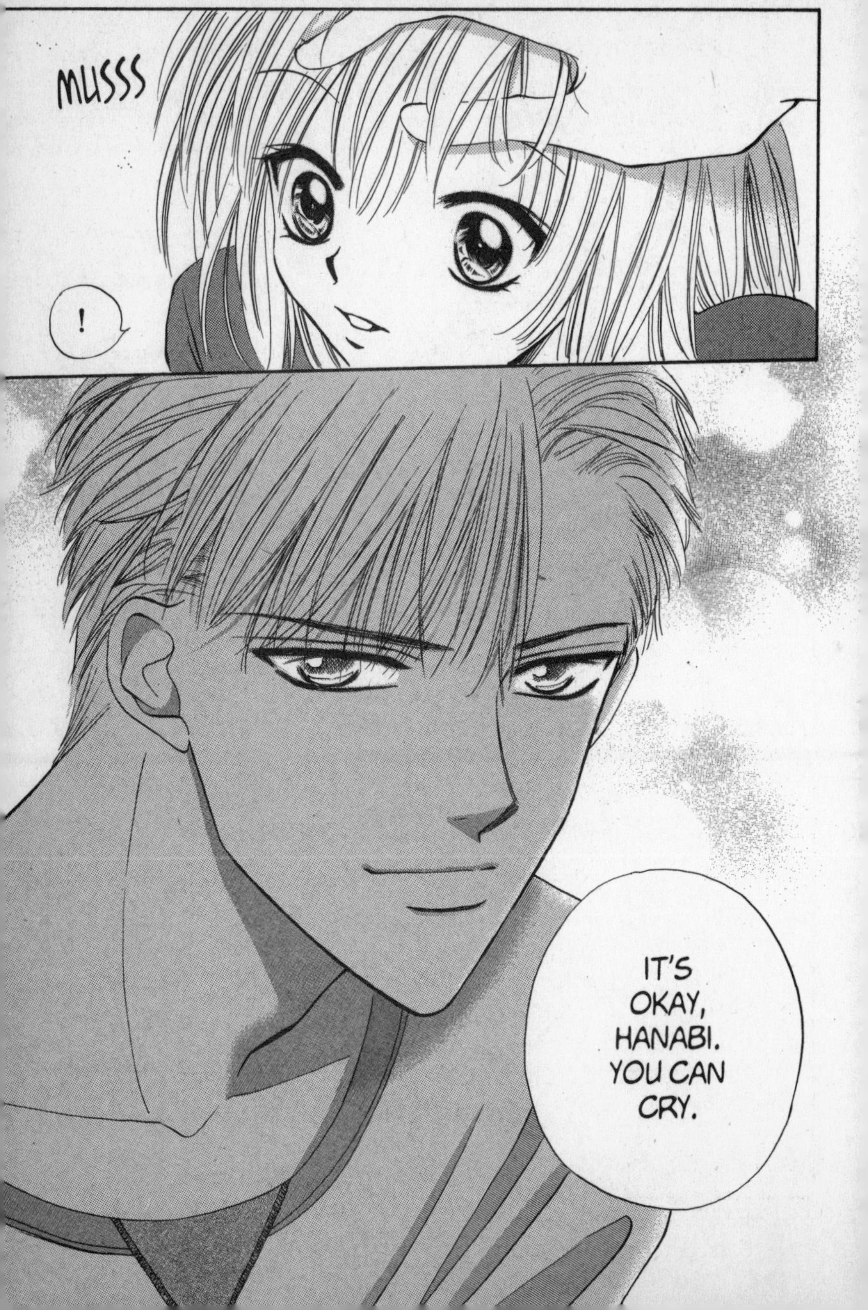
MUSSS
!
IT'S OKAY, HANABI. YOU CAN CRY.

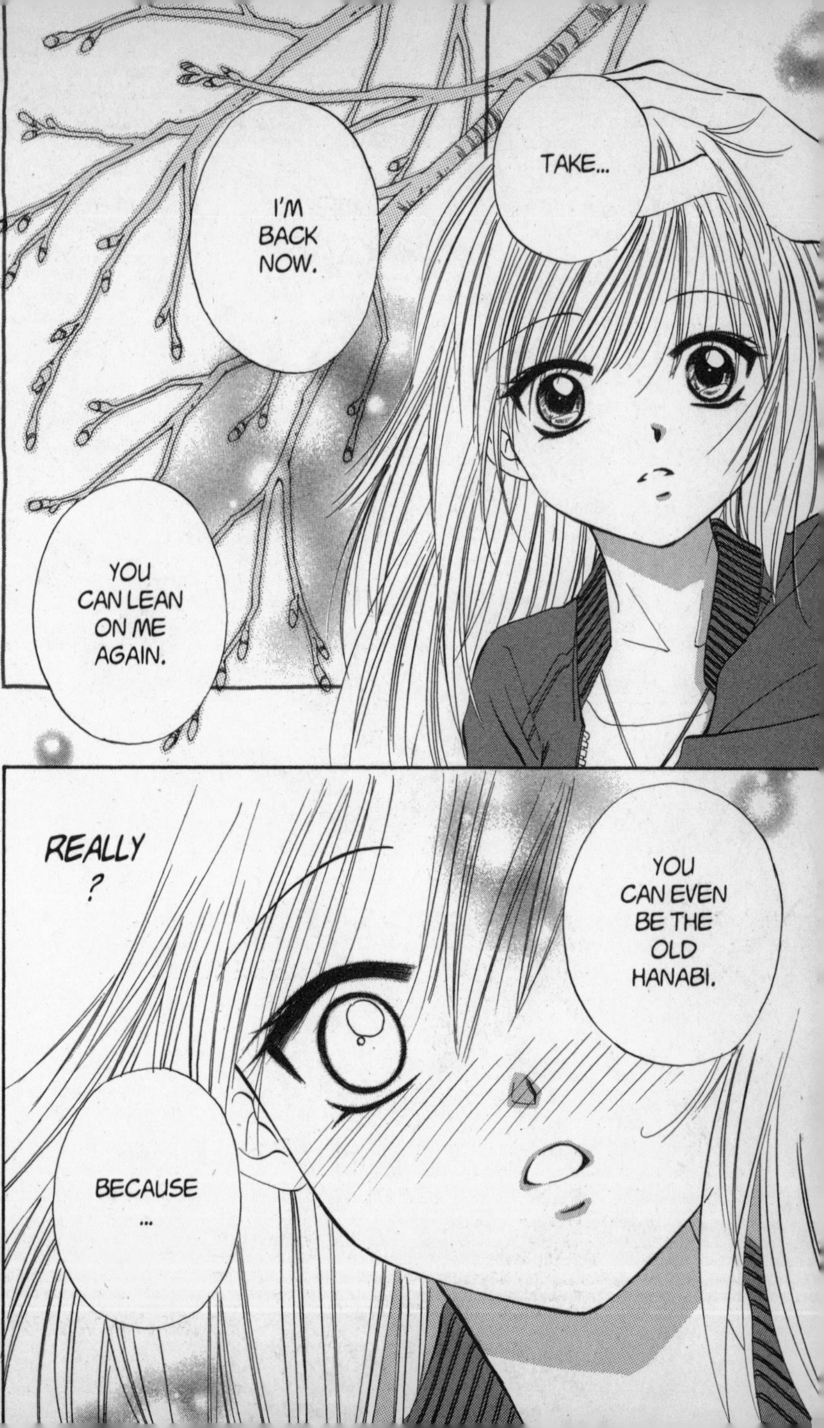
TAKE...
I'M BACK NOW.
YOU CAN LEAN ON ME AGAIN.
YOU CAN EVEN BE THE OLD HANABI.
REALLY ?
BECAUSE ...

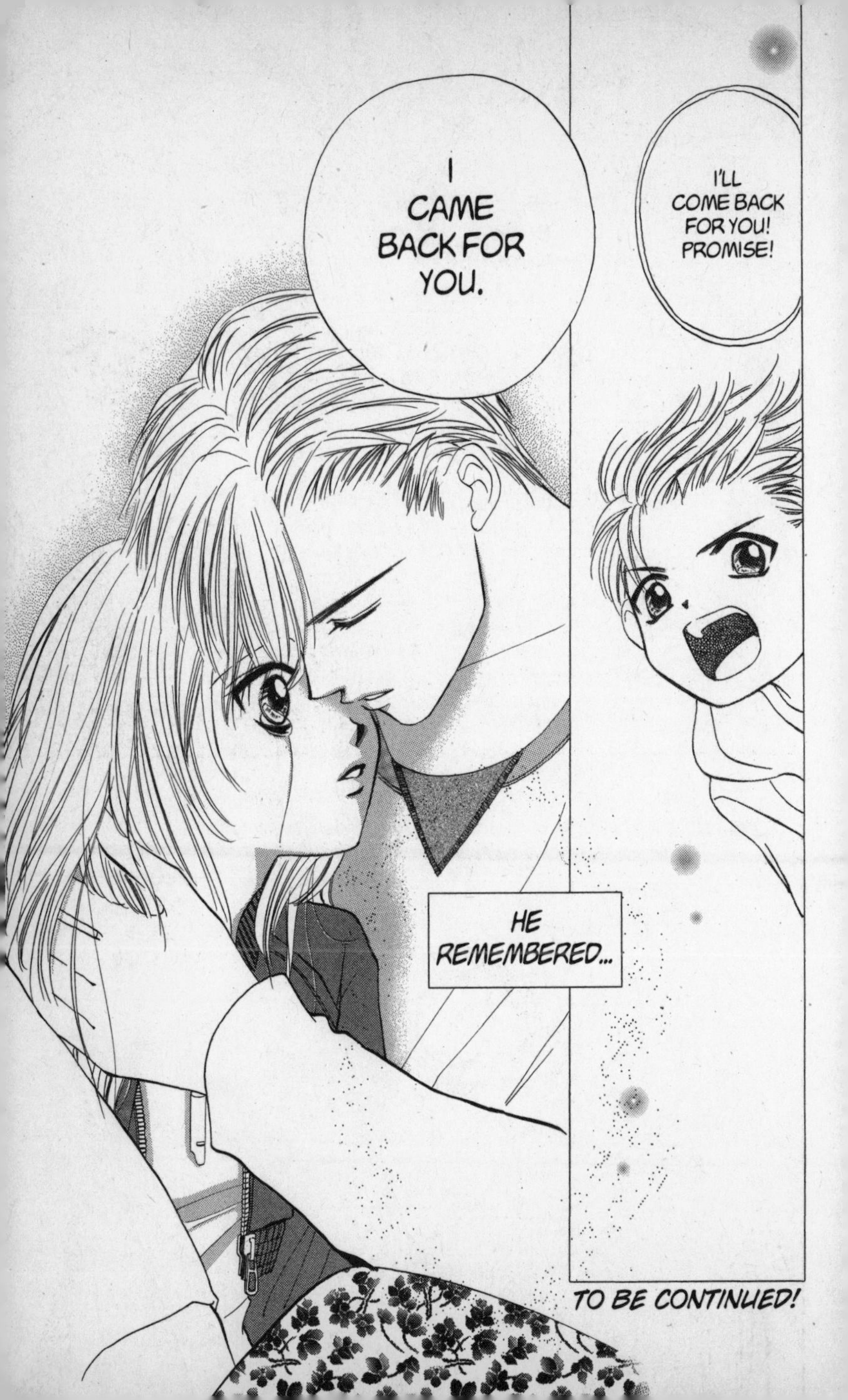
I'LL COME BACK FOR YOU! PROMISE!
I CAME BACK FOR YOU.
HE REMEMBERED...
TO BE CONTINUED!

HAPPY HUSTLE HIGH
Vol. 3

Story and Art by Rie Takada

English Adaptation/Janet Gilbert
Translation/June Honma
Touch-up Art & Lettering/Rina Mapa
Design/Izumi Evers
Editor/Kit Fox

Managing Editor/Annette Roman
Director of Production/Noboru Watanabe
Vice President of Publishing/Alvin Lu
Sr. Director of Acquisitions/Rika Inouye
Vice President of Sales & Marketing/Liza Coppola
Publisher/Hyoe Narita

Printed in the U.S.A.

Published by VIZ Media, LLC
P.O. Box 77010
San Francisco, CA 94107

10 9 8 7 6 5 4 3 2 1
First printing, August 2005

www.viz.com
store.viz.com

PARENTAL ADVISORY
HAPPY HUSTLE HIGH is rated T+ for Older Teen and is recommended for ages 16 and up. This volume contains strong language and sexual themes.

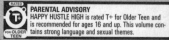

EDITOR'S RECOMMENDATIONS

If you enjoyed this volume of

HAPPY HUSTLE HIGH

then here's some more manga you might be interested in.

© 2000 Kaneyoshi IZUMI /
Shogakukan Inc.

Doubt!! by Kaneyoshi Izumi: A wise man once said, "There are only two kinds of people: those that make wide, sweeping generalizations, and those that don't." Unfortunately, body-image-challenged Ai definitely falls into the former category for, as she sees it, there are really only two kinds of girls: those who get noticed by boys, and those—like herself—who don't. Will an ultimate makeover change her luck with the fellas, or will she inevitably become just another vacuous slave to fashion?

© 2002 Kaho MIYASAKA /
Shogakukan. Inc.

Kare First Love by Kaho Miyasaka: Shy and oh-so-insecure Karin Karino is getting ready for her first shot at teenage love, but at what cost? It sure is great that the attractive and artistically inclined Kiriya has taken a fancy to her bespectacled charms, but things are bound to get messy when her classmate Yuka, in a fit of jealousy, pushes Karin down a staircase! They say love hurts, but this might be taking things a bit too far.

© 2001 Miki AIHARA /
Shogakukan Inc

Hot Gimmick by Miki Aihara: If some people have the misfortune of being born under an unlucky star, then Hatsumi Narita must've been born under an unlucky galaxy. Scheming neighbors and demented classmates are but a few of the many woes that befall this hapless heroine. But at least hope springs eternal...right? Not only is Miki Aihara's *Hot Gimmick* one of the most talked-about shôjo titles from Japan, it's rapidly becoming one of the most popular ones in the U.S. too!